IN MANY AND DIVERSE WAYS

Jacques Dupuis, S.J.
In his Eightieth Year
5 December2003

IN MANY AND DIVERSE WAYS

In Honor of Jacques Dupuis

Daniel Kendall
Gerald O'Collins
Editors

ORBIS BOOKS

Maryknoll, New York 10545

Copyright © 2003 by Daniel Kendall, S.J. and Gerald O'Collins, S.J.

Published by Orbis Books, Maryknoll, New York, U.S.A.

Manufactured in the United States of America.

Library of Congress Cataloging-in-Publication Data

In many and diverse ways : in honor of Jacques Dupuis / Daniel Kendall, Gerald O'Collins, editors.
    p.cm.
  Includes bibliographical references and index.
  ISBN 1-57075-510-8 (pbk.)
  1. Theology of religions (Christian theology)   2. Catholic Church—Relations.
3. Dupuis, Jacques, 1923-   I. Dupuis, Jacques, 1923-   II. Kendal, Daniel.   III. O'Collins, Gerald.
  BT83.85 .I5 2003
  261.2—dc21

                        2003010737

Contents

Contributors

Herbert Alphonso is Professor of Spirituality at the Pontifical Gregorian University, Rome.

Michael Barnes is Professor of Theology of Religions and Religious Studies at Heythrop College, London.

William R. Burrows is Managing Editor of Orbis Books.

Henry Sebastian D'Souza is the Archbishop Emeritus of Calcutta.

Doris Donnelly is Professor of Religious Studies and Director of the Cardinal Suenens Program at John Carroll University, Cleveland.

Avery Cardinal Dulles is the Lawrence J. McGinley Professor of Religion and Society at Fordham University, New York.

Archbishop Michael Louis Fitzgerald is President of the Pontifical Council for Interreligious Dialogue, Rome.

Claude Geffré is Professor of Religious Sciences at the Institut Catholique, and Director of the collection "Cogitatio Fidei" for Cerf, Paris.

George Gispert-Sauch is Professor Emeritus of Theology at Vidyajyoti, Delhi.

Robert Blair Kaiser is a writer for *Newsweek* and based in Rome.

Daniel Kendall is Professor of Theology at the University of San Francisco, San Francisco.

Franz Cardinal König is Archbishop Emeritus of Vienna.

Dorothy Lee is Professor of New Testament at Queen's College, Melbourne.

Terrence Merrigan is the editor of *Louvain Studies*.

Gerald O'Collins is Professor of Theology at the Gregorian University, Rome.

Peter Phan is Professor and Chair of Catholic Social Thought, Department of Theology, Georgetown University.

Samuel Rayan is Professor Emeritus of Theology at Vidyajyoti, Delhi.

Luigi Sartori is Professor of Ecclesiology at the Seminario Vescovile, Padua.

Francis A. Sullivan is Professor Emeritus from the Gregorian University, Rome, and currently teaches theology at Boston College.

Hans Waldenfels is Professor Emeritus of Fundamental Theology at the University of Bonn.

Abbreviations

AAS   *Acta Apostolicae Sedis*

AG   *Ad Gentes* (Vatican II, Decree on the Church's Missionary Activity)

ANF   *The Anti-Nicene Fathers*, A. Roberts and J. Donaldson (eds.)

ATI   Italian Theological Association

BCE   Before Common Era

CBCI   Catholic Bishops' Conference of India

CDF   Congregation for the Doctrine of the Faith

CE   Common Era

DH   H. Denzinger and P. Hünermann, *Enchiridion Symbolorum*, 37th edition (Bologna: Edizioni Dehoniane Bologna, 1995)

DM   *Dialogue and Mission*

DP   *Dialogue and Proclamation* (Letter of the Pontifical Council for Interreligious Dialogue [1991])

DV   *Dei Verbum* (Vatican II, Dogmatic Constitution on Revelation)

EN   *Evangelii Nuntiandi* (Apostolic Exhortation of Pope Paul VI [1975])

ET   English Translation

FABC   Federation of Asian Bishops' Conferences

GC   General Congregation

GS   *Gaudium et Spes* (Vatican II, Constitution of the Church in the Modern World)

Jesus Christ   J. Dupuis, *Jesus Christ at the Encounter of World Religions*

LG   *Lumen Gentium* (Vatican II, Dogmatic Constitution on the Church)

LXX   Septuagint

NA   *Nostra Aetate* (Vatican II, Declaration on the Relationship of the Church to Non-Christian Religions)

PDV   *Pastores Dabo Vobis*

Religious Pluralism   J. Dupuis, *Toward a Christian Theology of Religious Pluralism*

RH   *Redemptor Hominis* (Encyclical Letter of Pope John Paul II [1979])

RM   *Redemptoris Missio* (Encyclical Letter of Pope John Paul II [1990])

RTL   *Revue theologique de Louvain*

VJTR   *Vidyajyoti Journal of Theological Reflection*

UR   *Unitatis Redintegratio* (Vatican II, Declaration on Ecumenism)

Who Do You Say   J. Dupuis, *Who Do You Say I Am?*

Foreword

Henry D'Souza

My association with Father Jacques Dupuis, S.J., spans over 25 years. I have always trusted his theological skills and his competence for orthodox, accurate and clear expression. In the years before he left India, he had emerged as *the theologian* for the Catholic Bishops' Conference of India (CBCI). He would be invited as a matter of course for the general body meetings of the Conference. He would always be on the panel for examining theological issues. In those years, the question of inculturation, the new form of ministries and later the issues of rites were much debated. His advice was immediately sought and his guidance was invaluable for coming to decisions.

I would like to commend the behavior of Fr. Dupuis over the three years in which he was under a cloud. It was the last year of his teaching in the Gregorian and he withdrew from the course so as to remain loyal to his conscience and to respect the Congregation—a good example of Jesuit obedience, which could be admired and imitated by other theologians. Archbishop Fitzgerald of the Pontifical Council for Interreligious Dialogue has praised Fr. Dupuis for his work and for his conduct during these difficult years.

His book *Toward a Christian Theology of Religious Pluralism* has been the fruit of long study and experience. The area of interreligious dialogue is a delicate one and so very important at this moment of Christian history. With the present-day increased movement of peoples over the world, the presence of persons of diverse faiths and cultures is now ubiquitous. The need for understanding and for pastoral care of migrants of other faiths is also being more sharply felt. At the Synod of bishops during October 2001 in Rome, it was also clear that one of the fundamental roles of the bishop is to promote interreligious dialogue. For us in Asia, this is absolutely necessary. In the minutes of FIRA 4 (Fourth Formation Institute for Interreligious Affairs), held in Thailand August 20-25, 2001, we read among the theological reflections: "In most Asian countries adherents of various religions live in good neighborly relationships. Interreligious relationships or sharing is thus not so much an apostolate as a religious duty and commitment. Before we can build interreligious relationships and engage in sharing life with others, it is important that we develop an attitude of respect for the followers of other religions. We need to cultivate a more integrated spirituality of interreligious relationship and sharing."

Ecclesia in Asia states that "the Synod expressed encouragement to theologians in their delicate work of developing an inculturated theology especially in the area of Christology" (22). Theologians are grateful to the Congregation for the Doctrine of the Faith for the guidelines within which we are to understand God's mysterious workings in the history of humankind. They will surely help for future research. During the Asian Synod the bishops welcomed the Petrine office and its ministry in guaranteeing and promoting the unity of the Church. There were many voices calling for a greater sensitivity to the realities of Asia. This could be achieved in a more realistic way if there were more Asian theologians in the dicasteries of Rome.

It is my belief that Fr. Dupuis has contributed very abundantly for further research, reflection and understanding in the field of interreligious dialogue. His pioneering efforts in the new and complex issues of religious pluralism are very commendable. It is to be noted that *Dominus Iesus* (14) states: "Theology today in its reflection on the existence of other religious experiences and on their meaning in God's salvific plan, is invited to explore if and in what way the historical figures and positive elements of these religions may fall within the divine plan of salvation."

Fr. Dupuis has been striving to do just that. The example of Fr. Dupuis can give courage and confidence to go ahead with theological research.

Preface

It has been a great joy and a special privilege to put together this Festschrift in honor of our esteemed colleague and friend, Jacques Dupuis, S.J. (b. December 5, 1923). The title of our book, *In Many and Diverse Ways*, is drawn from the opening words of the Letter to the Hebrews and reflects the question with which Father Dupuis has grappled for more than fifty years: the mystery of God's plan to call all people through the Incarnate Word and the Holy Spirit to share forever in the divine life.

A number of the chapters which follow will tell something of his life and examine closely his thinking and writing. Here we wish to highlight only four major achievements. First, for thirty years Jacques Dupuis proved himself a discerning and efficient editor; his twelve years as editor of *Vidyajyoti Journal of Theological Reflection* (Delhi) were followed by eighteen years as editor of the *Gregorianum* (Rome). Very few theologians have ever served so long and so well as editor of two major journals. The bibliography at the end of this volume shows how much Father Dupuis also contributed to both *Vidyajyoti* (or, as it was formerly called, *Clergy Monthly*) and the *Gregorianum* by his articles and book reviews.

Second, seven editions of *The Christian Faith* form a further monument in his world-wide contribution to the life and thought of Catholics and others. In 1938 Josef Neuner and Heinrich Roos published in German a collection of major doctrinal documents of the Catholic Church: *Der Glaube der Kirche in den Urkunden der Lehrverkündigung*. They were assisted by two young Jesuits: Alfred Delp (1907-45), who preached against Nazism, assisted Jews to flee Germany, joined in drafting plans for a new German democracy, and was hanged with others who opposed Hitler; and Karl Rahner (1904-84). Rahner, along with many other theological activities, edited subsequent editions of this collection of documents, until Karl-Heinz Weger took over —from the eighth edition in 1971. Even though this work continued to have new editions in German and had also become available in other languages, Josef Neuner and Jacques Dupuis, the colleague with whom he was now teaching in India, realized that after Vatican II (1962-65) it was clearly desirable to prepare a fresh collection of the Church's doctrinal documents, which would leave out irrelevant texts and include more documents, in particular from conciliar and postconciliar teaching. The introductions to chapters and introductions to specific documents were written in the light of Vatican II's doctrine and the best current scholarship. Existing translations needed correction and in some cases had to be redone. New chapters were introduced to cover significant fields of modern teaching and theology, making in all 23 chapters, from "Revelation and Faith" (ch. 1) to

"Christian Fulfilment" (ch. 23), with an opening section of "Symbols and Professions of Faith." In doing this work, Neuner and Dupuis had the help of eight other professors of two faculties, Vidajyoti (Delhi) and Jnana Deepa Vidyapeeth (Pune). The result was *The Christian Faith*, published in 1973 by Theological Publications in India. From 1973 to 2001 the work went into seven editions, which were successively revised and brought up to date. The work has kept the same 23 chapters but has grown in length from 711 pages in the 1973 edition to 1135 pages in the seventh edition of 2001, from which an Italian translation was made in 2002. In preparing the sixth edition (of 1995) and the seventh edition, Dupuis enjoyed the help of ten collaborators from the Gregorian University. In its English version and Italian translation, *The Christian Faith* continues to prove a valuable instrument of theological learning—for Catholics, other Christians, and any persons interested in studying seriously the two thousand years of the Church's official teaching.

His 1997 book, *Toward a Christian Theology of Religious Pluralism*, is a further enduring monument to Dupuis's theological work. Contributors to the Festschrift offer many reflections on this work, which plunged Dupuis into several years of painful controversy but which pushed many Catholics and others into wrestling with the question of God's saving plan for the entire human race. It is hard to think of another work published after the Second Vatican Council which sparked off so many reviews, articles, and sections in books. Even as we write this preface in mid-2002, every week some new publication takes up the pros and cons of the case Dupuis argued. He has triggered, or at least put into focus, a worldwide debate which involves not only experts but also many vitally interested persons.

A fourth achievement might go unnoticed: Dupuis's inculturation into the Italian scene. Several of the contributors to the Festschrift explore the various ways Dupuis immersed himself in the cultural and religious scene of India, which became the creative matrix of his thought. But, after coming to Rome and settling at the Gregorian in 1984, he accepted many contacts with a whole range of Italian groups and audiences. He taught courses in Bologna and Florence, as well as being invited to give conferences all over Italy, from Venice and Udine in the North to Catania and Messina in the South. He was also asked to lecture in other European countries (Belgium, France, Portugal, Spain, Sweden, Switzerland, and the United Kingdom), the United States, South America, Asia and Africa. But he never neglected Italy, and received great encouragement and stimulation from the Italian public.

He has made some very good friends in Italy. The Italians prize him for his capacity for enduring friendship, as well as for his love of art and music. During his years at St. Mary's College (Kurseong, Northern India), he directed the choir in singing polyphonic compositions and Gregorian chant. One memorable holiday season he enjoyed packed audiences when he conducted Handel's *Messiah* at St. Joseph's College in nearby Darjeeling, the "queen of the hill stations." His eyes glisten when he recalls the military bands who played at parades in Delhi on August 15, the day of India's independence. As the sun was setting, the last item to be played was "Lead kindly light." "It was wonderful, wonderful," he says, when memory brings back the sound of the bagpipes and the sight of beautifully decorated elephants standing high on buildings and silhouetted against the sky

The eighteen chapters of this Festschrift are arranged in five sections. Avery Cardinal Dulles, who was a doctoral student in Rome with Fr. Dupuis, leads off the opening section of "Tributes." He shows how cautious developments in Vatican II teaching and subsequent developments provide ample grounds for fruitful interreligious dialogue. Franz Cardinal König, who has never met Fr. Dupuis face-to-face but strongly endorses his pioneering efforts in the theology of religious pluralism, questions not only the "procedural mechanism" but also "the discourteous and negative tone" adopted by the Congregation for the Doctrine of the Faith in its investigation of Fr. Dupuis's *Toward a Christian Theology of Religious Pluralism*. The section of "tributes" ends with Gerald O'Collins's account of the genesis of this book, the controversy it ran into, and some of the major issues in the controversy.

The second section on "Theological Reflections" brings together six experts from London, Paris, Louvain, Washington, Padua and Boston—in that order. It opens with Michael Barnes, who provided hospitality for Fr. Dupuis when he visited London in October 2001 to give a major address for the London *Tablet*. Barnes probes the challenges, limits and possibilities in recognizing the theological significance of Buddhism for Christian faith.

In paying homage to Fr. Dupuis's outstanding work in shaping a theology of religious pluralism, Claude Geffré highlights the novelty of interreligious dialogue in an age of globalization. He shows how serious dialogue and reflection can open the way for interreligious theology. Terrence Merrigan argues that Dupuis's option for "inclusive pluralism" not only belongs to a broader movement to redefine inclusivism but also responds to a real need in the theology of religions. God's plan for humankind entails not only Christ's role as universal Savior but also the roles of various religions.

Peter Phan's chapter examines Dupuis's use of the documents of official organizations of the Asian Churches. It then compares his theology of religious pluralism with those of two Asian theologians, one Catholic and the other Protestant. Phan concludes by suggesting how Dupuis's model of "inclusivist pluralism" can be extended further on the basis of Asian theologies. In Chapter 8, Monsignor Luigi Sartori explores the "subsists in" of *Lumen Gentium* 8. He shows how this key ecumenical principle can also be fruitfully applied to interreligious dialogue.

The second section concludes with Frank Sullivan's precise examination of the solution Clement of Alexandria offered to the question of those who lived and died before the coming of Christ. In fact this solution involved recognizing in ancient "philosophies" elements of truth which Clement attributes to the Divine Word, the source of all truth.

Herbert Alphonso begins the third section by examining the spiritual experience which is at the heart of any genuine interreligious dialogue. In particular, he shows how the *Spiritual Exercises* of St. Ignatius, with their masterly pedagogy, provide wonderful guidance for the common journey toward the fulfillment of God's kingdom. To this Doris Donnelly adds the role of interpersonal relationship in making possible and fruitful the mutual questioning and listening that interfaith dialogue requires.

George Gispert-Sauch evaluates the personal and intellectual contacts which Dupuis enjoyed with the contemplative Swami Abhishiktananda. Dupuis is one of the few serious interpreters in the West of the intuitions of the Indian-French sannyasi, whose life and experience in India partially coincided with Dupuis's own.

The Gospel of John is central to Dupuis's Trinitarian approach to interreligious dialogue—in particular, the theme of Christ as the Light of the whole human race. Dorothy Lee examines John's theme of the manifestation of Jesus' luminous glory which pervades the whole Gospel and seems to replace the story of the transfiguration narrated by the other Gospels.

Samuel Rayan concludes the third section by prayerfully reflecting on what it means for the divine-human encounter to acknowledge that God is Love and has loved into existence the whole cosmos and all human beings. Since the beginning of human history, God has been coming to people in many ways, with an offer of love and life.

The fourth section contains chapters on two Roman documents. First, Archbishop Michael Fitzgerald, from the perspective of Christian-Muslim relations, examines the enduring role of the 1991 *Dialogue and Proclamation*. That document called for specific studies with reference to different religions, and his chapter attempts to heed that call. Second, Hans Waldenfels evaluates *Ecclesia in Asia*, the Post-Synodal Apostolic Exhortation which appeared in late 1999. He directs attention to some crucial issues in Asia, in particular for the development and mission of the local churches.

The fifth and concluding section contains two further tributes, one from the editor of Orbis Books and the other from a journalist who covered Vatican II for *Time* magazine. William R. Burrows offers a moving appreciation of what he has personally learned from three books by Dupuis which he has edited and published. He understands Dupuis's work as explicitating theologically what Bede Griffiths, Abhishiktananda and others experienced in an intense life of interfaith dialogue. Robert Blair Kaiser provides a vivid picture of Dupuis, along with some reminiscences from his life's journey—from Belgium to India and, eventually, to Rome.

We want to thank all our contributors very warmly for writing their chapters and Orbis Books for agreeing to publish this book. Our gratitude goes out to Archbishop Henry D'Souza of Calcutta for agreeing to write a foreword. He and other members of his family have been for many years close friends of Father Dupuis. We should also add that this book was completed in mid-2002; by the time of its publication in late 2003 some details will obviously need to be updated and changed. We have planned this Festschrift not only as a tribute to an outstanding theologian, Father Jacques Dupuis, but also as a wide-ranging statement on something at the heart of his life: the many ways in which God mysteriously works through the Holy Spirit to bring all peoples home to the final kingdom of his Son.

Daniel Kendall, S.J., and Gerald O'Collins, S.J.
August 15, 2002

Part I

SOME TRIBUTES

1

World Religions and the New Millennium

A Catholic Perspective

Avery Cardinal Dulles, S.J.

I dedicate the following reflections to Father Jacques Dupuis, whom I have known as a friend and colleague since we were doctoral students together in Rome at the Pontifical Gregorian University. Since that time Father Dupuis has become a world-known expert on the subject here treated. I dare to hope that he will find my perspectives somewhat convergent, or perhaps fully concordant, with his own.

The relationship of Christianity to other living religions has varied with the passage of time. In the first 1500 years the encounter was predominantly hostile, even though significant attempts at dialogue were made by authors such as Justin, Abelard, and Nicholas of Cusa. Christian apologists wrote innumerable tracts with titles like "Against the Perfidy of the Jews" and "Against the Errors of the Mohammedans." In the sixteenth century, when Christianity entered into contact with the religions of Eastern Asia and America, some missionaries sought to find positive elements in these religions and even to incorporate indigenous elements into Christianity, as was done in the so-called Chinese and Indian rites. But the negative perceptions were too strongly rooted in Christian tradition for these efforts to be much appreciated.

In our own century the Second Vatican Council took up the question of the religions in a new context—that of an era of globalization. The Declaration on the Non-Christian Religions bears the title derived from its opening words, "In our age" (*Nostra aetate*). The first sentence states that at present the human race is being daily brought closer together and that contacts between different peoples are becoming more frequent. Recognizing that this closer contact contains dangers of renewed conflict, the Council sought to make a constructive

This paper is based on a lecture given at the University of St. Thomas, Houston, Texas, September 30, 1999.

contribution. But did it bring about a change in Catholic doctrine?

According to a rather widespread impression, Vatican II effected something like a Copernican revolution, displacing the Catholic Church from the center and turning all the religions into planets revolving about some vaguely defined divine center. It is sometimes supposed that Vatican II rejected the traditional doctrine of the necessity of the Church for salvation, that it renounced the privileged status of Christianity among the religions, that it affirmed the presence of grace and revelation in other religions, and that it acknowledged other religions as ways of salvation, thereby undercutting the importance of missionary endeavor. These perceptions can be illustrated from any number of contemporary authors.

Paul Knitter judges that Vatican II, especially in its Declaration on Non-Christian Religions, "stands as a watershed" between two eras.[1] Donald Nicholl writes that the Church at Vatican II "has expressed repentance (however muted) for its previous attitude toward other religions and now acknowledges 'seeds of the Word' in other religions and grants that adherents of these religions may come to salvation by way of their religion."[2] Pietro Rossano, former secretary of the Vatican Secretariat for Non-Christians, reads the Council documents as holding "that 'grace and truth' do reach or may reach the hearts of men and women through the visible, experiential signs of the various religions."[3] An Indian theologian, K. Kunnumpuram, reaches a similar conclusion: that according to the Second Vatican Council "non-Christian religions can serve as ways of salvation, in the sense that God saves these men in and through the doctrines and practices of these religions."[4] The Irish theologian Dermot A. Lane writes that the teaching of the Declaration on Non-Christian Religions has not yet been received by the people of God, and that, when the full import of the Declaration is perceived, it "may yet turn out to be the most radical of all the documents of the Second Vatican Council."[5]

Other interpretations of Vatican II are sharply opposed to the authors just quoted. The distinguished Dutch missiologist, Henrikus van Straelen, asserts that "no reevaluation of the non-Christian religions took place during the Second Vatican Council, and there was no talk of a Copernican revolution in this field."[6] A distinguished Catholic missiologist from Münster, Paul Hacker, calls attention to the negative aspects of the Council's assessment of non-Christian religions. This realization, he concludes, was doubtless the reason that "prevented the Council from stating that pagans are saved *through their religions* or that their religions as such have a *salvific significance*. The thesis of the 'legitimacy' of pagan religions," he concludes, "has received no sanction or support by the Council."[7]

In the same vein a Finnish Lutheran theologian, Mikka Ruokanen, in his monograph on the Catholic teaching concerning non-Christian religions, reaches the conclusion:

> . . . the common interpretation of the Council documents as recognizing non-Christian religions to be capable of specific mediation of God's saving grace is *invalid*. There is a legion of individual Catholic authors who recognize non-Christian religions as vehicles of divine revelation and

salvation or as expressions of supernatural Christological grace. But the official statements of the Council do *not* permit such a conclusion.[8]

The same author notes that the Council never speaks of "revelation" with reference to non-Christian religions and that it makes no mention of any possible contribution of the truth in other religions to the salvation of non-Christians. These religions, according to the Council, "do not add any supernatural dimension of revelation or grace to the natural condition of man."[9]

On my own reading, the Council documents are cautious and yet open to new developments that are consistent with Catholic tradition. They firmly uphold the creeds and dogmas of the Church and are solicitous to maintain the rationale for missionary evangelization.

With regard to the uniqueness of Christianity, the Council allows no room for debate. It teaches explicitly that God has established Christ as the source of salvation for the whole world (LG 17). It affirms that he is God's Word made flesh, "so that as perfect man he might save all men and sum up all things in himself. The Lord is the goal of human history, the focal point of the longings of history and civilization, the center of the human race, the joy of every heart, and the answer to all its longings" (GS 45). The Council quotes Paul to the effect that God's intention is "to reestablish all things in Christ, both those in the heavens and those on the earth" (Eph 1:10; GS 45). Vatican II, therefore, clearly rejected any kind of relativism or radical pluralism that would attenuate or negate the traditional teaching on the absolute primacy of Christ.

In speaking of revelation and salvation the documents of Vatican II frequently cite 1 Timothy 2:5 on the sole mediatorship of Jesus Christ. For instance, the Constitution on Divine Revelation describes him as the "Mediator and at the same time the fullness of all revelation" (DV 2). The Constitution on the Church calls Christ the one Mediator and the unique way of salvation (LG 14; cf. 49). The Decree on Missionary Activity quotes Paul to the effect that all human beings have sinned and fall short of the glory of God (Rom 3:23), and draws the consequence: "all have need of Christ as model, master, liberator, savior, and giver of life" (AG 8).

According to the Council the Church is involved in the salvation of all who are saved. It asserts: "Established by Christ to form a fellowship of life, charity, and truth, it [the Church] is also used by him as an instrument for the redemption of all, and is sent forth into the whole world as the light of the world and the salt of the earth (cf. Mt 5:13-16)" (LG 9).

Regarding the necessity of belonging to the Church, Vatican II reaffirms the positions of the modern popes since Pius IX—namely that full incorporation in the Church is the divinely established way of salvation. After asserting the unique mediation of Christ, the Constitution on the Church adds:

In explicit terms he himself affirmed the necessity of faith and baptism (cf. Mk 16:16; Jn 3:5) and thereby affirmed also the necessity of the Church, for through baptism as through a door men enter the Church. Whoever, therefore, knowing that the Catholic Church was made necessary by God through Jesus Christ, would refuse to enter her or to remain in her could not be saved. (LG 14; cf. AG 7)

Like Popes Pius IX and Pius XII, Vatican II taught that God's saving will extends to every human person and that his salvific design includes those who without fault on their part fail to accept Christ and the Church. Such persons may attain salvation without explicit faith in Christ and without formal membership in the Church. But to be saved, according to the Council, they must be moved by divine grace (LG 16); they must have the gift of faith (AG 7); they must strive to do God's will as known to them through the dictates of conscience (LG 16), and they must be associated, in a manner known to God, with the Paschal mystery (GS 22). In the absence of some kind of union with the Christ and the Church, at least by way of a dynamic orientation (*ordinatio*), salvation would be completely unattainable (LG 14-16). In enumerating the conditions for salvation of non-Christians, the Council makes no reference to their religions as mediators of revelation or grace.

In its statements on the other religions, the Council was, one might say, diplomatic and noncommittal. Unlike Dermot Lane, I fail to find anything radical in the Declaration on Non-Christian Religions. It teaches that religions everywhere "strive variously to answer the restless searchings of the human heart, proposing 'ways' that consist of teachings, rules of life, and sacred ceremonies" (NA 2). It goes on to say that the Church looks with sincere respect upon those ways of conduct and life, rules and teachings, "which often reflect a ray of that divine Truth which enlightens all men." Nevertheless the Church proclaims Christ as the way, the truth, and the life, in whom alone the fullness of life can be found. Quite unremarkably, the Declaration asserts that "the Catholic Church rejects nothing that is true and holy in these religions" (NA 2).

The expression "ray of divine truth" is perhaps deliberately ambiguous. It could mean revelation, but since Christ as the eternal Logos is the source of all truth, both natural and revealed, the reference could be simply to philosophical truth attainable by the right use of reason.

In several other texts the Council speaks of "seeds of the Word" in other religions (AG 11; 15). These seeds, I take it, would be providential gifts that could find their fulfillment in Christian faith. The expression does not imply the Word of God itself is present in these religions, for "there is a great difference between the seed of something and the thing itself."[10] These seeds, quite evidently, do not sprout spontaneously, but are planted by the divine Logos. To be fruitful, they have to be "watered by divine dew" (AG 22).

Among the other terms used by Vatican II that are sometimes misunderstood, one may mention "preparation for the gospel," an expression borrowed from the Fathers of the Church, especially Eusebius of Caesarea (LG 16; AG 9). Some have imagined that this term implies that the non-Christian religions are related to Christianity in the same way that ancient Judaism was, and that their Scriptures must therefore be inspired. But the Council evidently means that God providentially prepares people of other nations not for bringing forth the Savior, as Israel did, but only for the reception of the gospel.[11] In saying that the Church regards whatever goodness and truth is found among non-Christians as a preparation for the gospel (LG 16), the Council neither affirms nor denies that the goods in question are supernatural.

At no point does Vatican II characterize the religions as such as good, holy, or true. Indeed it recognizes that "rather often people, deceived by the Evil One, have become caught in futile reasoning and have exchanged the truth of God for a lie, serving the creature rather than the creator (cf. Rom 1:21, 25). Consequently, to promote the glory of God and procure the salvation of all such persons, and mindful of the command of the Lord, 'Preach the gospel to every creature' (Mk 16:16), the Church painstakingly fosters her missionary work" (LG 16). Evangelization, according to the Decree on Missionary Activity, frees the rites and cultures of the nations "from all taint of evil, and restores [them] to Christ their source, who overthrows the devil's domain and wards off the manifold malice of evil-doing" (AG 9). These sentences imply that the religions, far from serving as substitutes for the gospel, may indeed be in some ways obstacles to salvation.

For the Church to speak officially of non-Christian religions as containing elements of truth and goodness, as it did at Vatican II, is admittedly something new. This new posture would seem to be required for an adequate response to the world situation at the dawn of the third millennium. Christianity can no longer identify itself with a portion of the world where it holds uncontested dominance. Numerous religions are simultaneously present on every continent. In a country such as our own, Islam, Hinduism, and Buddhism, to name only three, are taking their places in public life alongside Judaism and Christianity.

In an earlier century this situation of religious pluralism might have brought on persecutions and religious wars. But the lessons of history have taught us that hostility and violence are contrary to the gospel of Christ and do not promote true religion. For the peace of civil society and the integrity of the religions themselves it is essential to cultivate an atmosphere of charity, esteem, and dialogue, as the Council tended to do.

Turning specifically to the theme of dialogue, it is striking that although dialogue is frequently recommended in the Decree on Ecumenism, it is scarcely mentioned in the texts dealing with non-Christian religions. In the Decree on Missionary Activity, the Council does say that missionaries "can learn by sincere and patient dialogue what treasures a bountiful God has distributed among the nations of the earth" (AG 11), and that future missionaries should be scientifically prepared for dialogue with non-Christian religions and cultures (AG 34). But there is no specific proposal that interreligious dialogues be conducted. The Declaration on the Non-Christian Religions entirely avoids the term dialogue, although it mentions in passing the desirability of conversations (*colloquia*) and collaboration with the followers of other religions. It exhorts Christians both to bear witness to the Christian faith and life and to recognize, preserve, and promote the spiritual, moral, and sociocultural values that are found among non-Christians (NA 2). None of the Council documents indicates that the presence of revealed truth in other religions might be a basis of dialogue.

Pope Paul VI is often mentioned as favoring interfaith dialogue. While Vatican II was still in session, he issued his first encyclical, *Ecclesiam Suam* (1964), calling for interreligious relationships animated by courteous esteem, understanding, and good will. Catholic Christianity, he declares, respects the moral and spiritual values of the great monotheistic religions, and desires to join with them in promoting common ideals of religious freedom, human brotherhood, sound culture, social welfare, and civil order (112). These common ideals, he suggests, could be made subjects of conversation (*colloquium*) with these groups. He does not use the term dialogue (*dialogus*) in this connection; still less does he recommend that the doctrines of God and redemption should be themes for dialogue.

Toward the end of his pontificate, Paul VI once more took up the question of interreligious contacts in the context of evangelization, the subject of his great apostolic exhortation, *Evangelii Nuntiandi* (1975). He there quoted Vatican II on the innumerable "seeds of the Word" in non-Christian religions, and stated that these seeds can constitute a true preparation for the gospel (53). He spoke of "natural religious expressions most worthy of esteem," but carefully avoided suggesting that the non-Christian religions were supernatural or revealed. The term "dialogue" never appears in this exhortation. The emphasis falls on the abiding necessity of missionary proclamation (EN 53).

Pope John Paul II, deeply rooted in personalist philosophy, appropriates the theory of dialogue expounded by Jewish thinkers such as Martin Buber, Abraham Heschel, and Emmanuel Lévinas. In his first encyclical he declared that the Church's self-awareness is formed in dialogue, which presupposes attentiveness to the others with whom one wishes to speak (RH 11). The Council, he added, correctly saw in the various religions so many reflections of the one truth, attesting that, though the roads may be different, there is but a single goal of the human spirit as it seeks the full meaning of life (ibid.).

When he reorganized the Curia in 1988, John Paul II gave the Secretariat for Non-Christians a new name: the Pontifical Council for Interreligious Dialogue. His encyclical *Redemptoris Missio* (1990) devotes several paragraphs to the idea of dialogue with other religions (RM 55-57). In his book *Crossing the Threshold of Hope* he includes a chapter on the multiplicity of religions, in which he gives some interesting reflections on the concept of "seeds of the word." There follow three chapters devoted respectively to Buddhism, Islam, and Judaism. And finally, in his apostolic letter on the coming great jubilee, *Tertio Millennio Adveniente*, the Pope asserts that the event of the year 2000 will provide an auspicious occasion for interreligious dialogue, in which conversations with Judaism and Islam ought to have a preeminent place (53).

Some interpret this summons to dialogue as a demand for radical changes in Catholic doctrine. They base this interpretation on a particular understanding of dialogue and on an agnostic or pragmatic theory of religious truth quite alien to Catholic conciliar and papal teaching. Contemporary religious pluralists (as they often call themselves) are at home in a culture that rejects any quest for transcendent truth as utopian, and settles for a pragmatic goal of peaceful coexistence.

But this relativistic theory has little in common with the classical concept of dialogue as a striving for truth—a concept that has come down from Plato and Augustine, and still lives on in the Catholic tradition.[12]

The writings of Paul Knitter and John Hick are illustrative of this new tendency. Knitter, an American Catholic, writes that "dialogue is not possible if any partners enter it with the claim that they possess the final, definitive, irreformable truth. Claims of finality set up a roadblock to any real growth in experience and understanding."[13] Dogma, he contends, must shed its unconditional character and present itself as a tentative opinion to be tested through dialogue and praxis. No religion can claim to hold more than a fragmentary glimpse of the ultimate.

A British Protestant, John Hick, holds that Christianity must today be seen as one of the streams of saving reality in which human beings can be salvifically related to the ineffable Reality that Christians call by the name of God.[14] In rejecting the unique superiority of Christianity and holding that all religions stand on the same level, Hick in effect rejects Christianity's self-understanding. His argument is unconvincing. By the same logic he ought to eliminate every claim to truth, since truth is always permanent, universal, and superior to its opposite. But if the dialogue partners did not have divergent views about truth, dialogue would hardly be necessary.[15]

After cautioning that divisive topics should not be broached until mutual trust has grown up between the participants, Cardinal Francis Arinze calls for frankness about the real differences:

> Accordingly, a Catholic who is meeting a Muslim should not soft-pedal beliefs in the Most Blessed Trinity (three persons in only one God), in Jesus Christ as the Son of God and God, in the Son of God becoming man and dying on the Cross for the salvation of all humanity, and in the Most Blessed Virgin Mary as the Mother of God. Muslims do not accept these doctrines. But a sincere, friendly Muslim dialogue partner should not get angry that Catholics hold them. On the other hand, a Muslim in dialogue should not hesitate to state that Muslims hold that the Qur'an is the last revelation from God and Muhammad the greatest and the last of the prophets.[16]

The popes, when they speak of dialogue, are following a properly theological concept in which dialogue is a necessary aspect of evangelization. According to Paul VI, Christ himself exemplifies the dialogue of salvation in which God himself comes to us in meekness, trust, and patient witness, respecting our freedom and our limitations. In our contacts with adherents of other faiths, in *Ecclesiam Suam* Paul VI declares, "honesty compels us to declare openly our conviction that there is but one true religion, the religion of Christianity. It is our hope that all who seek God and adore him may come to acknowledge its truth" (111).

Pope John Paul II in his encyclical on missionary activity, *Redemptoris Missio*, adopts a similar approach. "No one," he affirms, "can enter into communion with God except through Christ, by the working of the Holy Spirit" (RM 5). The Catholic, he contends, must take part in the dialogue "with the conviction that the Church is the ordinary means of salvation and that she alone possesses the fullness of the means of salvation" (RM 55). In dialogue we seek to identify signs of Christ's presence and of the Spirit's activity that may be present in other religions. But "those engaged in this dialogue must be consistent with their own religious traditions and convictions. . . . There must be no abandonment of principles nor false irenicism" (RM 56).

Of all the documents of the Holy See up to this time, the most positive on the value of other religions is probably the paper on "Dialogue and Proclamation" prepared by the Pontifical Council for Interreligious Dialogue in collaboration with the Congregation for the Evangelization of Peoples and published in 1991. It firmly upholds the principle that Christians must enter into dialogue without concealing their conviction that the fullness of revelation has been given to them in Jesus Christ, the only Mediator between God and man. But it reminds Christians that God has also manifested himself in some way to the followers of other religious traditions (DP 48). There are elements of truth and grace as well as of error and sinfulness in the religious traditions of the world. In the concrete order, says the paper, non-Christians may be responding to God's gracious invitation when they sincerely practice their own religion according to the dictates of their conscience. By so doing they receive the grace of Jesus Christ, who is their Savior even if they do not recognize him as such (DP 29).

Evangelization, according to this document of the Pontifical Council, cannot consist in dialogue alone. In addition to dialogue, evangelization includes proclamation, in which people are invited and urged to acknowledge Jesus Christ and become his disciples in the Church (DP 76). In situations that make overt proclamation practically impossible, the Church may still carry out its evangelizing mission to some degree through presence, witness, social action, and dialogue (DP 76).

A clear distinction between proclamation and dialogue can be very useful, I believe, in interfaith relationships. Through dialogue it may be possible to establish the interpersonal relationships of trust and understanding required for effective proclamation. Proclamation can often be conducted most fruitfully within a framework of dialogue. Within the process of dialogue there will normally be an element of mutual proclamation.

The choice of topics and rules for dialogue will depend very much on the particular identity of the participants. In dialogue it is normal to speak about themes that resonate with the traditions or experience of all the participants. In intra-Christian ecumenical dialogue themes such as God, Christ, and the Church will presumably be central. But in dialogue with non-Christians, especially those who are not monotheists, other themes may be preferable. Paul VI suggested discussion on common ideals, such as religious liberty, human brotherhood, sound culture, and civil order. One could imagine dialogues concerned with suffering and happiness, life and death, speech and silence, and more explicitly religious topics such as prayer, worship, and mystical experience. But it might be a mistake to rush abruptly into the themes of Christian dogma, such as Trinity, Incarnation, Church, and sacraments. To begin by presenting the full Christian position of these questions could hardly provoke anything but bewilderment and rejection. When a suitable groundwork has been laid, the time could come for these doctrines to be explained.

Whatever topics are chosen, it is important that all the participants be left free to express their real convictions and those of the communities they represent. A Catholic Christian could not be required to conceal or misrepresent the Catholic position on the topics under discussion.

Participants in dialogue must be prepared to face stubborn disagreements. Great patience is needed to accept the impossibility of arriving at full consensus on the basis of dialogue alone. Dialogue is not normally the place in which to propose the requirement of conversion, which may be necessary to overcome fundamental disagreements. Premature efforts to reach agreement can result in ambiguous formulations and in the falsification of the positions of the communities involved.

In summary, then, we may conclude that there are ample grounds for fruitful interreligious dialogue, since most if not all religions enshrine truths and cultivate virtues that are worthy of respect; they also sustain the human quest for reconciliation and union with the divine. The grace of Christ may be presumed to be present with those who sincerely worship within the framework of their own religions. These religions may indeed embody signs and symbols of God's gracious presence in communities that earnestly turn toward him, even without yet recognizing his full self-disclosure and redemptive action in Jesus Christ. These tokens may be called rays of divine truth, seeds of the Word, and preparations for the gospel.

We may conclude, further, that salvation is within reach of all human beings who with God's grace sincerely follow the biddings of their conscience. This is true whether they adhere to any religion or not. The possibility of salvation, therefore, does not require that the non-Christian religions mediate the grace of God, nor does it exclude the possibility that religions may play a salvific role in the process.

The presence of elements of truth and goodness in other religions, even if we suppose that these derive from revelation, does not eliminate the need for explicit Christian proclamation. Unless purified in the light of the gospel, human religions will inevitably contain serious errors and distortions that will hamper the journey to salvation. The fragmentary elements of truth and grace in these religions need to be purified, elevated, and completed by contact with Christ and the gospel.

Dialogue between Christianity and other religions can always be profitable. By learning about the religious traditions, sensitivities, and dispositions of their partners, Christians can find new ways of understanding and presenting the gospel, more suitable for a given audience, perhaps, than the ways previously known. In dialogue each party can explain why it adheres to its own religious heritage, insofar as this explanation may bear upon the particular theme under discussion. No party to the dialogue should be required to conceal or misrepresent its own distinctive doctrines.

If the dialogue takes up themes relating to the nature of God and salvation,

Christians, like others, will be expected to be straight-forward and honest. Their integrity as Christians will oblige them to speak of Christ as the incarnate Son of God, the sole mediator of salvation. In candidly expressing what the Church believes about Christ and his redemptive work, they will not be motivated by any sense of personal superiority. On the contrary, they will feel seriously inadequate to serve as representatives of so lofty a faith.

Dialogue, unlike proclamation, is not a direct call for conversion. It will put no pressure on the partners to change their religious affiliation, but it may help to prepare the ground for a future conversion. Confident that Christ is the way, the truth, and the life, Christians will hope that members of all religions may come to share their own faith.

Short of conversion, dialogue may generate an atmosphere of friendship and good will. As we enter the intense globalization of the third millennium, interreligious dialogue is not a luxury. It may be required to prevent disastrous collisions between opposed religious groups. The arrival of the great jubilee of the year 2000 provides an auspicious occasion for overcoming the religious hostility and violence of the past millennium and inaugurating an era of mutual esteem and cordial cooperation.

References

[1]Paul F. Knitter, *No Other Name?* (Maryknoll, N.Y.: Orbis, 1985), 123-24.

[2]Donald Nicholl, "Other Religions (*Nostra aetate*)," in Adrian Hastings (ed.), *Modern Catholicism: Vatican II and After* (London: SPCK, 1991), 126-34, at 132.

[3]Pietro Rossano, "Christ's Lordship and Religious Pluralism in Roman Catholic Perspective," in G. H. Anderson and T. F. Stransky (eds.), *Christ's Lordship and Religious Pluralism* (Maryknoll, N.Y.: Orbis, 1981), 96-110, at 103.

[4]K. Kunnumpuram, *Ways of Salvation: The Salvific Meaning of Non-Christian Religions according to the Teaching of Vatican II* (Poona, India: Pontifical Athenaeum, 1971), 91; quoted in Jacques Dupuis, *Toward a Christian Theology of Religious Pluralism* (Maryknoll, N.Y.: Orbis, 1998), 168.

[5]Dermot A. Lane, "Vatican II, Christology and the World Religions," *Louvain Studies* 24 (1999): 147-70, at 147-48.

[6]H. J. J. M. van Straelen, *The Church and the Non-Christian Religions at the Threshold of the 21st Century* (London: Avon Books, 1998), 277.

[7]Paul Hacker, *Theological Foundations of Evangelization* (Münster: Steyler Verlag, 1980), 72.

[8]Mikka Ruokanen, *The Catholic Doctrine on Non-Christian Religions according to the Second Vatican Council* (Leiden: Brill, 1992), 115; cf. van Straelen, *The Church*, 277-78.

[9]Ruokanen, *The Catholic Doctrine*, 100; cf. Dupuis, *Toward a Christian*, 166.

[10]International Theological Commission, "Christianity and the World Religions," §42; *Origins* 27 (August 14, 1997): 149-66, at 156.

[11]"Christianity and the World Religions," §85, p. 161.

[12]Cardinal Joseph Ratzinger, in an address to 80 bishops from mission countries, criticized Paul Knitter and John Hick as representatives of the current relativism in the

theology of the religions. See his "Relativism: The Central Problem for Faith Today," *Origins* 26 (October 31, 1996): 309-17, at 312-14.

[13]Knitter, *No Other Name?*, 211.

[14]John Hick, "The Non-Absoluteness of Christianity," in John Hick and Paul F. Knitter (eds.), *The Myth of Christian Uniqueness: Towards a Pluralistic Theology of Religions* (Maryknoll, N.Y.: Orbis, 1987), 16-36, esp. 22-23.

[15]"The truth as truth is always superior," says "Christianity and the World Religions," §104, p. 164. For a thorough critique of Hick see Gavin D'Costa, *Theology and Religious Pluralism: The Challenge of Other Religions* (Oxford: Blackwell, 1986), 22-51.

[16]Cardinal Francis Arinze, *Meeting Other Believers* (Huntington, Ind.: Our Sunday Visitor Publishing Division, 1998), 46.

2

Let the Spirit Breathe

Franz Cardinal König

Interreligious dialogue is vital in a pluralistic global culture. Thus Pope John Paul II in his recent apostolic letter *Novo Millennio Ineunte* (January 6, 2001) speaks of "the great challenges of interreligious dialogue to which we shall be committed in the new millennium." The dialogue "must continue," he urges forcefully. To which I would add—without peace among the world's religions there will be no peace among the nations.

Because too little was known about other civilizations, Christians used to see members of non-Christian religions as "heathens" or "idolaters" and their religions as superstitions or false religions. But interreligious dialogue has opened up new insights.

The Second Vatican Council was the first to take up the subject of interreligious dialogue and of religious pluralism—the interpretation of the significance of the variety of world religions. The Council's brief decree *Nostra Aetate* explains that in a world in which people are drawing closer together, the Church "is examining its relations with the non-Christian religions more carefully." The Council did not ask whether there were such "relations," but "what kind of relations" existed and should be encouraged. The question was significant, it explained, because it was the Church's duty to foster "unity and charity among nations."

With his invitation to the representatives of all the world religions to meet at Assisi with him in 1986, John Paul II opened people's eyes to what this meant. His action corresponded to the Council text: "The Catholic Church rejects nothing of what is true and holy in these religions." For this reason, *Nostra Aetate* explained, "the Church urges its sons and daughters to enter with prudence and charity into discussion and collaboration with members of other religions. Let Christians, while witnessing to their own faith and way of life, acknowledge,

This chapter originally appeared as an article in the April 7, 2001 issue of *The Tablet*. It is reprinted here with the kind permission of Cardinal König and the editor of *The Tablet*.

preserve and encourage the spiritual and moral truths found among non-Christians."

At the Council the Catholic Church opened itself in a positive way to other religious traditions and other religions, to a far greater degree than had ever been the case before. John Paul II has added emphasis on these positive appraisals by pointing to the ubiquitous presence of the Divine and of Jesus Christ and the Holy Spirit in the other non-Christian religions, as for example in his encyclicals *Redemptor Hominis* (1979) and *Redemptoris Missio* (1990).

The Second Vatican Council, however, did not adequately answer the question of what kind of relationship the Church has to the non-Christian religions. The theology of religious pluralism poses not only the question of human values, but also of religious values and their meaning—their significance for salvation. I personally feel that to recognize some salvific elements in other religions does not belittle the treasures of our own.

An extensive amount of literature testifies to the great interest which these new theological issues have aroused. The theology of religions and the theology of religious pluralism have come to be accepted as new disciplines alongside the philosophy of religion and comparative religious studies. Christians are now faced with additional questions which give rise to new difficulties, but should also make it possible to strengthen and deepen their own choice of the Christian faith.

The Vatican Congregation for the Doctrine of the Faith (CDF) has devoted a comprehensive document to the subject, entitled *Dominus Iesus*. This declaration draws attention to the difficulties which religious pluralism can cause for the missionary proclamation of the Christian message. The text goes into the difficulties and dangers of relativising this missionary proclamation. It insists on the "unique and universal salvation" accomplished through Jesus Christ: the universal salvific will of the one threefold God brought about the mystery of the Incarnation of the Son of God, who died on the Cross and rose from the dead.

Dominus Iesus does not reprove any authors, books or theological schools by name. And despite the warnings it expresses about relativising the Christian doctrine of salvation, thus endangering the Church's missionary proclamation, the CDF invites theologians to reflect on the existence of other religious experiences and on their meaning in God's salvific plan: they should "explore if and in what way the historical figures and positive elements of these religions may fall within the divine plan of salvation."

At the time that this CDF document was presented to the public (September 5, 2000), another, shorter text, a so-called *Notificatio* or notification, had already been prepared, which referred solely to one author, Fr. Jacques Dupuis, S.J., and to one of the books he had written, *Toward a Christian Theology of Religious Pluralism*, which he wrote originally in English and which is considered a pioneering achievement in the new and complex issues of religious pluralism. Until the investigation of his book started, Fr. Dupuis taught at the theological faculty of the Gregorian University in Rome. His book was first published in the autumn of 1997 and has since been translated into several languages and had numerous reprints. In dealing with Fr. Dupuis's book, however, the CDF did not proceed with the same open-mindedness toward interreligious dialogue and religious pluralism as in the passages from *Dominus Iesus* that I have quoted above.

On October 2, 1998, nearly a year after his book was published, the distinguished author was informed by his superior general that the CDF had accused it of containing serious doctrinal errors, whereupon Fr. Dupuis became utterly distraught. He was able, however, to reply to the CDF's detailed written list of questions on his book. But the CDF, on September 1, 2000, sent the author the first version of a notification that was to be published forthwith and which had already been signed by Pope John Paul II two and a half months previously, namely on June 16.

Meanwhile a theological adviser was able to prove that there was not a single passage in Dupuis's book which justified the CDF's accusation of serious errors pertaining to the faith. And indeed the first notification of the CDF had not actually pointed out which passages in the book it was referring to. Thus on December 6, 2000, a second, milder version of the notification was drafted, which had again been signed by the Pope on November 24. This version spoke only of "ambiguities" on matters of faith. This second version was altered yet again, and a third version drawn up which was officially made public on February 27, 2001. The Pope had signed this third version on January 19, 2001.

The first and second versions of the notification were both seen by Fr. [Peter] Hans Kolvenbach, the Jesuit superior general, and Fr. Gerald O'Collins, Dupuis's theological adviser. Today these versions are back in the CDF archives. The information I am reproducing here comes from a talk to journalists in Rome given by Fr. Dupuis after receiving the final version of the notification on February 26, 2001.

It is evident from the way the notification came into being that the CDF is experiencing difficulties with its procedural mechanisms. I have four chief points of criticism to make here. In this particular case it is shocking that Dupuis was informed of the CDF investigation by his superior general and not approached directly. The CDF procedure, which used to be inquisitorial, was altered and much improved by Paul VI on the last day of the Second Vatican Council—December 7, 1965. The idea of informing the superior general, if the member of a religious order was to be investigated, was meant to enable his entire order to come to his help. But Dupuis is a distinguished professor of theology and an expert in his field, who is as qualified as the members of the CDF. So why not inform him directly or simultaneously with his superior general, for courtesy's sake?

It was moreover far too soon for an investigation. The book had been published only nine months beforehand and interreligious dialogue is a relatively new, complicated and most important subject. Theologians and others working in this field must be given the greatest possible freedom. By investigating Dupuis so soon, the CDF risked narrowing the discussion down, discouraging those theologians who have taken it up and giving rise to a fear that the subject is "dangerous." One also wonders why three times in a row the notification was presented for the Pope's signature before the third and final version was published. Is that not confirmation that the CDF was proceeding over-cautiously and far too quickly?

A third important aspect is that no specific passages in the book were quoted. The CDF's accusations applied to the book as a whole. If I reject an entire book, that surely means that I do not think much of it, a negative assessment of interreligious dialogue which contrasts with the positive approach of the Pope and Vatican II.

And then there is the human aspect, which is perhaps the most important shortcoming of all. The CDF deals not only with books, but also with their authors who are human beings, in this case with a distinguished theologian who taught at a renowned university and had pledged himself to fidelity to the Church's teaching authority. The CDF hurt Fr. Dupuis deeply and the shock he received led to ill-health and depression, albeit, one hopes, only temporarily.

This brings us to the commentary the CDF published on the internet on March 2 ("Commentary on the Notification of the Congregation for the Doctrine of the Faith Regarding the Book *Toward a Christian Theology of Religious Pluralism* by Father Jacques Dupuis S.J."). It is on the Vatican website at www.vatican.va (see Congregations and then CDF). In this apologia the Vatican congregation defends itself against accusations of "undeserved harshness" as regards the Dupuis notification, pointing out that this is written in the traditional style in which CDF documents are always presented.

The fact that the CDF felt obliged to defend itself shows clearly that it has come in for sharp criticism because of the discourteous and negative tone it used. And indeed its words were often not only impersonal but withering, as if they had been taken from a sixteenth-century catechism. The congregation has neglected the human aspect, ignoring the deep hurt it has caused, all of which could have been avoided had it adopted a different approach. No one loses authority just because they are courteous.

I can only hope that the subject of interreligious dialogue and religious pluralism has not been adversely affected. Rather, we should press ahead and encourage interreligious dialogue all the more determinedly, especially from the Christian viewpoint. The CDF's right, and indeed its duty, to accompany these discussions with critical remarks goes without saying.

The CDF is correct, however, at least in this, that interreligious dialogue today is raising once more the ultimate question: was Jesus Christ a great religious leader, but in the last instance only human? Or was Our Father in heaven speaking through him in order to point to those all-important final questions which concern all humankind and to answer them? We Christians are convinced of the latter. Not only the Council of Nicaea but above all the Council of Chalcedon had to confront this question, which Jesus Christ himself first put to his apostles: "Who do you say that I am?"

Fr. Dupuis has always clearly confessed Jesus Christ as the Son of God and universal Savior. But this very confession—as is the case also with Pope John Paul II—encourages him to seek and acknowledge the active presence of Christ and the Holy Spirit in the religions and cultures of the world.

3

Jacques Dupuis

His Person and Work

Gerald O'Collins, S.J.

I first met Fr. Jacques Dupuis early in 1971 when I spent several weeks with him in a Jesuit theological college (St. Mary's, Kurseong) in north India near Darjeeling where he had been teaching theology since 1959. After a semester as a visiting professor at Weston School of Theology in greater Boston and a month's study in Rome, I had broken my flight home to begin a new academic year in Melbourne (Australia). I had been asked to teach a course on the theology of hope in Kurseong, one of the most beautiful places in the world, with its astounding views across rich forests and tea plantations to the majesty of Kanchenjunga rising to 28,000 feet. Besides his work as a professor of theology, Dupuis helped Tibetan and other refugees along the frontier of India. A luminous intelligence shone through the glasses perched on his oval face. Wiry and tireless, despite bouts of bad health, he was most energetically hospitable. On our free days he took me to meet a wide variety of people, including the Sherpa Tensing, who shared in 1953 with the New Zealander Edmund Hillary the first proven ascent of Everest; in the early seventies Tensing headed a mountaineering school. As Dupuis raced his Yugoslavian motorcycle along the narrow roads of the Himalayan foot-hills, I clung to him for dear life, and prayed not to fall down the sheer precipices so close to our wheels. When his theological college shifted to Delhi later in 1971, Dupuis rode his motorcycle right across northern India to his new home.

A strong friendship had been forged with "Jim," as I have always called him—the name by which he was known in India. At the invitation of René Latourelle, the dean of the Gregorian's theology faculty, Dupuis came to the Gregorian for a few weeks as a visiting professor. Then in 1984, at the request of Latourelle, he was transferred to Rome and joined our theology faculty. Dupuis quickly made his mark as a first-rate teacher in our two-year second cycle in theology; his classes often drew well over two hundred students. In 1985 he became the editor of our theological and philosophical quarterly, the *Gregorianum*, and we collaborated closely on the journal. As an interpreter he attended four synods held in Rome (1974, 1983, 1985, and 1987). He also served for ten years (1985-95) as a consultor for the Pontifical Council for Interreligious Dialogue, and made a major contribution to their 1991 document "Dialogue and Proclamation."

Dupuis's Books

Dupuis asked me, with the approval of the Gregorian University's Jesuit superior, to be the in-house censor for *Who Do You Say I Am?,* his study of Christian doctrine on Christ (1994) which followed his much acclaimed *Jesus Christ at the Encounter of World Religions* (1991). Both books appeared in English, French, Italian, and Spanish; *Who Do You Say I Am?* easily proved itself the best seller in the fifteen-volume series of basic texts in which it appeared. His next project was the sixth edition of doctrinal documents of the Catholic Church, *The Christian Faith* (1996). He had co-edited with Josef Neuner the five previous editions and they were helped by a team of colleagues working in India; the sixth edition was prepared with the help of eight other professors of the Gregorian. With that project off his hands, Dupuis set himself to complete his trilogy on Christ's person and redemptive mission by writing a major work on interreligious encounter.

Well ahead of time, and once again with our superior's approval, he asked me to take on the task of reading and censoring this third volume, on behalf of the Jesuit community at the Gregorian. He fed me the chapters over a period of three or four months, and I read the text closely, not only to check his theology but also to correct on occasions his English. Although French is his native tongue, after years in India he preferred to write in English. The result was the 447-page *Toward a Christian Theology of Religious Pluralism*, which appeared more or less simultaneously in French and Italian at the end of 1997. While Orbis Books (Maryknoll, N.Y.) was preparing the English edition, Dupuis had already passed his manuscript for translation into Italian and French to Queriniana (Brescia) and Cerf (Paris), respectively. The Portuguese and Spanish versions were published later.

In October 1997 Dupuis flew off to Paris for a presentation and a debate (featuring Claude Geffré and Joseph Doré, the newly appointed Archbishop of Strasbourg) on the French edition of the book; it had been chosen as number 200 in the renowned *Cogitatio Fidei* series. The Italian publishers, together with the Italian Theological Association (ATI) and the rector of the Gregorian, Father (later Archbishop) Giuseppe Pittau, also wanted to honor the appearance of this magisterial work with a celebratory launch. This happened at the Gregorian on the late afternoon of November 22, 1997. The big crowd of students, the speeches from Fr. Pittau, the secretary of the Pontifical Council for Interreligious Dialogue (Bishop Michael Fitzgerald), the president of ATI (Giacomo Canobbio), and myself, along with the carefully crafted response from Dupuis made it a lively, international event.

In 1998 Dupuis learned that *Toward a Christian Theology of Religious Plural-ism* had won an annual award from the Catholic Press Association in the United States. Numerous reviews were appearing in English, French, and Italian—the first, a very positive review, in the November 22, 1997, issue of *Avvenire*, which is owned by the bishops of Italy. My own review was published by the London *Tablet* in January 1998, and Dupuis began composing an article for the Naples-based *Rassegna di teologia*, as he wanted to continue dialogue with his review-ers, both the more favorable and the less favorable ones.

The Storm Breaks

At Easter 1998 a tiny cloud appeared—in the shape of a very negative article published by *Avvenire* in its April 14 issue. The author, a theologian who is a world expert on St. Anselm of Canterbury and teaches in Milan, vigorously mis-represented and misreported Dupuis, and the most charitable judgment was that the piece resulted from a rapid and careless reading of the book. Before summer began, the Congregation for the Doctrine of the Faith (CDF) had discussed Dupuis's book on March 30 and April 4, and heard strong criticism leveled against it. A further meeting of the CDF on June 10, 1998, an "ordinary congregation," voted in favor of taking action against the book. Dupuis knew none of this at the time. When I returned to Rome from the United States in early August, he was out of town but had left for my comments the article he had prepared for *Rassegna di teologia*. Before publishing his response to reviewers, Dupuis had decided to wait for comments not only from me but also from Monsignor Luigi Sartori, a leading Italian theologian with whom he had also shared the draft of his article for *Rassegna*. In a letter dated October 12, 1998, Sartori forwarded two pages of precise and constructive comment. But by that time Dupuis had been stunned by a communication that had reached him from the CDF on October 2, via the Jesuit superior general, Father Kolvenbach.

A nine-page, single-spaced document developed major questions and accusa-tions challenging *Toward a Christian Theology of Religious Pluralism*. Dupuis was given three months to reply. Fr. Kolvenbach suggested his dropping the op-tional course (for which over two hundred Gregorian students had enrolled) and also a seminar that Dupuis was due to begin teaching on October 19. This would ensure more time and greater peace in which to write his response to the CDF.

Dupuis began by spending two weeks in hospital. At the time I was away, enjoying a sabbatical semester at Marquette University in Milwaukee. On Dupuis's behalf the dean of theology phoned to ask me to become the one consultor the CDF allowed Dupuis, and I agreed. Throughout my four months in Milwaukee I was in constant touch with Dupuis, and by the end of my sabbatical semester was already receiving the first sections of his draft response to the CDF. I urged him to break up his paragraphs and insert as many headings as possible. An editorial in the London *Tablet* for November 21, 1998, led me to compose a letter, "In defence of Fr Dupuis," which appeared in the same journal on December 12,

1998. In that letter, among other things, I drew attention to the way he had developed at theological length themes that came from the Pope's teaching and example: for instance, the need for interreligious dialogue (which is simply not the same thing as a falsely tolerant pluralism), God as the only One who is truly absolute, the living actuality of the divine self-revelation whose definitive fullness will appear only at the end (*Fides et Ratio*, 2 [John Paul's encyclical on faith and reason of September 14, 1998]), a patently deep respect for all "the treasures of human wisdom and religion" (*Fides et Ratio*, 31), and a special interest in Indian "religious and philosophical traditions," to be drawn from with discernment and sound criteria (*Fides et Ratio*, 72). These were all major themes of Fr. Dupuis's book. I concluded my letter by saying: "Like John Paul II, Fr. Dupuis recognizes those treasures of religion through which millions of non-Christians will, we may confidently hope and pray, find salvation and be united with all the redeemed in the coming kingdom of the glorious Son of God. To condemn Dupuis's book would, I fear, be to condemn the Pope himself."

Once back in Rome at the Gregorian before Christmas 1998, I carefully read the whole of the 190-page response which Dupuis had prepared for the CDF and which he handed over to Fr. Kolvenbach for delivery to the CDF. In the meantime, Dupuis's *Toward a Christian Theology of Religious Pluralism* continued to be the theme of further reviews, articles, letters to editors, and sections in books. On January 16, 1999 the London *Tablet*, for instance, carried a two-page article, entitled "In Defence of Fr. Dupuis," written by Cardinal Franz König, the retired Archbishop of Vienna and a longtime advocate of interreligious dialogue. The Cardinal followed up his *Tablet* article with an extensive interview in the February issue of the Italian monthly *Trenta giorni*, now edited by the former Italian prime minister Giulio Andreotti. Shortly after that interview appeared the *Tablet* carried an English translation of an open letter written to Cardinal König by Cardinal Ratzinger, who had invited the London weekly to publish it. Among other things, Cardinal Ratzinger referred to the CDF's desire to "dialogue" with Dupuis and to "consult him personally."

In February 1999 Dupuis once again fell ill, and had to cancel a lecture trip to India and Japan—something to which he had been looking forward greatly. After he recovered, the Dominicans at Montpellier flew him to southern France to talk about his book. He also spoke in England at Douai Abbey to Benedictine leaders from around the world. Dupuis was the only theologian asked to give a paper at a remarkable meeting in Ferrara, which featured Claudio Abbado conducting Verdi's *Falstaff* and Jonathan Miller directing a play. Dupuis felt encouraged when he came across a well argued book, published in late 1998 by a Roman biblical scholar, Giovanni Odasso; it provided strong biblical underpinning for Dupuis's belief that the various religions belong to the one saving plan of God for all humanity, a plan that has its fullness and center in Christ and the Holy Spirit.

When I flew off to teach in the United States and Australia during the summer of 1999, Dupuis was about to take a holiday in Naples before a lecture tour in Bangladesh and India. In Melbourne on July 30 I received a fax from him to say that he had finally received a response from the CDF to the text he had handed over at the start of January. The July response began with a letter which welcomed the clarifications offered by Dupuis's document of December 1998, and included a shorter list of points detailing propositions which were considered "erroneous or ambiguous or insufficient." But there was bad news of Dupuis's health: he had been hemorrhaging and had been rushed to hospital. It turned out that he was not, as he feared, suffering from any cancer in his prostate or his kidneys. But he had to drop the trip to Bangladesh and India that had been scheduled to begin in late July. However, he was happy that his response to Italian reviews of *Toward a Christian Theology of Religious Pluralism* appeared at the end of October 1999 in *Rassegna di teologia*. In the same month *Louvain Studies* published his 52-page-long response to English and French reviews of the same book.

The Storm Ends

When I left the Gregorian at the end of June 2000 to lecture in the United States and return to Rome via Australia, Dupuis was still waiting for any reaction to the sixty-page reply (which he had submitted the previous November) to the second document received from the CDF. In the middle of August he contacted me by fax in Melbourne with the news that the CDF had prepared a "declaration" (*Dominus Iesus*) on Christ's unique and universal impact as Savior and a "notification" on his book. Cardinal Ratzinger had invited him to a meeting scheduled for Monday, September 4, the day before the publication of *Dominus Iesus*. This meeting, the one and only time Dupuis has ever met the Cardinal, was also attended by Archbishop Bertone, Fr. Angelo Amato of the Salesian University, the Jesuit Father General (Peter-Hans Kolvenbach), and myself. The agenda was the text of a "Notification" about Dupuis's book, which contained eight positive propositions (e.g. that Jesus Christ is "the unique and universal mediator of salvation for humanity"), with accusations against the book following six of these propositions. During the two-hour exchange, it became clear that the false opinions the "Notification" listed were not to be found in Dupuis's book; he could not retract what he had never held. There was never any argument about the eight positive propositions.

A second, much shorter, version of the "Notification" was presented to Dupuis's signature in November 2000. This text, somewhat modified and then dated January 24, 2001, was finally published in the *Osservatore Romano* on February 27, 2001. The CDF applauded Dupuis's "willingness to provide the necessary clarifications" and "desire to remain faithful to the doctrine of the Church and the teaching of the magisterium." But, the notification said, the book contains "notable ambiguities and difficulties on important points which could lead a reader to erroneous or harmful opinions." Dupuis was not asked to change a single line in subsequent editions of the book. Instead, the CDF requested that in any new editions or further translations which might appear, the text of the "Notification" should be included. This has been done.

The Issues

The literature and documentation, both published and unpublished, on Dupuis's book is vast. His article for *Louvain Studies* in 1999 took into account, for example, twenty reviews that had appeared in English and twenty-seven in French.[1] Some of these, such as the piece by Terrence Merrigan in *Louvain Studies* itself, entered into critical dialogue with Dupuis in a way that was admirable; others, such as an equally long piece in *Revue thomiste*, seemed a bizarre going back to a dead past. There have been many other reviews in German, Italian, Spanish, and other languages, as well as articles and chapters of books dedicated, in whole or in part, to a critical evaluation of his views. Clearly he has addressed a central question: how to profess and proclaim faith in Jesus Christ as the one redeemer of all humankind, while simultaneously following Pope John Paul II and recognizing the Spirit at work in the world's religions and cultures. Within a Christian perspective, what is the place of the other religions? As revealer and redeemer, Jesus is one and universal, but in practice the visible paths to salvation have remained many. Would Dupuis's views, if, as some said, "taken to their logical conclusion" (whatever that means), eliminate missionary work?

One might distinguish, but not separate, the issues that have emerged into terminological and substantial ones. Terms such as "distinguish," "separate," "absolute," "definitive," "complementary," the "Logos" qualified in various ways, and "pluralism" have recurred over and over again in reflection on Dupuis's work. The debate has essentially come down to the work of Christ, the Holy Spirit, and the Church for the salvation of all people. Let us look first at the terms, trying to "watch our language" in ways rightly encouraged by analytic philosophy but sadly often neglected by contemporary theology.

Some Terms

Over and over again Dupuis has insisted that he distinguishes but does not separate various things: for instance, the divine and human operations of the incarnate Son of God, or distinct paths of salvation within the one divine plan to save all human beings. In using this language to make such points, he has shown himself a faithful follower of the Council of Chalcedon and its vitally important language about the two natures of Christ being distinct but not separated. No critic has found a passage in Dupuis's book (or other writings) where he moves beyond a distinction and introduces a false separation, for example, between the incarnate Word's action within the Church and in the world at large. Critics have alleged that he separates the Word of God and the man Jesus into two separate subjects, but they have never produced chapter and verse to back up this accusation. What Dupuis has consistently argued is that within the one person of Jesus Christ we must distinguish the operations of his (uncreated) divine nature and his (created) human nature. Here he lines up with St. Thomas Aquinas, who championed the oneness of Christ's person but also had to recognize that Christ's "divine nature infinitely transcends his human nature (*divina natura in infinitum humanam excedit*)" (*Summa contra Gentiles*, 4. 35. 8).

Some reviewers puzzled over Dupuis calling Christ "universal" and "constitutive" but not "absolute" Savior and Redeemer, and speaking of the whole "Christ-event" as "decisive" rather than "definitive." Dupuis dislikes the inflationary use of "absolute" and "absolutely" which flourishes in much ordinary speech and in some theological talk. He maintains a firm, Thomistic line: only God, who is totally necessary, utterly unconditional, uncaused, and unlimited, is truly absolute. While Dupuis certainly has never wanted to reduce Christ to being one savior among many, he is sensitive to the limits involved in the historical incarnation of the Son of God, the created character of the humanity he assumed, and the specific quality of his redemptive, human actions. Moreover, the incarnation itself was a free act of God's love and not unconditionally necessary. As regards the other dimension of the divine self-communication in Christ, God's self-revelation which was completed with the resurrection and the coming of the Spirit, one should not so emphasize the "fullness" of this revelation as to ignore "the glorious manifestation of our Lord" still to come (*Dei Verbum*, 4). Our present knowledge of God as revealed to us in Christ is limited and neither "absolute" nor "definitive." Those who claim otherwise ignore the way the language of revelation in the New Testament is strongly angled towards the future (e.g. 1 Cor. 13:12; 1 John 3:2), as Cardinal Avery Dulles pointed out years ago in his *Models of Revelation*.[2] John Paul II said the same thing in his 1998 encyclical on the relationship between faith and reason, *Fides et Ratio*, where he wrote of "the fullness of truth which will appear with the final revelation of God" (2). We "see through a glass darkly" and not yet "face to face"; hence it is more accurate to call the revelation completed in Jesus Christ "decisive" rather than "definitive," a term that would too easily suggest (wrongly) that there is nothing more to come. A knee-jerk reaction characterized some who were upset by Dupuis's refusal to speak of God's historical self-communication in Christ as "absolute": "he must mean that it is only relative and there are various, more or less equal saviors and revealers." That was not what Dupuis meant; in declining to use "absolute" and "definitive," he was sticking closely to the language of Vatican II's *Dei Verbum* and, behind that document, the language of the New Testament itself.

As regards any "complementarity" between Christianity and other religions, Dupuis never intended to deny that the revelation which reached its fullness in Christ is somehow incomplete or imperfect, and so needs to be filled out by other religious traditions. Rather he used that term to indicate how some elements of the one divine mystery can be vividly expressed by the practices and sacred writings found beyond Christianity. In prayerful and respectful dialogue with other traditions, Christians may "hear" something which enriches them spiritually. They can receive as well as give, as the closing message of the 1977 synod of bishops in Rome recalled (5). Nevertheless, to express Christian faith in the unique fullness of the divine self-revelation in Christ, it may have been better for Dupuis to have qualified from the outset the kind of "complementarity" he had in mind. In his subsequent book, *Christianity and the Religions* (Maryknoll, N.Y.: Orbis, 2002), he called this complementarity "asymmetrical"—an adjective which brings out the Christian belief that in Jesus Christ the divine revelation enjoys a unique fullness and completeness and that there is no void to be filled by other revelations and traditions.

In *Toward a Christian Theology of Religious Pluralism* Dupuis distinguished the Logos *asarkos* (the Word of God *in himself* and not, or not yet incarnated) from the Logos *ensarkos* (the Word of God precisely as incarnated). Dupuis was surprised to find this distinction leading a few readers to conclude that he was "doubling" the Logos, as if he were holding that there were four persons in God! To avoid such odd misunderstandings, he has dropped the terms *asarkos* and *ensarkos*. However, he continues to distinguish between the Word of God *in se* and to be incarnated (*incarnandus*) and the Word of God precisely as incarnated. We must make such terminological distinctions. Otherwise we will finish up joining some critics in such a strange statement as "the Word of God *as such* is the Word incarnate." Those who fail "to watch their language" and use such an expression seem to attribute an eternal, real (and not just an intentional) existence to the humanity created and assumed by the Word of God at a certain point in the history of the world, as well as appearing to cast doubt upon the loving freedom of the Word of God in becoming incarnate for our salvation. Presumably such critics meant to write "the Word of God *de facto*/in fact is the Word incarnate." If so, they should have said just that.

Finally, the term "pluralism" has obviously raised a red flag to certain readers. Some link it at once to such "pluralists" as John Hick, who put Christ on a par with other religious founders or at least allege that he differs from them only in degree but not in kind. But "pluralism" means a range of things: above all "pluralism de facto" (which recognizes the fact of different religions) to "pluralism de iure" (which endorses a pluralism in principle). Now this latter pluralism in principle may take a soft, Hickian form: in principle all major religions have equal authority, and hence in principle are equally valid, separate paths to salvation. But pluralism *de iure* may take another form, as, for instance, when the declaration *Dominus Iesus* of September 2000, following the lead of John Paul II (e.g. in his 1990 encyclical *Redemptoris Missio*) acknowledges that God becomes present to peoples through the "spiritual riches" that their religions essentially embody and express (8). "The presence and activity of the Spirit" touch not only individuals but also "cultures and religions" (12); the "elements of religiosity" found in the diverse "religious traditions" come "from God" (21). Now, granted that God never acts merely "in fact" but always "in and on principle," such statements about the Spirit's activity in various religions and all that comes from God to the religions imply some kind of religious "pluralism" which exists in principle. Thus one needs to differentiate sharply between the "pluralists" and "pluralism," and then scrutinize very carefully what kind of "pluralism" Dupuis or anyone else endorses. Knee-jerk reactions to terminology are totally out of place here.

Central Questions

The first of the three central issues raised by Dupuis's book concerns the work of the incarnate Son of God for the salvation of all. Certain critics have attributed to Dupuis something he has never maintained: a personal distinction between the eternal Word of God and the historical Jesus of Nazareth. He has always upheld firmly the Word of God and Jesus are personally identical.

But Dupuis insists on distinguishing (but never separating) the two natures of Christ and their respective operations. Christ's finite human nature remains basically and integrally human, and is therefore incapable of states of being and operations which are strictly infinite and divine. The particular, created character of Christ's humanity in no way threatens his unique role in conveying divine revelation and salvation. That unique value derives from the *personal* identity of the Son of God, an identity which is not to be confused *tout court* with his two natures and their operations. In *Toward a Christian Theology of Religious Pluralism*, Dupuis might have cited the Third Council of Constantinople (680/81) in support of his position here: that Council distinguished not only between the two wills of Christ but also between the "energies and operations" of the two natures. In the incarnation the Son of God's divine nature does not lose its essential characteristics and functions. In subsequent publications Dupuis has drawn attention to the importance of this Council's teaching for reflection on the universal salvific activity of the divine Word before and after the incarnation.[3]

In particular, Dupuis argues that, while the human acts of his whole historical story enjoy an ever-present efficacy, the Word's universal divine operations are not canceled or restricted by his assumption of a human existence that has now been glorified through the resurrection. Both before and after the incarnation, the Word of God remains divinely present and active everywhere, and has not been somehow "eclipsed" by the assumption of a human nature. This vision of the Logos' activity draws support from the way some major exegetes understand John 1:9 ("the true Light that enlightens everyone, coming into this world"), from the writings on the Logos of such Church Fathers as St. Justin Martyr, St. Irenaeus, (St.) Clement of Alexandria, and St. Athanasius, and from such modern theologians as Avery Dulles, later Cardinal Dulles. In fact, Dulles anticipated the conclusion Dupuis wished to draw from the universal activity of the Logos:

> It need not be denied that the eternal Logos could manifest itself to other peoples through other religious symbols. . . . In continuity with a long Christian tradition of the Logos-theology that goes back as far as Justin Martyr . . . it may be held that the divine person who appears in Jesus is not exhausted by that historical appearance. The symbols and myths of other religions may point to the one whom Christians recognize as the Christ.[4]

Dupuis wants to add two points to such a position.

First, he repeats over and over again that the Word of God who remains universally operative is personally identical with Jesus of Nazareth. One must distinguish between the divine and human actions, but never between two personal agents. Second, along with all the distinctions to be drawn, there is only one divine plan of salvation. All people are called to share finally in the one divine life of the Trinity, through the gracious activity (both human and divine) of the incarnate Son of God and the divine activity of the Holy Spirit. I cannot understand how some readers of Dupuis's book could miss his insistence on the divine plan of salvation through Christ and the Spirit being undivided and not multiple. He excludes any talk of two "economies" of salvation: either in the form of an alleged pneumatocentric plan of salvation separated from a Christocentric one, or in the form of an economy of salvation in the Word as such which is separate from an economy of salvation in the incarnate Word.

Mention of the Spirit leads us to a second major issue. On the one hand, the Holy Spirit was poured out at Pentecost to give life to the Church in her mission to preach to all people the good news of Christ crucified and risen for our salvation. Dupuis values as much as anyone the ongoing power of the Spirit, working in and through the glorified Christ, both in the life of the Church (Vatican II, *Lumen Gentium*, 3-4) and in the whole world (Vatican II, *Gaudium et Spes*, 22). But, on the other hand, he also emphasizes that the action of the Spirit is not confined to acting in and through the risen humanity of Christ. Before the incarnation, the Spirit acted in a revelatory and salvific fashion (Vatican II, *Ad Gentes*, 4). With the resurrection and Pentecost the Spirit, while working in total communion with the glorified Christ, does not lose his/her universal, divine activity, so as to exercise his/her mission "ad extra" only through the mediation of Jesus' risen humanity. To allege that the Spirit's saving and revelatory action takes place exclusively through Christ's glorified humanity means maintaining the kind of Christomonism which Eastern Christians have often rightly denounced. If the visible incarnation did not mean the suppression of the divine powers of the Word, a fortiori the invisible, non-incarnate mission of the Holy Spirit did not entail limiting the divine nature of the Spirit (which is the only operative principle possessed by the Spirit—in common with the Father and the Son). What Dupuis has written about the universal mission of the divine Spirit fills out very nicely, I would argue, what John Paul II has taught about the Spirit operating beyond the visible Church and enriching the world's cultures and religions.

This activity of the Spirit reaches and enriches the members of various religions in and through their religious life and practice. There is no other way possible, since that is where Hindus, Muslims, Buddhists, and others live and worship. Since these religions contain elements of truth and goodness (Vatican II, *Nostra Aetate*) and the Spirit of God is mysteriously but powerfully present to them, adherents of these religions can reach salvation by following the ways proposed to them. In some sense their religions are ways of salvation for them. In a guarded way the International Theological Commission reached this conclusion in its 1997 document on "Christianity and the Religions": "Because of such explicit recognition of the presence of Christ's Spirit in the religions [the reference is to John Paul II's 1990 encyclical, *Redemptoris Missio*, 55], one cannot exclude the possibility that these [religions] *as such* exercise a certain salvific function" (84). This document went on to allow cautiously that the religions can be "a means which helps their followers to salvation" (86).

But Dupuis adds four qualifications to this picture. First, over and over again he relates the ways of salvation proposed by other religious traditions to the "event of Jesus Christ": that is to say, Dupuis never forgets the mysterious but real relationship of these "ways" to the incarnation, life, death, resurrection, present activity and future coming of Christ. Second, all this happens as foreseen and intended by God. Granted that under God the various religions have a positive role for the salvation of their adherents, there is only one divine plan of salvation for the whole world, a whole in which one can distinguish different parts: namely, the paths proposed by different religious traditions. In that picture it is God the Father who searches us out and saves us, through his (incarnate) Word and his Spirit; it is improper, or at best secondary, to speak of people being saved through any religious traditions. Here Dupuis can rightly appeal to the Council of Trent, which called God the Father "the efficient cause" of justification and salvation (DH 1529). Third, Dupuis has highlighted the *final* causality in the divine plan for salvation. In that one plan all things, all cultures, and all religions converge toward the final reign of God and the omega-point, the risen and glorious Son of God.[5] Fourth, Dupuis has repeatedly acknowledged that the fullness of the means of salvation is to be found only in the Church. But what then is the role of the Church for the salvation of those who are not baptized and go to God after a life spent in practicing their religious faith?

Most theologians remain grateful that the Second Vatican Council never repeated the old slogan of "outside the Church no salvation"—a slogan that many explained (or should one say explained away?) by talking of people being saved through "implicitly desiring" to belong to the Church or by an "implicit baptism of desire." The Council used rather the language of all people being "ordered" or "oriented" towards the Church (*Lumen Gentium*, 13-16).[6] What then is the "necessity" of the Church for the salvation of all human beings? To begin with, one should follow Dupuis in recognizing that the Reign of God is the decisive point of reference. The Church exists for the Kingdom and at its service, not vice versa. Second, one should join Dupuis in noticing how the official magisterium, from the time of Vatican II, is more cautious and less precise about the Church's role in the saving grace reaching those who are not baptized Christians (e.g. John Paul II, *Redemptoris Missio*, 9, 10); the mystery of God's plan to save all must be respected. Third, the Church mediates grace to her members principally, although not exclusively, through the proclamation of the Word and the sacraments, the center of which is the Eucharist; she intercedes for "the others." The eucharistic prayers distinguish between the invocation of the Holy Spirit to maintain the unity of the faithful and liturgical intercessions for "others" (intercessions which do not take the form of an *epiklesis*). Here the "law of praying" should encourage theologians not to blur the distinction between the Church's role for the salvation of her members and for the salvation of "the others."

At a special audience on April 6, 2001, to commemorate the 450 years of the

Gregorian University's existence, Pope John Paul II highlighted the importance of interreligious dialogue in today's world where believers of different religions and cultures live side by side. Jacques Dupuis, as a systematic theologian who spent nearly forty years of his life in India, offers a shining example in supporting such a dialogue—not only through his *Toward a Christian Theology of Religious Pluralism* but through other publications and activities. His theology of the religions converges with the official teaching and actions of John Paul II, and provides it with a massive theological underpinning.

References

[1]More than one hundred reviews appear in the bibliography on *Toward a Christian Theology of Religious Pluralism* at the end of this Festschrift.

[2]2nd ed. (Maryknoll, N.Y.: Orbis, 1992), 228-29, 240-42.

[3]"Le Verbe de Dieu: Jésus Christ et les religions du monde," *Nouvelle Revue Théologique* 123 (2001), 529-46, at 537-38. As well as invoking Constantinople III, Dupuis recalled in the same section of this article the importance of teaching from Leo the Great's *Tomus ad Flavianum* for distinguishing between the infinite, uncreated, divine activity of the Son of God and his finite, created, human activity. See also Dupuis, *Christianity and the Religions* (Maryknoll, N.Y.: Orbis, 2002), 144.

[4]*Models of Revelation*, 190.

[5]See the concluding remarks in *Toward a Christian Theology of Religious Pluralism*, 389-90.

[6]See ibid., 347-56.

Part II

THEOLOGICAL REFLECTIONS

4

On Being Theological

A Christian Encounter
with Buddhism

Michael Barnes, S.J.

Jacques Dupuis has long argued for a theology of religions which is relational in scope and intent; that is to say, one which opens up areas of complementarity and mutual enrichment between the religions. In recent years Christians have learned that it is no longer possible to understand their faith without reference to the faith of the Jews and to the Covenant of Sinai which has never been revoked. It may, therefore, be relatively uncontroversial to argue that Judaism has a substantive role to play in Christian self-understanding.[1] Christianity was formed in a particular historical milieu, in relationship with its "Jewish other," and will always betray the traces of that unique relationship. But what about other engagements with other religions which have developed in the course of history? Does not a similar process of inter-cultural and interreligious interrogation attend Christian faith wherever the Spirit leads Christians into new relationships with "other others?" In what sense may we speak of them as having something to do with the unfolding of God's providential purposes for humankind?

This possibility takes on a special significance when we consider the radical otherness of Buddhism—where difference appears to reach the point of incommensurability. It is one thing to speak of the intrinsically Jewish dimension of Christian faith; quite another to seek to relate that faith to a tradition whose doctrine of *anātmāvāda* appears radically to call into question the Christian conviction of being a unique individual called by God. Put in such a way, the crucial question is not the relatively straightforward probing of the limits of terminology and language but the more challenging issue of *how to be theological at all*? How are Christians to learn to speak with Christian integrity about the *theological significance* of Buddhism for Christian faith?

Persons in Relation

A recent collection of essays is revealingly asymmetrical in the way contributors speak about their experience of relating to the persons of Buddha and Jesus.[2] The Christians claim to admire the Buddha and to have benefited spiritually from their contact with Buddhism; the Buddhists, on the other hand, express a deep appreciation of Jesus' teaching but have little time for Christian confessions about his significance. Where Christians feel an imperative to explore possible "seeds of the Word" in the world of the other, Buddhists are content to follow a "Middle Way" which is suspicious of all speculative theory and sees no need to investigate, let alone incorporate, "other" ways. Yet underlying such disjunctions—which owe as much to expectations of the dialogue as they do to attitudes towards "the theological"—lies something more profoundly symmetrical about attitudes towards human flourishing and the nature of true personhood. Buddhism is anthropocentric; Christianity theocentric. Buddhism begins with the impersonal; Christianity with the personal. Whatever the truth in such popular disjunctions, a dialogue which begins with stereotypes rather than rooting itself in the *liberating experience which the language of tradition seeks to describe* is unlikely ever to get beyond polemic and caricature.

So much is obvious. If the first principle of dialogue is to see others as they see themselves, then it is clearly necessary to avoid the sort of projection which, at best, reflects back a Christian agenda and, at worst, represents a spiritualized version of the concerns of post-Enlightenment modernity. Paradoxically, it is often in the human relationship, where we may be confronted with a disarming sense of radical otherness, that we also find hope of better understanding and a more adequate theology. Instead, therefore, of asking how different ideas of personhood and human flourishing can somehow be made compatible, the question to ask is why particular ideas of personhood emerge in the first place. Otherwise Christians (if not Buddhists) will end up locked into the terms of the Enlightenment culture of what David Tracy calls "possessive individualism," the defense of some identifiable, substantive self in face of an ever-threatening "other."[3] The value of Tracy's "post-modern" engagement with Buddhism is that it highlights the extent to which the Christian account of the self is always likely to be reduced to a manageable sense of "given identity." The Buddhist account of the person as essentially *anattā/anātman*—lacking a substantive sense of self—is nothing if not a reminder that Christianity too is based on a sense of personhood which is only ever found by being lost. As Corless points out, in his juxtaposition of the two parables of spiritual progress from Julian of Norwich and the Lotus Sutra, spiritual progress is only ever made by confronting sin or ignorance, not by denying its reality.[4] In both traditions the fundamental "problem" of the human condition is the transience of all things. The paradox is that in understanding that truth correctly lies the solution. For the Christian it means the embrace of death, after the manner of Christ; for a Buddhist it entails a quite radical denial of "soul-theories" in imitation of the Buddha's enlightenment experience of seeing things "as they really are."

Clearly concepts of true personhood, ideals of what makes for human destiny or fulfilment, differ enormously—even within the traditions. But this does not mean that there is not a roughly similar *strategy* of achieving true human personhood at work. By confronting truth in the "here and now" and deliberately avoiding any would-be escape into a "safe haven," a comfortable "beyond," Buddhists and Christians ask the same questions—even though the philosophical and cultural roots from which they spring mean that they come up with radically different answers. For the *Theravādin* the person is a linguistic construct which is analyzed in the course of thorough introspective meditation; in the *Mahāyāna* liberation comes not through such "personless" self-effacement, but by working for a vision of the personal as always "inter-personal," in which the "I" can only be said to exist in so far as it exists in relationship with the other. In both schools there seems to be very little by way of an individual self; there is only the inter-connectedness of persons.

In Christianity, of course, the concept of person emerges more directly, and more strongly, from the biblical image of a humanity made "in the image of God." Human beings are essentially made for an eternal relationship with God. It may be possible to distinguish roughly between a more ecclesial or communitarian Catholic sense of how God's grace is "at work" in the world, and a more individualistic Protestant sense of personhood formed in response to God's Word. Yet both have their validity, reflecting two complementary sides of Judeo-Christian faith, that God calls each person "by name" and has formed a people for himself. For a Christian salvation, "human flourishing," is both personal or communitarian. But how to avoid the sort of extremes which lead to a "possessive individualism" or a totalizing inclusivism? Is there something to be learned from the way Buddhism steers a middle way between the extremes of "eternalism" and "annihilationism"?[5]

In Buddhism the human subject is analyzed in terms of the five *skandhas* or "aggregates," none of which has any ultimate value in itself. Any account of "the human" which would isolate some sort of essential *atman* is vigorously resisted. Instead the self-perception formed by mindfulness takes one out of the obsession with seeking an unchanging ultimate and develops the "counter-perception" of *pratītyasamutpāda*, the vision of a radical relatedness. In Christianity, human destiny is understood not as the survival of some separable "soul"-essence but in terms of *resurrection*, in imitation of the one whom God raised from the dead. In 1 Corinthians 15, for instance, Paul is attacking an early form of Christian "eternalism," some sort of Platonist belief in an enduring if not transmigrating "soul." He stresses how much Christian faith makes a radical challenge to such assumptions. The Resurrection is not just a demonstration of God's power over death and therefore a *motive for faith*; it is, more exactly, the self-revelation of God himself and therefore an *object of faith*. In other words, Christians believe in a God who has raised Jesus from the dead and now promises to do the same for all who believe and are therefore incorporated into Christ. The form which that incorporation takes is a new way of embodiment. This is the belief which makes Christians more than just another religious community whose identity lies in following a particular teaching. For Paul they are a new creation, the "Body of Christ." As the people of Israel were themselves called by God "from among the nations," so the disciples are constituted as Church, the beginnings and sign of what the world is to become. They find themselves "embodied in Christ" through the life-giving action of his Spirit. In Paul's terms what was once a "physical body" into which God breathed life is now re-created anew through the Spirit of Christ and made a spiritual body (1 Cor 15:44).

There is at least one way in which the Buddhist concept of *pratītyasamutpāda* reinforces rather than contradicts the Christian conviction of being called by the imageless God out of darkness. Everything exists "in dependence." Putting it in very un-Buddhist terms, there is never a self which can be set apart from the other. Rather the self is a self precisely *because of* the other. In Christianity the individual receives eternal value from responding to the call to enjoy a filial relationship with God. But salvation is always mediated through socially and culturally bound forms of human existence. God does not pluck us out of this world. In the manner in which God calls a people for himself is grounded the possibility of harmony in human relationships. Putting it another way, Christians meet in Christ, whose members they become and whose fellowship they seek to share with others. Indeed without that sharing—a Christian version of the Buddhist *karuna* or compassion—there is something crucially lacking to the practice of Christian faith. Christians are always being called to learn how to become persons who are not "mere" individuals but individuals who exist in relation to each other because they always exist in relation to God. Yet it must never be forgotten that this is *God's* initiative. God alone can form this new people, this new set of redeemed relations. Which is why theology, our attempt to risk speech about God, begins with an imperative—the "hear, O Israel" of the *Shema* or the words of Jesus to the disciples, "follow me," "come and see." For both traditions the first—and indeed last—experience of God is that God is Emmanuel, come to be "with us."

The Silence of God

Buddhism, notoriously, refuses even the speech which acknowledges this measure of a radical dependence. The Buddha's silence can be interpreted in a number of ways, from sheer agnosticism to a nihilistic insistence that language is only a source of mystification. But there is also the possibility that it should be treated in *apophatic* terms as a version of what in Christian terms is sometimes called the *via negativa*. This "negative way" is usually understood as reflecting the conviction that God is strictly "ineffable" or beyond grasping by human intelligence and therefore by human language. Put like this, it implies the *remoteness* of the Ultimate. That scarcely seems fair to the Christian mystical tradition where "darkness" is very often the image used to describe a *closeness* which, in its overwhelming superabundance of light, is positively blinding. The *apophatic* response does not, therefore, spring from a cool conviction that language is inadequate to describe the experience of God and must somehow be transcended; it arises from wonder at the sheer awesomeness of God. In Buddhism too the Buddha does not claim that he does not know; it is much more that words cannot contain everything that can be said.[6]

More specifically, of course, the Buddha refused to answer questions which he considered unhelpful. More so than the Christian mystics, he engaged in a critique of religious language, a critique he considered to be liberative. Immediately, of course, the Buddha was reacting against the religion of the Brahmanical sacrifice, its sheer "wordiness" and the human desire for hard and fast answers which it embodied. All too easily, words, images and symbols can become idols. This is not to say, however, that the Buddha denies "God" or Ultimate Reality. Rather he attempts to overcome the tendency to idolize some symbol or image of God by awakening people to a sense of their own contingency.

In both traditions, the *apophatic* has to be related to the *kataphatic*, the so-called positive way or way of analogy and images. In some way the former grows out of the latter, developing a sort of *docta ignorantia*. Literally, of course, this term means "taught ignorance," but in the light of Buddhism it might almost be translated as "enlightened silence." It seeks to follow the example of the Buddha himself who, according to the mythology, only decided to speak about Dharma out of compassion for suffering sentient beings and at the specific request of the god Brahma. The risk in speaking of God (in this sense, of course, the risk taken by any strictly *kataphatic* theology) is that words disfigure, that they turn the Ultimate into an object. To guard against this, the Buddha speaks not of the goal itself, but only of the *way* to the goal. Buddhism is called the "middle way" not just because it seeks to avoid extremes of practice but because it encourages an equanimity with regard to the goal. To be "in the middle" is enough.

According to Raimundo Panikkar, the Buddha's silence can only properly be understood within the context of meditation.[7] To put it again in Christian terms, theology is not speculation but a response to God which begins in contemplative wonder of God's call to be "with" him. Panikkar is thus undoubtedly right that it is only within the silence of the heart that this peculiarly Buddhist quality of "equanimity"—which leaves one, as it were, on the threshold of *Nirvāna*—can be experienced. But he also wants to point out how silence can assume a constructive role within all ritual, a role which sets it in a dialectical play with "word," the language which in some sense can be said to "command" or "control" the sacrifice.

According to an important myth "from pre-Buddhist times," Panikkar tells us, the god Prajapati tried to adjudicate between the claims of Word (*Vāc*) and Mind (*Manas*) as to which was the greater.[8] He came down on the side of Spirit because Word only "follows and imitates" what Mind is doing. Panikkar translates *Manas* as Spirit but the word refers more exactly to the human cognitional faculty, the inner heart or "spirit" of the person which *contemplates* Word rather than speaks about it or names it. Panikkar's point is that all words issue from silence and must return to silence. As a Christian would say, the Word is spoken out of the silence of the Father.

Ritual is, of course, based on a response which is expressed in words—through the liturgical action itself, hymns of praise, formal prayers etc. But it relies for its effectiveness on the silence which it encourages and to which ultimately it leads. No religion, as Panikkar reminds us, can afford to ignore the religious significance of silence. "Even in a tradition like the Judeo-Christian, in which praise is very often the dominant element in ritual, the observance of silence cannot be dispensed with when one comes face to face with God. And of course the tool par excellence of the contemplative life is the silence that hushes not only word but also, and especially, thought. Silence regards mystery."[9]

The Buddhist way is not normally thought of as a ritual but it is impossible to ignore many ritual-like elements in the practice of the Noble Eightfold Path, not just the central practice of meditation but the taking of the refuges[10] and precepts. What is being developed, however, through these formal elements is not some sort of speculative intellectual structure of faith but the silence which stills the restless mind. The particular insight behind *Madhyamika* practice, for instance, with its growing reflexive awareness that words reify and therefore condition our perceptions, is that the use of language to speak of ultimate reality is always likely to be self-defeating. But, since it is impossible to step outside the "webs" of language, the only way to overcome the betrayals of language is precisely *through* language. Like all ritual speech *about* God or ultimate reality, words have to give way to silence *before* God if the true end of ritual is to be realized.

This may give some clue as to how the *apophatic* and *kataphatic* dimensions are to work together. Looked at in Buddhist terms, Silence and Word are always "dependently co-arisen"; they depend on and enfold each other. What has to be learned are the "skillful means" which discern how the two levels of truth—conventional truth (*samvtisatya*) and ultimate truth (*paramārthasatya*)—are continually interacting, leading the meditator towards that level of mindfulness which sees things "as they really are." For the Christian mystic, of course, the key question is Christological. How to speak of Christ the Word (perhaps, more properly, how to allow the Word to speak) in the "light" of a mystic darkness? The classical account, mapped out by Greek Fathers like Origen, Dionysius the Areopagite and Gregory of Nyssa, speaks of the threefold purgative, illuminative and unitive ways. But this is not so much a rising to higher and higher stages but more a spiraling movement in which the original divine image in which human beings are made is restored. After the initial drawing into light, the mind has to come to terms not so much with the inadequacy of language but with the *vulnerability of the self* in the presence of God. Ultimately such an intimate restoration of the "sense of God" can be expressed only in terms of love. Not unlike the Buddha's insistence that one can speak only of the "middle way," not of the goal itself, so the Christian remains always "on the way," only ever *with Christ* in God.

Of the Form of God

Our reflections on the nature of a Christian faith which enters into serious engagement with Buddhism seem, almost inexorably, to raise questions about the theological value of *relationality* itself. Where—to oversimplify somewhat —is God Emmanuel in the Christian's relationship with his or her Buddhist other? The suggestion already advanced is that the mystery of the self-revealing God is to be discerned in the unfolding story of the Buddhist-Christian dialogue, especially in what Buddhists and Christians may learn *together* about the nature of humanity. Can we now go further and, however tentatively, suggest that the same mystery is also present within the *story which is Buddhism itself*—albeit in the form which Levinas would refer to as a "trace of the other"? The challenge here is to read the Christian and the Buddhist stories together—to let them develop echoes of each other or what, following some suggestive remarks of Christopher Brown, might be called "resonances."[11]

In this regard it is not unhelpful to discern Trinitarian "resonances." With the *parinirvāna* or final enlightenment of the Buddha, questions began to be asked about the nature of one who lived as a human being yet also transcended the human condition. Buddha himself stated that "he who sees the Buddha sees the Dharma, he who sees the Dharma sees the Buddha." He was also held to have acquired special yogic powers by means of which he could travel at will to other realms and preach the Dharma to all manner of sentient beings, including the gods. The earliest form of "Buddhology" seems to have recognized a distinction between the Buddha's *Rūpakāya* or "form-body" and the *Dharmakāya* or "transcendent body," the former focusing on the cult of relics, embodied in the burial mounds or *stupas*, and the latter on the Buddha's teaching. The two bodies can be understood as ways in which the Buddha's memory or influence can be said in some sense to continue. As speculation developed, especially under the influence of the *Mahayāna* practice of glorifying the *sūtras* (understood as "further" teachings of the Buddha taught by enlightened *bodhisattvas*), a threefold division emerged: the *Nirmānakāya* or "apparition body" by which the Buddha appears in human form and preaches the Dharma to human beings; the *Sambhogkāya* or "enjoyment body" which the Buddha assumes to preach to the heavenly *bodhisattvas*; the *Dharmakāya*, the unmanifest form or "transcendent body" which is the ultimate truth shared by all Buddhas.

There are some intriguing parallels between this emergent Buddhology and the way in which Christology and the doctrine of Trinity develop within Christianity. The Resurrection narratives express a similar quandary: the Risen Lord is now exalted to be with the Father, yet continues to bear the marks of crucifixion and his earthly life. A Christian will, however, see in the *Trikāya* Buddhology a docetism which makes the "historical" Buddha, Siddhartha Gautama, just one example of a projection into the world on the part of some sort of transcendent principle. To that extent any purely speculative attempt to draw an analogy between the Buddhist teaching and the Christian doctrine of the Trinity is bound to be misleading. But perhaps the dialogue, not to mention the cautions of the Buddha, are reminding us that metaphysical speculation is not the best place to begin?

Buddhist doctrine is not to be understood as the elaboration of some philosophical conundrum but primarily in terms of the concept of *upaya,* the "skillful means" by which the Dharma is taught. And, however much Christian theology may have been formed by the dialogue with Hellenistic culture, faith in the triune God is—to repeat—essentially a response to the call of the one who experienced God as Father and promised the coming of the Spirit of truth. If the context of a spiritual discipline (in Buddhism) and the life of discipleship (in Christianity) is borne in mind, then a suggestive, if somewhat inchoate, comparative "resonance" between the two traditions emerges. In Buddhism consciousness is formed by a discipline which moves from hearing the Dharma spoken by an enlightened one, through practices inspired by the memory of the enlightened one, to enlightenment itself. In Christianity the new identity of the disciples is formed by the action of the Spirit, in whom they confess that Jesus is Lord—the one whose life, death and resurrection manifests the God he calls Abba, Father. But in neither instance is the *summum bonum,* the ultimate truth about human nature and destiny, reducible to a *gnosis* or some sort of esoteric wisdom.

The fundamental point is that for both traditions truth is not to be identified as some "transcendent essence"—lurking, as it were, undetected in the metaphysical undergrowth—but is always *embodied or incarnated* in some form. Truth can never be limited to culture but is, nevertheless, *inseparable from* culture. Hence the need to find a way of differentiating between form, which implies limitation of some kind, and the unlimited or unconditioned to which form points or leads. Classical Christian theology has always used the concept of analogy to speak about God, always recognizing that, however much God may be thematized in human language, and thus be said to be "like" some human form, the "unlikeness" is always greater. This is why *Pneuma* must complement *Logos*—not so much to allow God somehow to function in two interdependent ways but, more profoundly, to remind us that *form can never be exhausted by the consciousness of form.* Thus when Jesus calls God Abba he is not turning God into some comforting icon or talisman. Nor as the face which reveals God's glory (2 Cor 4:6) does Jesus displace the God who surpasses all understanding. Rather, in Jesus is heard God's Word, the voice which speaks out of the silent depths of God.

Jesus thus introduces us into a *relationship* which itself expresses the very nature of God. At the same time, as Buddhists would remind Christians, to name that which is beyond all names is to risk idolatry. That is why it is only "in the Spirit of Christ" that we are able to speak of that relationship, because the Spirit witnesses not merely to the "naming" of God which takes place "in Christ" but also to the wider context of a discipleship, which leads the one who dares to use that name Emmanuel further and further into the infinity and inexhaustibility of the self-giving God. Put another way, the Spirit is the Spirit of Christ, because the Spirit is always the Spirit of love whose very nature is to go on witnessing to the continual unfolding of the mystery which is God.

In terms of the concept of *Pratītyasamutpāda,* the Father is Father *because of* the Son and the Son is Son *because of* the Father. There can be no isolated "given" identity which can somehow be separated from that which is other. Buddhists do not, of course, identify or name the "poles" of the relationship, still less do they speculate on the nature of the principle which, as a theoretical account of causality, can be said to hold the relationship in being. The Spirit is not to be interpreted, therefore, as a rather more dynamic or creative notion of the concept of *Pratītyasamutpāda.* Nor is the Spirit to be regarded as the *Sambhogakāya* to Jesus' more "explicit" human role as the *Nirmānakāya.* Nevertheless, some version of this "inner" differentiation within the single *Dharmakāya* or Buddha-nature may be helpful in explaining in Buddhist terms the mystery of the Incarnation—and, possibly, give some insight into the significance of the economic Trinity for Christian living.

Dharma is not to be equated in any purely speculative way with God, but that—to repeat—is the wrong place to start: with the search for word or concept equivalents. *Dharma* does not exist apart from Buddha; to be more precise, *Dharma is* Buddha—and what the Buddha says and does, in manifold and inexhaustible ways. If this is correct, then maybe in the dialogue with Buddhism it makes more sense to begin with the Spirit: not, that is, with preconceived notions about Ultimate Reality which have to be painfully and systematically deconstructed but with the glimpse of the mysterious *sunyata* of the everyday. Such a suggestion is implicit in Panikkar's account of the myth of *Vāc* and *Manas:* we may only utter the name of God because God inspires speech in us. This is the work of the Spirit. The Spirit initiates and orders the life of discipleship, leading the Christian community into the depths of the Paschal Mystery just as the same Spirit leads Christians back, as it were, to the one whom Jesus called Father. In this sense the guiding, enlivening, enabling Spirit of Christ, assumes something of the nature of the *Dharmakāya*—its compassionate skill-in-means, as it were. The Spirit leads us "into all the truth" by pointing in two directions at once. By living "in the Spirit" we see in the face of Jesus the memories which form our faith— *and* we also see the face of one whose features are reflected in myriad ways in other people, the poor and the suffering, those in joy and in pain, those whose faith rejoices in other names, and those whose faith demands a profound silence before the unnameable.

Conclusion: Ways of Speaking of God

According to David Tracy, the very "otherness" of Buddhist thought and the challenge it makes to Christian concepts of self and God have reinforced the sense of alienation which is typical of post-modernity.[12] But in another, perhaps somewhat surprising, way, the experience of the post-modern has enhanced the dialogue—not by commending plurality as such but by freeing up a certain capacity to retrieve what has been forgotten or ignored. At its best the post-modern deconstructs various modern myths about progress and power; it thus sets any

tradition within a wider historical context of social and political relations and allows key insights and concepts to stand out with greater clarity. Stephen Batchelor's
post-modern Buddhist reflections on "the way," for instance, remind us that the
original Buddhist image is of path-making through a wilderness, not building permanent highways.[13] In this light—a return to the context of spiritual practice—
Śūnyātavāda appears not as "nihilism" (essentially a nineteenth-century, Western
construction which effectively slots Buddhism into a spectrum of "grand narratives"), but in properly Buddhist terms as a correlate of *Pratītyasamutpāda*. Batchelor
thus concludes that "instead of seeing itself in opposition to other grand narratives that seem to contradict or threaten it, Buddhism remembers how in its vital
periods it has emerged out of its interactions with religions, philosophies and
cultures other than its own."[14] This should remind Christians that what both traditions hold in common is a quite profound capacity to adapt to culture. Indeed
both might almost be defined (if we may allow ourselves a very un-postmodern
move) by such a capacity.

It is, of course, true that Buddhism needs to be understood against its
Brahmanical background and Christianity through its Jewish roots. To that extent both are inseparable from very particular religious origins. But they are also
critiques of and, to some extent, reactions against these origins. In different ways
such a conscious distancing was provoked by the conviction of their *universal
significance*; the Gospel is Good News for all peoples while the Dharma is to be
preached for the welfare of all sentient beings. Both are "missionary" traditions,
committed to the communication of a message and therefore needing consciously
to find appropriate translation and what contemporary Christians might call
"inculturation." This has marked the way Buddhism and Christianity have developed and—despite (or possibly because of) various reform and reactionary movements—explains the proliferating forms they have taken historically. While Christianity may generally be more "prophetic" and Buddhism more "mystical" in
ethos, style and practice, both traditions exist only *in relationship* with "the other."
It is not possible to separate out some sort of "pure essence" of either Buddhism
or Christianity; both are bound up with and inseparable from particular symbolic
forms.

Some version of this principle must be present in all major religious traditions; the alternative, a straight identification of faith with culture, would reduce
a religion to a narrow tribalism. As Aloysius Pieris says, "each religion is a *singular* phenomenon and represents, in a way, a *judgment* passed on every other
religion."[15] There are, in other words, descriptive and normative elements in any
religion which intermingle with each other. Buddhism and Christianity as consciously universal religions make the point most strongly—which is why the
question of the theological significance of Buddhism for Christians is particularly difficult to assess. In the Buddhist-Christian encounter as outlined above,
we find ourselves dealing not just with two more or less comparable stories or
"language games," one drawing its inspiration from the Buddha, the other from
Jesus, but with two different norms or *meta-narratives*, claims to discern the
universal meaning behind or within any particular culture.

If this is correct, then there are clear limitations in a dialogue conceived as the correlation of concepts, in the comparing and contrasting of different languages. This may, however, turn out to be something of an advantage theologically. Whatever "resonances" between the traditions may be suggested will always have to be subsumed within a much greater context of distance and dissonance. Because of their entirely separate origins and history, Buddhism and Christianity remain, to use Pieris's term, radically *singular* phenomena. This does not mean, however, that they cannot challenge and critique each other and that they may not do so in ways which stimulate a deeper self-understanding. The future of the dialogue, therefore, will lie not in passing judgement on the adequacy of the other's concepts (though it may at times demand that) but, more importantly, in what Cobb calls a "*mutual* transformation."[16] Christians may not, in any particular instance, be in a position to pass judgement on the other; nor may it be appropriate to do so. But, if it is the case that Christian faith exists not in some "pure" state but always *in relationship*, then we will always be expected at least to listen to the other by seeking responsibly to read our own narrative in the light of similar Buddhist concepts.

To be avoided, however, is any "artificial convergence" which fits the other into "a broader scheme of ultimate reality."[17] To be cultivated is that generosity which respects the faith of the other and acknowledges with humility the possibility that God may be speaking *to Christians* through the other. If Buddhism is itself a critique of all narratives, then the dialogue should reinforce in Christians the proper sort of reticence—*care in the way we presume to speak about God*—which expresses the very best of the Christian tradition.

References

[1]This is the thesis developed in my *Theology and the Dialogue of Religions* (Cambridge: Cambridge University Press, 2002).

[2]Rita M. Gross and Terry C. Muck (eds.), *Buddhists Talk about Jesus, Christians Talk about Buddha* (New York: Continuum, 2000).

[3]See, for example, his *Dialogue with the Other: The Inter-religious Dialogue* (Louvain: Peeters Press, 1990).

[4]Roger Corless, "The Dramas of Spiritual Progress," *Mystics Quarterly* 11 (1985), 65-75.

[5]I have learned much from the thorough analysis of the Buddhist teaching of *anatta* (based on the *Theravāda* tradition) and the insightful theological critique of Lynn D'Silva's invaluable *The Problem of the Self in Buddhism and Christianity* (London: Macmillan, 1979).

[6]On the relationship between Buddhism and the Christian mystical tradition, see the provocative yet admirably lucid study by John Keenan, *The Meaning of Christ: A Mahayana Theology* (Maryknoll, N. Y.: Orbis, 1989).

[7]See, in particular, his *The Silence of God: The Answer of the Buddha* (Maryknoll, N.Y.: Orbis, 1989).

[8]See "Silence and the Word: The Smile of the Buddha," in *Myth, Faith and Hermeneutics* (Bangalore: Asian Trading Corporation, 1983), 257-276.

[9]See *The Silence of God*, 156.

[10][This refers to the threefold Buddhist "refuges": "I take refuge in the Buddha; I take refuge in the teaching; I take refuge in the community." Eds.]

[11]Christopher A. Brown, "Can Buddhism Save? Finding Resonance in Incommensurability," *Cross Currents* 49 (1999), 164-196.

[12]Tracy, *Dialogue with the Other*, 70 ff.

[13]Stephen Batchelor, "The Other Enlightenment Project: Buddhism, Agnosticism and Postmodernity," in Ursula King (ed.), *Faith and Praxis in a Post-modern Age* (London: Cassell, 1998), 113-127.

[14]Ibid., 126.

[15]Aloysius Pieris, *Love Meets Wisdom* (Maryknoll, N. Y.: Orbis, 1988), 17.

[16]John Cobb, *Beyond Dialogue: Toward a Mutual Transformation of Christianity and Buddhism* (Philadelphia: Fortress, 1982).

[17]Brown, "Can Buddhism Save?", 189.

5

From the Theology of Religious Pluralism to an Interreligious Theology

Claude Geffré, O.P.

The theology of religions has become one of the liveliest and most intensively worked chapters in contemporary theology. It is tempting to say that just as atheism could be the *horizon* against which the theology of the second half of the twentieth century reinterpreted the great truths of the Christian faith, religious pluralism is tending to become the *horizon* of the theology of the twenty-first century, and it is inviting us to revisit the major chapters of all dogmatic theology. It is the response to a new situation in history, and likewise the consequence of a key intuition of Vatican II, which for the first time in the history of the Roman magisterium has passed a positive judgment on non-Christian religions.

In the following pages I will begin by highlighting the newness of interreligious dialogue, which goes hand in hand with the planetary era of humankind. We will then look at the efforts of recent theology to take religious pluralism seriously as a theological issue and to seek to provide a theological foundation for interreligious dialogue. That will allow for a reflection on the evolution of the theology of religions, which has moved from being a theology of the salvation of unbelievers to a theology of religious pluralism. I will likewise pay homage to Father Jacques Dupuis, whose own work has been most outstanding in shaping that development. But within this logic of such a theology of religions, I will allow myself a further step by showing that it must move toward becoming an interreligious theology.

The Newness of Interreligious Dialogue

Over the centuries, religions have tended to stir up the violence of history. Interreligious dialogue is thus something new and an opportunity. But it is no coincidence that it has come at the same time as what Edgar Morin calls the fourth age of humankind, namely its planetary age, that is, the fact that men and women find themselves in solidarity in this tiny region of the universe that is our "planetary village." For the first time, humankind is aware that it holds its fate in its own hands. Thanks to the new human scientific and technological mastery we can place the very survival of the human species in jeopardy. The issue is not only the threats weighing on the future of the human genome; it also has to do with the perverse effects of the fantastic advances of which we are all today the fortunate beneficiaries. Sooner or later, they may degrade our environment to the point of rendering human life on earth utterly impossible.

Thus, despite their fundamental differences, the religions are not responsible solely for salvation after death in the form of immortality or eternal life. They are discovering their common responsibility toward the historic fate of human beings, and they are accordingly seeking to dialogue in order to better serve the great causes that call for the generosity of men and women of good will. In the age of globalization, we feel the need for a *global* ethic that can draw on the moral resources of the great religious traditions and the contributions of the various secular ethics.[1] We have reached a certain ethical consensus whose official expression is found in the declaration of human rights. The religions should thus allow themselves to be questioned by the new consciousness of the legitimate aspirations of the human being. But regardless of the extent to which many religions may have been historically perverted by way of fanaticism, obscurantism and even inhumanity, modern ethical reason can only benefit from listening to the lessons of wisdom of the great religious traditions which help us to better decipher the exigencies of the truly human. In particular, when faced with the ambiguities of globalization, interreligious dialogue represents an opportunity to the extent that it can remedy the perverse effects of a culture that is ever more uniform and marked by consumerism, obsession with profits, and easygoing hedonism.[2]

This is the context in which the truly historic importance of the Catholic Church's new post-Vatican II attitude toward non-Christian religions must be situated. The Declaration on the Relation of the Church to Non-Christian Religions (*Nostra Aetate*) contains this solemn statement: "The Catholic church rejects nothing of what is true and holy in these religions" (2). This new stance is embodied in the highly symbolic actions of Pope John Paul II: his visit to the chief rabbi in the synagogue in Rome, his speech to young Muslims in the stadium at Casablanca in 1985, and especially the well-known gathering in Assisi in October 1986. More recently, during the Jubilee Year 2000, the pilgrimage of the Bishop of Rome to Jerusalem, with the visit to Yad Vashem and the Wailing Wall, should not be underestimated, nor should the visit to the Umayyad Mosque in Damascus the following year be ignored. Bearing in mind the longstanding conflicts of the Catholic Church with both Judaism and Islam and its longstanding practical ignorance of the other religious traditions, it is no exaggeration to speak of a truly revolutionary development.

But even after forty years, Catholic theology has barely begun to take seriously the properly theological implications of this new attitude of the Church. If the Church regards the other religions positively, it is not simply because we live in the age of tolerance and respect for the freedom of all human beings, regardless of their religious allegiance. It is not simply because we have a more positive view of the possibility of salvation outside the church. One did not have to wait for Vatican II to have a less rigorous interpretation of Saint Cyprian's well-known adage, "Outside the church no salvation,"[3] and not to plunge into the outer darkness all human beings of good will who are inculpably ignorant of God and of Jesus Christ. Indeed, the Declaration *Nostra Aetate* primarily proposed a certain ethic of dialogue with other religions. It did not provide a theological basis that could clearly justify the dialogue encouraged by the Church. The council document presents a positive judgment on non-Christian religious but it does not explicitly take a position on the positive relationship that the different religions may have toward the Absolute. It refers to the patristic teaching on the "seeds of the Word, " without elaborating a true theology of the religions. [A clear reference to the "seeds of the Word" comes elsewhere in the conciliar documents (e.g. *Ad Gentes,* 11)—eds.]

For some decades Catholic theologians have been striving to get beyond a theology of the religions which would be simply an extension of a theology of the "salvation of unbelievers," which still remains on the level of the subjective intentions of the members of other religions, and which does not take seriously the challenge posed to Christian faith by the multiplicity of religious traditions considered as factual reality. The theology of religions is thus increasingly tending to become a theology of *religious pluralism* that inquires into the meaning of this multiplicity of religious traditions within God's plan and that wonders whether, beyond the subjective intentions of people of good will, the great religions of the world do not have in their historic reality a positive relationship to the Absolute.[4] It is in fact the only way to ascribe a theological basis to the interreligious dialogue that has been insistently called for by the top leadership of the Church.

Toward a Theology of Religious Pluralism

Even before the council, Catholic theologians like Jean Daniélou, Henri de Lubac, and Yves Congar had developed a *theology of fulfillment* in which the pagan religions were regarded as distant evangelical preparations for the one true revealed religion which is Christianity.[5] This theology is the one that underlies the Declaration *Nostra Aetate* and the Decree on the Church's Missionary Activity (*Ad Gentes*). It is in continuity with the Constitution *Lumen Gentium* which says that non-Christians are "ordered to the people of God" and that "whatever of good or truth is found amongst them is considered by the Church to be a preparation for the Gospel and given by him who enlightens all men and women" (16, 17). Thus, the religions can play the role of "preparation for the Gospel" for all who have not yet encountered Jesus Christ. This is not simply a matter of claiming that people of good will can be saved in other religions. Rather, as would be made explicit in the council texts, the suggestion is that the great religious traditions can be bearers of saving values that prepare for the recognition of the fullness of truth found in Christianity. It is tempting here to invoke the Hegelian idea of Christianity as "absolute religion" which ultimately transfigures the historic embodiments of the various religious traditions of humankind.

Within the same logic of the theology of fulfillment, in the 1960s Karl Rahner developed the theory of *anonymous Christians*.[6] By virtue of the supernatural existential present in every human being, the orientation to the Absolute, i.e., to the God who bestows grace, is as it were the quintessence of being truly human. Explicit faith in Christ as saving reality can entail a kind of implicit, *anonymous,* hidden fulfillment, being embodied only in the upright conduct of life. Where the religions are sincerely lived out by men and women of good will, they are like seeds in relation to that fullness of grace which is justification before God. The religions are thus a kind of anonymous option for Christ, conditioned by the fundamental prior orientation of every human being to the Absolute. Finally, the Church's mission is that implicit Christianity become explicit and thus come to itself.

The *anonymous Christians* thesis has been the object of numerous criticisms from theologians as different as Hans Küng and the future Cardinal Ratzinger.[7] It has been censured for operating on the basis of an abstract and overly optimistic view of the religions. By making them embodiments of God's universal will of salvation, it does not emphasize enough the fundamental ambiguity of the religions, which are also the expression of sinful human blindness. Moreover, the theory of *anonymous Christians* does not take seriously enough the newness of Christian existence with relation to human nature as a prior condition for grace. In particular, it may be asked whether Rahner does not sacrifice too much the unique privilege of the Judeo-Christian revelation as historic revelation, as differentiated from *transcendental* revelation, i.e., the communication of grace that God makes to every human being.

These criticisms have some weight and they are taken up by many contemporary theologians who denounce this idea for containing a hidden imperialism, as though all members of non-Christian religions who lead an upright life according to the imperatives of their own religious tradition were already unwitting Christians. But it should be noted that Rahner simply pushes to its extreme consequences what is already inscribed in the very logic of the theology of fulfillment, according to which everything that is just and good in the other religions can only be a degradation of—or better, a distant preparation for—what is found in its fullness in Christianity.[8] What is not taken seriously is the otherness of the other religious traditions in their irreducible difference. On the basis of the universality of the mystery of Christ, the uniqueness of Christianity is conceived as a unity of *inclusion* which embraces all the values of truth and goodness that other religions may bear. That is why the most promising theological current within Catholicism is that seeking to move beyond a theology of fulfillment toward *a theology of religious pluralism* which, while not compromising the uniqueness of the mystery of Christ, i.e., a *constitutive* Christology, does not hesitate to speak of an *inclusive* pluralism in the sense of the acknowledgment of the values proper to the other religions. Here the balanced position of Jacques Dupuis is acknowledged. But in order to do so, one must begin by taking the risk of theologically inquiring into the reason why there are multiple ways to God.

Religious Pluralism as Theological Question

As has been observed, Vatican II has begun a new era in theology inasmuch as, reversing a narrow ecclesiocentrism, it has officially issued a positive judgment on non-Christian religions by acknowledging that they can be bearers of saving values. But the council did not go so far as to consider them "ways of salvation," and it was careful not to issue a theological judgment on the meaning of religious pluralism. It is precisely the task of a hermeneutically oriented theology whose starting point is the Church's new historic experience to reinterpret our vision of God's plan of salvation. Dupuis himself has deliberately opted for an inductive theology as opposed to a deductive theology. The Church must face a religious pluralism that in human eyes seems insurmountable, and it must do so just when, at the outset of the third millennium, it is much more acutely aware of the historic particularity of Western culture, that culture which has been dominant and has underlain its theology for twenty centuries. Indeed, it is increasingly confronted with very old cultures which are inseparably bound to great religious traditions. Hence it is not surprising that a certain number of eminent Catholic theologians—I am thinking especially of Edward Schillebeeckx and Jacques Dupuis—seriously question whether this pluralism might not in fact force us to face a pluralism in principle or by right that would be mysteriously willed by God.[9]

Even if a theologian like Karl Barth thought that such a theological question was in vain because scripture offers no answer to such an enigma, the question may be regarded as inevitable, and indeed very fruitful because it helps us expand our view of salvation history. In any case, it is the only way to deal with the major intuitions of many council texts and to assess what I call getting beyond the age-old problem of the theology of the salvation of unbelievers.

As is well known, the Declaration of the Congregation for the Doctrine of the Faith, *Dominus Iesus*, on the uniqueness and saving universality of Jesus Christ and the Church (September 5, 2000) condemns indiscriminately all theologians who are willing to distinguish between a *de facto* pluralism and one that is *de iure* or by right (see 4). That is not surprising inasmuch as the entire document signed by Cardinal Ratzinger intends to warn us against the relativism of which certain contemporary theologians would be guilty, when, under the pretext of encouraging interreligious dialogue, they allow the unique character of Christ's mediation to be called into question and are inclined to relativize Christian revelation as complete and definitive revelation. But it would be easy to prove that many theologians, Catholic and non-Catholic, who are willing to make a distinction between de facto religious pluralism and a pluralism by right, in no way surrender to the ideology of a pluralism that despairs of any objective truth, and they would be very surprised to discover that this distinction inevitably leads to regarding as obsolete the truths listed in number 4 of the Declaration: in particular, the complete and definitive character of Christian revelation, the inspiration of scripture, the personal unity between the eternal Word and Jesus of Nazareth, the uniqueness and universality of the mystery of Christ, and so forth. Without claiming to know the reason for the multiplicity of ways to God, these theologians are simply seeking to interpret an apparently insurmountable pluralism in the light of what we know of God's universal will of salvation. This pluralism cannot be simply the consequence of culpable human blindness over the centuries, and even less the sign that after twenty centuries the Church's mission has met defeat. Hence, it is theologically permissible to interpret it as a pluralism that corresponds to a mysterious divine design.

It is true that biblical revelation does not provide a clear answer to the question of why religious pluralism exists; it only witnesses to the profound ambiguity of the religious history of humankind. According to *Lumen Gentium* 16, religious differences may be "the manifestation of developments, of falls of the human spirit tempted by the spirit of evil in history," but they may also be the expression of the genius and spiritual riches that a generous God has distributed among the nations (see 11 of *Ad Gentes*). On the part of Paul, for example, there are apparently contradictory statements: on the one hand, he passes a very negative judgment on those who have not recognized God in creation and who have fallen into idolatry and superstition (Rom 1:18-32), but, on the other hand, he displays a positive attitude toward the Gentiles, as attested by his speech to the Athenians: he admires the religious spirit of the pagans and he proclaims to them that which they adore as the unknown God without knowing him (Acts 17:22-34). In any case, whatever might be the Bible's pessimistic judgment on the religions of the pagans that often lead them to idolatry, the diversity of the religious phenomena ought to be interpreted in the light of the New Testament assertion of God's universal saving will, a will that extends to all human beings since the beginning: "God . . . desires everyone to be saved and to come to the knowledge of the truth " (1 Tim 2:4). Likewise, in his speech to the pagans in Acts, Peter declares "I truly understand that God shows no partiality, but in every nation anyone who fears him and does what is right is acceptable to him" (Acts 10:33-35). Thus, religious pluralism may be regarded as a mysterious design of God, the ultimate significance of which is beyond us. That is what is suggested by a beautiful council text which, after stating that the Holy Spirit offers everyone the possibility of participating in Christ's paschal mystery, adds "in a way known to God" (*Gaudium et Spes* 22).

Beyond the ambiguities of what is attested in scripture, the extremely harsh judgment of the Church Fathers on the pagan religions of their times could always be invoked against the very idea of religious pluralism in principle. They regard them as idolatrous religions that fall into magic and superstition, and they do not hesitate to consider them to be inspired by the devil. But the Fathers should be placed in their own historic context. By definition, they could not take a stance toward a religion like Islam, which arose in the early seventh century, and they were very poorly informed about the great religions of the East, even if certain texts, of Origen in particular, indicate that Brahmanism had reached as far as a city like Alexandria.[10] Rather it should be noted that at the very same time that they are extremely pessimistic about the great pagan religions of their time, they pass a very positive judgment about what they freely call "the wisdom of the nations," that is, in accepting the legacy of Greek philosophy. They are ready to recognize in the wisdom of the philosophers some *semina Verbi* or indeed reflections of the light of the Logos, the very Word of God. This idea is found among the great theologians of the Eastern Church, such as Justin, Clement of Alexandria, Origen, and so forth. For them these seeds of the Word, or these reflections of the eternal Truth, are like a preparation, a prefiguration, of the fullness of revelation that will coincide with the coming of Jesus Christ.

We have already seen that the council text *Ad Gentes* refers directly to the patristic doctrine of the seeds of the word. With the passage of time, it seems to me that the Catholic theology of religions has realized better that Vatican II applied to the non-Christian religions a teaching that was concerned primarily with the treasures of Greek philosophy. The issue is not only the seeds of truth, goodness, and even holiness that may dwell in the soul and heart of men and women of good will but also positive values that may be found in the constitutive elements of non-Christian religions, namely doctrines, rituals, or moral attitudes. *Nostra Aetate* is particularly eloquent in this regard: "The Church . . . has a high regard for the manner of life and conduct, the precepts and doctrines, which although differing in many ways from its own teaching, nevertheless often reflect a ray of that truth which enlightens all men and women" (2). An especially clear assertion is made in the Decree *Ad Gentes* on the missions: "Whatever goodness is found in people's minds and hearts, or in the particular customs and cultures of peoples, far from being lost is purified, raised to a higher level and reaches its perfection for the glory of God. . . ." (9). The document *Dialogue and Proclamation*, which was published in 1991 in the wake of the encyclical *Redemptoris Missio*, states that "it will be in the sincere practice of what is good in their own religious traditions and by following the dictates of their conscience that the members of other religions respond positively to God's invitation and receive salvation in Jesus Christ, even while they do not recognize or acknowledge him as their savior" (29).

The Theological Foundation of Interreligious Dialogue

Finally, the theological foundation of religious pluralism that legitimizes the new interreligious dialogue encouraged by the Church is the idea that the economy of the incarnate Word is the sacrament of a broader economy which is coextensive with the religious history of humankind.[11] When seeking to justify interreligious dialogue theologically, one is always brought back to the mystery of the incarnation. It is true that human history has always been subject to receiving the seeds of the eternal Word of God and to the inspirations of the divine Spirit. But after the Word has taken flesh in Jesus of Nazareth, it is the mystery of Christ, he who has passed through death and resurrection, who has universal significance for all human history. In other words, human history has never been left to itself. Since the emergence of that threshold, which is the human spirit, the history of freedoms is a history of sin and grace, and it is impossible to distinguish which portion is the religious genius of human beings and which portion is God's gift. Universal history is simultaneously the history of the human pursuit of the Absolute that we call God and God's pursuit of human beings. According to Karl Rahner's intuition, the religions may be regarded as embodiments of God's universal will of salvation. The upshot is that despite their limits in the order of knowledge and their imperfections in the moral order, they can be clumsy and stammering attempts in search of the true God. The created spirit is defined as a spirit in relation to God, not only the creator God, but the God who gives grace and seeks maximum self-communication. Thus the historic revelation, which coincides with the history of the people of Israel and reaches fulfillment in the history of the people of the New Covenant, is the sacrament of that transcendental revelation that is coextensive with human history.

From the outset, God's creative design is a design of salvation in Jesus Christ. Despite their errors and imperfections, the many expressions of the religious phenomenon converge toward better manifesting the inexhaustible fullness of the mystery of God. As Edward Schillebeeckx is fond of saying, God ceaselessly narrates himself in history.[12] Instead of the slogan, "Outside the Church, no salvation," what should be said is, "Outside the world, no salvation." In his speech to the Cardinals after the October 1986 Assisi meeting, John Paul II declared that the commitment to interrreligious dialogue encouraged by council is not justified unless religious differences do not necessarily diminish God's plan. He added that "they are less important than the oneness of that plan."[13]

The difficult task of a theology of the religions is accordingly that of thinking about the multiplicity of ways to God without compromising the uniqueness of Christ's mediation and without selling short the unique privilege of Christianity, which only makes sense in reference to Jesus Christ who is more than the founder of a religion because he is God come to live among human beings. The Declaration *Dominus Iesus* could be interpreted as a halt to the most promising research in Catholic theology. It is nothing of the sort. It need only be accepted as a very serious warning addressed to certain theologians who for the sake of interreligious dialogue are tempted to call into question the saving universality of Christ. But it is rather the deepening of the *paradox of the incarnation* that enables us to respect the irreducible value of the other religions without sacrificing anything of the uniqueness of the mystery of Christ and Christianity.

In their desire to establish a dialogue on an equal plane with the other religions of the world, certain American theologians like Paul Knitter and Roger Haight[14] as well as certain Indian theologians are understandably tempted to adopt a so-called *pluralist* position which abandons an inclusive Christocentrism for a radical theocentrism, according to which all religions including Christianity revolve around this sun which is the mystery of God or of the ultimate Reality of the universe whatever be the name given to it. They thus go beyond the line traced by the recent document of the Roman magisterium. Under the pretext that "Only God saves" they are tempted to relativize salvation in Jesus Christ. Christ would thus be a *normative* way for Christians but would not be the constitutive way of salvation.

According to the clearest New Testament teaching, we are told that from the very instant of creation God has willed to connect his eternal plan of salvation to the Christ who is the Alpha and Omega. However, that has never meant that Christ's mediation excludes other ways of salvation, provided it be likewise added that these other ways of salvation, and the world's religions in particular, are simply *derived* mediations (*Dominus Iesus* speaks of *participated* mediations), which have saving efficacy only in reference to their secret connection with the mystery of Christ. This is the teaching of John Paul II's encyclical on the missions: "Although participated forms of mediation of different kinds and degrees are not excluded, they acquire meaning and value *only* from Christ's own mediation, and they cannot be understood as parallel or complementary to his" (*Redemptoris Missio* 5).

Thus it is possible to reconcile a *constitutive*[15] and not simply normative Christology and what might be called an *inclusive* pluralism insofar as, in keeping with the Council's teaching, the positive values or even "the elements of truth and grace" (see *Ad Gentes* 9) found in the other religious traditions are taken seriously. Christocentrism need not inevitably be abandoned for a vague theocentrism in order to allow for dialogue with the other religions. It could indeed be objected that Christianity's claim to the universal betrays a certain imperialism toward the members of other religions. But I believe that we will be increasingly invited not to confuse the universality of the Christian religion with the universality of the mystery of Christ. And only a deepening of the paradox of the incarnation can help us to respect this difference. One may properly regret that the Declaration *Dominus Iesus,* in its concern to hunt down any sort of relativism, is too much in thrall to a logic of absolutization and tends to place the universality of Christ on the same plane as that of the Church or Christianity. If Christianity can dialogue with the other religious, it is because it bears in itself its own principles of limitation.[16] In order to understand it, the theology of religions has not finished meditating on the mystery of the Word made flesh.

The Church has been confessing Jesus as Son of God since the apostolic age. But a self-aware theology ought to be careful not to identify the historical and contingent element of Jesus with his Christic and divine element. The manifestation of the absolute of God in the historic particularity of Jesus of Nazareth helps us to understand that the uniqueness of Christ does not rule out other manifestations of God in history. God is indeed identified in Jesus (according to the strong expression of the Epistle to the Colossians 2:6): "the fullness of the divinity dwelled in him, bodily." But this identification itself sends us back to the inaccessible mystery of God who eludes all identification. Christianity thus does not exclude other religious traditions which identify the ultimate Reality of the universe in another manner.

It is by insisting on the very paradox of the incarnation, that is, the union of the absolutely universal and the absolutely concrete, that one is in a position to deabsolutize Christianity as a historic religion and to verify its dialogical nature. After twenty centuries, no Christianity in history can claim to incarnate the essence of Christianity as a religion of the complete and definitive revelation of the mystery of God. Thus the universality of Christ as Word incarnate may not be confused with the universality of Christianity as a historic religion. Christ's universality is coextensive with all history. By contrast, Christianity is itself relative. In opposition to certain contemporary currents, the Declaration *Dominus Iesus* has correctly sought to insist on the complete and definitive character of Christian revelation. Nevertheless, contrary to all false absolutization, its historical and relative character must be maintained, at least in the sense that it remains accessible to human intelligence and thus does not exhaust the fullness of the riches of the mystery of Christ. One thus may rightly say that Christian truth is neither exclusive nor even inclusive of any other truth in the religious realm. It is *unique* and relative to the portion of truth borne by other religions.

The upshot is that the seeds of truth and goodness sown in the other religious traditions may be the expression of the Spirit of Christ ever at work in history and in human hearts. I therefore find it inadequate to speak of implicitly Christian values simply according to the logic of preparation and fulfillment. It is preferable to speak of *Christic* values.[17] They attest to something irreducible in the realm of the religious. It is in their very difference that they will find their final fulfillment in Jesus Christ, even if they do not become explicitly visible in Christianity. Theologians increasingly will have to endure intellectually the enigma of a plurality of religious traditions in their irreducible difference. They do not easily lend themselves to being harmonized with Christianity, and it would be to misunderstand the unique value of Christian revelation to seek to complete it through the incomplete truths of the other religions. But the more we become familiar with the proper riches of the doctrines and practices of other religions, the more we are in a position to undertake an enriching reinterpretation of the truths which have to do with Christian uniqueness. According to God's own pedagogy in salvation history, the *foreigner* may prophetically serve for a better understanding of one's own identity. It is true of the knowledge of God who is always greater than the names that we give him, and it is true of the relation to God that it ought to tend to the perfection of worship in spirit and truth.

The Meaning of an Interreligious Theology

The theology of religions has undergone a profound evolution in the past thirty years. It is tending more and more to become a theology of religious pluralism which inquires about the meaning of the significance of the multiplicity of religious traditions within the single plan of God. But that is still saying too little. As this theological shift continues, the new paradigm of religious pluralism seems to be inviting us to reflect on what true *interreligious theology* or even a *dialogical* theology might be. This is still a work in progress. But so as not to stay with a purely programmatic vision, out of an epistemological concern, I would like at least to lay out some rules. First of all, the difference between an interreligious theology and a comparative theology of religions should be stressed. Moreover, questions should be asked about the notion of truth underlying such a theological project. And one may already glimpse the consequences of the paradigm of religious pluralism for what is taught in the main theological treatises.

Toward an Analogical Imagination

There is no theology of religions without employing some procedure for comparing Christianity and the other religions. But the comparative method, which is already undergoing a certain declining prestige within religious studies (by what criterion is one definition of religion to be privileged?), is even more ticklish in the theology of religions.[18] How is the irreducible difference of each religion to be respected if the sole standard of comparison is Christianity regarded as the archetype of any religion? Even so, there is a legitimate usage of comparative procedure which avoids falling into apologetics, if one does not stop with comparing term by term the structuring elements of each religion with regard to teachings, rites, and practices, by underlining the differences from, and similarities with, Christianity. One may indeed very quickly be tempted to judge that which is different either as a degradation, or as a distant prefiguration of what is achieved in perfection in the Christian religion. I think that an interreligious theology ought to be able to be faithful to Christian uniqueness while striving to respect the originality of each religion.

In order to do that, it is desirable, as has been noted, to move beyond the simple logic of promise and fulfillment and the facile distinction between the implicit and the explicit. As Raimundo Panikkar suggests, *intrareligious* dialogue consists of embracing the other's standpoint while not renouncing one's own identity.[19] This means that rather than remaining at a phenomenological standpoint where one compares term by term the constitutive elements of each religion in order to evaluate their respective merits, one must grasp each element within the totality of the religious system to which it belongs and verify how it serves communion with that Absolute which Christian faith names as the God revealed in Jesus Christ. In other words, one would be well advised to invoke what David Tracy calls an *analogical imagination*, that is, that ability to discern similarity in difference.[20] This properly hermeneutic understanding is particularly valuable when dealing with religious universes so as to avoid both hasty convergences and irreconcilable discontinuities. At the very moment when I ascertain a certain religious irreducibility that is alien to me, I likewise discover how it helps me explore new possibilities of meaning within my own Christian identity.

Another Status of Truth in Theology

If interreligious dialogue is tending to become the horizon of theology in the twenty-first century, it is clear that we will be called to reinterpret the concept of truth which underlies our ordinary theology. Theology has claimed for itself such an absolutistic conception of truth according to the logic of contradictory propositions that it does not think it can recognize different truths without thereby compromising its claim to truth. It could at best regard them as degraded truths or as distant anticipations of the truth over which it has the monopoly and which it identifies with a truth of excellence and integration. It is significant that the Declaration *Dominus Iesus* seems to be incapable of invoking the fundamental truths of Christian faith on the uniqueness and universality of salvation in Jesus Christ except while remaining trapped in an insurmountable dilemma between absolutism and relativism. Yet it seems that the theology of the future will have to show that the truth to which it bears witness is neither exclusive nor inclusive of the truths of which the other religions may be bearers. Because we always conceive the relative to be the opposite of the absolute, we do not have words for calling a Christian truth *relative* in the sense of *relational* to the part of the truth that is inherent in other religions.

An interreligious theology will have to display the harmonies of a truth that is closer to truth in the biblical sense. Classical theology understood as metaphysical theology has normally privileged *truth-as-correspondence* in Aristotle's sense, that of judgment, namely the correspondence between intelligence and reality. In that case, the opposite of the true can only be the false. It seems desirable to invoke a more primal truth, *truth-as-manifestation* in its difference from a fullness of truth that still remains hidden. Even if Heidegger exhibits a strange ignorance of truth in the Hebraic meaning, it is not rash to effect a rapprochement between *a-létheia* and truth in the biblical meaning.[21] The primal essence of truth is the property of that which does not remain hidden. Thus, rather than interpreting the different truths of the religious traditions in terms of contradiction, their historic and textual contingency must be taken into account each time. In the age of religious pluralism, the historic vocation of Christian theology is to highlight the eschatological meaning of its own language as language of truth. Then despite divergences that are difficult to overcome, interrreligious dialogue could lead each dialogue partner to the common celebration of a fullness of truth beyond the partial character of each particular truth.

Another Practice of Theological Teaching

Within the perspective of interreligious theology, the impact of interreligious dialogue on the major treatises of a dogmatic theology will have to be shown. We may not be content to insert into the theological curriculum a new course devoted to the theology of religions. This dimension is coextensive with theology in its entirety and leads to a new reinterpretation of the great truths of the faith in keeping with the rays of truth to which the other religious traditions give witness. I have already called attention to the paradox of the incarnation on which the dialogical character of the Christian religion in some fashion is based. Here I will simply suggest how we could approach the mystery of God and the central notion of salvation.

How can we reflect on the mystery of the triune God without taking into account the strict monotheism to which both Judaism and Islam give witness? Christian monotheism as Trinitarian monotheism must not compromise on the issue of the divine oneness while protecting itself from the two symmetrical temptations of tritheism and modalism. But at the same time, it is the benefit of an interreligious theology that it highlights better how much God-the-Trinity invites us to move beyond a monolithic conception of God's oneness understood in terms of absolute Being to think of a unity that assumes differences. The transcendence of a God who is self-communicating to the point of taking on the flesh of a man is a transcendence of love and not simply of being. Moreover, dialogue with the great religions of the East which refuse to designate the Absolute as a personal transcendence can help us to move beyond the still anthropomorphic representation of a *created self* and a divine *Thou*. In the register of personal experience, there are real convergences between *advaïta* as thought of non-distinction and the deeper intuitions of Christian wisdom under the banner of negative theology.

Salvation as liberation of the human being is the common goal of all the world's religions. It will be characteristic of an interreligious theology to show an analogy between the way in which the constitutive elements of each religion are related to this common aim which is salvation.[22] The originality of Christian salvation in Jesus Christ must be shown as liberation from sin and death and especially as gift of eternal life which has already begun. But at the same time, a greater familiarity with the other religious traditions, especially those of the East, put us on our guard against a conception too exclusively polarized on salvation as liberation from sin. In terms of the confused expectation of our contemporaries, it is important to spell out better all the virtualities of Christian salvation, not only as reconciliation with God, but as healing of the affliction of the human condition and as life wisdom, that is, as reconciliation with oneself and with all creation.

In short, the point is not to complete the Christian message with positive elements displayed by other religious traditions but to open oneself up to a mutual fertilization that leads to a better deciphering of the resources hidden in the revelation that has been gratuitously entrusted to us by God.

References

[1]For this global ethic, see the declaration published at the close of the Parliament of Religions held in Chicago in August 1993, spearheaded by the theologian Hans Küng, found in Hans Küng (ed.), *Yes to a Global Ethic* (New York: Continuum, 1996).

[2]I have sought to justify this historic opportunity presented by interreligious dialogue vis-à-vis globalization in my article "Pour un christianisme mondial," *Recherches de Science Religieuse* 86 (1998), 53-75.

[3]On the meaning of this formula resituated in its historic and ecclesial context, one may consult the now old article of Yves Congar, *Catholicisme*, vol. 5 (Paris: Letouzey, 1959), col. 948-56, and especially the very well documented study by Jacques Dupuis in his book, *Toward a Christian Theology of Religious Pluralism* (Maryknoll, N.Y.: Orbis, 1997), 84-109.

[4]The now classic work of Jacques Dupuis that I have already cited attests decisively to this evolution in the Catholic theology of religions. It should be completed with his more recent book aimed at a larger public, *Christianity and the Religions* (Maryknoll, N.Y.: Orbis, 2002). I myself have reached the point of writing that religious pluralism as horizon of theology constituted a *paradigm shift* for Christian theology. See in particular my article, "Le pluralisme religieux et l'indifférentisme ou le vrai défi de la théologie chrétienne," *Revue théologique de Louvain* 31 (2000), 3-32.

[5]For Henri de Lubac, one may consult particularly his book, *Le fondement théologique des missions* (Paris: Seuil, 1946), and for Yves Congar, *The Wide World My Parish: Salvation and Its Problems* (London: Darton, Longman & Todd, 1961).

[6]See K. Rahner, "Anonymous Christians," in *Theological Investigations*, vol. 6 (New York: Crossroad, 1982), 390-98, and *Foundations of Christian Faith: An Introduction to the Idea of Christianity* (New York: Seabury, 1978), 176.

[7]See in particular, Hans Küng, *On Being a Christian* (Garden City, N.Y.: Doubleday, 1976), 97-98, and Joseph Ratzinger, *Principles of Catholic Theology: Building Stones for a Fundamental Theology* (San Francisco: Ignatius Press, 1987), 162-66, 169-71 .

[8]For a fair evaluation of criticisms made of Rahner's proposal, one may profitably read the brief observations of Michel Fédou, *Les religions selon la foi chrétienne* (Paris: Cerf, 1996), 72-78.

[9]Among Catholic studies on the theology of religions, in addition to the already cited work of Jacques Dupuis, I would mention in particular the book of Edward Schillebeeckx, *Church: The Human Story of God* (New York: Crossroad, 1990).

[10]On this topic one may consult Michel Fédou's very detailed study, *Christianisme et religions païennes dans le* Contre Celse *d'Origène* (Paris: Beauchesne, 1988).

[11]The very compact formulation of the theological basis for interreligious dialogue proposed in the document of the International Theological Commission, *Christ and the Religions*, may be cited: "Interreligious dialogue is based on the common origin of all human beings created in God's image, in their common destiny which is fullness of life in God, in the unique divine saving plan through Jesus Christ, in the active presence of the Holy Spirit among those who follow other religious traditions" (n.° 25).

[12]That is what he intended to express in the Dutch title of his already cited *Mensen als verhaal van God,* which appeared as *Church: The Human Story of God* (New York: Crossroad, 1990).

[13]"The differences are less important than the unity, which, by contrast, is radical, fundamental, and decisive"; *La Documentation catholique*, n.° 1933, February 1, 1987.

[14]For Paul Knitter, one may consult, among his works, *No Other Name? A Critical Survey of Christian Attitudes Toward World Religions* (Maryknoll, N.Y.: Orbis, 1981), and for Roger Haight, his latest work, *Jesus, Symbol of God* (Maryknoll, N.Y.: Orbis, 1999) must be cited. As is well known, the principal initiator of a pluralistic theology of religions was the British theologian John Hick: see in particular his book, *God Has Many Names* (Philadelphia: Westminster Press, 1980).

[15]Father Jacques Dupuis has always advocated a *constitutive* and not simply a *normative* Christology. Even if the Declaration *Dominus Iesus* could have in mind certain positions set forth in his book *Toward a Christian Theology of Religious Pluralism*, it is well known that the examination of his book by the Congregation for the Doctrine of the Faith, which lasted almost three years, ended with what in legal terminology is called dismissal for lack of evidence. The Notification dated January 24, 2001, does not point to errors properly so-called, but to notable "ambiguities and difficulties on important points."

[16]I have developed this idea particularly in my article, "La vérité du christianisme à l'âge

du pluralisme religieux," *Angelicum* 74 (1998), 171-92.

[17]In any case this is the expression which I have often invoked (see chapter 5 of my book *Croire et interpréter: Le tournant herméneutique de la théologie* [Paris: Cerf, 2001]). The same idea is also found in many writings of Raimundo Panikkar.

[18]I have explained my position on the difference between comparative history of religions and comparative theology of religions; see my study, "Le comparatisme en théologie des religions," in F. Boespflug et F. Dunand (eds.), *Le comparatisme en histoire des religions* (Paris: Cerf, 1997), 415-31.

[19]See Raimundo Panikkar, *The Intrareligious Dialogue* (New York/Mahwah, N.J.: Paulist Press, 1978).

[20]I refer to his classic work, *The Analogical Imagination. Christian Theology and the Culture of Pluralism* (New York: Crossroad, 1981). He has applied such a principle in his small work, *Dialogue with the Other. The Inter-religious Dialogue* (Louvain: Peters Press, 1990).

[21]I have attempted to explain my position on the relevance of this approach in my article, "La vérité du christianisme à l'âge du pluralisme religieux," 171-92.

[22]In a special issue devoted to salvation, I have tried to sketch what a comparative theology of salvation in the religions might be under the title, "Un salut au pluriel," *Lumière et Vie* n.° 250 (April-June 2001), 21-38.

6

Jacques Dupuis and the Redefinition of Inclusivism

Terrence Merrigan

Jacques Dupuis and the Theology of Religions

It has become more or less customary to organize the many "theologies of religion" on offer in terms of the threefold typology of "exclusivism," "inclusivism," and "pluralism."[1] *Exclusivism* consists in the claim that no one can be saved who does not make an explicit confession of faith in Jesus Christ. *Inclusivism* insists on neither an explicit confession of Christ nor explicit membership in the Christian Church, but it does claim that Christ is always implicated in the salvific process and regards explicit Christian faith as the completion of every religious system. *Pluralism* claims that salvation is possible in and through a variety of independent and more or less equally valid religious traditions. Since the appearance of this typology in 1983, a number of alternatives have been proposed, some of them remarkably complex. Nevertheless, the threefold typology continues to hold sway, if only as a foil for the new proposals.

Seeking to situate his own approach within the prevailing framework, Jacques Dupuis has observed that "the most appropriate term" to describe it "would seem to be that of an 'inclusivist pluralism' that holds together the constitutive and universal character of the Christ-event in the order of human salvation and the salvific significance of religious traditions in a *de iure* plurality of religious traditions within the one manifold plan of God for humankind."[2] Since Catholic theology of religions has nearly always been described as (if not simply identified with) the inclusivist approach, Dupuis's self-description is quite daring, since it would seem to represent a break with Catholic tradition. The controversy surrounding his work indicates that some are inclined to believe that this is indeed the case.

In what follows, I do not intend to pursue the question of Dupuis's "orthodoxy."[3] Instead, I would like to situate his option for an "inclusivist pluralism" against the background of the development of the theology of religions since

Vatican II. By doing this, I hope to make two points. The first is that Dupuis's position must be seen as part of a broader movement to redefine inclusivism. Within the framework of this movement, Dupuis's self-description is less radical than it initially appears. The second point is that Dupuis's participation in this movement is as much a matter of necessity as of choice. I have argued elsewhere that Dupuis's great contribution to the theology of religions is his willingness to "explore the frontiers," i.e., the limits, of prevailing views.[4] Here I hope to situate his approach within a broader framework, with a view to demonstrating that his explorations are a response to a real need and not the work of a reckless loner.

The Challenges Facing the Theology of Religions

Much of recent theology of religions (certainly in Catholic circles) has been a response to the pluralist paradigm. The pluralists have, so to speak, concentrated theological minds on a number of issues which might otherwise have never received the attention they have been given. These issues are: (1) the demand to take religious pluralism seriously as a cultural and religious fact (i.e., religious otherness as a *fact*); and (2) the demand to recognize the "spiritual and moral goods" ("bona spiritualia et moralia"—*Nostra Aetate,* 2)[5] found in other traditions (i.e., religious otherness as a *value*). In both cases, what is being "demanded" is not a halfhearted acknowledgment of the others' right to exist, or of the relative merits of what they have achieved. Instead, what is being demanded is wholehearted recognition of their intrinsic right to be "other," and of the intrinsic value of their "otherness." To honor the former demand means to accept the fact that most people in the world are not and are never likely to be Christian. To honor the latter demand means to accept that other religious traditions can match Christianity in terms of the practice of virtue which they engender, the profundity of the doctrine which they produce, and the depth of the spirituality which they inculcate.

It seems fair to say that most contemporary inclusivist theologians have taken these demands seriously, and attempted to do them justice. Indeed, it is possible to sketch the state of contemporary inclusivism by examining the theological response to these two challenges. Of course, the character of this response has been fragmentary and uneven. Depending on who is speaking, one finds a concern to address one or both of these themes, and a greater or lesser willingness to adjust traditional thinking in order to do so. Let us examine the nature of these responses and Dupuis's position via-à-vis the other major players.

The Demand to Account for the Fact of Religious Otherness

Among those theologians who acknowledge an inclusivist bias, so to speak, it is possible to identify four major theological responses to the fact of religious otherness. These can be arranged in ascending order, according as they approach the pluralist position.

Religious Otherness as an Expression of the Human Quest for Meaning

The minimalist position sees the world's religions as the expression of humankind's quest for ultimate meaning and value. According to this view, religious otherness is the fruit of humanity's fundamentally religious nature, i.e., our orientation toward the (as yet unnamed) transcendent reality, but it is not possessed of any intrinsic theological value. This position can be discerned in Vatican II (see especially *Ad Gentes*, 3) and a number of commentators have in fact argued that this is the most adequate reading of the council's basic attitude.[6] However, as Dupuis points out, the council's teaching in this regard is not unambiguous and a case can be made for a more positive appraisal of the non-Christian traditions.[7]

Religious Otherness as an Occasion for "Self"-Discovery

A development of the minimalist position portrays religious plurality as an opportunity for Christianity to come to a more profound understanding of the truth contained in its own tradition—in and through dialogue with the "other." Here, the other performs, as it were, a maieutic function. The premise underlying this approach is the conviction that the Holy Spirit is at work outside the confines of the Jewish-Christian dispensation, so that the encounter with other traditions might be the occasion for "an even deeper penetration, understanding and application of the truth of God's triune self-revelation entrusted to the church."[8] Recently a case has been made for the view that this is the position of Pope John Paul II, especially in *Redemptoris Missio* (1990).[9]

Religious Otherness as Evidence of God's Historical Engagement with Humankind

The next step is to see religious pluralism as evidence of God's continual engagement with humankind throughout history. Here, the religions are viewed as the concrete expression(s) of God's search for humankind and humankind's response to God (however partial and contaminated by sin that response may be). This view is reflected in Karl Rahner's understanding of the non-Christian religions. In this view, religious diversity is an inevitable consequence of humanity's historical nature. Christianity, the true religion, can only take root gradually. In the meantime, God employs the other religions to realize his salvific will in history (which, of course, is not to say that these religions, as such, are willed by God). The upshot of this view is that while religious pluralism is a good, it is only a provisional good and ought—ideally—to be overcome.[10]

Religious Otherness as an Integral Element of God's Universal Salvific Will

A fourth position, which stops just short, as it were, of the pluralist claim that the world's religions are more or less equivalent as ways of salvation, is the view that religious pluralism is willed directly by God and that it is possessed of a lasting significance in the economy of salvation. This is the view expressed by Dupuis in his controversial study of 1997 (*Toward a Christian Theology of Religious Pluralism*). There Dupuis writes that he intends "to look at religious pluralism not merely as a matter of course and a fact of history (pluralism de facto) but as *having a raison d'être in its own right* (pluralism de iure or 'in principle'). The question no longer simply consists of asking what role Christianity can assign to the other historical religious traditions but in searching for the root-cause of pluralism itself, for *its significance in God's own plan for humankind.* . . . "[11] What separates this position from pluralism pure and simple is the conviction that while the other religions have a vital—indeed indispensable—role to play in the economy of salvation, their effectiveness is rooted in the God revealed in Jesus Christ. In other words, Christ continues to function as the universal mediator of salvation.[12]

Reviewing the Options

Clearly, all of these approaches reflect a concern to integrate the fact of religious pluralism (pluralism *de facto*) into an inclusivist framework. Moreover, all are able to discern some good in the existence of a diversity of religions. In the case of Dupuis, this good is very nearly "intrinsic" to the non-Christian traditions. He is careful, however, never to ascribe any independent (i.e., independent of Christ) validity to them.[13] Nevertheless, Dupuis's attempt to account for "the fact of religious otherness" carries him to the frontiers of inclusivism. These frontiers are to be located where the discussion begins regarding the way in which the universal salvation realized in the Christ-event is mediated to humankind.[14] There can be no doubt that the traditional view was that the Church is the exclusive instrument of such mediation. Dupuis's interest in Vatican II's reformulation of the relationship between non-Christians and the Church indicates his conviction that this approach no longer suffices, and that taking the reality of other religions seriously means moving beyond the view that they are, so to speak, incidental to salvation history.[15]

Let us now turn to the second issue raised by pluralist theology.

The Demand to Recognize the "Spiritual and Moral Goods" of Other Religious Traditions

The second issue which I have identified is the demand to recognize the "spiritual and moral goods" of other traditions. Here, as in the case of the first issue considered, we are dealing with a demand that is inspired as much by a cultural shift as by theological considerations (though these have since been developed).[16] Here, too, we can identify a range of views and, once again, these can be arranged in an ascending order.

The "Spiritual and Moral Goods" of Other Traditions as Propaedeutic Tools

The minimalist position regards the positive elements of other religious tradi-tions as traces or fragments of that fullness of the divine presence which is given in Christ. These elements are possessed of a propaedeutic value. That is to say, "they can at times be regarded as leading towards the true God or as paving the way for the gospel message" (*Ad Gentes*, 3). Their presence in other religious traditions may be portrayed as incidental or even "accidental," but more often than not they are regarded as divinely willed. Vatican II suggests both approaches. So, for example, on the one hand, the Council speaks of those human "efforts" which "need to be guided and corrected" (*Ad Gentes*, 3) if they are to realize their propaedeutic potential, and acknowledges that elements of the doctrine, ethics, and ritual[17] of non-Christian traditions "frequently reflect a ray of that truth which enlightens everyone" (*Nostra Aetate*, 2). On the other hand, it describes "what-ever truth and grace [that] are already to be found among peoples" as "a secret presence of God, so to speak" (*Ad Gentes*, 9), and encourages missionaries to "discover the seeds of the Word which lie hidden" in the "national and religious traditions" of those to whom they are sent (*Ad Gentes*, 11, 15).[18] Pope John Paul II has invoked this tradition in a number of his official pronouncements.[19]

The "Spiritual and Moral Goods" of Other Traditions as an Occasion for Insight into Trinitarian Mystery

Clearly, this view of things obtains among theologians who regard the Trinity as the ultimate goal of humankind's religious aspirations. However, as we shall see, this does not mean that they all necessarily hold that all religious men and women attain this goal. As the title of this subsection indicates, the leitmotif of this view is the inexhaustible richness of the Trinitarian God whose very nature is mystery. The theme of "mystery" is common among pluralist theologians. They, however, would never identify the Trinity as the ultimate goal of all human reli-gious striving.[20] According to the view of things under discussion here, other religious traditions can bring into sharper focus dimensions of God which are underdeveloped, or have been obscured, within Christianity. There is even some suggestion that non-Christian traditions might highlight insights into God that have not yet been appropriated within Christianity (though, in the final analysis, these insights must be judged in the light of what is already known). Representa-tives of this position include Catholic theologians like Dupuis and (to a lesser degree) Gavin D'Costa, and the Protestant theologian S. Mark Heim.[21]

Of the three, Dupuis displays the greatest appreciation of the "spiritual and moral goods" of other traditions. So, for example, he speaks of the non-Christian religions "as representing in their own right distinct facets of the self-disclosure of the Absolute Mystery,"[22] and claims that one may discover "in other saving figures and traditions, truth and grace not brought out with the same vigor and clarity in God's revelation and manifestation in Jesus Christ." The "truth and grace found elsewhere," he observes, "represent additional and autonomous benefits." Indeed, he asserts that "more divine truth and grace are found operative in the entire history of God's dealings with humankind than are available simply in the Christian tradition."[23]

Heim's trinitarian theology is more sophisticated than Dupuis's, but he is less insistent as regards the "novelty," so to speak, of the "spiritual and moral goods" contained in other traditions. According to Heim, "the life of the Trinity manifests three dimensions," namely, impersonality, undifferentiated unity, and differentiated personality.[24] Encounter with the triune God can take either of three forms, depending on the dimension of the divine life which is "accessed," so to speak. There are, accordingly, "three types of relation with God, one marked by impersonal identity, one marked by iconographic encounter [with either "a transcendent order or a transcendent person"], and one marked by personal communion."[25] From a Christian perspective, the supreme "religious end" (which Christians call "salvation") is communion with the differentiated personality of the triune God. Other religions, however, may focus on one of the other two dimensions of the trinitarian life as the most appropriate "religious end." So, for example, some forms of Buddhism might be said to be oriented towards God's impersonality, while Islam is directed to the undifferentiated personality of the Creator. Heim acknowledges the legitimacy of these other religious ends but they are—from a Christian point of view—inevitably partial.[26] He does, however, allow that, precisely in their limitation, other traditions may promote "an intensified realization of one dimension of God's offered relation with us."[27] Hence, in "particular veins of relation," the other religious traditions "exhibit greater purity and power than are usually manifest in Christianity," and may therefore further insight into the triune mystery.[28]

D'Costa is more reticent about the positive values to be found in other religions. However, in view of the universal presence of the Spirit of Christ, he does allow for the "possibility of God's gift of himself through the prayers, practices, insights, and traditions found within other religions." This gift might not be immediately discernible, and its appropriation by Christianity may "involve radical discontinuity," but it can be the occasion for "greater holiness, truth, and goodness."[29]

What unites these three positions is the conviction that the trinitarian character of God allows for real diversity in the ways of his presence to men and women. While Christ remains the primary analogue, so to speak, for determining God's "whereabouts" throughout history, it would be wrong to limit his presence to the incarnation. Nevertheless, in the final analysis, whatever is good, and true, and holy in the world's religions will reveal something of the divine life in which Christ shares.

A slight variation on this theme also deserves to be mentioned. There is a growing tendency, especially among theologians of an inclusivist persuasion (e.g., Paul Griffiths, Gavin D'Costa, Mark Heim and, to a lesser extent, Dupuis), to insist on the "tradition-specific" character of religious beliefs and practices.[30] This means that particular elements of a religion must not be seen in isolation from the comprehensive religious system of which they are part. This more "holistic" approach to other traditions would seem to be inspired by two factors: (i) an appreciation of the nature of the all-embracing character of religious commitment (so Griffiths and Heim);[31] (ii) and/or a post-modern tendency to acknowledge the historical particularity (and even the incommensurability) of distinctive (narrative-) traditions (so D'Costa).[32] The upshot of this sensitivity is that theologians are increasingly reluctant to claim that particular elements in non-Christian traditions correspond to (or are isomorphic with) similar elements in Christianity. Among inclusivists, it has led to a greater caution in claiming that "Christian" truths are contained in other religions, and a willingness to approach these religions as being *potentially* possessed of insights which Christianity has not yet appropriated.[33]

As far as the Catholic Church is concerned, Paul Griffiths has recently argued that the tradition allows for the view that "it is possible that alien religions teach truths of religious significance to the Church; and that some of these are not yet explicitly taught or understood by the Church." Griffiths describes this as "open inclusivism," and contrasts it to "closed inclusivism," which holds "that all alien religious truths (should there be any) are already known to and explicitly taught by" the Church.[34]

The "Spiritual and Moral Goods" of Other Traditions as an Opportunity for Mutual Cross-fertilization

This third possible approach to the "spiritual and moral goods" of other traditions is emerging in the Asian context.[35] Here the overwhelming presence of other religions means that it is Christians who constitute the "other" and who are, therefore, called to give an account of themselves rather than to call others to account. Asian theologians and the Federation of Asian Bishops' Conferences have made it clear that, in the Asian context, pluralism is, in the first place, a starting point for theological reflection, not an object of such reflection.[36] Pluralism here denotes more than the mere fact of religious diversity. As the Theological Advisory Commission of the Federation of Asian Bishops' Conferences (1987) pointed out, "its experience of the other religions has led the Church in Asia to [a] positive appreciation of their role in the divine economy of salvation. This appreciation is based on the fruits of the Spirit perceived in the lives of the other religions' believers: a sense of the sacred, a commitment to the pursuit of fullness, a thirst for self-realization, a taste for prayer and commitment, a desire for renunciation, a struggle for justice, an urge to basic human goodness, an involvement in service, a total surrender of the self to God, and an attachment to the transcendent in their symbols, rituals and life itself. . . . "[37] In line with this experience, the Federation has called for "a stance of receptive pluralism," i.e., "an attitude of openness to and acceptance of the working of the Spirit beyond the boundaries of the Church as such, and the Asian social and religious context, in particular, becomes a theological resource, a locus theologicus, where the divine presence needs to be discerned."[38] Interreligious dialogue, in the spirit of "receptive pluralism," becomes the means to this end. This dialogue is above all a matter of sharing, of exchange, with partners who represent impressive systems of religious thought and practice. It means taking their claims and their self-understanding seriously. One instance of this approach is the development of what is called interfaith or multifaith hermeneutics in the reading of the Bible and the sacred texts of the dialogue partners. Rather than taking the Bible "as a yardstick to judge the sacred texts of other religions," the Bible is read "in light of other sacred texts and vice versa, for mutual cross-fertilization." As Peter Phan observes, "the purpose of such reading is not to prove that the Christian Bible and the sacred scriptures of other religions are mutually compatible, [or] to find linguistic and theological parallels between them for some missiological intent, but *to enlarge our understanding of both* [our emphasis], to promote cross-cultural and cross-religious dialogue, to achieve a 'wider intertextuality.' "[39] Here, the aim is not, in the first place, to situate the other against the horizon of the Trinity, but to achieve a deeper appreciation of the other in their "otherness." This does not mean that Christians must abandon their particular faith perspective, but it does mean that they open themselves to be enriched by the distinctiveness of the other.

Reviewing the Options

I said at the outset that the demands being made on the theology of religions are as much cultural as they are theological. Clearly, in our day, it is increasingly unacceptable to approach the "religious other" simply in function of one's own religious project. For that reason, the purely propaedeutic approach to the "spiritual and moral goods" of other religions will no longer suffice. Those theologians who advocate a trinitarian perspective are clearly testing the limits of "classical" inclusivism,[40] at least if this paradigm is understood (as it traditionally has been) in essentially Christological terms. They have discovered, within the tradition of trinitarian theology, the resources to develop a genuine "theological pluralism," so to speak. The Asian theology of religions, which is being forged in a predominantly non-Christian context, supplements this "theological pluralism" with the "religious and cultural pluralism" of Asian experience. The attempt to integrate these "pluralisms" into a comprehensive vision will be the major preoccupation of the theology of religions in the years to come.

Concluding Remarks

Jacques Dupuis's work has been characterized by a concern to do justice to both the traditional doctrine of faith and the reality of our pluralistic context. In its thoroughgoing Trinitarianism and its determination to incorporate the Asian experience, it might be said to have anticipated the shift in the theology of religions that is now becoming visible. Dupuis's description of himself as an "inclusivist pluralist" can only be correctly understood against the background of this shift. By juxtaposing these terms and applying them to himself, Dupuis has not emptied the threefold typology of content. Instead, he has chosen once again to take up a position on the frontier, that is to say, the region "in-between." In doing so, he encourages all of us to forego some of our certitudes and to accept the challenge of finding our bearings between the Other revealed in Christ, and those others whose demands and achievements can no longer be ignored or minimized.

References

[1]The precise content of these three "types" is a subject of debate. I will use the terms in the sense indicated in the body of the text.

[2]Jacques Dupuis, "Trinitarian Christology as a Model for a Theology of Religious Pluralism," in *The Myriad Christ: Plurality and the Quest for Unity in Contemporary Christology*, ed. T. Merrigan, J. Haers, Bibliotheca Ephemeridum Lovaniensium, 152 (Leuven: University Press & Peeters, 2000), 97. See also Dupuis " 'The Truth Will Make You Free': The Theology of Religious Pluralism Revisited," *Louvain Studies* 24 (1999), 226, 227, 228, 246. On p. 226, Dupuis explains that this model "would mean that, while keeping to the inclusivist position by holding fast to Jesus Christ as universal Saviour, one may affirm at the same time a plurality of religious paths having some salvific value for their adherents; not, however, without being essentially and organically related to the Christ event in accordance with the one divine plan of salvation for humankind." The tripartite division is usually associated with Alan Race, *Christians and Religious Pluralism* (Maryknoll, N.Y.: Orbis, 1983).

[3]Dupuis has provided an extensive reply to critics of his position in " 'The Truth Will Make You Free'," 211-63.

[4]Terrence Merrigan, "Exploring the Frontiers: Jacques Dupuis and the Movement 'Toward a Christian Theology of Religious Pluralism,' " *Louvain Studies* 23 (1998), 338-39; reprinted in *East Asian Pastoral Review* 37 (2000), 5-32.

[5]All references to the conciliar documents will be taken from *Decrees of the Ecumenical Councils*, ed. Norman P. Tanner, 2 vols. (London & Washington: Sheed & Ward and Georgetown University Press, 1990), 2:969. Tanner translates "bona spiritualia et moralia" as "spiritual and moral good things." For stylistic reasons, I prefer to use my own formulation in this particular instance.

[6]Dupuis discusses these authors in *Toward a Christian Theology of Religious Pluralism* (Maryknoll, N.Y.: Orbis, 2000), 162-65.

[7]Ibid., 168-70; see also Jacques Dupuis, *Jesus Christ at the Encounter of World Religions* (Maryknoll, N.Y.: Orbis, 1991), 98.

[8]Gavin D'Costa, *The Meeting of Religions and the Trinity* (Maryknoll, N.Y.: Orbis, 2000), 114.

[9]For a detailed defense of this reading, see ibid., 101-9. For a more critical reading of *Redemptoris Missio*, see Aloysius Pieris, *Fire and Water: Basic Issues in Asian Buddhism and Christianity* (Maryknoll, N.Y.: Orbis, 1996), 67, 76, 84, 155.

[10]Karl Rahner, "Christianity and the Non-Christian Religions," *Theological Investigations*, vol. 5 (Baltimore: Helicon, 1966), 115-34; "Anonymous Christians," *Theological Investigations*, vol. 6 (Baltimore: Helicon, 1969), 390-98. For a detailed discussion, see Dupuis, *Toward a Christian Theology of Religious Pluralism*, 143-49.

[11]Dupuis, *Toward a Christian Theology of Religious Pluralism*, 11. (Our emphasis).

[12]Dupuis makes much of the document, *Dialogue and Proclamation: Reflections and Orientations on Interreligious Dialogue and the Proclamation of the Gospel of Jesus Christ*, published jointly by the Pontifical Council for Interreligious Dialogue and the Congregation for the Evangelization of Peoples (May 19, 1991). See his *Toward a Christian Theology of Religious Pluralism*, 178-79; and "A Theological Commentary: Dialogue and Proclamation," in *Redemption and Dialogue: Reading* Redemptoris Missio *and* Dialogue and Proclamation, ed. W. R. Burrows (Maryknoll, N.Y.: Orbis, 1993), 119-58. In *Toward a Christian Theology of Religious Pluralism*, 178, Dupuis describes *Dialogue and Proclamation* as "a first among documents of the Church's magisterium on the subject of members of other religions and their traditions." It "goes beyond whatever Church documents have stated before regarding the role played by religious traditions in the salvation in Jesus Christ of their followers." The text (n.° 29) declares that "the mystery of salvation reaches out to [those who 'remain unaware that Jesus is the source of their salvation'], in a way known to God, through the invisible action of the Spirit of Christ. Concretely, it will be *in the sincere practice of what is good in their own religious tradition* and by following the dictates of their conscience that the members of other religions respond positively to God's invitation and receive salvation in Jesus Christ, even while they do not recognize or acknowledge him as their Saviour" (emphasis Dupuis). Dupuis acknowledges that the statement is a "guarded one," but he also claims that "a door seems to be timidly opened here, for the first time, for the recognition on the part of the Church authority of a 'participated mediation' of religious traditions in the salvation of their members. With such a statement we seem to be definitely moving from the 'fulfillment theory' to that of an active presence of the mystery of Jesus Christ in the traditions themselves" (pp. 178-79).

[13]Merrigan, "Exploring the Frontiers," 354-56. In view of the discussion surrounding Dupuis's ecclesiology (see n. 15), it is interesting to note that he distinguishes the fulfillment of the non-Christian traditions in the religion of Christianity (a position which he apparently rejects) from their fulfillment in the Christ-event (a position which he endorses). See " 'The Truth Will Make You Free,' " 228.

[14]I have suggested elsewhere that the theme of "mediation" might be a helpful tool for understanding the various approaches to the theology of religions. See Terrence Merrigan, "'For us and for our salvation': The Notion of Salvation History in the Contemporary Theology of Religions," *Irish Theological Quarterly* 64 (1999), 339-48.

[15]Dupuis has come under fire for allegedly separating the salvific work of Christ from the Church. He provides a discussion of this criticism and a response in "The Truth Will Make You Free," 222-24, 228, 250-55. See also *Toward a Christian Theology of Religious Pluralism*, 84-109, 330-57; and *Jesus Christ at the Encounter of World Religions*, 95-99.

[16]The appeal to the pluralistic character of the modern world is probably the most important argument invoked by pluralists to defend their views. Though this argument is supplemented by other, more properly theological, arguments, it does seem to have pride of place among pluralist thinkers. See, for example, Paul Knitter, "Preface," in *The Myth of Christian Uniqueness: Toward a Pluralistic Theology of Religions*, ed. J. Hick and P. Knitter (Maryknoll, N.Y.: Orbis, 1987), ix. I have discussed the pluralist arguments at length in Terrence Merrigan, "Religious Knowledge in the Pluralist Theology of Religions," *Theological Studies* 58 (1997), 686-707.

[17]The conciliar text speaks of "teachings and rules of life as well as sacred rites."

[18]Francis A. Sullivan, *Salvation Outside the Church? Tracing the History of the Catholic Response* (London: Geoffrey Chapman, 1992), 164-68.

[19]See Dupuis, *Toward a Christian Theology of Religious Pluralism*, 173-79; 360-62;

Paul Griffiths, *Problems of Religious Diversity* (Oxford: Blackwell, 2001), 61; D'Costa, *The Meeting of Religions and the Trinity*, 105-09.

[20]Merrigan, "Religious Knowledge in the Pluralist Theology of Religions," 693-98.

[21]In addition to their shared Trinitarian approach, all three authors can be described as "inclusivists," in line with the understanding of this term offered at the outset of this paper. See S. Mark Heim, *The Depth of the Riches: A Trinitarian Theology of Religious Ends* (Grand Rapids: William B. Eerdmans, 2001), 7, 8, where Heim declares that he "affirms the legitimacy of Christian confession of Christ as the one decisive savior of the world," and describes himself as a "convinced inclusivist." In *The Meeting of Religions and the Trinity*, D'Costa seeks to "deconstruct" the threefold typology of exclusivism, inclusivism and pluralism, but continues to defend Christ's role as constitutive and universal savior. See especially 127-29.

[22]Dupuis, *Toward a Christian Theology of Religious Pluralism*, 210.

[23]Ibid., 388. See also p. 382: "Through the experience and testimony of the other, [Christians] will be able to discover at greater depth certain aspects, certain dimensions, of the Divine Mystery that they had perceived less clearly and that have been communicated less clearly by Christian tradition. At the same time, they will gain a purification of their faith." However, Dupuis's claims in this regard need to be weighed against other remarks, such as the claim that that, while there are "surely . . . elements of other faiths that are in harmony with Christian faith and can be combined and integrated with it, . . . there may be other elements . . . that formally contradict the Christian faith and are not assimilable" (381). See also Merrigan, "Exploring the Frontiers," 354-58.

[24]Heim, *The Depth of the Riches*, 185. For a discussion of the three dimensions of trinitarian life, see especially 185-207, 210-13.

[25]Ibid., 210. The text between square brackets is from p. 197.

[26]Ibid., 229, 255, 264.

[27]Ibid., 179.

[28]Ibid., 198; see also pp. 167, 179, 182-87, 198, 213, 219, 220, 227, 229. Heim acknowledges Dupuis's critique of the theory of diverse religious ends (see ibid., 243; Dupuis, *Toward a Christian Theology of Religious Pluralism*, 309-13). It is, however, important to note that Dupuis was responding to Heim's earlier work, *Salvations: Truth and Difference in Religion* (Maryknoll, N.Y.: Orbis, 1995).

[29]D'Costa, *The Meeting of Religions and the Trinity*, 115, 128, 130, 133. See also pp. 109, 114.

[30]Regarding Dupuis, see, for example, *Toward a Christian Theology of Religious Pluralism*, 384. Regarding Griffiths, Heim and D'Costa, see nn. 31 and 32.

[31]Griffiths, *Problems of Religious Diversity*, 7-12; Heim, *The Depth of the Riches*, 21-35.

[32]D'Costa, *The Meeting of Religions and the Trinity*, 19-24.

[33]See J. A. DiNoia, "Varieties of Religious Aims: Beyond Exclusivism, Inclusivism, and Pluralism," in *Theology and Dialogue: Essays in Conversation with George Lindbeck*, ed. Bruce D. Marshall (Notre Dame: South Bend, Ind.: University of Notre Dame Press, 1990), 254-58; DiNoia, *The Diversity of Religions: A Christian Perspective* (Washington, D.C.: The Catholic University of America Press, 1992), 56-64, 88-94.

[34]Griffiths, *Problems of Religious Diversity*, 63, 59.

[35]For an extensive treatment of the contribution to the theology of religions by Asian theologians, see Peter Phan, "Doing Theology in the Context of Cultural and Religious Pluralism: An Asian Perspective," *Louvain Studies* 27 (2002) 36-98. I am greatly indebted to Phan's article for the discussion of the Asian approach to the theology of religions.

³⁶For an overview of the thought of the Federation of Asian Bishops' Conferences and its significance for interreligious dialogue, see A. Alangaram, *Christ of the Asian Peoples: Towards an Asian Contextual Christology—Based on the Documents of the Federation of Asian Bishops' Conferences* (Bangalore: Asian Trading Corporation, 1999), 177-208. See especially pp. 180-82, 185-86, 200-01. Dupuis's *Toward a Christian Theology of Religious Pluralism* is peppered with references to the documents of the Federation and to the work of Asian theologians and theological bodies. For a reflection on the critical questions which the Asian experience poses to traditional theology of religions, see Paul Knitter, "Catholics and Other Religions: Bridging the Gap Between Dialogue and Theology," *Louvain Studies* 24 (1999), 319-54, especially 333-35.

³⁷Quoted in Dupuis, *Toward a Christian Theology of Religious Pluralism*, 220. The text is taken from a document of the Theological Advisory Commission of the Federation of Asian Bishops' Conferences (FABC), entitled "Theses on Interreligious Dialogue," *FABC Papers* 48, Hong Kong, 1987, p. 7. The "Theological Advisory Commission" is now known as the "Office for Theological Concerns." Regarding the organization of the FABC, see Alangaram, *Christ of the Asian Peoples*, 7-8.

³⁸For a reflection on the Asian context, see Samuel Rayan, "Reconceiving Theology in the Asian Context," in *Doing Theology in a Divided World*, ed. V. Fabella and S. Torres (Maryknoll, N.Y.: Orbis, 1985), 124-42; Aloysius Pieris, "Christ Beyond Dogma: Doing Christology in the Context of the Religions and the Poor," *Louvain Studies* 25 (2000), 187-231.

³⁹Phan, "Doing Theology in the Context of Cultural and Religious Pluralism," 64-65; regarding the "'wider intertextuality'," see George M. Soares-Prabhu, "Two Mission Commands: An Interpretation of Matthew 18:16-20 in the Light of a Buddhist Text," in *Voices from the Margin*, ed. R.S. Sugirtharajah (Maryknoll, N.Y.: Orbis, 1995), 319-38. See especially pp. 323, 324, and 325. This article originally appeared in *Biblical Interpretation: A Journal of Contemporary Approaches* 2 (1994), 264-82.

⁴⁰This is perhaps reflected in D'Costa's proposal to abandon the model of inclusivism altogether, since it can never do justice to the others in their otherness. See *The Meeting of Religions and the Trinity*, 23.

7

Jacques Dupuis and Asian Theologies
of Religious Pluralism

Peter C. Phan

In his assessment of the review of his book *Toward a Christian Theology of Religious Pluralism* by the editorial board of *Revue Thomiste*, Jacques Dupuis mentions its disparaging remark about the "myth of the superiority of 'the man on the spot.' "[1] Since he has never claimed to possess superior knowledge on the basis of his life and experiences in India from 1948 to 1984, Dupuis takes the criticism to refer to the fact that he has quoted with approval the documents published under the patronage of the Federation of Asian Bishops' Conferences and the Catholic Bishops' Conference of India. Dupuis is one of the very few Western Catholic theologians who are conversant with the teachings of the magisterium of the Asian Churches, whom he holds in high respect. He is also familiar with the works of many Asian theologians, with whom he enters into a fruitful dialogue.

This essay will first examine Dupuis's dialogue with Asian theologies, in particular that expressed in the documents of various official organizations of the Asian Churches. It will next compare his theology of religious pluralism with those of two Asian theologians, one Catholic and the other Protestant. It will conclude with suggestions on how Dupuis's model of "inclusivist pluralism" can be extended further on the basis of Asian theologies.

Dialogue with Asian Theologies

Over thirty years of living and teaching theology in India cannot fail to leave permanent imprints on anyone's religious outlook and theological vision, the more so if one, like Jacques Dupuis, is a first-class intellectual with a capacious mind, a generous heart, and a prolonged exposure to Asian realities. Life in Asia, according to Sri Lankan Jesuit Aloysius Pieris, is pervaded by massive poverty and deep religiousness. Nowhere are these two features more pronounced and visible than in India, and there is little doubt that they have shaped Asian theologians',

72

as well as Dupuis's, theological agenda in terms of inculturation, liberation, and interreligious dialogue.[2] In what follows I will explore how the Asian context and Asian theologies have influenced Dupuis's theological method, his understanding of interreligious dialogue, and his theology of religious pluralism.[3]

A New Way of Doing Theology

One of the strident critics of Dupuis, Léo Elders, blames his alleged Christological errors on his method. For Elders, the only valid theological method is the deductive one, which takes the data of revelation and tradition as first principles from which to draw theological conclusions.[4] In contrast, Dupuis advocates a combination of the deductive and inductive methods.[5] He acknowledges the necessity and the limitations of both the dogmatic-genetic and the inductive methods and argues for a combination of both into a new way of doing theology which, following Claude Geffré, Dupuis calls "hermeneutical theology." In such a method, there is an interaction between three realities: the "text" (the data of faith), the "context" (the total reality, including its sociopolitical, economic, cultural, and religious dimensions), and the "interpreter" (both the individual theologian and the community).

Such a method is particularly applicable to a Christian theology of religious pluralism which, according to Dupuis, must not start from the teachings of the Bible or Tradition but ought to be rooted in an actual praxis of dialogue with non-Christian religions. Only such a dialogue can go beyond the mere fact of religious diversity (a "theology of religions") and help Christian theologians understand the root-cause of pluralism itself and its potential significance in God's plan of salvation (a "theology of religious pluralism"). Accordingly, Dupuis notes with approval the change that the Indian Theological Association made in the wording of its annual meeting from "Towards a Theology of Religions: An Indian Christian Perspective" in 1988 to "Towards an Indian Christian Theology of Religious Pluralism" in the following year. Again, he appreciates the observation made by the same association in 1991 that in India "to be religious is to be interreligious."[6]

Furthermore, because of the twin phenomena of massive poverty and deep religiousness in Asia, Dupuis, following Aloysius Pieris, argues that interreligious dialogue must go hand in hand with actions in favor of the liberation of the Asian poor.[7] Finally, because of this imperative of interreligious dialogue in Asia, Dupuis acknowledges that the lead to construct a theology of religious pluralism belongs to the churches in Asia.

Interreligious Dialogue and Evangelization

Another area in which Asian theology influences Dupuis's thinking is the connection between interreligious dialogue and evangelization. There is no need here to follow Dupuis's detailed and instructive account of the changes in the Church's understanding of evangelization—from Vatican II through Paul VI's *Ecclesiam Suam* (1964) and *Evangelii Nuntiandi* (1975) to John Paul II's *Redemptoris Missio* (1990) and the joint document of the Pontifical Council for Interreligious Dialogue and the Congregation for the Evangelization of Peoples, *Dialogue and Proclamation* (1991). Evangelization is an umbrella term for the mission of the Church in its totality comprising several distinct activities such as witness, proclamation, conversion, sacramentalization, founding of churches, inculturation, interreligious dialogue, and human development. The problem is how to conceive the exact relationship between the two activities of evangelization, namely, proclamation and interreligious dialogue.[8]

Basically, for Dupuis, today it is necessary to affirm (1) that interreligious dialogue (understood not simply as a spirit of respect and friendship but also as a fourfold activity of sharing a common life, joint work for justice and peace, intellectual exchange, and sharing of religious experiences) is an intrinsic dimension of evangelization; (2) that interreligious dialogue and proclamation (understood as the invitation to non-Christians to explicitly accept Jesus and join the Church) are distinct elements in the Church's evangelizing mission and must neither be confused with nor separated from one another; and (3) there is a tension between these two activities insofar as the Church is both "already" and "not yet" the Kingdom of God: the former makes proclamation possible, the latter interreligious dialogue necessary.[9]

Again, my interest here is not to expound Dupuis's theology of interreligious dialogue but to show how it is based on Asian theologies. On the necessity of interreligious dialogue in Asia, Dupuis appeals to the International Theological Conference on Evangelization and Dialogue in Asia which was held at Nagpur, India, in 1971. He praises the Nagpur Conference's positive theology of non-Christian religions and cites with appreciation its statement that "the religious traditions of the world can be regarded as helping them toward the attainment of their salvation. . . . The different sacred scriptures and rites of the religious traditions of the world can be, in various degrees, expressions of divine manifestation and can be conducive to salvation."[10] This positive attitude toward non-Christian religions Dupuis also finds in the First Plenary Assembly of the FABC held at Taipei (Taiwan) in 1974, which affirms that Christian mission in Asia "includes a dialogue with the great religious traditions of our peoples."[11]

With regard to the relationship between proclamation and dialogue, Dupuis admires the position, championed by D. S. Amalorpavadass at the 1974 Synod of Bishops on evangelization, which affirms that "while evangelization and the dialogue are theologically distinct, they are nevertheless joined together in a single life, in the case of many Christians."[12] Dupuis also quotes at length from the FABC Theological Advisory Commission's document *Theses on Interreligious Dialogue* (1987) to the effect that dialogue and proclamation are not opposed to one another, inasmuch as proclamation is the Church's awareness of God's special mission in the world, while dialogue is its awareness of God's presence and action outside its visible boundaries.[13] Again, he quotes with appreciation the speech of Bishop F. M. Fernando of Chilaw, Sri Lanka, during the 1985 Extraordinary Synod of Bishops, in which Bishop Fernando affirms that "the interreligious dialogue should be regarded as an integral element of the Church's evangelizing mission."[14] In addition, with regard to the intimate link between interreligious dialogue and liberation, Dupuis finds support for it in the 1989 document *Liberative Praxis and Theology of Religious Pluralism* of the Indian Theological Association, which affirms that the combination of these two activities is "the significant *locus theologicus* and term of reference for a theology of religions from a liberative perspective."[15]

Religious Pluralism and Asian Christologies

Dupuis's indebtedness to Asian theologies is even more evident in his Christology and theology of religious pluralism. In the first half of his book *Jesus Christ at the Encounter of World Religions* Dupuis begins a lengthy discussion of what he calls the "Unbound Christ" of Neo-Hinduism by expounding six Christological models found in the Hindu Renaissance: Mahatma Gandhi's moral approach to the Christ of the Sermon on the Mount and the Beatitudes, Keshub Chunder Sen's devotional (*bhakti*) approach to Christ, Sarvepalli Radhakrisnan's Neo-Vedantine approach to Christ as the end-point of humanity's self-development and cosmic evolution, Swami Akhilananda's ascetical approach to Christ as an avatar, Manilal C. Parekh's theological approach to Christ as the *yogi*, and Bhamanbandhab Upadhyaya's mystical approach to Christ as the teacher of the *advaitic* or non-dualistic experience of Brahman.[16]

Dupuis highlights both the strengths and the weaknesses of these six Christologies, and on the basis of their positive insights, proposes to view Christ as the teacher of Christian yoga and the mystic of the *advaita* experience of Brahman. Dupuis argues that New Testament data support the contention that Jesus performed all the three levels of yoga: i.e., the manifold psychophysical exercises, the mental exercises of meditation and concentration, and the pure consciousness of God. Thus Jesus can be said to have introduced the way of Christian yoga for his followers.[17] In addition, Jesus is also reported to have a unique consciousness of his identity with God the Father. Jesus' affirmation that "I and the Father are one" (Jn 10:30) seems to be the equivalent of the two fundamental formulas of *advaitic* Hinduism: *Aham brahmasmi* [I am Brahman] and *tattvamasi* [That art thou]. Dupuis is careful to point out that Jesus was also aware of being distinct from his Father, and in this sense Jesus' identity is not the same as the identity envisaged by *advaitic* Hinduism in which all duality vanishes. Nevertheless, Jesus' identity-in-distinction and communion with the Father represents the supreme realization of the *advaita* in the human condition affirmed by the seers of the *Upanishads* but scarcely imagined possible even by them in a particular human being.[18]

Again, the point here is not to present and assess Dupuis's Christology but to show how it has been shaped by Asian-Christian and even Hindu theologies. In this respect, it is also interesting to note how Dupuis has a deep admiration for the Hindu-Christian monk Swami Abhishiktananda (Henri Le Saux), especially the latter's attempt to unite in himself the "two forms of a single faith." For Dupuis, Abhishiktananda's experience "opens an important avenue toward a Christian theology of religious traditions that would be based on an existential encounter with these traditions in interreligious dialogue."[19]

Furthermore, in developing his own theology of religious pluralism, which he terms "inclusivist pluralism" or "pluralistic inclusivism," on the basis of a Trinitarian Christology, Dupuis often appeals to Asian theologies. In arguing for the possibility of viewing non-Christian religions as ways of God's revealing and saving action, he cites the statement of the FABC's First Plenary Assembly in Taipei, 1978: "How then [could] we not acknowledge that God has drawn our peoples to himself through them [non-Christian religions]?"[20] He also quotes at great length a 1987 statement by the Theological Advisory Commission of the FABC which bases this positive regard for other religions on the fact that God has only one plan of salvation for humanity.[21] Another lengthy text of the FABC's Institute for Religious Affairs is also quoted to show that the theological basis of religious pluralism is the self-manifestation of the Triune God in history (the "Immanent Trinity").[22] Again, Dupuis appeals to the statement of the Thirteenth Annual Meeting of the Indian Theological Association (December 1989), which affirms that diversities among religions become "complementarities" and divergences "pointers of communion."[23]

With regard to the "inspired" character of the Scriptures of other religions, Dupuis adopts the affirmative position of the Research Seminar on Non-Biblical Scriptures held in Bangalore, India, in September 1974, citing a long passage from its final statement.[24] He also endorses the same seminar's later recommendation, made at its meeting in December 1974, to make use of these sacred books in the liturgy.[25]

Finally, concerning the relationship between the Kingdom of God and the Church, Dupuis quotes extensively from three statements of the FABC to support his position that the Kingdom of God is larger than the Church and is found in non-Christian religions, a key element of his theology of religious pluralism.[26]

Jacques Dupuis, Aloysius Pieris, Choan-Seng Song

So far I have shown that there exist between various Asian theologies and Dupuis convergences and even influences of the former upon the latter with regard to theological method, interreligious dialogue, and the theology of religious pluralism. To arrive at a sharper delineation of Dupuis's theology, it would be helpful to compare and contrast him with two major Asian theologians whose works Dupuis has frequented cited, Aloysius Pieris and Choan-Seng Song.

Dupuis and Aloysius Pieris

Aloysius Pieris (1934-), a Sri Lankan Jesuit, has acknowledged that his own theology is inspired by two fundamental personal experiences: his immersion in

Buddhist studies and his exposure to Asia's massive poverty.[27] This double experience corresponds to the two major features that, according to Pieris, characterize the Asian situation: pervasive religiousness and dehumanizing poverty. In Pieris's view, how the Asian Churches meet the challenges posed by these two realities will determine the future of Christianity in Asia, that is, whether the Christian Churches will remain simply *in* Asia or will become *of* Asia. For Pieris, Christianity will achieve real inculturation in Asia and become *of* Asia only by receiving, like Jesus, a double baptism, that is, at the "Jordan of Asian Religiosity" and on the "Calvary of Asian Poverty." In the first baptism, the Churches will be immersed in the deep religiousness of Asia's non-Christian religions and will, humbly and willingly, learn from these religious traditions; in the second, the Churches will, by voluntary poverty, embrace the enforced poverty of the masses and join in their struggle for liberation. Interreligious dialogue and liberation, practiced conjointly as a unified process of inculturation, the one authenticating the other, are the only way by which Christianity will find a real home in Asia. This is one of the basic themes running throughout Pieris's theological works.[28]

Another key and recurrent thesis of Pieris's theology is that Christianity and Buddhism represent two fundamental religious quests of humanity, namely, for love (*agape*) and wisdom (*gnosis*) respectively. For Pieris, these two quests are not mutually exclusive; rather *agape* and *gnosis* are each by itself inadequate to experience and express the Ultimate and therefore need each other as complementary idioms to mediate the experience of salvation and liberation. Hence the necessity of a "core-to-core" dialogue, a "*communicatio in sacris*," in which Christianity's *agape* will be enriched by Buddhism's *gnosis* ("gnostic agape"), and vice versa, Buddhism's *gnosis* will be enriched by Christianity's *agape* ("agapeic gnosis").[29]

From this dialogue between Buddhism and Christianity emerges a third key idea in Pieris's theology, namely, the parallel between the process by which Jesus became, that is, is interpreted as the Christ (Christology) and that by which Gautama became, that is, is interpreted as the Buddha (Buddhology). Needless to say, parallels between these two processes render problematic any claim to uniqueness made by both Christians and Buddhists for either the Christ or the Buddha. Pieris's proposed solution to such competing claims is to distinguish three dimensions of the mystery of salvation of which both Gautama and Jesus spoke: the *source, medium*, and *force* of salvation. Whereas Buddhists and Christians diverge in their ideas about the source and the force of salvation, they converge in their affirmation of the necessity of the mediation/mediator of salvation, that is, *agape* and *gnosis*. An Asian theology of liberation which combines both, according to Pieris, will be able to produce "a Christology that does not compete with Buddhology but complements it by acknowledging the *one path* of liberation on which Christians join Buddhists in their *gnostic detachment* (or the practice of 'voluntary poverty') and Buddhists join the Christian *agapeic involvement* in the struggle against 'forced poverty' as it truly happens in the basic *human* communities in Asia."[30]

My intention here is of course not to offer a comprehensive presentation of Pieris's theology but to compare it with Dupuis's theology of interreligious dialogue and religious pluralism. Dupuis discusses at length and sympathetically Pieris's position that the Churches *in* Asia must become *of* Asia by being immersed in the double baptism of Asian religiousness and poverty, that is, they must be engaged in interreligious dialogue and liberation as a unified process of inculturation.[31] Dupuis also agrees with Pieris that "a combined interfaith liberative praxis is an urgent task of evangelization—and a *locus theologicus* for a theology of religious pluralism."[32] However, though affirming the appropriateness of "hyphenated Christians," that is, Christians who embody in themselves different religious traditions, Dupuis emphasizes more explicitly and strongly than Pieris the necessity of discerning "elements . . . that formally contradict the Christian faith and are not assimilable."[33]

In addition, Dupuis subscribes to Pieris's notion of different but converging paths to salvation, in particular the complementarity between Christian *agape* and Buddhist *gnosis* and his proposal of a core-to-core dialogue between Christianity and Buddhism.[34] However, Dupuis seeks to clarify an ambiguity in Pieris regarding the relationship between the "medium" of salvation and Jesus. Whereas Pieris merely identifies this mediating reality with the Word, Dupuis goes further to affirm that the Word has become flesh in Jesus and that this Word that "enlightens every human being" (Jn 1:9) is the "source of the 'enlightenment' of Gautama-the-Buddha."[35]

Finally, with regard to the challenge to the Christian claim of uniqueness posed by the parallel process of "deification" of Jesus and Gautama, Dupuis agrees with Pieris that the language of "uniqueness" has become problematic and that the categories of exclusivism, inclusivism, and pluralism are not ultimately helpful.[36] However, he finds unacceptable Pieris's distinction between "the Word of God who saves" and "the Word-of-God-made-flesh," that is Jesus Christ, who does not. For him, "the anticipated action of the Word of God is related to the event of Jesus Christ in which God's plan for humankind comes to a climax. The Word-to-be-incarnate and the Word incarnate are one indivisible reality."[37]

Dupuis and Choan-Seng Song

C. S. Song (1929-), a Presbyterian, has spent most of his life outside his native country Taiwan, in Europe and especially in the U.S.A. He has made the construction of a truly Asian theology—or, as he put it, planting the Cross in the land of the Lotus—the main goal of his theological project. One of the distinctive features of his theological method is the use of stories. Indeed, Song's prolific writings offer a narrative theology par excellence.[38] By stories Song means the stories of Asian people, especially of children, women, and men who are poor, oppressed, and marginalized. These stories are correlated with the master story, namely, the story of Jesus which reveals his message about the Reign of God. From this story of the Reign of God in the life and ministry of Jesus, Song moves backward to the stories of the Reign of God in the Hebrew Scriptures and forward to the stories of the people outside the Christian Church. It is important to note that Song does not see the relation between the story of Jesus, on the one hand, and the stories of the Hebrew Scriptures and those of the Asian people, on the other hand, in terms of promise and fulfillment but in terms of the *presence* of God's reign in all three sets of stories.

Central to Song's theology are the reality of the Reign of God and Jesus' role within it. That the Reign of God and Jesus are intrinsically intertwined is indicated by the title of the second volume of Song's Christological trilogy: *Jesus & the Reign of God.* Indeed, for Song, the stories about the Reign of God constitute the key to understanding who Jesus was and is. In explicating Jesus' message about the Reign of God, Song repeatedly privileges its sociopolitical and economic aspects: "The heart of Jesus' message is the reign of God (*basileia tou theou*). In all he said and did he was at pains to make clear that God's reign is primarily concerned with the people victimized by a class-conscious society and a tradition-bound religious establishment. God's reign, in the light of what Jesus said and did, inaugurates an era of people."[39] At the center of God's reign stand the "people" who reveal who Jesus is: "*People are now the clues to who the real Jesus is*—people who are poor, outcast, and socially and politically oppressed. What Jesus has said and done is not comprehensible apart from men, women, and children who suffer in body and spirit."[40]

This view of the Kingdom of God shapes Song's Christology. Song has made a vigorous critique of what he calls "church-centered Christology" and "Christ-centered Christology." By "church-centered Christology" he means the theology of Christ devised to serve the Church's interests, especially its economic and political power, often in alliance with colonial and secular powers. Theologically, according to Song, this Christology is undergirded by the *heilsgeschichtlich* interpretation of history which operates according to the promise-fulfillment scheme and which draws a straight line from Israel to Jesus to Church. Such a historical interpretation relies on the concept of divine election of a particular people (i.e., Israel, now replaced by the Christian Church) to the exclusion of other peoples, the "pagan" ones. Over against this exclusivistic Christology Song develops his universalist theology based on the unified doctrines of creation and incarnation/redemption.

By "Christ-centered Christology" Song means the images of Christ that various Christian theological traditions have presented of Jesus to serve the interests of the Church, both as an object of worship and as a theme for metaphysical speculation. This Christology, too, is characterized by exclusivistic claims, implied in the term "centered."

In contrast to "church-centered," "Christ-centered," and even "Jesus-centered" Christologies, Song proposes a "Jesus-oriented" Christology. "Orientation" connotes, according to Song, relation and inclusion. Such a Jesus-oriented Christology does not need to choose between Christocentrism and theocentrism, because one cannot know God except through Jesus and one cannot know Jesus except through God. Methodologically, such a Christology is constructed out of the stories of

God which, according to Song, cannot be limited to the stories of the Bible and Christianity but include the "stories outside the Christian community as well as inside it—stories of people around us, stories of the human community to which the Christian community is closely related, and stories of Asia, for example, to which Christians in Asia belong. The world these stories represent is infinitely larger than the 'Christian world.' "[41] In a word, a Jesus-oriented Christology emerges out of the stories of the Reign of God. Furthermore, because these stories are those of oppressed, marginalized, and poor people, Song says in the arresting title of one of his books, Jesus is "*the Crucified People*."

To explain the universality of this Jesus, Song proposes a "creation-redemption paradigm" in which God's creation, incarnation, and redemption are seen simply as "equiprimordial" aspects or moments of one and the same action of God in the world, thereby annulling any special election of a group of people on God's part which would exclude the non-chosen peoples. The particularity of God's action is guaranteed by what Song calls the "death-resurrection paradigm," which assures the connection of God's action with the concrete history of Jesus of Nazareth. But this second paradigm is included in the first which obtains primacy.[42]

Dupuis discusses Song's theology far less extensively than that of Pieris. Most of his comments refer to Song's theology of the Reign of God; with the refusal to identify the Kingdom of God with the Church he heartily agrees.[43] Dupuis welcomes Song's emphasis on the universality of the Reign of God. He cites with approval Song's interpretation of the parable of the Great Banquet (Lk 14:15-24; Matt 22:1-14) as expressing Jesus' "global vision" of the Kingdom of God.[44] He also subscribes to Song's reading of Jesus' two healing miracles in favor of non-Jews, i.e., the daughter of the Canaanite woman (Matt 15:21-28) and the servant of the Roman centurion (Matt 8:5-13) as indicating that the Reign of God extends beyond the boundaries of the Church.[45] Dupuis also welcomes Song's remark that Jesus by intentionally crossing into Samaria, without needing to, on his way back from Jerusalem to Sychar (Jn 4:1-42) indicates the universality of the Reign of God.[46] Similarly, Song's observation on the irony of the fact that Jesus' disciples were unable to drive out demons while someone not of their circle was able to (Mk 8:28; 38) and of its implication for the universality of the Reign of God finds a sympathetic hearing with Dupuis.[47]

With regard to the relationship between the Reign of God and non-Christian religions, Dupuis finds plausible Song's view that the audience to whom Jesus preached his Sermon on the Mount included not only the intimate circle of his followers and disciples but also all the crowds coming from Judea, Jerusalem, and the coastal region of Tyre and Sidon (Lk 6:17), and therefore Jesus' message and blessings are directed to all.[48] Finally, Dupuis cites at length with approval Song's argument that the apparently exclusivistic text of Acts 4:12 refers only to an intra-Jewish debate regarding who has the power to save ("By what power, and by whose name have you men done this?" [Acts 4:7]), and cannot legitimately be extended to the question about the possibility of salvation outside the Church.[49]

While Dupuis's discussion limits itself to Song's theology of the Reign of God with which he is by and large in agreement, and does not extend to Song's Christology, there is no doubt that Dupuis would take issue with Song's unilaterally sociopolitical interpretation of Jesus' message about the Kingdom of God. Nor will he accept Song's aversion to the use of metaphysical categories in Christology. Nor would he accept Song's rejection of the possibility of a special election of a particular people by God on the ground that this would imply an exclusion of other peoples. Above all, Dupuis would certainly object to Song's preferred manner of speaking: Jesus as the "prototype" or "archetype" of God's love and as the "supreme concentration" of God's incarnating dynamics falls short of the Christian profession in Jesus' divinity.[50] Indeed, for Dupuis, an orthodox Christian theology of religious pluralism must be based upon the faith conviction of Jesus' "unique divine filiation."[51]

Further Elaborations

At the end of his lengthy discussion of the reviews of his undeservedly controversial book, Dupuis acknowledges that his "inclusivist pluralism" of religions "certainly needs further elaborations and requires to be studied more thoroughly."[52] We have shown how Dupuis's theology of religious pluralism, based on a "Trinitarian Christology," has found strong echoes in Asian theologies, and how it also has many divergences from the thought of two major Asian theologians.

In the concluding pages I will highlight some areas in which Dupuis's inclusivist pluralism can receive further elaborations from the insights of the Asian theologies from which he himself has drawn.

1. In terms of methodology, Dupuis's insistence on the need to combine the deductive and the inductive approaches is well taken. Whereas the deductive approach accepts as non-negotiable principles certain Christian assertions (e.g., Jesus' ontological divine filiation), the inductive approach tests the meaning and significance (not the truth-value) of these affirmations in the cauldron of interreligious dialogue. For Dupuis, as we have seen, this interreligious dialogue is complex: it is a constitutive dimension of evangelization; it is inextricably linked with liberation; and it takes four forms: dialogue of life, of common work, of theological exchange, and of spiritual communion.[53] However, in developing his theology of religious pluralism, Dupuis has privileged, and inevitably so—one must acknowledge in all fairness—the dialogue of theological exchange.

Out of this intellectual give-and-take, Dupuis has been able to break new ground, though recognizably within the boundaries of Christian orthodoxy, by offering fruitful insights into the universality of the Kingdom of God (beyond ecclesiocentrism), the presence of the Holy Spirit in non-Christian religions (beyond Christomonism and the older fulfillment theory which sees other religions as "stepping-stones" or "seeds" or "preparation" for Christianity), the "limitedness" or "relationality" of Jesus' revelatory and redemptive work, and the lasting role of the Logos beyond Jesus (beyond Jesuology).

All this makes for a dynamic and open theology of religious pluralism (not only the mere fact of religious diversities—"de facto pluralism"—but also the "de iure pluralism" which is accorded a place in God's plan). However, one can wonder what kind of Christology and theology of religious pluralism would emerge if the dialogue were carried out in the other three modalities and if a theology of religious pluralism were articulated as the result of such a different dialogue. In other words, to adopt Pieris's suggestion, what if the dialogue were to take place not *between* the Christian community and other non-Christian communities but *in* and *among* basic *human* communities? Of course, even in such a dialogue, no Christian truth should be denied, nor will any of the theses of Dupuis's theology be necessarily gainsaid. But there is the real possibility that these Christian truths and Dupuis's reinterpretations of them will be modified and enriched in unforeseeable ways. For example, it is highly likely that through a dialogue in such basic human communities, the possibility of recognizing that the Spirit is saying something *different* from (albeit not contradictory to) what Jesus has said would be heightened. As a result, the complementarity between Christianity and other religions will be more clearly seen. In other words, in addition to Dupuis's Trinitarian Christology, a more robust Spirit Christology, which should not sever the Spirit from Christ but allows the Spirit a genuine autonomy from Christ, is still to be developed.[54]

2. Another area where Asian theologies can open up further explorations in the theology of religious pluralism is the Asian concept of harmony, a word that resonates with all Asian cultures and religions.[55] First of all, it is important to state what harmony is not. As the FABC's Institute for Interreligious Dialogue, in its meeting in New Delhi, India, on October 24-28, 1995, says: ". . . Harmony does not consist in leveling off differences in order to arrive at consensus at any cost. Avoiding controversies and bypassing disagreements do not pave the way to harmony."[56] The fundamental reason why this way of conceiving harmony is wrong is that "Reality is pluralistic."[57] According to the Institute, harmony is "the spiritual pursuit of the totality of reality in its infinite diversity and radical unity. . . . Harmony evolves by respecting the otherness of the other and by acknowledging its significance in relation to the totality."[58]

In this understanding of harmony as reconciled diversity, a theology of religious pluralism might have to go beyond or at least modify substantially the model of pluralistic inclusivism which ultimately still maintains the superiority of one religion over others and the inclusion of other religions into this one superior religion. Perhaps, another model is more appropriate which lays more stress on pluralism than on inclusivism. As the FABC's Institute puts it intriguingly, "The unique significance of every religion is gratefully and critically perceived within the context of the universal spiritual evolution of humanity. Beyond the extremes of inclusivism and exclusivism, pluralism is accepted in resonance with the constitutive plurality of religion. Religions as they are manifested in history are complementary perceptions of the ineffable divine mystery, the God-beyond-God. All religions are visions of the divine mystery. No particular religion can raise the claim of being the norm for all others."[59]

Dupuis would perhaps object to these further elaborations and with his characteristic scholarly circumspection, his loving fidelity to the Tradition, and his instinctive prudence, would take issue with this or that proposal. For our part, we are deeply grateful to him for opening up the path, with great courage and at painful personal costs, so that others can travel further in the quest for understanding the marvelous and indeed stubborn fact of religious pluralism.

References

[1]Jacques Dupuis, " 'The Truth Will Make You Free': The Theology of Religious Pluralism Revisited," *Louvain Studies* 24 (1999), 216. The review by the editorial board of *Revue Thomiste* is " 'Tout récapituler dans le Christ'.: À propos de l'ouvrage de J. Dupuis, *Vers une théologie chrétienne du pluralisme religieux,*" 106 (1998), 591-630. There is irony in the fact that the followers of Saint Thomas look askance at the epistemological advantage of "being on the spot," given the fact that according to their master all knowledge starts from experience.

[2]According to the FABC, the Church not only *in* but also *of* Asia must engage in a triple dialogue: with Asia's people, especially the poor (liberation), their cultures (inculturation), and their religions (interreligious dialogue). These three dialogues are not separate activities but are intrinsically related to each other. The FABC was founded in 1970, on the occasion of Pope Paul VI's visit to Manila, Philippines. Its statutes, approved by the Holy See *ad experimentum* in 1972, were amended several times and were also approved again each time by the Holy See. For the documents of the FABC and its various institutes, see *For All the Peoples of Asia: Federation of Asian Bishops' Conferences. Documents from 1970 to 1991*, ed. Gaudencio Rosales and C. G. Arévalo (New York/Quezon City: Orbis/Claretian Publications, 1992), and *For All the Peoples of Asia: Federation of Asian Bishops' Conferences. Documents from 1992 to 1996*, vol. 2, ed. Franz-Josef Eilers (Quezon City: Claretian Publications, 1997).

[3]Of Dupuis's major works, *Who Do You Say I Am? Introduction to Christology* [*Who Do You Say*] (Maryknoll, N.Y.: Orbis, 1994) shows the least influence by Asian theologies; *Jesus Christ at the Encounter of World Religions* [*Jesus Christ*] (Maryknoll, N.Y.: Orbis, 1991) shows the most influence; *Toward a Christian Theology of Religious Pluralism* [*Religious Pluralism*] (Maryknoll, N.Y.: Orbis 1997) and *L'Incontro delle religioni* [*Incontro*] (still to be published in English) lie somewhere in between.

[4]See Léo Elders, "Les théories nouvelles de la signification des religions non-chrétiennes," *Nova et Vetera* 3 (1998), 97-117 and *Sedes Sapientiae* 68 (1998), 64-100.

[5]See *Who Do You Say*, 5-8; *Jesus Christ*, 4-7; *Religious Pluralism*, 13-19; *Incontro*, 8-11.

[6]*Religious Pluralism*, 11.

[7]Ibid., 19. We will come back to this point later.

[8]See *Jesus Christ*, 207-29; *Religious Pluralism*, 360-70; *Incontro*, 195-204.

[9]See *Jesus Christ*, 226-29.

[10]Ibid., 213-14.

[11]Ibid., 215.

[12]Ibid., 216.

[13]See *Religious Pluralism*, 371-72.

[14]*Jesus Christ*, 225.

[15]*Religious Pluralism*, 375-76. Dupuis also cites the works of Aloysius Pieris, Felix Wilfred, and the collective volume edited by S. Arokiasamy and G. Gispert-Sauch, *Liberation in Asia: Theological Perspectives* (Anand, Gujarat, India: Gujarat Sahitya Prakash, 1987).

[16]See *Jesus Christ*, 18-45.

[17]See ibid., 48-55.

[18]See ibid., 55-66 and *Religious Pluralism*, 268-74.

[19]*Jesus Christ*, 90. Dupuis's exposition of Abhishiktananda is found on pp. 67-90. In addition to Abhishiktananda, another figure who attempted to blend "East" and "West" and who is much admired by Dupuis is Bede Griffiths. See *Religious Pluralism*, 152-53, 267-68, 278-79.

[20]*Religious Pluralism*, 220.

[21]See ibid., 220.

[22]See ibid., 314, n. 6.

[23]Ibid., 199-200.

[24]See ibid., 248.

[25]See ibid., 253.

[26]See ibid., 341-42.

[27]See A. Pieris, "Two Encounters in My Theological Journey," in *Frontiers in Asian Christian Theology: Emerging Trends*, ed. R. S. Sugirtharajah (Maryknoll, N.Y.: Orbis, 1994), 141-46.

[28]Pieris's many essays are collected in three major works: *An Asian Theology of Liberation* (Maryknoll, N.Y.: Orbis, 1988); *Love Meets Wisdom: A Christian Experience of Buddhism* (Maryknoll, N.Y.: Orbis, 1988); and *Fire & Water: Basic Issues in Asian Buddhism and Christianity* (Maryknoll, N.Y.: Orbis, 1996).

[29]See Pieris, *Love Meets Wisdom*, 110-124.

[30]Ibid., 135.

[31]See *Religious Pluralism*, 19; 374-75.

[32]Ibid., 375.

[33]Ibid., 381.

[34]See ibid., 9; 326-28; 381.

[35]Ibid.,, 328; *Incontro*, 76-77.

[36]See *Religious Pluralism*, 199; *Incontro*, 79.

[37]*Religious Pluralism*, 196. Similarly, Dupuis is opposed to any "Spirit-Christology" that separates the historical Jesus and the Spirit: "One needs to affirm clearly the universal action of the Spirit throughout human history, either before or after the historical event Jesus Christ. But Christian faith has it that the action of the Spirit and that of Jesus Christ, though distinct, are nevertheless complementary and inseparable. Pneumatocentrism and Christocentrism cannot, therefore, be construed as two distinct economies of salvation, one parallel to the other" (197).

[38]Among his many works the following are most noteworthy: *Third-Eye Theology: Theology in Formation in Asian Settings* (Maryknoll, N.Y.: Orbis, 1982; rev. ed. 1990); *The Tears of Lady Meng: A Parable of People's Political Theology* (Geneva: World Council of Churches, 1981; Maryknoll, N.Y.: Orbis, 1982); *The Compassionate God* (Maryknoll, N.Y.: Orbis, 1982); *Tell Us Our Names: Story Theology from an Asian Perspective* (Maryknoll, N.Y.: Orbis, 1984); *Theology from the Womb of Asia* (Maryknoll, N.Y.: Orbis, 1986); his Christological trilogy entitled "The Cross in the Lotus World": *Jesus the Crucified People* (New York: Crossroad, 1990); *Jesus & the Reign of God* (Minneapolis: Fortress, 1993); *Jesus in the Power of the Spirit* (Minneapolis: Fortress, 1994); and *The*

Believing Heart: An Invitation to Story Theology (Minneapolis: Fortress, 1999). For a presentation of Song's theology, see Karl H. Federschmidt, *Theologie aus asiatischen Quelle: Der theologische Weg Choan-Seng Songs vor dem Hintergrund der asiatischen ökumenischen Discussion* (Münster: LIT Verlag, 1994) and Peter C. Phan, "Experience and Theology: An Asian Liberation Perspective," 101-03; 114-18; idem, "Jesus the Christ with an Asian Face," *Theological Studies* 57 (1996), 417-21.

[39]C. S. Song, *Jesus & the Reign of God*, ix. Again: "The reign of God for him [Jesus] is very much more a social and political vision than a religious concept. It has to be the texture of a society. It must be the foundation of a community. The reign of God is, thus, a cultural happening" (57).

[40]C. S. Song, *Jesus the Crucified People*, 12.

[41]*The Believing Heart*, 66.

[42]See C. S. Song, *Christian Mission in Reconstruction: An Asian Analysis* (Maryknoll, N.Y.: Orbis, 1977) .

[43]See *Religious Pluralism*, 343; *Incontro*, 24.

[44]See *Incontro*, 22; Song, *Jesus & the Reign of God*, 26.

[45]See *Incontro*, 23; Song, *Jesus in the Power of the Spirit*, 77-78.

[46]See *Incontro*, 25; Song, *Jesus in the Power of the Spirit*, 103-106.

[47]*Incontro*, 26; Song, *Jesus in the Power of the Spirit*, 200-26.

[48]See *Incontro*, 27: Song, *Jesus in the Power of the Spirit*, 214-20.

[49]See *Incontro*, 36-38; Song, *Jesus in the Power of the Spirit*, 244-45.

[50]Indeed, sometime Song's language seems *prima facie* to deny Jesus' divinity: "Jesus lived with this kind of love. He dedicated his entire life to it and shared it with others. . . . He practiced, lived, and died for it. He personified it. In this love which is Jesus we Christians come to know that God is love. Jesus is not God. He is flesh and blood just as we are. But he reflects God as he reflects this kind of love" (*The Believing Heart*, 294). The most Song is willing to affirm of Jesus is that Jesus is *in* God and God is *in* Jesus, or better, that "Jesus was in God *through the power of the Holy Spirit* and that God was in Jesus, also *through the power of the Spirit*" (*The Believing Heart*, 63).

[51]*Jesus Christ*, 195. Dupuis is critical of Hans Küng's merely functional Christology that describes Jesus as "God's representative" or God's "plenipotentiary, advocate, spokesman, representative, deputy, delegate—all functional terms that fall short of the decisive assertion of his unique divine filiation."

[52]J. Dupuis, " 'The Truth Will Make You Free,' The Theology of Religious Pluralism Revisited," 261.

[53]In interreligious dialogue in Asia today, many Christians consider "the priority in dialogue to be that of the dialogue of life" (*For All Peoples of Asia* [1997], 169).

[54]It has been suggested that Dupuis, "contrary to his intentions," is still "subordinating the Spirit to the Word in Jesus after all." See Paul F. Knitter, *Theologies of Religions* (Maryknoll, N.Y.: Orbis, 2002), 104.

[55]For an exposition of the Asian understanding of harmony, see "Asian Christian Perspectives on Harmony," in *For All the Peoples of Asia* (1997), 143-82; 229-98.

[56]Ibid., 158.

[57]Ibid., 155.

[58]Ibid., 157.

[59]Ibid., 157-58.

8

"Subsistit in"

Criterion of "Truth and History" in Interreligious Dialogue

Luigi Sartori

It is a common belief among scholars, that the radical and crucial problem raised by religious pluralism is the problem of "historicity" or the "historical sense," of the truths relating to the transcendent world. As with every kind of human knowledge—especially that searching for the eternal and religious truths which expresses itself out of the conscience of the subjects who understand and communicate such truths—it is necessarily bound to the historical and cultural limits which characterize every language or semantic world belonging to temporalities. Until now, at least within the universe of Christian faith, the problem of historicity has been normally discussed from the point of view of change: historicity in its legitimate or even necessary changes and successive novelties, and in its plurality of cultural forms or languages, even within the continuity of the same tradition of faith. According to some scholars of the history of dogma and heresies (Yves Congar), the first Christian millennium was characterized by a youthful missionary drive, a courageous embodiment of faith in various and new cultural universes: i.e. change understood as innovation. Hence the heretics were those people who remained behind and put the brakes on: they were not able to follow the innovation of the Church within the orthodox tradition. After many centuries of consolidation and tired conservation of the results of previous inculturation, the second millennium showed instead an almost opposite image: the orthodox are conservative people, i.e. those who a priori suspect novelties, while people who want to innovate are too easily accused of heresy. To be sure, this evaluation sounds a bit hasty and one-sided. But we cannot deny that in Catholic theology (the theology codified in scholastic manuals, the theology I studied in my youth) the word "novatores" had become almost synonymous with "heretics." Right up to Vatican II modernity was mistrusted: official documents in defense of orthodoxy specialized in condemning errors and deviations from the path of truth. At the height of the crisis the significant word "Modernism" dominates: it is a short period of time (at the end of the nineteenth century and the beginning of the twentieth century), but its negative consequences have been long-lasting.

Nowadays, following Vatican II, after the Church has solemnly committed itself to renewal and dialogue, it is necessary above all to follow the path of "reconciliation with modernity." "Modernism" is a word alluding to excesses we must avoid, but this is not so with the word "modernity." It is necessary to recover lost time, obviously with balance and not without giving in to excesses.

It seems at this point that the experience of verifying the scheme of the four circles of dialogue, which we find in the encyclical *Ecclesiam Suam* and *Gaudium et Spes* (GS) 92, shows that the fourth level of dialogue, that with the humanisms, seems to be wider than the dialogues more directly concerned internally with the Christian faith (between the subjects of the Catholic world, with the other Christian confessions, and with the other religions). The aim is to reconcile two mentalities rather than two opposite doctrinal universes. After centuries of mutual aversion two radically contrasting ways of interpreting and living history collide with each other: the first considers history "eternity *of* times," rather than "eternity *in* times" (some times must be preserved as if they were eternity); the other resolves eternity into an "eternal changing of everything" (historicity as historicism or mere relativism). This is the risk generated by secular modernity, which withdraws from faith. In my opinion it is important to emphasize that the *mens* of conservatism has had more time and more ways to consolidate itself; while the new *mens* of a genuine sense of history and of authentic historicity, leading an adequate and deep renewal, must be verified.

Therefore in my opinion we should think again about the meaning and value of that expression from the Council, which more than other statements appeals to historicity as the basis for dialogue. I am referring to the already famous *"subsistit in,"* article 8 of the *Lumen Gentium* (LG), which is taken up in other texts of the Council. Nowadays its true meaning is still vigorously discussed.[1] I think I can give a more convincing and useful interpretation. I think Congar is right: according to him, the "subsistit in" is the most innovative principle of the Council's ecumenism, while according to some Protestants (e.g. Oscar Cullmann) the most important principle is the "hierarchy of truths" in article 10 of *Unitatis Redintegratio* (UR).[2] The "subsistit in" establishes the principle of the historicity of dogma and of any other ecclesial reality.

It is true that the "subsistit in" forms the basis of specific ecumenism. But I want to demonstrate that it can and should also be applied to dialogue with other religions. That is the precise aim of this article, structured in two parts.[3] The first deals with the exegesis and interpretation of the "subsistit in " in relation to the ecumenism for which the "subsistit in" was originally adopted; the second part aims at demonstrating that it can also be legitimately adopted in relation to other religions. At the end I will weigh the arguments for and against my proposal.

The *"Subsistit in"* (LG 8) Principle of Historicity
of Truth for Ecumenism

Lumen Gentium 8

The exegesis and interpretation of the expression "subsistit in," which we find for the first time in article 8 of LG, continues to provoke rather bitter debates. I do not want to repeat the precise information offered by Frank Sullivan; his study is still the most pertinent and best documented account of the "case." To begin with, he points out that the identity of the author who changed "est" to "subsistit in" in the text concerning the relation between the "mystery" of one and only one Church and the Roman Catholic Church is still unknown. The Theological Commission did not offer explicit reasons for making this change, which resulted in the Council's dialogue with the non-Roman Catholic Churches. In my opinion the discussion has concentrated too exclusively on the meaning of the verb "subsist." Sullivan notes the interpretations which reduce it to a new way of repeating that only the Roman Church can claim the exclusive dignity of being the "only true Church," and also the interpretations which link it with philosophical or theological theses concerning the relation between "essences" or universal ideas and real individual subjects which give them concrete existence, or which link it with the relation between the one "divine nature" and the three persons of the Trinity. According to Sullivan both these interpretations are unsuitable. The first line of interpretation seems to characterize Cardinal Ratzinger's opinion, which he steadily repeated down to the recent document "Dominus Iesus"; above all since he raised objections against Leonardo Boff, who seems to support the second line of interpretation, which at least at first sight makes all churches and confessions equal.[4]

On the contrary I think we should underscore and emphasize the preposition *"in;"* the perspective of historicity is evident in this preposition. To affirm that the reality of the true Church *exists*, is found, and is present within the Roman Church, even apart from paying particular attention to non-Catholic Churches, means that we see things from a space and time perspective which must distinguish two aspects: the divine *contents* (or what is derived from God), and the *container* (formed by concrete human factors, i.e. by culture and not only by nature).

The context encourages us to highlight this line of interpretation, which is also what Sullivan does, even if he does not turn to account the preposition "in." The Doctrinal Commission, which modified the text, says at least one thing: it aimed to make the text more suitable for the next sentence, where it is admitted that "many elements of truth and grace are also found outside the Roman Church." With this a new thesis has begun: the thesis that compares "fullness or completeness" (the Catholic Church) with "not fullness and not completeness," or a larger or smaller "percentage" (the other Churches); instead of the previous thesis that compares a curt "yes" with a flat denial, by opposing "true church" to "false churches" ("only the Roman Church is the true Church").

Therefore it is important to pay attention to "historicity," to "there is" ("is present"), in place of "it is." The divine and unchanging element is distinct from the human element that appears also as "culture or the dress of nature" in the variety and diversity, not only of colors and expressions, which preserved the identity and continuity of truth, but also of historical forms which allow the embodiment of truth. This founds the principle which supports and leads an ecumenical openness to a substantial legitimacy of various historical forms of Church and tradition. This principle must obviously be associated with the other very important principle, that of the so called "hierarchy of truths," on which basis we must not even put the many, distinct divine gifts which build the Church. I have already referred to the dispute between Congar and Cullmann. As a Protestant, Cullmann emphasizes the principle of "concentration," the essential and what is primary: therefore he fears the exuberance of historical developments which appeal to God. But the importance of historicity implicit in the "subsistit in" seems more radical and universal, and Congar emphasizes it: he refers to the efforts for renewal and reform which concern all the ecclesial realities, and which hold good for all the churches in all historical periods. It will always be necessary to distinguish between what is "contained in" or the substance of the divine gift and what is only the "historical human container," because this usually involves short-lived elements or at least elements subject to change and renewal.

In my earlier comments on article 8 of LG[5] I have always underlined three principal limits of that ecumenical passage. First of all, everything is seen from the point of view of a quantitative comparison; the totality and completeness are measured almost wholly on the basis of the material number of the elements: in the Roman Church there are all the elements one hundred percent; in the other churches only a certain higher or lower percentage. This does not take into account that the mystery, even in its historical dimension, is intrinsically spiritual and of a qualitative order. Secondly, only the "being there" seems decisive for these elements, as if it were less important that they are truly experienced and operating and as if it were sufficient to preserve them and to keep them at our disposal (like food inside the refrigerator and not on the table or like money inside a safe or in a bank, money that we do not invest). Thirdly, our text refers to the Church rather than to Christ; those values derive from the Church and *de iure* belong to it (the Roman Church?). And do outsiders enjoy them as if they were stolen goods? These valuable elements should go back or encourage others to go back to the original Church. What is at stake is merely a question of justice: that of establishing the legitimate owners and restoring the items to them.

But shortly afterwards (in LG 15) we begin to move significantly beyond this. The point of view is decidedly Christological. Rather than the measurable quantity of ecclesial elements present elsewhere, their intrinsic characteristics are important. Hence LG takes care to underline the highest, primary, and most fundamental goods. The principle of the "hierarchy of truths" is already at work. The end of the subjective moment is emphasized: i.e. the real life of people, who on the basis of those values are raised to bear the precious fruit of a genuine faith and even witness the sanctifying action of the Holy Spirit to the point of martyrdom.

The logical conclusion of the doctrinal teachings offered by LG, articles 8 and 15, can be at once verified in the Council: in particular the decree UR 3 recognizes that the Holy Spirit can act even in the churches with only a few ecclesial elements (but with central and not marginal elements!). The decree even has recourse to the concept of the "Sacrament Church," which has already been rectified in the first chapter of LG, by affirming that the Holy Spirit does not refuse to use them [the churches which are not Roman Catholic] as a means for salvation.

Therefore we can at least deduce from these texts a new theological thesis. We cannot say anymore that only the Roman Catholic Church *is* the true Church: we must instead profess that it is the true Church in *fullness and totality*, and do so specifying that we refer only to the objective presence of the divine gifts (further dimension of "subsistit in"), and we make no pre-judgments as to their effective exploitation and subjective fullness. (In the Church these are all gifts, but it is not said that all subjects can show the fruits of these gifts.)

We must underline two aspects. The immediate context places in the foreground the subject "Church as institution," i.e. all the visible and historical elements, or means of a supernatural life, and not the Church as a mystical essence or transcendent reality (even if the background and the overall context of the first chapter of LG is rather that of the "Church as mystery"). Thus the problem of the comparison between "totality-fullness" and "incompleteness-percentage" is limited to the presence of these elements. This is perhaps the reason why (we turn our attention to the second aspect) many interpreters, even authoritative ones, have disregarded the significance of "historicity" in their interpretation of the "subsistit in," and insisted on that of "real consistency."

The result has been that the attention to other parallel texts of the Council has been somewhat poor. (We may refer to two texts: article 4 of UR, and article 1 of *Dignitatis Humanae*). So some, (e.g. Ratzinger[6]) even deny *tout court* the qualification and dignity of "Church" to those historical subjects who lack quantitatively some ecclesial elements. They even marginalize that solemn text, article 3 of the UR, which speaks of Churches where the Holy Spirit acts as a Sacrament also in relation to those other Churches which do not have all the complete elements which only the Roman Catholic Church enjoys. They also marginalize the final passage of article 4, where it is admitted that the Roman Catholic Church, in its historical reality is poor and limited because it cannot express perfectly and totally its treasure of completeness and fullness with which it is gifted (again an echo of "there is" and "subsistit in"), until it becomes one with all the other Churches.

Other Texts of the Council

First of all the principle emphasized for the first time by John XXIII in his speech at the opening of the Council (October 11, 1962): "the substance of faith is one thing; its form of expression is another."[7] We find again this principle taken up in UR 6; it is also applied in articles 14-17 to the historical and cultural varieties of "traditions in the one Tradition." Articles 14-17 thus try to spell out the specific characteristics of the spiritual "mentality" proper to the sister Churches of the East. Thus we also find this principle in GS 62 (the chapter on Gospel and culture). But it is the whole Constitution which should be considered as articulating a basic hermeneutical principle of the Council, precisely because it emphasizes the relation between Church and history—i.e. the theme of "Church in history" and "history in the Church." Thus it maintains not only that the Church "gives" to history (to concrete humanity), but it also "receives" from history (GS 44).

At the end, GS 92 synthesizes the famous four moments of dialogue which had been already suggested by Paul VI in *Ecclesiam Suam* and which I mentioned above: dialogue between the various ecclesial subjects within the Church, with non-Catholics, with non-Christians, and with humanity (or with the cultures). According to Congar, the new concept of "reception" must begin from here. Reception must constitute the privileged factor in the existence and life of the Church, not only in order to form within the Church particular communities or families of communities which might fully express the communion of charisms and ministries, and therefore the richness of legitimately diverse subjects of true ecclesial existence, but also to actualize the fullness of catholicity from the point of view of the dialogue ratified by the Council. Thus we can acquire elements of truth and vitality also in and from the exchange with non-Roman Catholics and even with non-Christians or atheists.[8]

In Ecumenical Theological Dialogue

At this point we can appeal to that "reception" of the principle of historicity which emerges in the area of ecumenical theology. We can affirm that nearly all the texts concerning theological dialogue offer a kind of verification of the criterion of "subsistit in" with regard to various doctrinal themes: biblical exegesis, Christological dogma, that of the Trinity, the doctrines concerning grace, the sacraments, the papacy, and the structures of the Church. In each sector the guiding principle is always that of unity *in* and *from* diversity. In the past the appeal to diversity seemed dangerous, almost as if it were logically destined to justify only negative fruits and separations. Today, instead, we tend to consider diversity as at least a possible note of hope and sign of positive complementarity, in view of a final goal of authentic richness and fullness in communion and unity. In fact, history now presents itself as a terrain where different and even positively original cultures are born and reach maturity. From them various, legitimate traditions of faith and ecclesial life can gain expression and confirmation. Here is the miracle of "a great Tradition which subsists *in* many traditions." One should no longer regard a priori all changes and innovations with suspicion.

I shall indicate only a few texts. In 1971 the Joint Working Group of Rome and Geneva (made up of the Catholic Church and the World Council of Churches) issued a "Joint Study on Catholicity and Apostolicity" in which basic themes are reconsidered: "Identity, change and norm," and "Unity and plurality."[9] Nine years later (1980) the same Joint Working Group produced a document on faith

(*Toward the Confession of a Common Faith*, 905-25), in which the problem of historicity is examined in the most delicate area, that of the doctrine of faith; and here, too, reflection is entirely guided by the two ecumenical criteria which I have mentioned before: that concerning the "hierarchy of truths" and that concerning the distinction between "the essential nucleus of faith" and the "historical form of its expression." I should like merely to quote a new and original practical caveat:

> Churches for which the content of faith is expressed in a fuller form must not a priori consider other churches, whose doctrinal traditions are less explicit, as betraying the wholeness of the Christian heritage. In their turn, clearly, Churches which are more restrained in their doctrinal affirmations must be on their guard against considering a priori that other churches, with richer formulas of faith and rites, are polluting the purity of faith with adventitious or parasitical additions.[10]

Let me emphasize, in particular, the reference to life experience and to the implicit way of living the expansion of truth; in one passage we read: "*one must trust what is implicit and the life experience which it permits*" (*Toward the Confession of a Common Faith*, 924). In any case, the Lutheran brothers in dialogue with Catholics have also made a great contribution to fixing and consolidating reflection concerning historicity, in order to construct ecumenical theological dialogue. The numerous, profound texts which express this insist on communion as a most concrete reality of "*the universal Church* in *particular churches*," of the "*Church* of *churches*," and they point to a progressive pathway leading to a goal of "organic unity" (a theme dear to Catholics), but always interpreting such unity in terms of a "communion of churches."[11] Perhaps it is precisely that approach which constitutes the most crucial, arduous problem for Catholic theology today, particularly for official theology.

At the end of this section, I should like to indicate at least one of the specifically theological works by Catholics who have attempted to widen discussion concerning the verification and practical applications of the "subsistit in" (and its associated principle of the "hierarchy of truth"): the well-known volume by Karl Rahner and Heinrich Fries, *Einigung der Kirchen—reale Möglichkeit.*[12] For several years this work almost seemed subject to censorship, given the critical reactions by Catholics and by Protestants as well; but now it seems to have revived and become extremely relevant. Let us hope that this is a sign of widespread maturity—slow but unstoppable—in the mentality of dialogue. For this reason I propose to extend the thought of this book to the area of interreligious dialogue.

"*Subsistit in*" Applies also to Interreligious Dialogue

As pointed out earlier, the "subsistit in" of LG 8 applies above all to the specific area of ecumenism: that is, to dialogue between the Christian confessions.

However, the unity of the entire Second Vatican Council demands that the harmony between all the Council texts be made to emerge, according to the more general principle of analogy, even if this also means that we take into account not only the aspects of identity or commonality between the various subjects being discussed, but also those implying difference and diversity.

In any event, we must respect a certain order between the conciliar documents. For our purposes we should above all commit ourselves to starting out from those set in an historical and doctrinal context of greater universality. It is right here that religious pluralism, by its very nature, is situated; indeed, it is here that the Council brings up the theme of the Church. I refer to GS and, even more, to DH, the declaration concerning religious freedom. In general, GS is entirely committed to allowing adequate room for the "anthropological" dimension of the Church, and even Christian truth. However, DH is the text which, more than any other, accentuates the radical theme of man's universal relationship to truth. That is why I wish to set out from this text.

Dignitatis Humanae

DH is quite a brief, seemingly marginal text; one may risk neglecting it, also because it seems to refer almost exclusively to the area of politics. States, in their relations with churches and religions, must safeguard and promote not just one single faith, giving it discriminating privileges with respect to others, but rather they must actuate relations in harmony with the principle of religious freedom. However, DH also has a higher, more universal meaning: it bases its entire reasoning on certain ideas regarding human relationship with truth. In so doing it touches on philosophical areas, such as the gnoseological question and, more globally, on anthropology. On the other hand it is the only text which, after LG 8 and UR 4, expressly takes up the expression "subsistit in." Regarding this point, I believe we should thank Pope John Paul II who, nearly alone, has recalled this trait of DH. He has taken it up repeatedly, even—I would say—with obstinacy. In the encyclical *Ut unum sint* (1995), he often invokes it (articles 2, 8, 18, 32), with the purpose of giving a solid foundation to the ecumenical commitment. Even in the solemn liturgy of the "Mea culpa" during the Jubilee of 2000 (March 12),[13] he recalled it to everyone's surprise in his prayer for the second of the seven confessions: the one relating to sins committed by recourse to methods of violence in the desire to safeguard and promote the truth. In that second "mea culpa," Cardinal Ratzinger's initial reference had been limited to characterizing such sins in terms of failures in the duty of being inspired by the Gospel even while reiterating the holy duty of defending truth. Instead, immediately afterwards, the Pope inserted in his prayer a doctrinal theme—that of the universal historicity of the truth—quoting DH, whose text points in the following direction: "Truth can impose itself on the mind of man only in virtue of its own truth, which wins over the mind with both gentleness and power" (DH 1). People have the duty to seek it out (it always remains something to be discovered!), and they must do so together (that is, with the participation of everyone, even those who have yet not reached certainties, but can only give opinions), by proposing—according to the text—"what they believe to be the truth, and strive toward the goal of universal consensus; this, indeed, could become normative" (DH 1-2).

We might therefore infer that, for the Pope, even what is a reality of faith and the Church should be inserted into such a context of humanity's global journey towards the truth, so that it can be fully understood, interpreted, expressed and communicated. This necessarily demands constant adaptation by hermeneutics.

Dei Verbum

We can then take up again the theme of Christian Revelation (*Dei Verbum*), since it is closely linked to the theme of truth: the Word of God communicates to us a specific truth, that of God; and this implies the problem of the humanization of the "Mystery-Truth." The Word (the Logos) is not given in its intrinsic immediacy; it does not yet present itself now with the evidence of the beatific vision, but enters history; indeed, it becomes history. No one has ever seen God, not even the holy prophets or the sacred writers who have transmitted his word of truth. They, before anyone else, had to draw it from its embodiments; they grasped it through the mediation of events and words of a human order, and they had to commit themselves to a true work of interpretation, translation, understanding and transmission. Jesus himself, though he was the high point of revelation, offers us his own Mystery wrapped in historical, human veils. We might say, with Rahner, that the "*symbolic*" character intrinsically and necessarily characterizes every divine Word which becomes hearable and communicable; only a part of it, one side of it, becomes accessible to us and then only as a "translation" within the limits of our language and our history. Its best part, that of the side turned toward God, still remains beyond our reach, even though in some way that side is not only a "part" or "fragment," but also "a whole within the fragment." At this point "subsistit in" re-emerges: the appeal to prefer "*there is*" to "*is*" applies also to the Word as revealed. Rather than affirm that "it *is* the Truth in its fullness," let us say that "*within it there is* Truth in its fullness" (and take note: not "*a* truth," but *the* Truth"). The Mystery manifested and given to us remains always hidden in the most intimate secret of God; and this is so precisely because of the "mediations" that "translate" it into our language. Those are right who insist on the paradox of a "God who manifests himself even while hiding himself"!

All that now turns out to be a common belief when we deal with the Word of God in relationship to the sacred texts of Christian faith, and even more in relationship to its tradition. The historical-human extent of "symbolic" mediation gradually grows both in breadth and depth as the transmission of the Word passes through the times which stretch from the beginning to the end. But one must insist on the initial times and the first moment in which the Word is entrusted to the mediation of the prophets. It is already there that one must know how to recognize and receive both the values and the limits in the humanization of the Truth and Mystery of God. Unity and eternity enter into the diversity and variety of human cultures and languages. The "subsistit in" involves the unity that one must attain *"in* and *from* diversity,"* and the permanence *"in* and *from* change."* We can never forget that we have one Book in many books, one Gospel in four gospels, one Tradition in various traditions, one Church in different churches, and one Faith in its various professions.

Knowledge as Interpretation

Certainly the Christian faith makes an original contribution to discussion regarding the historicity of the Mystery which reveals itself. The "symbolic" history of God's truth is not suffocated within the unsurmountable limits of the finite—as if diversity were only the equivalent of a dividing wall, and change were something implying separation and breakage. Instead, the final point of arrival can only be a sublimating, divine harmony: that of the Unity and Eternity of God. We ask ourselves: when will this happen? Only after history? Only beyond everything which is reality in time? No! For the Christian faith the value of the human, of creation and history, is so great that it can even contain and ensure a real "anticipatory prolepsis," a seed of that final perfection and fullness which is eschatological. This is the mystery of Christ who "recapitulates everything" even now, since he is the apex of communion between the Creator and the creature, between God and man. As one might say, the "discourse" of the Word of God does not limit itself to providing only accumulations of words and sentences, always various and new as they might be, each one singularly rich with meaning. But even now this "discourse" ensures at least the intuition of synthesis, and reveals the perfection and fullness of its own nucleus and its own end.

All this means that, as far as truth is concerned, the primacy does not belong to mere rational knowledge, made up of abstract concepts and of words which are spoken and listened to; but to the *person who lives the truth* in the historical event, and who reaches the truth and nourishes himself on it by way of experience. Jesus himself shows that he favors the criterion of *"doing the truth in order to come to the light,"* that is, verification or the experienced truth. In the foreground stands the person who seeks the truth, who draws it out from listening and dialogue, and who knows how to clothe it in his own words, translating the words that others transmit to him, above all if they are said in the name of God. To receive from witnesses is in order to become witnesses. To be a gift received is also to be reciprocated. A "We" of community that gathers in fraternal intimacy all the single "I's", all those who are smitten through by a common passion for the Truth, which thus becomes a passion for faith.

But in order to accept the other as incarnate truth, we also need to heed the cultural forms in which he or she incarnates the truth which is sought for, received, assumed and expressed. This entails knowing how to distinguish between the container and the contents of truth (and here we get back to "subsistit in"!). Otherwise, any a priori, indiscriminate acceptance or refusal of the other's offer or proposal of truth, exposes us to the risk, the sometimes dramatic risk, of identifying the means with the end, the thing with the person, the provisional with the eternal. (Let us remember the well-known paradox about "throwing out the clean baby with the dirty bath water"). Thus it is not sufficient to keep alive the different cultures which currently clothe faith, that is, the Christian truth. As far as possible, we should also foster the rebirth of past cultures, call back to life the dead cultures, all of them. For only if there are many interpreters of the Word given by the Mystery does it become easier to approach a little the goal of the full and perfect comprehension of that truth. This is conditioned, of course, on the interpreters' real communion being based on a constant, robust pedagogical promotion of each person as to the meaning of the mystery. This entails bringing them to the historical meaning and critical meaning of the truth, so that every person constantly remains committed to reciprocal brotherly correction, to mutual support, and, above all, to reciprocal stimulus to a saintly competition in striving to outdo one another, as we race toward the total and final Truth. What greatly matters, then, is constructing a dialogical hermeneutical subject which is plenary and universal, so that each and every person may be fit to encounter God the Truth.

The Plenary Hermeneutical Subject[14]

What could be, then, the most adequate hermeneutical subject; or rather, the least inadequate one? And to what degree can it be truly plenary and universal? It will only be the fruit of dialogue, providing that (since we are dealing here with believing Christians whom the Council and world ecumenism address) each single, particular subject vitally takes up the dialogue within unlimited horizons. Such dialogue will not have to respond merely to provisional, reduced functions of a "political" or "pedagogical" order, even if we should also aim at the honest goals of being reliable and deserving the esteem of "others." On the other hand, neither should we use dialogue as an expedient in order to guarantee or predispose merely a sort of common ground on which to carry out useful and adequate discussions. Rather, dialogue must have the value of an internal process inspiring believers, in their faith and theology, to rise toward an ever increasingly penetrating understanding of that Mystery which, however, remains the infinite, transcendent richness of Truth. Let us repeat: the Truth is always found incarnated in forms of human language and translated into finite expressions, and thus must always be sought out and rediscovered beneath and beyond the events and words of humans (here, again, "subsistit in") that offer it. We need the humility to invoke and accept the help of all in such an arduous hermeneutical task—not only the help of those who are "generically" competent in rationality, but even more of "experts and specialists" in experienced religious faith. The individual subject/believer reaches maturity only if he or she grows, be it only step by step—and so by degrees—toward full availability and "inclusive" capacity and toward being inclusive to the greatest degree, so as to enter into that transcendent "We" ("We who believe and think," almost an analogy with the We of the Trinity) that goes beyond but does not jeopardize the identities of the individual "I's." On the contrary, this guarantees for those identities a higher, wider (hypothetically unlimited!) capacity to obtain and grasp the fullness of those aspects of the Truth which God offers.

While walking in this direction, each religious faith should likewise accept a number of concrete tasks: to acquire and refine, by way of constant experimentation, the willingness to listen to the other in order to succeed in understanding him or her with authenticity and depth; to translate the other's gift into our language; to actuate "true reception" by way of mutual exchange; in a word, to verify truth in lived experience, so that it does not remain merely "truth which is only enounced or only written." At that point believers and churches will become credible; at that point their long-declaimed appeal to the character of subjects confessing themselves as being *"creatures of the Word and creatures of the Spirit,"* who are permanently and wholly *"under* the Word and *under* the Spirit," will become truly sincere and meaningful.

Certainly we must not suppose a priori that the affirmations of truth which come to us Christians from non-Christian brothers who believe are entirely free of ambiguity; we cannot expect their beliefs to be entirely in harmony with ours, or homogeneous with ours. But it is always possible and legitimate to recur a priori to the criterion of "analogy:" that is, we can be certain that, at least in part, there exist points in common, especially if we refer to the "subsistit in," upon which we have so repeatedly insisted up to now. That is, we refer to the fact the "the contents" of religious truths are not wholly identifiable with their "expressive containers." Some years ago, for example, the Catholic Church of India (at a meeting where Father Dupuis was present) seriously discussed the problem of the holy scriptures of Hindu tradition. The participants asked: "is it possible to think of 'gifts of revelation and inspiration' outside the Christian Bible?" They reached a positive conclusion, having recourse to the criterion of analogy: "yes, even outside we find holy texts touched by divine inspiration, which are a gift of revelation, *at least to a partial degree and in an analogical sense!* "[15]

Of course, the pathway opening up before us now is nearly all untrodden. We are just at the beginning. We must let time take its course. Without haste, we must experiment with dialogue and accumulate the treasures of experimentation, before expecting to gain valid normative conclusions. Therefore even the ecclesiastical authorities should consent to favoring patience, a climate of peace and freedom for this type of work, which is very difficult but also very urgent; precisely because such work cannot exclude contributions from adequate, sincere, lively debate.

It will thus be useful to reconsider—as Father Dupuis attempts to do—certain theological theses relating to the Trinity and Christ: How should we interpret the action of the Word and the action of the Holy Spirit in the universal history of the cosmos and humanity? How can we creatively define Jesus' participation in humanity, without forgetting the immeasurably long time during which the effective historical reality of the incarnation did not show up? Is it really necessary to annul the creaturely limits of that participation, assigning to it only the divine traits of absoluteness and infinity? And again: couldn't Jesus Christ's most singular uniqueness as mediator and savior be interpreted in such a way as not to exclude other, subordinate mediators? I believe that exploring this territory of "inclusion" with the aim of assigning value to "religious pluralism"—also *ex parte Dei*—cannot help but lead to a better, richer, deeper affirmation of that truth *"which is in"* (which underlies) the ideas of Christian dogmas. In my opinion, the root issue is to know how to and wish to believe authentically. Question: are we really entrusting ourselves to the light of the Holy Spirit which "guides the Church to the fullness of truth?" Or instead, do we claim that our dogmatics has already reached absolute perfection, and that, so to speak, it has now "exhausted," or explored to the point of exhausting, the gift of the Holy Spirit, which is "inexhaustible?"

Be this as it may, the current challenge of religious pluralism prompts us as well into knowing how to return always to the sources. The criterion of faith, which that great pioneer of specifically spiritual ecumenism, Father Couturier, expressed in inaugurating the new form for the " Week of Prayer for Christian Unity," applies also to the vaster horizon of dialogue. He proposed a prayer asking that we may accept the task of working toward Christian unity, but he saw that this goal is still remote in time. Therefore, he said, we should live in the awareness that unity can only be a gift of God, and that it will be given us *"only when and in the manner that he shall choose."* Even more, the definite and final convergence of religions into unity (or rather "toward communion") will long remain a secret hidden in the heart of God; in the future, only his hands can make it come true, "when and in the manner that he shall choose."

Conclusion

I should like to emphasize only a few points. It now seems necessary—urgent, indeed—to work so that the faithful and theologians can become increasingly aware of the *limits* and *incompleteness* which inevitably characterize the subjective moment (of the expression and formulation—today we say—of the incarnation and inculturation) of one's faith. Consequently, each Christian culture has an absolute need for *relations of dialogue and exchange* with the others, with other subjects of faith and culture, in order to walk toward a fullness and perfection—even in history—within one's own knowledge and life of faith; this dialogue must express a constant, authentic "give-and-take." Indeed, it must insist above all on the willingness to receive, so that the willingness to give will appear as credible and acceptable. Give-and-take: also as regards brotherly correction, spurring one on to strengthen the center or nucleus of one's faith and the faith of others. This, however, presupposes a radical *intentio fidei* which truly urges us to look ahead; indeed, to aim toward perfection and eschatological fullness. That is why we are pressed toward "true conversion": that is, *not to a déjà vu kind of ecumenism*, nor one based on mutual pacts ("you come to me! I'll come to you!"); but rather toward the need to *"walk ahead together, all of us."* All toward an Omega point urging us on, all of us!, toward superseding self and the phase now reached. . . .

That is why full openness toward the "other" is required: the other, understood more as a person or a concrete community than "the truths or abstract doctrines of others." Otherwise we run the risk of remaining victims of "ideologies": persons and communities would also be reduced to objects (or numbers!), to simple tools for the task of safeguarding and promoting abstractions. God cannot be lowered to the level of a mere "ideal value" or mere "formal absolute." Therefore, accepting the other should mean paying great attention as well to his culture and historical situation. It should mean considering the complexity of psychological, sociological and cultural factors, as well as their mysterious intertwining on which the concrete process of human life depends.

Of course, a serious question emerges at this point: are we not perhaps running the risk of compromising the truth of belief and the identity of the believer? Concretely speaking: the identity of the Christian and Catholic faith? True, the new situation of dialogue brings great problems; it easily causes difficulties for those who are "weak in faith" (learned persons may be such as well; even theologians and pastors!). Such persons today might be tempted to flee toward comfortable, unilateral choices; they might give in to indifference (which is now highly fashionable!), saying that all religions are the same. Even remaining outside any religion has its fascination, at least as great as that of adhering to a faith: "the only thing that counts is moral honesty" Or those who are weak in faith might shore up their defenses against other proposals of faith; they might take the road of integralism and sectarian fundamentalism. Today it seems almost too hard to bear the burden of knowing how to live fully and deeply a faith that we hold to be true, while at the same time keeping that faith open to dialogue and to encounter and exchange with other faiths! It is almost as though we were being asked to remain healthy and unharmed—indeed, to continue walking and running—while we actually are moving along a razor's edge. A miracle? Heroism? Perhaps it is; perhaps this is what we are asked to do in order to live our faith from now on. But doesn't Christianity's originality and its identity truly consist in this paradoxical radicality? Here is the apex of grace and commitment. To live "divinely" is the specific gift from that Jesus who is, for us, the supreme icon of God, and at the same time, a sublime model for ourselves. He intends to become immanent *in* us even in order to live "humanly" *with* us and *like* us.

References

[1] In several studies, as well as in those which support and reflect on J. Dupuis's writing concerning the pluralism of religions, I have already underlined the "subsistit in." Compare my editorial *'Dominus Iesus' scuote l'ecumenismo*, in *Studi Ecumenici* 19 (2001), 7-20; and my earlier comment on *Ut unum sint: Ecumenismo del terzo millennio: Considerazioni sull'enciclica 'Ut unum sint,'*, in *Studia patavina* 3 (1995), 3-26. See the insistence on this point in the *Commento alla Dichiarazione*, published by the "Congregation for the Doctrine of the Faith," *Documenti e Studi*, 18 (Vatican City: Libreria Editrice Vaticana, 2002). My present chapter aims at developing and deepening the points made in my article mentioned above—this time in honor of my dear friend Father Dupuis.

[2] See Y. Congar's thesis in *Regno-Documenti* 15 (1977) 377-96, an issue which reports the papers delivered at Lausanne in May 1977, as the official commemoration of the 50th

anniversary of "Faith and Order" (W. A. Visser 't Hooft, Y. Congar, N. Nissiotis, J. Moltmann); Congar's contribution (pp. 383-88) is entitled: *Cinquant'anni di ricerca dell'unità*. For O. Cullmann's thesis, see comment on the Decree on Ecumenism, edited by A. M. Javierre, *Promozione Conciliare del dialogo ecumenico* (Turin: Elle Di Ci, 1965), 226-27; Javierre draws on the ecumenical comment on *Unitatis Redintegratio*, reported in *The Ecumenical Review* 17 (1965), 226-27.

[3]See F. A. Sullivan, "In what sense does the Church of Christ 'subsist' in the Roman Catholic Church?" in R. Latourelle (ed.), *Vaticano II. Bilancio e prospettive venticinque anni dopo (1962-1987)*, vol. 2, (Assisi: Cittadella, 1982), 811-24.

[4]For the opposition of the Congregation for the Doctrine of Faith (Cardinal Ratzinger) against L. Boff's theses, see my article: *Ratzinger: la memoria non vada perduta! Boff: Ma per la profezia!*, in L. Sartori, *Per una teologia in Italia. Scritti scelti*, vol. II, (Padova: Messaggero, 1997), 285-94.

[5]See my "Lumen Gentium," *Traccia di studio* (Padova: Messaggero, 1994), 43-44.

[6] See Declaration *Dominus Iesus*, 16 with the note 56. In the commentary (already mentioned in note 1) edited by the Roman Congregation, D. Valentini tries to open up a less rigid exegesis.

[7] See *Enchiridion Vaticanum,* 10th edition (Bologna: EDB, 1976), 55.

[8] See "Atti del Colloquio internazionale di Salamanca 1996," *Recezione e comunione tra le chiese* (Bologna: EDB, 1998), and especially with reference to Congar, G. Routhier, *La recezione nell'attuale dibattito teologico* (pp. 27-63); and J. A. Komonchak, *L'epistemologia della recezione: a Y. Congar con gratitudine* (pp. 205-28).

[9] See *The Ecumenical Review* 23 (1971), 51-69.

[10]See *The Ecumenical Review* 32 (1980), 309-17, at 316.

[11]See in particular the document "L'unità davanti a noi" (1984), *Enchiridion*, 1548-1709.

[12]Freiburg: Herder, 1983. I presented a critical review of this work in my book, *L'unità della chiesa. Un dibattito e un progetto* (Brescia: Queriniana, 1989), 121-41.

[13]For texts celebrating March 12, see *Regno-Documenti* 7 (2000), 223 ff.: especially the first confession of sins committed in the service of truth (Cardinal Ratzinger and Pope John Paul II), p. 229.

[14]I believe that the hermeneutical dimension of theology and of faith itself constitutes a problem which demands today attention from Catholic thinkers. I confess that I often dedicate many lectures and specific courses to this theme in my personal commitment as a teacher of theology. The bibliography in this field is immense.

[15]See D. S. Amalorpavadass (ed.), *Revelation and Inspiration. Research Seminar on Non-Biblical Scriptures* (Bangalore: National Biblical, Catechetical, and Liturgical Centre, 1974). I specifically examined this book in *Credere-oggi* 6 (1989), 87-96.

9

Clement of Alexandria on Justification through Philosophy

Francis A. Sullivan, S.J.

A question that was put to the early Christians by their contemporaries to whom they proclaimed Christ as the savior of humanity was: "If Christ is the savior of all, how is it that he came only recently into the world? What about the salvation of all those generations of people who lived and died before he came?"

An early Christian writer who took this question seriously, and offered a unique answer to it, is Clement, the predecessor of Origen in the development of Christian theology at Alexandria. Clement shared with Justin Martyr and Irenaeus their conviction about the universal presence of the divine Logos, who before the coming of Christ had enlightened all people, giving them the possibility of knowing God and obeying his law written in their hearts. What was unique in the answer that Clement of Alexandria gave to the question was his assertion that as God had made a covenant with the Hebrews and given them the Law, so he had made a covenant with the Greeks and had given them philosophy as a means for their justification.

As Jacques Dupuis has observed, Clement's answer raises a number of questions. For instance, he has asked: "What does Clement intend by 'philosophy' when he states that God has made with philosophy a covenant destined to lead the Greeks toward Christ?"[1] Dupuis has also raised "the decisive question of the theological significance of the pre- and pro-Christian divine pedagogy operative through the Logos in terms of the bestowal upon persons of divine life and grace, whether before the Christ-event or after it, outside the boundaries of the Christian fold."[2] This "decisive question," when applied to Clement of Alexandria's theory, involves the further question whether he understood the justification which could be achieved through philosophy as the "bestowal of divine life and grace." Surely that is what "justification" means in classical Christian theology? However, it is another question whether this is what Clement meant when he spoke of the Greeks being justified by philosophy.

My intention in this essay is to take up some of the questions that are raised by

Clement of Alexandria's theory about the role that philosophy played in the divine plan of salvation for Gentiles before the coming of Christ. As far as possible, I intend to let Clement speak for himself, by quoting passages of his writings in which he has treated these questions. The two works that I shall cite are entitled *Protrepticus* ("Exhortation") and *Stromata* ("Miscellanies"). The *Protrepticus* is an apologetic treatise, consisting of a lengthy and severe critique of Greek religion, and an eloquent exhortation to his pagan contemporaries to abandon such folly and accept the true worship of God and the salvation offered by the Christian Gospel. The name *Stromata*, which literally means a kind of patch-work quilt, aptly describes this work in which Clement does not follow an orderly progression of themes, but moves freely from one topic to another. Because of the peculiar nature of the *Stromata*, which is his major work, I think it will be a useful exercise to gather together in some orderly fashion what Clement has said concerning God's provision for the salvation of those who had lived before the coming of Christ.

Clement had no doubt about the universality of God's salvific will. The following statement is one among many that sound this theme:

> For God is not only Lord of the Jews, but of all men, and more nearly the Father of those who know him. . . . So I think it is demonstrated that God being good and the Lord powerful, He saves with a righteousness and equality which extend to all that turn to Him, whether here or elsewhere.[3]

It was clear to Clement that since God is Lord not only of the Jews but of all men, one must ask what means of salvation he has given to the Gentiles. His answer was: as God gave to the Jews the Law and prophets, to the Greeks he gave philosophy.

Philosophy, the Gift of God to the Greeks, to Prepare Them to Receive the Gospel

Since this is the unique answer of Clement of Alexandria to the question about the way that God had provided for the salvation of the Gentiles who had lived before Christ, it seems worthwhile to cite a number of passages in which he has put forth and explained his view. Perhaps the briefest expression of his theory is the following: "But as the proclamation [of the Gospel] has come now at the fit time, so also at the fit time were the Law and the Prophets given to the Barbarians, and Philosophy to the Greeks, to fit their ears for the Gospel."[4] Clement's use of the term "Barbarians" reflects the way in which Greek speakers of his day referred to those who spoke other languages; here it obviously refers to the Hebrews.

In the following passage, Clement at first distinguishes between the two Testaments as primary gifts of God and philosophy as a secondary gift, but then suggests that philosophy too was a primary gift to the Greeks:

For God is the cause of all good things; but of some primarily, as of the Old and New Testament; and of others, by consequence, as philosophy. Perchance, too, philosophy was given to the Greeks directly and primarily, till the Lord should call the Greeks. For this was a schoolmaster to bring the Hellenic mind, as the Law, the Hebrews, to Christ. Philosophy, therefore, was a preparation, paving the way for him who is perfected in Christ.[5]

Clement insists that philosophy was a gift of Divine Providence to the Greeks:

Further, if the practice of philosophy does not belong to the wicked, but was accorded to the best of the Greeks, it is clear also from what source it was bestowed—manifestly from Providence, which assigns to each what is befitting in accordance with his deserts. Rightly, then, to the Jews belonged the Law, and to the Greeks Philosophy, until the Advent; and after that came the universal calling to be a peculiar people of righteousness, through the teaching which flows from faith, brought together by one Lord, the only God of both Greeks and Barbarians, or rather of the whole race of men.[6]

Hence Clement argues: "So there is no absurdity in philosophy having been given by Divine Providence as a preparatory discipline for the perfection which is by Christ. . . ."[7]

A further development of Clement's thought about the providential role of philosophy was to describe it as a "covenant" which God had given to the Greeks.

And in general terms, we shall not err in alleging that all things necessary and profitable for life came to us from God, and that philosophy more especially was given to the Greeks, as a covenant peculiar to them—being, as it is, a stepping-stone to the philosophy which is according to Christ. . . .[8]

In the following passage, we see that Clement not only saw philosophy as one of the "different covenants of the one Lord," but also saw some of the philosophers as "prophets" whom God had raised up for the Greeks.

And further, that the same God that furnished both the Covenants was the giver of Greek philosophy to the Greeks, by which the Almighty is glorified among the Greeks, is clear from this. Accordingly, then, from the Hellenic training, and also from that of the Law, are gathered into the one race of the saved people those who accept faith: not that the three peoples are separated by time, so that one might suppose three natures, but trained by different covenants of the one Lord, by the word of the one Lord. For that, as God wished to save the Jews by giving them prophets, so also by raising up prophets of their own in their own tongue, as they were able to receive God's beneficence, He distinguished the most excellent of the Greeks from the common herd.[9]

The extraordinary esteem that Clement of Alexandria had for philosophy, reckoning it as a gift of God to the Greeks comparable to the gifts of the covenant, the law and prophets to the Hebrews, was based on his judgment as to the benefits that philosophy had conferred on the Greeks. The benefit that he most stressed was that it had taught the Greeks the practice of virtue and piety.

Only a Philosophy That Taught Virtue and Piety Was Worthy of the Name

In the first Book of his *Stromata*, Clement gave the following explanation of what he meant by philosophy:

> And philosophy—I do not mean the Stoic, or the Platonic, or the Epicurean, or the Aristotelian, but whatever has been well said by each of those sects, which teach righteousness along with a science pervaded by piety,—this eclectic whole I call philosophy.[10]

In the following, more lengthy description of philosophy, it becomes clear that for Clement, since philosophers are those who love wisdom, there are "philosophers among us," just as there are "among the Greeks." It was obvious to him that if philosophy is what teaches righteousness and piety, what Christians had been taught by the Lord and the prophets eminently deserved that name.

> As we have long ago pointed out, what we propose as our subject is not the discipline which obtains in each sect, but that which is really philosophy, strictly systematic wisdom, which furnishes acquaintance with the things which pertain to life. And we define wisdom to be certain knowledge, being a sure and irrefragable apprehension of things divine and human, comprehending the present, past and future, which the Lord hath taught us, both by His advent and by the prophets. . . . This Wisdom, then—rectitude of soul and of reason, and purity of life—is the object of the desire of philosophy, which is kindly and lovingly disposed toward wisdom, and does everything to attain it. Now those are called philosophers, among us, who love Wisdom, the Creator and Teacher of all things, that is, the knowledge of the Son of God; and among the Greeks, who undertake arguments on virtue. Philosophy, then, consists of such dogmas found in each sect (I mean those of philosophy) as cannot be impugned, with a corresponding life, collected into one selection; and these, stolen from the Barbarian God-given grace, have been adorned with Greek speech.[11]

Clement's conviction about the divine origin of all teaching that led to a life of virtue is brought out by his description of the Lord as the source "not only of the different covenants, but also of the modes of teaching, both those among the Greeks and those among the Barbarians, conducing to righteousness."[12] This last phrase brings out Clement's conviction that genuine philosophy did not consist merely of theory about virtue; it would lead people to righteousness. One way he believed it would do this was by helping them to abstain from evil. As he put it: "Philosophy is from God, He having willed it to be such as it is, for the sake of those who not otherwise than by its means would abstain from evil."[13] On a more positive note, he was convinced that philosophy would make people virtuous.

How absurd, then, is it, to those who attribute disorder and wickedness to the devil, to make him the bestower of philosophy, a virtuous thing! . . . Philosophy is not, then, the product of vice, since it makes men virtuous. It follows, then, that it is the work of God, whose work it is solely to do good.[14]

As we have seen just above, Clement expressed his positive view about the providential role of philosophy by describing it as a "mode of teaching which leads to righteousness." The Greek word which the ANF version has translated "righteousness," is *dikaiosune*, which is derived from the Greek verb *dikaioun*, "to justify,"and can also be translated as "justification." We shall now see some passages in which Clement spoke of philosophy as the source of justification for the Greeks.

"Philosophy Has Justified the Greeks"

We have seen above that Clement gave the name "philosophy" only to "what has been well said by each of those sects which teach righteousness along with a science pervaded by piety."[15] Here, as elsewhere in the ANF translation, the Greek word rendered as "righteousness" is *dikaiosune*. It is not surprising, then, that Clement could say: "For those who have been justified by philosophy (*upo philosophias dedikaiomenois*), the knowledge which leads to piety is laid up as a help."[16] He goes on to say: "Accordingly, before the advent of the Lord, philosophy was necessary to the Greeks for righteousness" (= justification: *pros dikaiosunen*).[17] The following passage, however, makes it clear that the justification to which philosophy could lead was not complete.

Although at one time philosophy justified the Greeks, not conducting them to that entire righteousness (*eis ten katholou de dikaiosunen*) to which it is ascertained to cooperate, as the first and second flight of steps help you in your ascent to the upper room, and the grammarian helps the philosopher.[18]

Here we arrive at the question that Jacques Dupuis raised, and to which commentators on Clement of Alexandria have given different answers: How did Clement understand the justification to which he believed philosophy had led the Greeks? In what sense was it "incomplete"? Did those justified by philosophy share in faith, grace, divine life, but in a way that was deficient in comparison with those justified by Christian faith? I suggest that the first point to note in approaching an answer to these questions is that for Clement salvation could be obtained only through faith in Christ.

Salvation Only through Faith in Christ

The following passages make it clear that for Clement of Alexandria, no one, whether Jew or Greek, could be saved without faith in Christ.

> Men must then be saved by learning the truth through Christ, even if they attain philosophy. For now that is clearly shown "which was not made known to other ages, which is now revealed to the sons of men."[19]
>
> Accordingly, then, from the Hellenic training, and also from that of the Law, are gathered into the one race of the saved people those who accept faith. . . .[20]
>
> Rightly then, to the Jews belonged the Law, and to the Greeks Philosophy, until the Advent; and after that came the universal calling to be a peculiar people of righteousness, through the teaching which flows from faith, brought together by the one Lord, the only God of both Greeks and Barbarians, or rather of the whole race of men.[21]
>
> For, having furnished the one with the commandments, and the other with philosophy, He shut up unbelief to the Advent. Whence every one who believes not is without excuse. For by a different process of advancement, whether Greek or Barbarian, He leads to the perfection which is by faith.[22]

The problem these texts raise, however, is that they suggest that in Clement's view, salvation through faith was possible only since the coming of the Lord and the subsequent preaching of the Gospel. This leaves unsolved the question about the nature of the justification that could be achieved with the help of philosophy before the Advent. I suggest that the answer to this question can be found in Clement's interpretation of the early Christian tradition about the preaching of the Gospel to the dead.

Before considering his interpretation, it would be worthwhile to recall the sources on which he based it. The canonical source is the 1 Peter 3:18-20, and 4:6. The non-canonical source on which Clement also relied is the second-century Christian writing known as *The Shepherd of Hermas*. Hermas was a lay member of the Roman Church who claimed to have had visions and received instructions from heavenly messengers, and wrote this work to share what he had learned with his fellow Christians. The book consists of five visions, twelve mandates and ten parables. Its primary message is a call to repentance on the part of Christians who have not lived up to their calling. Clement of Alexandria and Origen both expressed high regard for this work, even considering it inspired, though not part of the canonical Scriptures. In the ninth parable, Hermas speaks of people who had died, having in their lifetime practiced such virtues as self-control, patience, sincerity, innocence, purity and love. However, not having been sealed with the name of the Son of God, they could not enter the kingdom of God. For this reason, the Shepherd explained to Hermas:

> When the apostles and teachers who preached the name of the Son of God fell asleep in the power and faith of the Son of God, they preached also to those who had previously fallen asleep, and they themselves gave to them the seal of the preaching. Therefore they went down with them into the water and came up again. But these went down alive and came up alive, whereas those who had previously fallen asleep went down dead and came up alive. So they were made alive through them, and came to full knowledge of the name of the Son of God. This is why they also came up with them and were fitted together with them into the structure of the tower, and were joined together without being hewn, for they fell asleep in righteousness and in great purity, only they did not have this seal.[23]

Clement's Interpretation of the Tradition about the Preaching to the Dead

The passage in which Clement expressed his thought on this matter is rather lengthy, but I think it worthwhile to give the main points of it in his own words.

> But as the proclamation [of the Gospel] has come now at the fit time, so also at the fit time were the Law and the Prophets given to the Barbarians, and philosophy to the Greeks, to fit their ears for the Gospel. . . . For to those who were righteous (*dikaios*) according to the Law, faith was wanting. Wherefore also the Lord, in healing them, said, "Thy faith hath saved thee." But to those that were righteous (*dikaios*) according to philosophy, not only faith in the Lord, but also the abandonment of idolatry, were necessary. Straightway, on the revelation of the truth, they also repented of their previous conduct. For this reason the Lord preached the Gospel to those in Hades. . . . For who in his senses can suppose souls of the righteous (*dikaion*) and those of sinners (*amartolon*) in the same condemnation, charging Providence with injustice? . . . And it has been shown also . . . that the apostles, following the Lord, preached the Gospel to those in Hades. For it was requisite, in my opinion, that as here, so also there, the best of the disciples should be imitators of the Master; so that He should bring to repentance those belonging to the Hebrews, and they the Gentiles; that is, those who had lived in righteousness (*dikaiosune*) according to the Law and Philosophy, who had ended their life not perfectly, but sinfully (*amartetikos*). For it was suitable to the divine economy, that those possessed of greater worth in righteousness, and whose life had been preeminent, on repenting of their transgressions, though making their confession in another place, should be saved, since they too belong to almighty God, each according to his own knowledge. And as I think, the Saviour also exerts His might because it is His

work to save; which accordingly He also did by drawing to salvation those who became willing, by the preaching [of the Gospel] to believe in Him, wherever they were. If, then, the Lord descended to Hades for no other end but to preach the Gospel, as He did descend, it was either to preach the Gospel to all or to the Hebrews only. If to all, then all who believe shall be saved, although they may be of the Gentiles, on making their profession there. . . . If, however, Christ preached only to the Jews, who lacked the knowledge and faith of the Saviour, it is plain that, since God is no respecter of persons, the apostles also, as here, so there, preached the Gospel to those of the heathen who were ready for conversion. And it is well said by the Shepherd . . . "Those who had fallen asleep descended dead, but ascended alive." . . . One righteous man *(dikaios)*, then, differs not, as righteous, from another righteous man, whether he be of the Law or a Greek. For God is not only Lord of the Jews, but of all men, and more nearly the Father of those who know Him. . . . What then? Did not the same dispensation obtain in Hades, so that even there, all the souls, on hearing the proclamation, might either exhibit repentance, or confess that their punishment was just, because they believed not? And it were the exercise of no ordinary arbitrariness, for those who had departed before the advent of the Lord, (not having the Gospel preached to them, and having afforded no ground from themselves, in consequence of believing or not) to obtain either salvation or punishment. For it is not right that these should be condemned without trial, and those alone who lived after the advent should have the advantage of the divine righteousness. . . . If, then, He preached the Gospel to those in the flesh that they might not be condemned unjustly, how is it conceivable that He did not for the same cause preach the Gospel to those who had departed this life before his advent?[24]

From the foregoing passage I would draw the following conclusions regarding Clement's understanding of the sense in which philosophy had "justified" the Greeks. First, the justification of Hebrews through the Law, and of Greeks through philosophy, clearly was not enough for their salvation. The Jews who were justified still needed faith in Christ; the Greeks needed both faith and the abandonment of idolatry. Second, their justification prepared them to hear the Gospel, and assured them of an opportunity to hear it, which "sinners" did not deserve and did not receive. (It would seem obvious that by "sinners" here Clement meant those whose lives had been altogether lacking in virtue and piety.) Third, the salvation of the just still depended on their repentance for such sinfulness as Clement evidently considered compatible with righteousness, and on their free response of faith to the Gospel. In the case of those who had been "righteous according to philosophy," it also depended on their abandonment of idolatry, which would seem to mean that Clement saw idolatry as due to ignorance and compatible with righteousness in the case of Greeks who had not been enlightened by the Gospel.

The conclusion I would draw from this, with regard to the meaning of the justification that Clement believed could be attained through philosophy, is that he thought of it simply as a way of life characterized by virtue and piety. As we have seen, this is what he believed would be taught by any philosophy worthy of the name. On the other hand, it is clear that while a life of virtue had prepared both Jews and Greeks to hear the Gospel, and in a sense had given them the right to hear it, their salvation still depended on their free response to it. Clement clearly shared what was to be the common Christian belief through the middle ages, that after Christ had come and the Gospel had been preached, there was no salvation without explicit faith in Christ. In fact, he believed that this was true also for those who had lived before the coming of Christ, who, if they had lived virtuously, would be given the opportunity to believe in Christ after death, and thus be saved.

Jacques Dupuis has quoted C. Saldanha, who has explained the justification which Clement said could be attained through philosophy as a participation in faith, grace and salvation, occupying a kind of middle ground between non-justification and Christian justification.[25] I agree with Dupuis when he says: "Keeping to the evaluation of the early Fathers, it must be said that the *qualitative* difference between pre-Christian justification and Christian grace, as well as the *intermediate* state of pre-Christian justification without the remission of sin, besides lacking in precision, fails to convince."[26] I think that when Clement of Alexandria spoke of justification through philosophy, he was using the term with a meaning that was different not merely in degree, but in kind, from the meaning it has in common Christian usage. According to the "Joint Declaration on the Doctrine of Justification" recently accepted by the Lutheran World Federation and the Roman Catholic Church, justification means that "by grace alone, in faith in Christ's saving work, and not because of any merit on our part, we are accepted by God and receive the Holy Spirit, who renews our hearts while equipping and calling us to good works." Clement of Alexandria no doubt believed in such justification, but he also believed it could be had only through explicit faith in Christ. He saw the Law and philosophy as gifts of God to the Hebrews and the Greeks, which had helped them to live lives of virtue and piety. He even described people who had lived that way as "justified." But it is obvious that he did not think that by grace they had already been accepted by God and had received the Holy Spirit. For that they would have to hear the message of the Gospel and freely respond to it. It was for this reason that the Gospel had to be preached to the "justified" who had died before the coming of Christ.

Subsequent Christian theology has not followed Clement of Alexandria in his belief that the salvation of the just who had died before Christ came would depend on their freely responding to the Gospel when it was preached to them in Hades. The traditional interpretation of 1 Pet 3:19 and 4:6 is that Christ preached to the just who had died before he came, simply to announce the fulfillment of the promise of salvation to those who were already assured of it. The common tradition has rejected the idea that a person's salvation could depend on a free choice that he or she would make in the after-life. However, the fact that Clement of

Alexandria's idea about the significance of the preaching of the Gospel in Hades has not survived, by no means precludes a positive answer to the final question of this essay.

Does Clement of Alexandria Say Anything That Is Pertinent to the Modern Discussion of the Salvific Function of Non-Christian Religions?

As I have mentioned above, one of Clement's works, the *Protrepticus* ("Exhortation") consists in large part of a severe critique of Greek religion. At first sight, this fact would seem to exclude the possibility that he said anything that would favor a positive view of the salvific role of non-Christian religions. However, I think that further light on this question may be gained by examining the grounds on which he based his critique of the religion which he was exhorting his pagan contemporaries to abandon.

Chapter Two of the *Protrepticus* offers a caustic description of the Greek mystery religions, which Clement described as being celebrated in "shrines of impiety"and "caverns full of monstrosity."[27] After naming those who were said to have been the founders of the various mysteries, Clement concludes: "These I would instance as the prime authors of evil, the parents of impious fables and of deadly superstition, who sowed in human life that seed of evil and ruin—the mysteries.[28] Further on he excoriates those who, "not understanding that it is God who does us good, have invented saviours in the persons of the Dioscuri, and Hercules the averter of evil, and Asclepius the healer." He adds:

> These are the slippery and hurtful deviations from the truth which draw man down from heaven, and cast him into the abyss. I wish to show thoroughly what these gods of yours are like, that now at length you may abandon your delusion, and speed your flight back to heaven. . . . The most of what is told of your gods is fabled and invented; and those things which are supposed to have taken place, are recorded of vile men who lived licentious lives.[29]

In the following chapter, Clement further develops his argument that the gods are more wicked than the worst of men, and are really demons.

> Well now, let us say in addition, what inhuman demons, and hostile to the human race, your gods were, not only delighting in the insanity of men, but gloating over human slaughter,—now in the armed contests for superiority in the stadia, and now in numberless contests for renown in wars providing for themselves the means of pleasure, that they might be able abundantly to satiate themselves with the murder of human beings. And now, like plagues invading cities and nations, they demanded cruel oblations. . . . I can readily demonstrate that man is better than these gods of yours, who are but demons. . . .[30]

Clement, who was well acquainted with Greek literature, also invoked the critical portrayal of the gods by the Greek dramatists: "Let the strictures on your gods, which the poets, impelled by the force of truth, introduce into their comedies, shame you into salvation."[31]

What I would point out, in Clement's sharp attack on Greek religion, is that his condemnation of it was based largely on his conviction that it was bound to have a deleterious effect on the morals of those who participated in it. He saw the mystery religions as "sowing in human life the seeds of evil and ruin." The gods the Greeks worshiped were not models of virtue, but rather of licentiousness and inhuman cruelty. Clement was convinced that the practice of such religion would have an effect on its devotees that would be the very opposite of the effect that the practice of philosophy would have. Rather than teaching them virtue and piety, as a genuine philosophy would do, the practice of the mystery religions and the worship of the gods could only lead people into vice and impiety.

However, in contrast to Clement's scorn for the pagan religions of his day, is his esteem for what he called the "philosophy" that "flourished in antiquity among the barbarians." Here is his account of it.

> Thus philosophy, a thing of the highest utility, flourished in antiquity among the barbarians, shedding its light over the nations. And afterwards it came to Greece. First in its ranks were the prophets of the Egyptians; and the Chaldeans among the Assyrians; and the Druids among the Gauls; and the Samanaeans among the Bactrians; and the philosophers of the Celts; and the Magi of the Persians, who foretold the Saviour's birth, and came into the land of Judaea guided by a star. The Indian gymnosophists are also in the number, and other barbarian philosophers. And of these there are two classes, some of them called Sarmanae, and others Brahmins.... Some, too, of the Indians obey the precepts of Buddha; whom, on account of his extraordinary sanctity, they have raised to divine honours.... Of all these, by far the oldest is the Jewish race; and that their philosophy committed to writing has the precedence of philosophy among the Greeks, the Pythagorean Philo shows at large.[32]

When Clement spoke of "their philosophy committed to writing" he was obviously referring to the Jewish religion as contained the Bible. However, rather than calling it their religion, Clement called it their "philosophy." Similarly, Clement speaks of "philosophers of the Celts," and "other barbarian philosophers," referring to those whom we would think of as the founders of various religions. The fact that he spoke of them as "philosophers," and their religions as "philosophy," shows that in his judgment their teaching belonged to what he called "the eclectic whole that teaches righteousness along with a science pervaded by piety." That this was his judgment is shown by his description of the "philosophy that flourished in antiquity among the barbarians" as "a thing of the highest utility," and as "shedding its light over the nations."

No doubt one may wonder how much Clement really knew about the doctrines taught by the "prophets" and "philosophers" of the Egyptians, Chaldeans, Druids, Indian "gymnosophists," and Brahmins. His high regard for them may simply reflect his respect for what he considered the "wisdom of antiquity," such as was to be found above all in the Hebrew Scriptures. In any case, he was convinced that Greek philosophy owed a great deal to the more ancient philosophy of the barbarians. What is more important is that he did not hesitate to attribute the portion of truth taught by each philosophy, whether Greek or barbarian, to enlightenment by the Divine Word, the source of all truth.

> Since, therefore, truth is one (for falsehood has ten thousand by-paths); just as the Bacchantes tore asunder the limbs of Pentheus, so the sects both of barbarian and Hellenic philosophy have done with truth, and each vaunts as the whole truth the portion which has fallen to its lot. But all, in my opinion, are illuminated by the dawn of Light. Let all, therefore, both Greeks and Barbarians, who have aspired after the truth—both those who possess not a little, and those who have any portion—produce whatever they have of the word of truth. . . . So then, the barbarian and Hellenic philosophy has torn off a fragment of eternal truth not from the mythology of Dionysius, but from the theology of the ever-living Word. And He who brings again together the separate fragments, and makes them one, will without peril, be assured, contemplate the perfect Word, the Truth.[33]

Conclusion

We have asked whether Clement of Alexandria says anything that is pertinent to the modern discussion of the salvific function of non-Christian religions. It seems to me that he does, by his readiness to recognize the presence of "fragments of the truth" in all those ancient "philosophies," and to attribute their elements of truth to the Divine Word, the source of all truth. It is true that he did not speak of those "barbarian philosophies" as "religions," as we would do. However, he called them "philosophies" precisely because he saw them as part of that "eclectic whole" that taught people to abstain from evil and to practice virtue and piety. And more importantly, he recognized every such "philosophy," whether Greek or barbarian, as a work of Divine Providence, serving as a "stepping-stone to the philosophy which is according to Christ."

References

[1]*Toward a Christian Theology of Religious Pluralism* (Maryknoll, N.Y.: Orbis, 1997), 70-71.

[2]Ibid., p. 74.

[3]*Stromata* 6:6; translation in *The Ante-Nicene Fathers*, Alexander Roberts and James Donaldson (eds.), vol. 2 (Grand Rapids: Eerdmans, 1979), 491A. Hereafter: ANF.

[4]*Stromata* 6:6, ANF 2, 490A.

[5]*Stromata* 1:5, ANF 2, 305B.

[6]*Stromata* 5:17, ANF 2, 517B-518A.

[7]*Stromata* 6:17, ANF 2, 516A.

[8]*Stromata* 6:8, ANF 2, 495B.

[9]*Stromata* 6:5, ANF 2, 489B-490A.

[10]*Stromata* 1:7, ANF 2, 308A.

[11]*Stromata* 6:7, ANF 2, 493A.

[12]*Stromata* 6:8, ANF 2, 495A.

[13]*Stromata* 6:17, ANF 2, 517A.

[14]*Stromata* 6:17, ANF 2, 517B.

[15]See above, n. 9.

[16]*Stromata* 1:4, ANF 2, 305B.

[17]*Stromata* 1:5, ANF 2, 305B.

[18]*Stromata* 1:20, ANF 2, 323B.

[19]*Stromata* 5:14, ANF 2, 465A.

[20]*Stromata* 6:5, ANF 2, 489B-490A.

[21]*Stromata* 6:17, ANF 2, 517B-518A.

[22]*Stromata* 7:2, ANF 2, 526A.

[23]*The Shepherd of Hermas* Parable 9:16; trans. by J. B. Lightfoot *et al.*, *The Apostolic Fathers* (Grand Rapids: Baker Book House, 1992), 499.

[24]*Stromata* 6:6, ANF 2, 490A-492A.

[25]Jacques Dupuis (*Toward a Christian Theology*, p. 75) quotes a statement to this effect by C. Saldanha, *Divine Pedagogy: A Patristic View of Non-Christian Religions* (Rome: Libreria Ateneo Salesiano, 1984), 157.

[26]*Toward a Christian Theology*, p. 76.

[27]*Protrepticus* 2, ANF 2, 174B.

[28]*Protr.* 2, ANF 2, 175B

[29]*Protr.* 2, ANF 2, 178B.

[30]*Protr.* 3, ANF 2, 183A-B.

[31]*Protr.* 6, ANF 2, 193A.

[32]*Stromata* 1:15, ANF 2, 316B.

[33]*Stromata* 1:13, ANF 2, 313A-B.

Part III

SPIRITUAL AND PASTORAL DIMENSIONS

10

Authentic Spiritual Experience

A Vehicle of God's Spirit for Interreligious Dialogue

Herbert Alphonso, S.J.

Introduction

It was in early 1995 that the XXXIV General Congregation (GC 34) of the Society of Jesus issued, while offering a renewed orientation to the apostolic mission of Jesuits in the Church and the world of today, a significant series of Decrees: *Servants of Christ's Mission* (Decree 2), *Our Mission and Justice* (Decree 3), *Our Mission and Culture* (Decree 4), and *Our Mission and Interreligious Dialogue* (Decree 5). These Decrees, together with all the other work of GC 34,[1] were promulgated by Fr. General Peter-Hans Kolvenbach, S.J., on September 27 1995, and took effect on that same day.

Barely two years later, Fr. Jacques Dupuis's pioneering and carefully researched work, *Toward a Christian Theology of Religious Pluralism*, underscored from the vantage point of highly qualified theological investigation, the emphatically pointed relevance of GC 34's Decree 5 on *Our Mission and Interreligious Dialogue*. Not surprisingly this book of Fr. Dupuis, which dares to explore in original fashion some fundamental, yet delicate, theological issues involved in the whole area of religious pluralism and interreligious dialogue, has raised serious, but nonetheless significantly pertinent, questions for the ongoing progress of theological science. The Congregation for the Doctrine of the Faith issued a "Notification" on this very book dated January 24, 2001. Very Rev. Fr. Peter-Hans Kolvenbach, S.J., Superior General of the Society of Jesus, issued a statement straight after the "Notification" was made public, not only acknowledging the "seriousness," "richness," and "originality" of Fr. Dupuis's research, but positively encouraging the author to pursue his pioneering investigation in the field he had opened up to the increasingly pastoral challenges facing "interreligious dialogue" in the Church's evangelizing mission for the Third Millennium.

This chapter forms part of a volume honoring a distinguished Catholic whom I have had the joy of knowing, admiring and being a friend of, right from our days together at St. Mary's Theological College, Kurseong, in the late 1960s. I am delighted, then, to express my great appreciation for his unstinted and generous service to the Church in my own beloved country, India, for over 30 years—not only in the field of theology, but also in that of the renewed postconciliar liturgy, and even pastorally through his publications, not the least of which have been his editing of, and contributing to, *The Clergy Monthly* and later *The Vidyajyoti Journal*, which reached out extensively to so many priests and religious, and later even to the committed laity, all over the Indian subcontinent.

My contribution here reflects on some specifically *spiritual* dimensions which, although often neglected, are at the very heart of a genuine interreligious dialogue. As such, therefore, it focuses on certain nuances from the distinctly characteristic perspective of Spiritual Theology.

Spiritual Theology: The Crucial Role of Spiritual Experience

It is only over the last six to seven decades that what is now commonly called *Spirituality* as a theological discipline, or more technically *Spiritual Theology*, has come into its characteristically own.

While it is true that Spiritual Theology has regularly stressed the existential reality of Christian life, not a few spiritual theologians, even among the pioneers of this specific theological discipline, in making sure that they were solidly grounded in dogmatic theology, were content to express their teaching of *Spiritual Theology* very largely, if not exclusively, as practical applications of dogmatic theology to the concrete situations of daily Christian life. The fairly recent "anthropological turning-point" given to the whole range of theological disciplines clearly showed up the inadequacy of such a manner of individuating and distinguishing the specific nature of Spiritual Theology. It came to be recognized that such an approach left Spiritual Theology totally bereft of its own specific object or "focus" of study, research, and development; it was an edifice being built up as it were on "alien soil," *not* on its own proper fundamental principles.

To focus on only a couple of serious drawbacks entailed in such an approach as detailed above, no account is taken, and much less scientifically rendered, of the great variety of spiritualities that have flourished down the ages even in the Christian tradition, to limit ourselves just to the history of Christian spirituality. Besides, any serious student of *such* a formulation of "Spiritual Theology" inevitably comes up against a formidable barrier: how does one explain and scientifically structure the dynamic development of the spiritual life in persons, groups and communities with its extraordinary capacity for constant progress and renewal?

Little wonder, then, that only fairly recently have the foremost spiritual theologians not only scientifically structured the specific discipline of *Spiritual Theology* on the sure foundations of revealed doctrine, but also fixed attention *spe-*

cifically on the study of *spiritual experience*[2] as such, with its immense variety, ongoing development and progressive deepening, in persons and groups.

To explain all this in terms of a recently deceased master in the field, Fr. Charles André Bernard, S.J.,[3] we could do no better than quote from the "Preface" to his much-acclaimed *Teologia Spirituale*:

> This whole work hinges on the notion of *spiritual experience*. What we mean by this term is the becoming aware or conscious of the vital reality inserted into our spirit (for us Christians, it is that supernatural reality which stems from a sharing in the divine life), which is then sustained by an inherent dynamism which leads it on to an ever deeper and fuller realization by means of our free cooperation.
>
> How does such a Christian experience manifest itself? We should avoid singling out only some privileged forms of such an experience: a true Spiritual Theology should take into consideration, and give account of, the extraordinary capacity which such experience has of renewing itself constantly, and of manifesting itself in individual persons in an endless variety of ways. On my part, I have striven to pay attention to the totality of spiritual experience (within the limits of my knowledge), without excluding that sprung up and grown outside the Christian sphere.
>
> In such a sphere, spiritual experience can well be termed, without being tautological, *an experience in the Holy Spirit.* Thus, the accent is placed on the personal aspect of the Christian spiritual life: its principal agent is the Spirit of the Father and the Son who leads us to the knowledge of Christ, pouring into our hearts charity or God's own kind of loving. On our part, we respond to the constant action of the Spirit by collaborating with it through the commitment of our whole being.
>
> Summing up in a few words the central theme of this study, we could say with St. Paul: "If we live by the Spirit, let us also walk according to the Spirit" (Gal 5: 25).[4]

"Spiritual experience," thus understood and specified as "experience in the Holy Spirit" or "experience animated, permeated by the Spirit of God," raises the issue of *authentic* spiritual experience.

St. Ignatius Loyola: Pedagogue of Authentic Spiritual Experience

Ignatius Loyola is acknowledged in the Church as one of the truly great masters, if not *the* greatest master, of "spiritual discernment," or what is biblically termed the "discernment of spirits."

Ignatius was no professional theologian or philosopher or psychologist, even though scholars discover in his writings profound theological insights, philosophical intuitions and even a great deal of psychological perspicacity. His proper place in the Church, as a spiritual master, is that of a *spiritual pedagogue*, indeed a consummate spiritual director. And this, not primarily because he had painstakingly done his studies in philosophy and theology, especially in the Faculties of Arts and of Theology at the University of Paris, even obtaining the highest academic degree in Arts that that University then granted, the *Magister Artium*, in March 1534.[5] He learned to be an expert "pedagogue" in *his own personal experience* under the guidance of God, the Divine Pedagogue himself. So he confesses in his *Autobiography* (speaking, as he does right through this narrative, in the third person):

> God treated him . . . just as a schoolmaster treats a child whom he is teaching. Whether this was because of his lack of education and of brains, or because he had no one to teach him, or because of the strong desire God Himself had given him to serve Him, *he believed without doubt and has always believed that God treated him in this way. Indeed, if he were to doubt this, he would think he offended the Divine Majesty* (*Autob.* 27; italics mine)

This divine pedagogue Ignatius translated into a living experiential pedagogy for others in his "tiny but immense book" of the *Spiritual Exercises*,[6] as he himself acknowledged toward the very end of his *Autobiography,* when he recounted to Luis Gonçalves da Câmara how he had composed the *Exercises*. It is this confidant himself who shares with us Ignatius's frank acknowledgement in characteristically modest accents of childlike simplicity, so proper of Ignatius whenever he spoke of his own person or his own experiences.[7]

In the *Exercises*, Ignatius underscores the crucial role of *spiritual experience* in two little sentences which contain the very marrow of his spiritual pedagogy: "It is not much knowledge that fills and satisfies the soul, but the inner experience and relish of reality (*el sentir y gustar de las cosas internamente*)" (*Sp. Exs.* 2/5). And again: " if in any point I find what I desire, there I will remain quietly, without any eagerness to go on till I have been satisfied" (*Sp. Exs.* 76/3)—and "satisfied" here must be understood as "fills and satisfies."

That Ignatius is focusing on "inner experience," indeed on "affective experience," is plain from his use of the words *sentir internamente* and *gustar internamente.* This is no chance language: anyone familiar with Ignatius's use of "interior knowledge" (*conocimiento interno*) and its equivalents right through the *Exercises*,[8] is aware that Ignatius is contrasting such "interior knowledge" with mere "conceptual knowledge." "Interior knowledge" is "felt or experiential" knowledge, "knowledge of the heart." Indeed, Ignatius is so unambiguous about the need of "inner experience" for any significant growth that he does not mince his words; he communicates his conviction in vigorously straightforward language:

> When the one giving the Exercises perceives that the exercitant is not experiencing any spiritual movements in his/her soul, such as consolations or desolations, or is not being moved one way or another by the different spirits, the director should question the exercitant much about the Exercises:

whether he/she is making them at the appointed times, how they are being made, and whether the Additional Directives are being diligently observed. The director should ask about each of these items in particular (*Sp. Exs.* 6).

In other words, not to have any inner experiences or inner movements over a period of time is a kind of "alarm signal," which is why the director is to ply the exercitant with questions, seek out the causes of such a state, and help to posit its remedies.[9]

An attentive reading of the book of the *Exercises* shows that, very far from seeking to achieve their objective through a process of cold intellectualism or lifeless voluntarism, the *Exercises* place a heavy premium on inner affective experience, fostering in fact what we have termed earlier an "experience in the Spirit."[10]

If we have vigorously underscored Ignatius's insistence on the crucial role of inner affective experience in the progressive pedagogy of his *Exercises,* we have not thereby meant to insinuate that for Ignatius our "hearts" or affective experience should be allowed to run away with us—no holds barred, as it were![11] By no means! We want, in fact, to emphasize that Ignatius highlights with equal force the need to educate and purify inner or affective experience. This is no different from the great St. John of the Cross in *The Ascent of Mount Carmel* and *The Dark Night* with their successive stages of the "night of the senses" and the "night of the spirit"—all of it so typically captured in his "*Nada . . . nada!*" Nor different, for that matter, from that extraordinary woman, often called the "greatest teacher of prayer in the Church," St. Teresa of Avila, both in her *Way of Perfection* and especially in her *Mansions of the Interior Castle*, in which she spells out progressively those ever more profound stages of spiritual growth—even if expressed in terms of prayer—which are all directed to refining inner spiritual experiences toward more and more intimate union with God.

What is singularly characteristic of Ignatius's spiritual pedagogy, as evidenced in the *Exercises,* is that it is a progressive education and refining of inner affective experience which is *purposefully geared to an insightfully calibrated training for spiritual discernment*—that ever-deepening dynamic of discernment so effectively inculcated in the *Exercises*. It is the particular art of "discerning," in the midst of the *maelstrom* of real-life inner experiences, of that which is *authentic, genuine, sterling* spiritual experience.

Such a perceptive training can best be described as a pedagogy of deepening inner or spiritual freedom, even though Ignatius never literally speaks of his *Exercises* as a process of "liberation" or "inner freedom."[12] What Ignatius, rooted as he was in the Gospel (see Mt 16:24: "If anyone will come after me, let him/her renounce self, take up his/her cross and follow me"), literally spelt out in his time as "getting out of self-love, self-will and self-interest" (*salir de su propio amor, querer e interés*), could well be translated in contemporary language as a deepening process of spiritual/inner freedom. Ignatius has captured in markedly symbolic language, in his "Two Standards Meditation" (*Sp. Exs.* 136-47), the sole criterion of Christian discernment so consistently inculcated in the New Testament—indeed, in the whole biblical tradition: the movement and orientation towards self-gift/self-surrender out of love characterize the Spirit of Christ (of God); that towards closing in on self in self-sufficiency/self-righteousness is clearly distinctive of the counter-spirit. It is an "inner freedom" not merely on the obvious level of sin, imperfection and disorder (First Week of the Exercises), but more profoundly on the level of the exercitant's value system and criteria of living (Second Week, with the contemplation of the mysteries of Christ, in which Christ's values, standards and criteria constitute *the* challenge to those of the exercitant). Indeed, such a process is further pursued to penetrate even the deepest existential levels of the exercitant's subtle and jealously guarded securities of life (the characteristic Ignatian exercises of the "Two Standards," the "Three Classes of Persons" and the "Three Kinds of Humility" applied *respectively*, with profound psycho-spiritual insight, to the securities in the obscured recesses of the intellect, the subtle motivations of the will, and the hidden folds of the heart).

What is remarkable in this typical Ignatian approach to educating inner affective experience toward progressively deepening inner freedom, appears amazingly modern to our contemporary psychological sensibilities and desire to integrate psychology *and* spirituality for effective growth. We had long been taught to deal with our inner affective experiences by running away from them, by getting afraid of them, or by suppressing or repressing them—and this sometimes with tragic results, because in its wake comes a whole host of newer, deeper and more vexing problems. How, indeed, does one educate something by first making a *tabula rasa* of it? There is only one positively effective way for realistic growth: this is what Ignatius, taught by God in the school of his own experience, was able to communicate through his *Spiritual Exercises*. A pedagogical process which begins by *becoming conscious* of one's inner affective experience, then moves on to *accepting* it for what it is,[13] and finally, through that consciously accepted experience, *opens up to the* freeing, healing, transforming *touch of God*. This pedagogical process is none other than the training for, or dynamics of, *spiritual discernment* so diligently instilled in the course of the Ignatian *Exercises*. Taught in his own personal experience of the efficacy of this "divine pedagogy," Ignatius has passed on to us this very process, with its above-detailed three successive steps, in the form of what we are calling today the "Consciousness Examen"[14]—in Ignatius's language, the "Examen of Conscience" (*Examen de Conciencia*). In Ignatius's understanding and practice of it, the *Consciousness Examen* is the *daily* exercise of discernment, in effect the most efficacious means of being and remaining interiorly free in the midst of the bustle of even hectic daily life, experience and activity.

The Inward Journey to the "Heart": Proper Goal of Spiritual Formation

What comes to my mind when we focus on the issue of spiritual formation, is a whole series of spiritual practices, like personal and community prayer, reading of the Word of God or "lectio divina," the celebration and reception of the sacraments, ascetical and penitential practices, devotional exercises like recitation of the rosary, monthly recollections and retreats—a whole required program of spiritual initiation and deepening through practices and exercises. While this is certainly an aspect, even an indispensable aspect, of spiritual formation, we may miss the mark with regard to the distinctively spiritual character of such formation unless we spotlight the purpose of all such exercises and practices: namely, the acquiring of a "style or quality of life," a "spirit" which effects unity and integration of life, a "new heart and new spirit" in biblical terms, or what is often designated today as an all-embracing life-"*horizon*" or perspective.

An example may illustrate what we are getting at. An expert dancer on the stage, or an accomplished pianist performing in a concert hall, evokes in us such admiration that we spontaneously exclaim: "how *freely,* how *gracefully* he/she dances!" Or, "what an amazing *grace* and *freedom* with which this pianist is performing, almost making the piano talk!" Where does such astonishing *freedom* and *grace* come from? From hours and hours on end, day-in and day-out, of submitting self to the grinding discipline of the ground rules of dancing or of piano-playing. But neither the dancer nor the pianist submits self to this grinding discipline for its own sake—no! Its whole purpose is to release a "flexibility," a "freedom," a "personal *style, art and grace*" which characterizes the expert and accomplished artist, the master pianist or the professional dancer. The ground rules of dancing or the laws of piano-playing are no longer merely within the books which expound them at length nor even in the scholarly teacher who explains them. They have become for the accomplished artist an *interior law,* an interiorized, assimilated, personalized "*heart and spirit,*" a personal style, which is what "inner freedom" is all about.

But there is *even more* to be drawn out from the illustration. Let us take two highly skilled pianists who are both playing the same masterpiece of Beethoven (B) or Chopin (C). We often say: "Oh! This master pianist has *his own* personal 'interpretation' of the very same piece by (B) or (C)." What we are *really* saying is in fact: "The first master pianist is expressing his *unrepeatably unique self* in playing this piece of (B) or (C); and the other skilled pianist is giving expression to her *unrepeatably unique self* in playing the very same piece. What comes through in each single accomplished artist's performance is the *secret of his/her inner freedom*—that is, his/her *truest and deepest self,* his/her *unrepeatably unique self.*[15]

What, then, is the process of discovering and *discerning* this unrepeatably unique self of a person, which is his/her personal secret of inner freedom? The *process*, we now gather, has *three* major steps: first, the *exercise(s)* of submitting to the discipline of the ground rules of dancing or piano-playing; second, taking note of the *experience(s)* gathered from the exercise(s) in a review and evaluation of what went on in the course of the exercises or practices; and finally, guided by a trainer or teacher, *tracing* through the succession of such ongoing experiences the *emergence of one's own* characteristically *personal* "*style or art*" of performing—that is, one's "true self," where one is interiorly free and uninhibited to be one's truest and deepest self—in our example, through the medium of the performing arts of dance or piano-playing.

We can apply all this to our subject of *spiritual formation*. The pedagogical initiation or apprenticeship through the series of the varied spiritual *exercises and practices* is the necessary starting-point for such a process of training or formation. But unless these exercises are then geared through the two further steps of *experience* resulting from the exercises and then the *evaluation* or *discernment*, under competent guidance, of such experiences to *trace* and discover in their ongoing succession *an emerging pattern* of that *inner "heart and spirit"* which unifies and integrates all of life, the training or formation remains what it was at its starting-point: no more than a series of fragmented, disparate disciplinary exercises and practices—in honest truth, a form of "slavery," where the person being formed has still not matured and has not yet found his/her life-center and true self, his/her "heart" or inner secret of freedom.

What we have just spelt out as the process of genuine *spiritual* formation is, in truth, the paschal passage from the Old Testament dispensation of "slavery" to the New Testament dispensation of the "freedom of the children of God" (see Gal 4-5; Rom 8). Indeed, did not God reveal through the prophets (see Jer 31: 31-34; Ezeck 11: 17-20; 36: 24-28) that he would take the law that was written on tablets of stone and put it within our hearts in the new dispensation when he would give us "a new heart and a new spirit"—*his* Spirit, that makes us "free children of God?"

A "new heart and a new spirit," a person's secret of inner freedom which, once discerned in depth, impels a person *from within* to express himself/herself—that is, that person's truest and deepest self—in those precise external exercises and practices that make up each day the Christian spiritual life. Only—and this is the crucial difference—it is no longer a fragmented discipline to which one submits wearily from the "outside" but a joyous uninhibited freedom *from within* the core of one's *authentic self*.

To conclude this section on *spiritual formation* we now append an eminently pertinent citation from Pope John Paul II's post-synodal apostolic exhortation *Pastores Dabo Vobis* (PDV), even if its context explicitly refers to priestly spiritual formation:

> And just as for all the faithful *spiritual formation* is *central* and *unifies* their *being* and *living as Christians*, that is *as new creatures in Christ who walk in the Spirit*, so too for every priest his *spiritual formation* is the *core* which *unifies* and *gives life* to his "being" a priest and "acting as" a priest (*PDV* 45c—italics mine).

"Heart" Speaks to "Heart:" Core of True Dialogue

To anyone familiar with the documents of Vatican II, it is evident that they set forth a "theological anthropology." Indeed, they all hinge on, are built around, one central conviction: the profound awareness of the *God-given dignity of the human person*. For example, after scrutinizing the signs of the times in its Introductory Statement on "The Situation of Men and Women in the Modern World," *Gaudium et Spes* dedicates its entire first chapter precisely to "The Dignity of the Human Person," as though this Pastoral Constitution of Vatican II wanted to spotlight the *God-given dignity of the human person* as the sign of our times. No wonder, too, that the very opening words of the far-reaching "Declaration on Religious Freedom" singles out the same awareness as peculiarly characteristic of modern man's/woman's sharpened sensibilities:

> A sense of the dignity of the human person has been impressing itself more and more deeply on the consciousness of contemporary man and woman (*Dignitatis Humanae* 1).[16]

Among the attitudes which characterize contemporary man and woman, a highly accentuated personalism is the major salient trait, so much so that it affects almost every area of human living. We would like to focus, for instance, on the *insatiable need for dialogue*—so very pronounced in its expressions that it is often publicized as the "panacea" for all human ills! Is it not in the mutual recognition by people of their *God-given dignity as human persons* that the genuine theological basis for dialogue actually lies? The immense popularity of the Jewish philosopher Martin Buber's *Ich und Du (I and Thou)*, especially after its first English translation by Ronald Gregor Smith appeared in 1937 and even more after Buber's death in 1965, bears ample witness to the amazing potential of "dialogue" in contemporary life. Very much of the wide-ranging contemporary renewal in theology and catechesis has been effected largely, if not universally, along "dialogal" and "interpersonal" lines: we need only consider present-day Christology, sacramental theology and the theology of revelation and faith.

In a world revolutionized and somewhat shrunken to the dimensions of a global village by the explosion of the communications media and the spectacular advances in information technology, calling attention to the crucial need for "dialogue" may appear to be thumping the obvious! And yet, paradoxically—indeed, ironically—we who are in the field of "spiritual counselling and formation" are painfully aware that in our world, there is tragically less and less of real and genuine communication. And *this* is the specific point we wish to make.

When the highly developed technology of communication takes over to the point of stifling the "human person," authentic communication fizzles out and breaks down. There can be no "communion" without communication; what is perhaps becoming increasingly obscured is that there can be no "communion" or community without the animating center and spirit of "person." For person and community, far from being mutually exclusive terms, are in fact intimately correlative. As experimental psychology has demonstrated, a "person" becomes a person only within community; but equally to be stressed is the no less experimentally established truth that a "community" is a genuine community only if it is made up of living, responsible persons who, each of them, make the community goals and tasks responsibly their own.

We sense, then, in the sacred dignity of the "human person" being progressively swallowed up in all spheres of human life by the computerized "automaton," one of the gravest risks facing contemporary civilization. There is but one decisively responsible way of "stemming the rot": and that is getting back to the "center" of "person," or what I have earlier phrased as the "inward journey to the heart." "Heart," we know, in biblical language connotes the "center" of human personality: where a being is most profoundly itself, where the "unity of being" is effected, where this being is capable of giving itself, where life-decisions are taken.[17]

This is why the pedagogical process detailed earlier as the process of authentic spiritual formation—in biblical terms, the paschal passage from the Old Testament dispensation of "slavery" to the New Testament dispensation of the "freedom of the children of God"—is that interiorization and personalization of the "external law" which, in the Bible, is termed God's putting in us a "new heart" and "a new spirit." It is the leading to that "core" which effectively unifies and vivifies a person's "being" and "acting."

The sages of old formulated the very essence of genuine and true communication in the maxim: "Cor ad cor loquitur!" ("Heart" speaks to the "heart"!) If the "heart" we are here focusing on is that *unrepeatable uniqueness* of each human person as "called by name" by God—that radical and fundamental God-given *identity* of every single human person—then we begin to grasp in depth that *this heart* is, in fact, the true "core" of all dialogue and human communication.

I have found in Pope Paul's first encyclical *Ecclesiam Suam* on "the ways in which the Catholic Church is in the present circumstances to carry out its mission,"[18] a significantly new and fresh content and context—indeed, a vast and profound theological horizon—opened to the world of "communication," and specifically to the understanding and depth of "dialogue." Paul VI opens this encyclical with a section on the Church's "awareness of her identity": "Church of Christ, who are you?" is the key question the Pope asks, and makes all of us ask. Only after becoming aware, in the light of revelation and the living tradition of the Church, of her "identity," can the Church meaningfully face the challenge of its reform and renewal—and this is the encyclical's second section on "renewal": that never-ending renewal of all sectors of the Church's life and activity, in order that she may increasingly be shaped in accord with her God-given identity. Only then, in the third and final section does Pope Paul confidently embark on the urgency of "dialogue"—the ongoing dialogue of the Church with the modern world, dialogue with all humankind and with the cosmos itself.

It is, therefore, from the rootedness in authentic God-given identity, followed by an ever-deeper measuring up, through reform and renewal, to this identity, that genuine, effective communication and dialogue emerge and move forward in ongoing depth. Against the background of all I have just developed, the inner abode of such "rootedness in identity" may well be *spiritually* designated as "heart." "Heart," then, speaks to "heart" as the vital core of genuine dialogue and communication!

The "Spirit" of Interreligious Dialogue

Though Pope Paul VI did not, in his encyclical *Ecclesiam Suam* of 1964, focus specifically on what we term "interreligious dialogue," except in what he described as the "second circle" of those with whom the Church, in her universal mission, is to dialogue (that is, "believers in God" [*Ecclesiam Suam*, nos. 107-108]), his wider-ranging reflections on the profound inner principles animating all true dialogue were later explicitly elaborated in the Constitutions, Decrees and Declarations of Vatican II—particularly in the Dogmatic Constitution on the Church (*Lumen Gentium*), the Pastoral Constitution on the Church in the Modern World (*Gaudium et Spes*) and the Declaration on the Relationship of the Church to Non-Christian Religions (*Nostra Aetate*)—as well as in the subsequent teaching of the Church specifically related to "interreligious dialogue."

It is in the Joint Document of the Pontifical Council for Interreligious Dialogue and the Congregation for the Evangelization of Peoples, *Dialogue and Proclamation* (DP) of March 19, 1991, that we have for the first time, even though citing from an earlier document of 1984, a kind of official definition or description of interreligious dialogue: ". . . in the context of religious plurality, dialogue means 'all possible and constructive interreligious relations with individuals and communities of other faiths which are directed at mutual understanding and enrichment' (from *Dialogue and Mission* [DM] 3, document of the Secretariat for Non-Christians of May 10, 1984), in obedience to truth and respect for freedom" (9).

The same Joint Document (DP of 1991) went on to enumerate, while once again referring to that earlier 1984 document DM (nos. 28-35), *four* principal and interrelated forms of interreligious dialogue: the dialogue *of life,* that *of action,* that *of theological exchange* among specialists/experts, and *the dialogue of religious experience.* It is on this last form, in the context of our present contribution, focussed as it is on spiritual experience, that we wish to dwell for a moment.

This dialogue of religious experience is paraphrased in both DM (1984) and DP (1991). "At *a deeper level,*" says very significantly DM 35, "persons rooted in their own religious traditions . . . *share their experiences* of prayer, contemplation, faith, and duty, as well as their expressions and ways of searching for the Absolute." Whereas this is reproduced in abbreviated form by DP 42, it is noteworthy that this 1991 DP text rephrases the DM text to read: "persons, rooted in their own religious traditions *share their spiritual riches,* for instance with regard to prayer and contemplation, faith and ways of searching for God or the Absolute."

Is there an implicit, perhaps unconscious, acknowledgment of the very contention of this our contribution: namely, specifically *spiritual experience*—indeed *authentic spiritual experience*—as *a vehicle of God's own Spirit for interreligious dialogue?* We are inclined to answer this query in the affirmative.

Be that as it may, the reasons for our firm conviction are plain. It is the Second Vatican Council that has decisively led us in the Church to a positive appraisal and assessment of religious and spiritual traditions other than our Christian one (see DP 14-15). Doubtless, the Council reaffirmed the traditional doctrine according to which salvation in Jesus Christ is, in a mysterious way, a reality open to all persons of good will. Christ, the New Adam, through the mystery of his incarnation, death and resurrection, is at work in each human person, whose heart is free and open, to bring about interior renewal. The Council teaches: "All this holds true not only for Christians, but for all persons of good will in whose hearts grace works in an unseen way (see LG 16). For, since Christ died for all (see Rom 8:32), and since all are in fact called to one and the same destiny, which is divine, we must hold that the Holy Spirit offers to all the possibility of being made partners, in a manner known to God, in the paschal mystery" (GS 22).

Little wonder, then, that Pope John Paul II's encyclical on the Church's missionary activity *Redemptoris Missio* of December 7, 1990, the 25th anniversary of the promulgation of Vatican II's Decree *Ad Gentes*, laid particular stress on the presence and activity of the Spirit of God at all times and in all places (see RM 28). Explicitly citing Vatican II's documents, notably *Gaudium et Spes* (nos. 10, 15, 22, 26, 38 and 41), the Pope is eloquently forthright on this theme: ". . . the presence and activity (of the Spirit) are universal, limited neither by space nor time. The Second Vatican Council recalls that the Spirit is at work in the heart of every person, through the 'seeds of the Word' to be found in human institutions— including religious ones. . . . The Spirit offers the human race 'the light and strength to respond to its highest calling': through the Spirit, 'humankind attains in faith to the contemplation and *savouring* of the mystery of God's design.' . . . The Church 'is aware that humanity is being continually stirred by the Spirit of God and can therefore never be completely indifferent to the problems of religion.' . . . The Spirit, therefore, is at the very source of the human person's existential and religious questioning. . . . The Spirit's presence and activity affect not only individuals but also society and history, peoples, cultures and *religions*" (RM 28, italics mine).

Such a presence and activity of the Spirit of God, vigorously affirmed even beyond the boundaries of the visible Church, makes us confidently believe that the authentic spiritual experience or "experience in the Holy Spirit," as we have designated it, is an effective vehicle for fruitful "interreligious dialogue" on our common journey with brothers and sisters of other religious and spiritual traditions toward the fullness of the Reign of God.

Conclusion: Toward the Fullness of the Kingdom

It is precisely the ongoing fruitful presence and work of the Spirit of the Risen Jesus that opens up the eschatological horizons of the journey of all humankind toward the fullness of the Kingdom. For "God's Spirit, with a marvellous providence, directs the unfolding course of the ages, and renews the face of the earth" (GS 26).

Committed as we, apostles of the Kingdom, are to the action of the Holy Spirit both in human hearts and in the unfolding history of the world, we must live in ways which look to the fullness of the Kingdom in which justice, peace, reconciliation and love will hold sway. "Working for the Kingdom," Pope John Paul II said in *Redemptoris Missio*, "means acknowledging and promoting God's activity which is present in human history and transforms it. . . . In a word, the Kingdom of God is the manifestation and realization of God's plan of salvation in all its fullness" (RM 15).

The Federation of Asian Bishops' Conferences (FABC), faced as it has been by the serious and delicate theological issues raised by the Asian situation, where the Church lives and carries out her mission in the context of cultural, religious and therefore spiritual pluralism, has on more than one occasion had to reflect on the Asian Church's life and mission in terms of "the journey toward the fullness of the Kingdom." Thus, for example, in the Theological Consultation organized by the FABC Office of Evangelization in Thailand (November 3-10, 1991), its *Major Conclusions* spotlighted the role and mission of the Church within a wider perspective of the Kingdom or Reign of God.[19]

> The Paschal mystery in which the Christ-event culminates . . . ushers in the renewal of creation and marks the decisive step in the establishment by God of his Kingdom on earth. It has cosmic implications and universal significance. . . .
>
> The Kingdom of God is therefore universally present and at work. Wherever men and women open themselves to the transcendent divine mystery which impinges upon them and go out of themselves in love and service of fellow humans, there the Reign of God is at work."

Quoting from the 1991 DP 29 to the effect that from the mystery of the unity of all humankind, "it follows that all men and women who are saved share, though differently, in the same mystery of salvation *in Jesus Christ through his Spirit.* . . . The mystery of salvation reaches out to them (non-Christians), in a way known to God through the invisible action of the Spirit of Christ," this FABC document draws out a whole series of theological conclusions. "Thus they (non-Christians) become sharers of the kingdom of God in Jesus Christ unknowingly. This goes to show that the Reign of God is a universal reality extending . . . beyond the visible boundaries of the Church. . . . In this universal reality of the Reign of God, the Church has a unique and irreplaceable role to play. . . . The focus of the Church's mission of evangelization is building up the Kingdom of God and building up the Church to be at the service of the Kingdom. The Kingdom is therefore wider than the Church. The Church is the servant of the Kingdom, making it visible, ordained to it, promoting it, but not equating itself with it."

In spelling out these theological conclusions, the FABC document makes a very timely reference to Pope John Paul II's encyclical *Redemptoris Missio* issued less than a year earlier:

It is true that the Church is not an end unto herself, since she is ordered towards the Kingdom of God of which she is the seed, sign and instrument. Yet, while remaining distinct from Christ and the Kingdom, the Church is indissolubly united to both. . . . The result is a unique and special relationship which, while not excluding the action of Christ and the Spirit outside the Church's visible boundaries, confers upon her a specific . . . role (RM 18).

The Reign of God, then, is sacramentally present in the Church in a special manner; she is "the seed, sign and instrument" of the Reign of God toward which she is ordered.

Within the framework of our particular contribution to the volume in honour of Jacques Dupuis, we conclude, within the context of these final reflections of "journeying together towards the fullness of the Kingdom," with a remarkable text from Vatican II's Dogmatic Constitution on Divine Revelation (*Dei Verbum*), where the Council speaks specifically of the *"spiritual experience of believers"* as a very significant means and instrument, *made use of by the Holy Spirit of God* in the Church's journeying towards the fullness of truth or *"authentic spiritual experience."*

Treating of the "transmission of Divine Revelation," the Council says:

This tradition which comes from the apostles develops in the Church with the help of the Holy Spirit. For there is a growth in the understanding of the realities and the words which have been handed down. This happens through the contemplation and study made by believers, who treasure these things in their hearts (cf. Lk 2:19, 51), *through the intimate understanding of the spiritual things which they experience (tum ex intima spiritualium rerum quam experiuntur intelligentia)*, and through *preaching. . . . For as the centuries succeed one another, the Church constantly moves forward to the fullness of divine truth until the words of God reach their complete fulfilment in her. . . . And thus God, who spoke of old, uninterruptedly converses with the Bride of His beloved Son;* and the *Holy Spirit, through whom the living voice of the gospel resounds in the Church, and through her, in the world . . .* makes the word of Christ dwell abundantly in them (cf. Col 3: 16) (DV 8: italics mine).

It seems to us that, while this text offers a profoundly integrated vision of Christ, the Church and the work of the Spirit in the journeying towards the fullness of truth—and, therefore, towards the fullness of the Kingdom—its even wider and deeper implications for a *spiritual* theology of interreligious dialogue have still to be further probed and fathomed.

References

[1]Though all of GC 34's work was promulgated on September 27,1995, Decrees 21, 22, 23 (A, B, C, D) and *The Constitutions of the Society of Jesus as annotated by GC 34, with*

their Complementary Norms were to take effect on January 1, 1996, the Titular Feast of the Society of Jesus: see "Letter of V. Rev. Fr. General 'To The Whole Society' " (September 27,1995), *Acta Romana Soc. Iesu* XXI (1995), 346.

[2]The most comprehensive study on the theme of "spirititual experience" is that of Jean Mouroux, *The Christian Experience* (New York: Sheed and Ward, 1954) who significantly distinguished the term "experimental" from that today commonly called "experiential," which is pertinent to our topic. See. also: "Expérience spirituelle," in *Dictionnaire de Spiritualité Ascétique et Mystique* IV/2, 2004-6.

[3]Charles A. Bernard, S.J., died suddenly after a brief illness, at the age of 78, on February 1, 2001. He had devoted the last 35 to 40 years of his life—most of them spent with us at the Pontifical Gregorian University, Rome—to the study and teaching of *Spirituality*, to tireless research in this field, and particularly to its ongoing development and recognition as an authentic and specific theological discipline.

[4]English translation mine, from the Italian original of Charles A. Bernard, 4th ed., *Teologia Spirituale* (Cinisello Balsamo, Milano: Ediz. Paoline, 1987), 7-8.

[5]See *Monumenta Soc. Historica Iesu*, Vol. 115: *Fontes Documentales*, 396.

[6]It is Pope Pius XI who first characterized the Ignatian book of the *Exercises* as "piccolo di mole, ma grande e prezioso di contenuto" (small in size, but great and precious in its contents) in his encyclical *Mens Nostra* of December 1929. This encyclical dealt entirely with the Ignatian *Spiritual Exercises.*

[7]"After these things had been narrated, I asked the pilgrim . . . about the Exercises . . . as I wanted to know how he had drawn them up. He told me that he had not composed the Exercises all at once, but that, when he noticed some things in his soul and found them useful *(las encontraba útiles)*, he thought they might also be useful to others *(le parecía que podrían ser útiles también a otros)*, and so he put them in writing" *(Autob.* 99). It is striking that Ignatius who regularly expressed all "apostolic activity" as "helping souls" *(ayudar a las ánimas)* speaks here of what he found useful (or helpful) in his own personal experience *(some things in his soul)*, and so he put it down in writing because he thought it "might be useful/helpful" to others. . . . The Preface to the first edition of the *Exercises* (1548), attributed to Polanco (Secretary of the Society of Jesus under Ignatius as General), clearly says: "Haec documenta ac spiritualia exercitia . . . non tam a libris, quam ab unctione Sancti Spiritus et ab interna experientia et usu tractandorum animorum edoctus, noster in Christo Pater M. Ignatius de Loyola . . . composuit" *(Monumenta Hist. Soc. Iesu*, Vol. 100: *Exercitia Spiritualia*, p. 79). (Our Father in Christ Master Ignatius Loyola . . . drew up these documents and spiritual exercises, taught not so much by books, as by the unction of the Holy Spirit, by his own inner experience and his practice of guiding souls).

[8]See, for example: *Sp. Exs.* 63; 65; 104; 233. Very worthwhile in this context is Divarkar's spelling out of the dynamics of the *Exercises* in terms precisely of "interior knowledge": see Parmananda Divarkar, S.J., *The Path of Interior Knowledge* (Anand, Gujarat, India: Gujarat Sahitya Prakash, 1990, and Rome: Centrum Ignatianum Spiritualitatis, 1983).

[9]This state must not be mistakenly equated with what the spiritual masters call "aridity" or "dryness," which for them is an authentic spiritual category: that is, the absence of experience only on the sense-level. Numerous examples in the history of Spirituality bear witness to such "aridity," sometimes lasting over a long period of time (see, for example, Teresa of Avila, *Autobiography*, c. 4, n.7 or c. 11, n.11). The sense-level of experience is only one elementary level; there exist deeper levels of experience, such as the level of faith, even a whole "affectivity of faith," attested by the so-called "Prayer of Faith." For all of this, see Herbert Alphonso, S.J., "To Love and Serve in All Things: Everyday Life as Prayer,"

in Herbert Alphonso, S.J. (ed.), *Esperienza e Spiritualità: Miscellanea in onore del R.P. Charles André Bernard, SJ* (Romae: Pomel, 1995), 362-68.

[10]The entire book of the *Spiritual Exercises* is literally laden with expressions of affectively charged inner experience (see e.g. nn.° 2, 6, 15, 17).

[11]In that age of fairly widespread "Illuminism" Ignatius Loyola came under fire at Alcalá, Salamanca, Venice, and finally at Rome in 1538 (cf. ibid., 98). Not only Ignatius was suspected of leanings towards "illuminism" because of the stress he laid on inner affective experience; the same suspicions were directed against such spiritual masters of the time as St. John of the Cross or St. Teresa of Avila, who laid an equally strong emphasis on inner affective experience.

[12]And yet, tucked away in somewhat latent fashion, nearly halfway through the book of the *Exercises* is that key sentence which, in the mind and heart of Ignatius, sums up the entire dynamics of his *Spiritual Exercises*. It is the very last sentence of his documents on "Election"——that is, on "Choice" or "Decision" effected through Discernment: "Let everyone keep in mind that in all things that concern the spiritual life, progress is in proportion to divesting oneself of self-love, self-will and self-interest" (*Sp. Exs. 189/10*).

[13]It is well worth stressing the fact that "acceptance" is *not* "approval." "Approval" or "disapproval" is a judgement; "acceptance" or "non-acceptance" is an affective attitude. There is a world of difference between the two, and not a few serious problems in human-spiritual growth stem from a confusion of these two worlds. God does not and cannot "approve" of so many things I say or do; yet, I am absolutely sure that in those very same words and actions of mine God "accepts" me *unconditionally*. This unshakable assurance of my Christian faith is based on the entire witness of the Word of God, as constantly grasped by the living tradition of the Church.

[14]For a fuller understanding of the "Consciousness Examen" and its efficacy in daily discernment, see: Herbert Alphonso, S.J., *The Personal Vocation: Transformation in Depth through the Spiritual Exercises*, 8th ed. (Rome: Pontificia Università Gregoriana, 2002), 62-63; 72-80; or again, in its American edition, *Discovering Your Personal Vocation: The Search for Meaning through the Spiritual Exercises* (New York/Mahwah, N.J.: Paulist Press, 2001), 47-48; 56-64.

[15]For a detailed spelling-out of what is here called a person's *truest and deepest self* or *unrepeatably unique self*, see my book mentioned in the previous note 14 which is entirely dedicated to this subject—*The Personal Vocation* or its American edition, *Discovering Your Personal Vocation*.

[16]Even that which appears to be, in the hierarchy of the documents of Vatican II, the "least" document, the simple and unpretentious "Declaration on Christian Education," builds all its recommendations on this one foundation. Its very first number, following on the introduction, starts off with: "Since every human being of whatever race, condition and age is endowed with the dignity of a person, he/she has an inalienable right to an education corresponding to his/her proper destiny and suited to his/her native talents, sex, cultural background and ancestral heritage" (*Gravissimum Educationis* 1).

[17]See Xavier Léon-Dufour (ed.), "Heart," *Dictionary of Biblical Theology*, 2nd ed. (Boston: St. Paul's Publications, 1988), cols. 228-29.

[18]This encyclical was issued on 6 August 1964, that is, in the interval between the second and the third periods of the Second Vatican Council: see AAS 56 (1964), 609-59.

[19]See *For All the Peoples of Asia: Federation of Asian Bishops' Conferences. Documents from 1970 to 1991*, ed. Gaudencio Rosales and C. G. Arévalo (New York/Quezon City: Orbis/Claretian Publications, 1992).

11

On Relationship as a Key to Interreligious Dialogue

Doris Donnelly

The first thing to acknowledge is immense gratitude. Jacques Dupuis has pioneered the fields of Christology, theology of the Trinity, and theology of religions into uncharted regions with uncommon insight for decades. He has done so with loving care for the tradition that has grounded him and with profound respect for the Holy Spirit who routinely has shaken that very same ground from under his feet. In the service of the Spirit, he has been led to unexpected places for glimmers of truth in the company of other theologians who are seeking to hold together their faith in Jesus as the universal savior of humankind, while affirming that other religious traditions, in God's eternal plan, have a positive significance as ways, means and channels of salvation for their followers.

Christian scriptures assure us that the truth sets us free, but they neglect to emphasize that the road to freedom is sometimes bumpy and hazardous, even with divine protection. We can all be grateful that Jacques Dupuis has been such a willing traveler on the unpredictable trajectory of the Spirit. He has not only coasted in fair weather but also has borne the bruises of occasional turbulence with what Ernest Hemingway has fittingly termed "grace under pressure."

The second thing to acknowledge is sheer astonishment. At a point in his life when he could anticipate a quiet retirement (I picture in my imagination a Jesuit villa in Tuscany or on the Costa del Sol—and hope such places exist!), he is, instead, as prolific as ever. I know first-hand that his proverbial "dance card" is full and that universities and academic societies the world over need to book well in advance to secure his presence. Characteristically, when he arrives on the scene he is not content simply to review the old. For him, the past is prologue. There are not only personal belongings but also fresh ideas to unpack. There are theological connections to be made and then tested for strength, durability and orthodoxy.

I am indebted to Mary Boys—friend and religious educator—for guiding me to so many sources regarding interreligious dialogue. This article depends on her for so many generous acts of kindness.

There is still work bearing on fruitful interreligious dialogue to be done. A quiet determination energizes his intellect, heart and (apparently) his computer. Once a mentor for university professors and serious students of theology, he is now, additionally, a role model for those free from professorial responsibilities as they move into other productive chapters in their lives.

What audiences and publishers are most eager to hear and read from Jacques Dupuis concerns the universal relevance of Jesus Christ and a God who saves in various ways. They wonder whether our language—indeed, our ways of thinking—are adequate to accommodate a radically fresh Trinitarian approach that preserves the essential unity of the salvific economy while recognizing the diversity that is part of our plural religious history. Is there a way to understand pluralism, in David Tracy's words that echo Dupuis, "as a responsible and fruitful option because it allows (indeed demands) that we develop better ways as selves, as communities of inquirers, as societies, as cultures, as an inchoately global culture to allow for more possibilities to enrich our personal and communal lives?"[1] And how does interreligious dialogue happen under circumstances that honor the integrity of all parties while these other questions are being sorted out?

As intriguing as all of these questions are, it is the last one that is the focus of this chapter. My interests lie in the urgency of inter-faith dialogue, the attitudes necessary for it, and in identifying places where encounter and dialogue between the religions is already a reality. In particular, I am interested in the category of relationship as the key to effective dialogue and I have found the work of Diana Eck, Mary Boys, and Sara Lee, among others, most helpful in this regard. I am aware, of course, that my concern is shared by many.

Why Interreligious Dialogue?

There are many reasons for the current intense interest in both the messenger Jacques Dupuis and his message. Certainly the catastrophic events of September 11, 2001 have been a four-alarm wake-up call. But long before 9/11 there was a growing consciousness that we live—all of us—as citizens of the global village. The availability of international travel and the presence of the media, including the omnipresence of CNN, have allowed people, other than theologians, religious leaders, missionaries, and diplomats to experience world religions first-hand. In fact one need not go outside one's local neighborhood. My own city of Cleveland, Ohio has synagogues, mosques, temples and shrines in abundance; my own neighbors drink their spiritual nourishment from many springs.[2] What some call "the dialogue of daily life" takes place in ordinary ways on a regular basis. In addition, many Christians have assimilated a paradigm shift with regard to the diversity of other religions surrounding them. To put it simply: they see that other religions are not only here to stay but also that many of them are growing by leaps and bounds. Not that long ago the response to the vitality of other religions might have been panic and frantic efforts to convert those outside the fold. But an alternative attitude now seems to be at work to explain why, after so many centuries of missionary activity, so few people have become and remain Christian. It would seem, as Monika Hellwig puts it, that "there are many paths of salvation, many ways of naming and worshiping the same ultimate, transcendent reality, many languages and rituals by which peoples search for communion with the divine and respond to the outreach of the divine in creation. If there are many such ways, then it is of overwhelming interest to know more about them, to see what we as Christians can learn from them, and to offer them a respectful exchange of all that makes up our faith-tradition and theirs."[3]

We have also come to recognize the holiness of people whose lives are enriched in other faiths. Some have celebrity status: the Dalai Lama, Mohandas Gandhi, Thich Nhat Hanh, Abraham Heschel. But often enough we see goodness in ordinary people doing ordinary things under extraordinary circumstances— people whose lives are a powerful witness to their faith. To her amazement as a twenty-year-old student in Benares, India, Harvard University professor Diana Eck recalls when she became aware for the first time that "Christians did not have a corner on love, wisdom and justice. Christians were not the only ones nourished by their faith to work to change the world."[4] Yet Eck believes it is precisely her faith experience of God, Christ and the Spirit that enabled her to acknowledge God's presence in a Hindu temple and in the lives of Hindus.[5] She says, "I would even say that it is Christ who enables Christians—in fact, challenges us—to recognize God especially where we don't expect to do so and where it is not easy to do so."[6]

Jacques Dupuis appreciates the giftedness of other religions as a manifestation of the fruits of the Spirit perceived in the lives of believers. In his study of Dupuis's work, Terrence Merrigan writes that "the willingness to accord the other religions a positive role in the divine economy of salvation—a willingness inspired by the actual experience of the fruits of the Spirit visible among them—is a major feature of Dupuis's own approach."[7] For Dupuis, the world religions possess "a lasting role and a specific meaning in the overall mystery" of the relationship between God and humankind.[8] If that is so, the basic question that intrigues us is what God is saying in and through other religions. Or to put it another way: What is the significance of pluralism in God's plan for humankind? What does God want us to hear? What does God want us to know?

Of course, the interest in the theology of religions and interreligious dialogue receives continual encouragement from Pope John Paul II. A relentless focus of his pontificate has been to repair bridges of trust and understanding that were damaged or destroyed in the past.

The positive strokes of the Second Vatican Council and its Declaration on the Relation of the Church to Non-Christian Religions (*Nostra Aetate*)[9] may have remained in mothballs had it not been for the single-minded mission of John Paul II. His appeal for a reconciled humanity in *Tertio Millennio Adveniente*, his insistence on interreligious dialogue in *Redemptoris Missio*, and his passionate plea for dialogue in *Novo Millennio Ineunte* are part of his enduring legacy. Karol Wojtyla sensed from the moment he accepted the vote of his brother cardinals to become the 265th pope that there is more at issue than common courtesy or diplomatic finesse in advancing interreligious dialogue. In *Redemptoris Missio*, he wrote: "Dialogue will be especially important in establishing a sure basis for peace and warding off the dread spectre of those wars of religion which have so often bloodied human history."[10] Without rehearsing the sorry history of the capacity for religions to become ideological tools for oppression and violence, we can concentrate, as Jacques Dupuis encourages us to do, on "an open and constructive theology of the religions of the world (as) a pressing need if we wish to foster an interreligious dialogue conducive to universal peace."[11] The ante is as high as it has ever been to learn, to understand, and to be in conversation with others.

It must be admitted, however, that as important as official Vatican statements are, it is the personal witness of Pope John Paul II that stirs the imagination of what the future could be. Seared into our collective consciousness are visual memories of the pope at the Wailing Wall in Jerusalem, with the Serbian Orthodox representatives in Sarajevo, with Muslims in Kazakhstan. The list goes on and on.[12] And who among us can forget the occasion orchestrated by the pope at Saint Peter's Basilica in Rome on March 12, 2000, with members of the Roman Curia, Cardinal Joseph Ratzinger among them, asking pardon for sins committed in the name of the Church?[13]

John Paul II personalized inter-faith dialogue. His unprecedented travel schedule, meticulously chronicled by the media, sends a message of openness and determination about the importance of dialogue that no document has done or will ever be able to do in the same way. Putting flesh and blood into his commitment is a symbolic act that speaks as no official statement on paper is able to do. His actions as much as his words reflect the optimism of the Council about salvation and *Nostra Aetate*'s universal affirmation of one God who created all and wills salvation for all. One is reminded of Karl Rahner's felicitous choice of the word *Heilsoptimismus,* "holy optimism," which recommends we "think optimistically" about the possibility that those outside the Church are "positively included in God's plan of salvation."[14] Rahner provided this historical perspective: "In more than a millennium of struggle, theology has overcome Augustinian pessimism in regard to the salvation of the individual and reached the optimism of the Second Vatican Council, assuring supernatural salvation in the immediate possession of God to all those who do not freely reject it through their own personal fault. Our question now must be whether theology can regard the non-Christian religions with the same optimism."[15]

There are theologians, Jacques Dupuis front and center among them, seeking ways of thinking and the language to carry *Heilsoptimismus* to its next level.

How Interreligious Dialogue Happens: The Primacy of Relationship

Interfaith dialogue does not begin with propositions and theories but with experience and relationships. Fittingly, Diana Eck calls her book, *Encounter with God*, "a theology with people in it."[16] A professor of religion at Harvard University and director of the Pluralism Project there, Eck grew up as a Methodist in the small town of Bozeman, Montana (population 12,000). As a second year student at Smith College in Massachusetts, an announcement for a year's study in India caught her eye. What followed was the first of many years visiting and re-visiting a place and people she came to love. "They are the people I have encountered in my studies of the history of religion, in my fieldwork in India, and in my travels throughout the world. I cannot think about Christianity and about my faith without hearing their voices, so it makes sense to give them narrative space in my theological thinking. What questions do they ask of me? What questions do I have of them? This mutual questioning and listening is what is meant by interfaith dialogue."[17]

Mary Boys, a Roman Catholic religious educator committed to interreligious dialogue, collaborated with Sara Lee, a Jewish religious educator (who is also committed to interreligious dialogue), in a project involving twenty-two Catholic and Jewish professional educators who met six times a year over a period of 18 months. They knew *learning about* the other was important, but they designed their colloquium "to facilitate encounter with *the tradition as embodied in the other.*" They wrote: "Our interest lay in providing ways participants might meet Judaism or Catholicism *as it was lived* by informed, committed Jewish and Catholic educators.[18] Their style was unmistakably relational.

Relationship is not a technique, although good relationships require skills, dispositions and attitudes to be life giving. The fundamental non-negotiable requirements of a relationship in the context of interreligious dialogue include a sense of self so that one is not dominated by another. It involves respect for the other as a religious person loved by God, not as a benighted believer to whom wisdom and insight must be dispensed. It assumes reciprocity—a natural give and take that leads to understanding that invariably leads to wider horizons, enhanced perspectives, and sometimes to an altered world view and a change of heart and mind.

Mutual transformation may be the long-range goal of interreligious dialogue,[19] but, on the other hand the starting point is understanding. David Lochhead explains it this way:

> The purpose of dialogue is understanding. . . . Understanding comes first. Yet if we think of understanding as something that happens in our heads and something that is confined to our heads, then understanding is not adequate to express the goal of dialogue. The word "integration" is intended to point to the fact that genuine understanding has implications for our life and practice. Integration is something that happens "in our guts." In dialogue, more than just our theory is transformed.[20]

If understanding comes first, it happens best when we hear our dialogue partners in their own voice. We know the power of sin to distort; we know how easy it is to cling to prejudices, stereotypes and "pre-mature" absolutes. The alternative is to listen to the self, to an understanding of the other and to welcome our dialogue partners with openness and trust. John Cobb offers this counsel:

We trust God for the needs of daily life. . . . We also trust that when we are truly open, when we surrender our defensiveness, when we allow the distortions of self-interest and fear to be set aside, we are led into deeper truth. The fullness of truth comes at the end. Now we see through a glass darkly. We must not absolutize what we see now for the sake of worldly security. We must be open to its change and transformation as we are led by the Spirit into new truth. Faith involves all of that. It cannot be clinging to the familiar, however comfortable that is.[21]

Half a century ago, the religious world took to heart Martin Buber's distinction between "I-Thou" and "I-It." The former is characterized by honesty, trust and openness, and the latter by a self-centeredness that does not allow room for the other and does not recognize the other as a person blessed by God.[22] With regret, the insight of Buber has not always been evident in inter-faith dialogue, but a permutation of his thought has surfaced in the thought of Thomas Green, and it seems to be catching on. Green writes of a "hermeneutic of the affections" and a readiness to listen "to the loves of others." He understands that listening to and understanding the other, even when we are disposed to do so, is not easy. The task is labor intensive. Strange texts, rituals, and traditions stretch our intellects but also at stake is a stretch of the affect: learning to hear with the ears of one's heart and to appreciate what the other "holds dear" in an encounter of commitments.[23]

The experience of encountering another tradition at the level of intensity proposed by Green, Cobb, Boys and Lee is often disorienting and destabilizing. For this reason Leonard Swidler proposes that "dialogue can take place only between equals—as Vatican [Council] II put it, *par cum pari*."[24] To their surprise, however, Mary Boys and Sara Lee found that some participants in the Catholic-Jewish Colloquium, even after careful screening before their acceptance, did not know their tradition as well as they thought. As a result, some experienced difficulty in addressing questions that presumed an entire context or that had a considerable degree of "affective attachment."[25] One participant wrote: "As I look at the roots of what I have believed and professed for all my life there are some very problematic areas which emerge. . . . This is, in many ways, frightening, threatening, uneasy, and at the same time exciting, challenging, and perhaps a new beginning."[26] To the disappointment of those who prefer a religion "with all the answers," this moment of enlightenment can open up an experience of "holy insecurity." While the term belongs to Martin Buber, Sandra Lubarsky uses it to refer to the recommitment we make to our own faith tradition after being challenged by questions from others and clarifying for ourselves our own beliefs.[27] The paradoxical nature of the term reflects the paradoxical nature of the experience.

Interreligious Dialogue: Real or Imagined Concerns?

As I write, I am aware that words like "holy insecurity," "religious pluralism," "openness to other faith traditions," and "mutual transformation" cause some people to feel uneasy because they equate these terms with "a wishy-washy relativism in which everyone has to agree on a watered-down version of something."[28] But these terms, according to John Cobb, do not mean "that faith is chasing after every ephemeral novelty in search of kicks. [They do] not mean that any of the deeply held convictions shaped by past Christian experience and reflection will be lightly set aside. [They do] not mean rebelliousness against the authority of the Church. [They do] not mean casual criticism of the Bible. [They do] not mean relativism."[29]

When she speaks about pluralism, Diana Eck clearly rejects relativism "when it means the lack of commitment to any particular community of faith." For relativists of this ilk, "there is no beloved community, no home in the context of which values are tested, no dream of the ongoing transformation of that community."[30] The pluralism of which Eck speaks is light years removed from relativism understood in this fashion. Pluralism results from dialogue by persons who have roots in a particular tradition, and in fact, it happens best with that grounding. Mary Boys phrases the equation this way: "A genuine religious pluralism depends upon a responsible particularism."[31]

Boys and Eck, among others, are aware that intellectual and spiritual formation and participation in one's religious tradition are part of a critical, intricate life-long process filled with tension and ambiguity. On one hand, because the formation process shapes our religious identity, it needs form, substance, structure and boundaries. But structures and boundaries ought not imprison us and close us in upon ourselves in a constricted world. Such impregnable boundaries link up with a fortress mentality where the goal is to protect and defend both people and things within the structure from people and things on the outside.

Significantly, one of the most popular images connected with the Second Vatican Council is of opened windows, pulled back draperies, and fresh air circulating in the Church. The clear message of the Council and Pope John XXIII was not to fear that either the structure or we would collapse by exposure to the world around us. In fact, an opposite optique pertained: we saw with God's eyes the enormous potential of the world to mirror more fully the love, compassion and justice of its Creator. Certainly we need boundaries or our identity evaporates. But by the same token, the boundaries cannot be so rigid, fixed and parochial that we suffocate.

Boys prefers the expression "permeable boundaries" to reflect the best of both worlds. Boundaries root us—they frame for us what we believe and what we do not believe. Boundaries are the invitation to personal appropriation of a life of faith—and for the Christian this means a life of relationship with God, Jesus and the Holy Spirit. But because the boundaries are permeable, a graceful reciprocity allows us to enter the differences in other religions. The "other," in David Tracy's way of looking at this give-and-take, becomes a disclosure of a new possibility and a new truth. In the context of interreligious dialogue, Tracy writes:

> In the to-and-fro movement of the game of conversation where the question
> or subject matter is allowed to "take over," we learn to abjure our constant

temptation to control all reality by reducing all difference to the "same" (viz., what "we" already believe). In that same to-and-fro movement of conversation, we learn to allow the other, the different, to become other for us—i.e., as a genuinely *possible* mode-of-being-in-the-world, as other, as different, as possible, thus as a similiarity-in-difference, an analogy.[32]

Mary Boys and Sara Lee write of an unexpected experience of the to-and-fro movement of which Tracy speaks. In the Catholic-Jewish Colloquium members of both traditions experienced "holy envy." It does not appear that New Testament scholar Krister Stendahl, who coined this expression, documented a definition of it in print, but Mary Boys educes from oral testimony that it has to do with "an experience of something so profound in the beliefs, rituals, polity, or practices of another tradition that one wishes her or his own community of faith also had (or practiced) it."[33] In the follow-up to the Catholic-Jewish Colloquium, a Jewish participant wrote of "holy envy" for the ease with which Catholics spoke of their spiritual lives; a Catholic participant experienced "holy envy" for the seriousness with which Jewish colleagues took the intellectual study of their tradition.

Although he does not use the term, Archbishop Joseph Pittau, S.J., captures the spirit of "holy envy" when he writes from twenty-nine years spent in Japan—as professor and rector-president of Sophia University, as Jesuit Provincial for Japan, as General Councillor and Regional Assistant for East Asia for the Jesuits—of an appreciation for the Buddhist tradition "of copying their sacred books, or else writing some ideograms, or even just one ideogram that has a profound significance. For example: love, life, joy, happiness."[34] He explains his involvement in this exercise:

> Each year, the students of Sophia University used to organize an exhibition of Japanese calligraphy. They would almost constrain me so that each year I, too, had to write something. It is an experience of prayer, because, before taking the brush in your hand, you have to sit on your heels, crouch down, turn into yourself, contemplate, then, almost as if inspired, as if touched by something, take the brush and write. They were simple things, however they were symbols that welled up from my heart and that seemed to touch the hearts of others.[35]

He wishes the practice could be adapted (or more accurately, recovered) in the Christian tradition.

Pittau also writes how living in Japan challenged him "to pray with the body, to form a body that prays." While attention to the body is not a novelty in the Judeo-Christian tradition, Pittau was introduced as a child to prayer at a time in our history when "the soul was idealised; the poor body was considered as an inferior—and dangerous—part." Living in Japan helped him "to understand that prayer is essentially an activity of the whole human person and that the posture of the body, the respiratory system, the bones, the blood, the head, the hands, the feet—all belong to God and all must be used in and for prayer."[36]

Clearly, relationships among people, and in prayer with God, also involve the emotions as our beliefs and values are disclosed, probed and challenged, or as we probe and challenge the beliefs of others. In one exercise with participants at the Catholic-Jewish Colloquium, Boys and Lee report on the use of the terms "First" and "Second" Testaments. As project leaders, they selected the terms because of their neutrality but they were unprepared for the fact that some Catholic educators had come to the colloquium with the assumption that the New Testament "fulfilled" the Old. They were caught off guard by the Jewish response to what sounded like a revival of supersessionist thinking. Emotions were on the alert, but a high enough degree of trust had developed among the participants so that serious engagement, even in difficult situations, was not only possible but ultimately growth producing.

In writing about emotional authenticity in dialogue, Nicholas Burbules emphasizes the critical role of "communicative virtues": perseverance, patience, receptivity to criticism, ability to be critical of another, self-control, and willingness to be a good listener.[37] Confrontations, cognitive and affective dissonance, disagreements, frustrations, tensions, anxieties, misinterpretations and personality conflicts are all part of life and therefore will be found in inter-faith dialogue. Perseverance and sustained commitment are key to any relationship, including the relationship that is part of the interreligious dialogue.

So, too, is humility. Having our deepest commitments tested, being open to other worlds, other visions of the transcendent, engaging in a to-and-fro dialogue that may lead to "holy insecurity" requires humility. Brazilian religious educator Paulo Freire speaks of it this way:

> How can I dialogue if I always project ignorance onto others and never perceive my own? How can I dialogue if I regard myself as a case apart from others—mere "it's" in whom I cannot recognize other "I's"? How can I dialogue if I consider myself a member of the in-group of "pure" men and women, the owners of truth and knowledge, for whom all non-members are "these people" or the "great unwashed"? How can I dialogue if I start from the premise that naming the world is the task of an elite and that the presence of the people in history is a sign of deterioration, and thus to be avoided? How can I dialogue if I am closed to—and even offended by—the contribution of others? How can I dialogue if I am afraid of being displaced, the mere possibility causing me torment and weakness? Self-sufficiency is incompatible with dialogue.[38]

In addition to providing wisdom and insight, Paulo Freire, as a citizen of Brazil, reminds us there is another world: the world of the poor, disenfranchised, and dispossessed. Is it possible that the religions of the world could reach out in relationship to this often forgotten world? Is it possible for a "liberative praxis," in the words of Paul Knitter, to inspire Hindus, Buddhists, Jews, Muslims and Christians to enlarge their frames of reference and work together to understand, analyze, and offer solutions to global injustices? Knitter proposes that if religions joined together in a common cause of changing the structures of oppression into communities of cooperation and unity, we would understand each other's scriptures and beliefs anew. He writes:

> Having heard and seen, for instance, how the Four Noble Truths or the nirvanic experience of *pratitya-samutpada* are enabling and directing Buddhist partners in the transformation of village life in Sri Lanka, Christians can come to appreciate and appropriate such beliefs/experiences in genuinely new and fruitful ways. And Buddhists will better grasp the Kingdom of God or resurrection-faith of Christians having experienced how it sustains their efforts for justice or their readiness to risk.[39]

Focusing the energies and imaginations of diverse religious traditions would allow for a dialogue based on compassion and care. "Progress" would be evaluated not by the canons or belief system of a particular religion but by the poor themselves. Knitter calls this the "hermeneutical privilege of the poor." "In the actual process of dialogue, what decides whether a particular symbol or belief or practice does promote liberation and welfare is not simply how strong a religion has claimed that it does, but what the poor and oppressed think of it—how much they find that it frees them or promotes their welfare."[40]

In a similar vein, Michael Amaladoss, S.J., reminds us that every religion has an inbuilt prophetic structure.[41] Certainly at this point in our collective history, with violence the daily fare in too many places in our world, prophetic voices need to be encouraged. It would be a most fitting time for prophets from all religions to voice a collective regard for humankind and to raise the level of interreligious dialogue in the cause of peace.

There are hard messages of conversion, forgiveness, and reconciliation to be announced by the prophets. And there are difficult messages to be appropriated and acted upon by the rest of us. But the Spirit of God has always been with us to enliven, sustain, empower, enlighten, comfort, fill, and support our efforts. The word for Spirit in Hebrew is *ruach*, which means breath or wind. Diana Eck reminds us that "it is a feminine noun, and it is employed in the first verses of Genesis to speak of the mothering, life-giving Spirit of God that hovered, brooded over the deep at the dawn of creation."[42] Never abstract, Spirit language is intimate, personal and relational. Heribert Mühlen calls the Spirit a "we-maker,"[43] and Bishop John V. Taylor appropriates similar relational terminology by referring to the Holy Spirit as "the go-between God."[44]

Our world needs a "we-maker" to counter those who would divide us by race, nationality or religion. And our world needs a "go-between God" to bind wounds, so that healing, wholeness and strength guide religions in the fragile dialogue taking place. Most of all, perhaps, we need the Spirit to brood with us, as new language and new ways of thinking about our religious partners are born.

References

[1]David Tracy, "Christianity in the Wider Context: Demands and Transformations," *Religion and Intellectual Life* 4 (1987), 9.

[2]See Diana Eck, *A New Religious America: How a "Christian Country" Has Become the World's Most Religiously Diverse Nation* (San Francisco: HarperSanFrancisco, 2001). Eck writes about Cleveland: "One of America's spectacular new mosques is in the suburbs of Cleveland" (21).

[3]Monika K. Hellwig, "The Thrust and Tenor of Our Conversations," in Leonard Swidler, John B. Cobb, Jr., Paul F. Knitter, and Monica K. Hellwig, *Death or Dialogue?: From the Age of Monologue to the Age of Dialogue* (London: SCM Press, 1990), 51.

[4]Diana Eck, *Encountering God: A Spiritual Journey from Bozeman to Banares* (Boston: Beacon Press, 1993), 16.

[5]But recognition of God's presence does not always happen. Eck writes: "Recognizing God is not an easy task. It is not the simple affirmation that all these visions of God are the same—they are not. And there are places and communities where I as a Christian do not have the experience of recognition. For me to recognize God as I know God in Vishnu or Shiva and for Mr. Gangadaran to recognize Shiva in Christian worship and language . . . can only be the fruit of a real encounter. There are no easy, uncritical theological equations here. Yet as we are open to real encounter in the give-and-take of learning and un-learning our recognition of the one we call 'God' can only become larger and clearer" (*Encountering God*, 80).

[6]Eck, *Encountering God,* 79.

[7]Terrence Merrigan, "Exploring the Frontiers: Jacques Dupuis and the Movement 'Toward a Christian Theology of Religious Pluralism,' " in *Louvain Studies* 23 (1998), 338-59.

[8]Jacques Dupuis, *Toward a Christian Theology of Religious Pluralism* (Maryknoll, N.Y.: Orbis, 1997), 211.

[9]Documents of Vatican Council II are available at the Vatican web site: www.vatican.va. All official documents of John Paul II including Apostolic Constitutions, Apostolic Exhortations, Encyclicals, Homilies, Letters, and Messages are likewise available through the Vatican web site.

[10]*Redemptoris Missio,* no. 56.

[11]Jacques Dupuis, "The Storm of the Spirit," *The Tablet* (October 20, 2001), 1484.

[12]The travels of Pope John Paul II are chronicled on the Vatican web site: www.vatican.va.

[13]See "Day of Pardon, 12 March, 2000," on the Vatican web site: www.vatican.va.

[14]*A Rahner Reader*, edited by Gerald A. McCool (New York: Seabury Press, 1975), 183.

[15]Karl Rahner, "On the Importance of the Non-Christian Religions for Salvation," *Theological Investigations*, vol. 18 (New York: Crossroad, 1983), 291.

[16]Eck, *Encountering God*, 16.

[17]Ibid.

[18]Mary C. Boys and Sara S. Lee, "The Catholic-Jewish Colloquium: An Experiment in Interreligious Learning," *Religious Education* 91 (1996), 425.

[19]John B. Cobb, Jr., uses the language of "mutual transformation" as the goal of interreligious dialogue. See his *Beyond Dialogue: Toward a Mutual Transformation of Christianity and Buddhism* (Philadelphia: Fortress Press, 1982).

[20]David Lochhead, *The Dialogical Imperative: A Christian Reflection on Interfaith Encounter* (Maryknoll, N.Y.: Orbis, 1988), 65, 67.

[21]John B. Cobb, Jr., "Dialogue," in John B. Cobb et al., eds., *Death or Dialogue*, 7.

[22]Martin Buber, *I and Thou* (New York: Charles Scribner's Sons, 1958).

[23]Thomas Green, cited in James Wiggins, *In Praise of Religious Diversity* (New York: Routledge, 1996), 95.

[24]Leonard Swidler, "Interreligious and Interideological Dialogue: The Matrix for All Systematic Reflection Today," in *Toward a Universal Theory of Religion*, in Leonard Swidler (ed.) (Maryknoll, NY: Orbis, 1987), 15. See also Leonard Swidler, "A Dialogue on Dialogue," *Death or Dialogue: From the Age of Monologue to the Age of Dialogue*. Swidler writes that any level of knowledge or education, as long as these are equal for the partners in dialogue, is acceptable. But he cautions that it is important "that the dialogue partners be more or less equal in knowledge of their own traditions, etc. The greater the asymmetry, the less communication will be two-way, that is, dialogic" (60).

[25]Boys and Lee, "The Catholic-Jewish Colloquium: An Experiment in Interreligious Learning," 438.

[26]Ibid.

[27]Sandra Lubarsky, "Dialogue: Holy Insecurity," *Religious Education* 91 (1996), 545.

[28]"One Nation under Which God?" An Interview with Diana Eck, *U.S. Catholic*, September 2001, 23. Eck responds to an interviewer's question about the document *Dominus Iesus:* "Since the Second Vatican Council, the Catholic Church has moved forward very significantly in interreligious relations on several fronts. The Pontifical Council for Interreligious Dialogue has done some very careful work on thinking about proclamation and witness in relation to other religions. And the Church has also made great strides through participation in intermonastic dialogue.

"At the same time this has made some people like Cardinal Ratzinger very nervous. Like his office's earlier document condemning Buddhist- or Hindu-oriented meditation for Catholics, *Dominus Iesus* is meant as a word of caution in a Church that actually is not at all cautionary in other ways.

"The Catholic Church and the Vatican, like all communities, can sometimes seem like a hydra-headed being—with one mouth it's producing *Dominus Iesus* while another head is profoundly engaged in intermonastic encounter. To some extent, the response of *Dominus Iesus* is a barometer of the fact that inter-faith encounter is a major issue in the Catholic Church today" (23-24).

[29]Cobb, "Dialogue," 7.

[30]Eck, *Encountering God*, 195.

[31]Mary C. Boys, "The 'Other' as Partner," *Encounter* 59 (1998), 327.

[32]Tracy, "Christianity in the Wider Context: Demands and Transformations," 18. See also David Tracy, *Plurality and Ambiguity: Hermeneutics, Religion, Hope* (New York: Harper and Row, 1987), and *Dialogue with the Other: The Inter-Religious Dialogue*, Louvain Theological and Pastoral Monographs 1 (Louvain: Peeters Press, 1990).

[33]Mary C. Boys, *Jewish-Christian Dialogue: One Woman's Experience* (New York/Mahwah, N.J.: Paulist Press, 1997), 57.

[34]Joseph Pittau, S.J., "Western Prayer and Eastern Prayer," an address given at The Second International Conference for Rectors of Roman Catholic Major Seminaries sponsored by *The Cardinal Suenens Center*, John Carroll University, in Rome, Italy, 22 January, 2002. The complete text of his address may be found on our web site: www.suenens.org.

[35]See above, Pittau, "Western Prayer and Eastern Prayer." At the same time that he writes appreciatively of this prayerful exercise of calligraphy in Japan, Pittau is aware of the history of the transcription of the Bible done entirely by hand by Christian monks.

[36]Ibid.

[37]Nicholas C. Burbules, *Dialogue in Teaching: Theory and Practice* (New York: Teachers College Press, 1993), 42.

[38]Paulo Freire, *Pedagogy of the Oppressed* (New York: Seabury, 1970), 78-79.

[39]Paul F. Knitter, "Interreligious Dialogue: What? Why? How?," in *Death or Dialogue: From the Age of Monologue to the Age of Dialogue,* 35.

[40]Ibid., 38.

[41]Michael Amaladoss, S.J., "Religions for Peace," *America*, December 10, 2001, 6. See also idem, *Life in Freedom: Liberation Theologies from Asia* (Maryknoll, N.Y.: Orbis, 1997), and *Mission Today: Reflections from an Ignatian Perspective* (Rome: Centrum Ignatianum Spiritualitatis, 1989).

[42]Eck, *Encountering God*, 120.

[43]Heribert Mühlen, *L'Esprit dans l' Eglise*, traduit de l'allemand par A. Liefooghe, M. Massart et R. Virron (Paris: Cerf, 1969).

[44]John V. Taylor, *The Go-between God: the Holy Spirit and the Christian Mission* (London: SCM Press, 1972).

12

Jacques Dupuis and Swami Abhishiktananda

George Gispert-Sauch, S.J.

This contribution to a work honoring Fr. Jacques Dupuis takes for granted what all his readers will have noticed at least in passing: that his theological output is intimately linked to his thirty-six year experience of India and its theological tradition. Unlike most western theologians, Dupuis studied, thought and taught in India. It is normal but important to be aware that his theological thinking has been partly shaped by this country. A look at his bibliographies will reveal how even in his later academic career in Rome he has kept in contact with the Indian theological output.

More specifically, I shall try to bring out here his personal and intellectual contacts with the contemplative Swami Abhishiktananda. Dupuis is one of the few serious interpreters in the West of the intuitions of the Indian-French *sannyasi* whose life and experience in India partially coincided with Dupuis's own, even though, if I am not mistaken, it was largely in the last four years of Abhishiktananda's life that the two came into personal contact and, one dares to say, became attached to each other.

Two Parallel Lives Meet

Exactly one year after India's Independence, on August 16,1948, Dom Henri Le Saux, O.S.B., arrived in South India, after sailing from Europe to Colombo, a mature 38-year-old monk, with nearly twenty years experience of contemplative life and thirteen of priesthood. He came at the invitation of the bishop of Tiruchirappalli to start a contemplative ashram with his compatriot Abbé Jules Monchanin. They envisaged it in the tradition of St. Benedict, but wholly Indian in style. Soon the Indian experience transformed Dom Le Saux into Swami Abhishiktananda, a wandering *sannyasi* in search of the ultimate experience the Upanishads offer. This solitary monk, an expression of India's flesh and spirit, became a symbol of the human search for experiencing the Divine, until he attained *samadhi* on December 7, 1973.

A Belgian Jesuit scholastic thirteen years younger than the French Benedictine, Jacques Dupuis landed in the then Calcutta (now Kolkata) a few months after Abhishiktananda reached South India, and was at once put to learn Bengali and to teach in one of the schools the Jesuits run in the large metropolis. He had been eight years a Jesuit and joined a century-old Jesuit mission, at the time consisting of some 200 members from India and such other countries as Belgium, Canada, Croatia, Italy, Luxembourg and Malta. His vocation would remain essentially institutional and creative, at the service of the Church and its mission. But it was forever marked by his early contact with Bengal, its language and culture, and sharpened by his years of theological studies (1952-1955) in St. Mary's College, Kurseong (hundreds of miles north of Calcutta and in sight of the Himalayas), where he was ordained a priest in 1954. Here he would become, after his doctorate in Rome, a theologian of the Asian Church, helping it in the transition from the pre-Vatican to the post-Vatican eras. He taught theology in India from 1959 until 1984, eleven years beyond Swamiji's death, when he was called to teach theology in the Gregorian University of Rome. He kept a close contact with the happenings on the Asian scene and, from his chair at the Gregorian, directed many doctoral theses and other pieces of research on Asian and on specifically Indian themes.

If I am not mistaken, Abhishiktananda and Dupuis first began close contacts in October 1969 at the ecumenical *Jyotiniketan Ashram* founded by the Rev. Murray Rogers, his wife Mary and friend Heather, near Bareilly in North India. There Dupuis, Abhishiktananda and Rogers discussed a possible follow-up of the Church in India Seminar that had been held in Bangalore in May of the same year. Dupuis showed interest in the project of setting up what Abhishiktananda called an Ashram seminary and was later referred to as a "pilot seminary." At this stage the plan envisaged an ecumenical ashram (possibly a continuation of *Jyotiniketan* enlarged with Roman Catholic members), a center for priestly formation run in the spirit of Indian ashrams, and a dialogue center. As James Stuart says, "Fr Dupuis was specially interested in having a center where experiments could be made in training clergy on new lines."[1] Swamiji had been long involved in inculturation for an Indian Mass. The new project, however, went far beyond liturgical innovation: it envisaged a center where priests would be formed with a radical inculturation. The proposal, eventually presented to the bishops, was not found feasible. The idea, however, remained floating in the Indian Church and took different forms as when, after the report of an Inculturation Commission they had appointed, the Jesuits began from 1978 onwards to set up regional theological centers and forms of seminary formation closer to the people.

Abhishiktananda in the Opus of Dupuis

Even before their contacts increased in 1969, Dupuis knew Abhishiktananda and his writings, which had begun appearing in the fifties. Dupuis's cyclostiled class notes on Christology (a very rich text completed in early 1967) mention *Sagesse hindoue mystere* [sic] *chretien* which had been published in Paris in 1965.

In 1971 Dupuis completed his class notes on the Trinity: here he not only includes *Sagesse hindoue et* [sic] *mystique chretienne* in the bibliography of the section on "Hindu presentiments of the Trinity," but also in the section on "Trinity and Religious Dialogue" he explains some of the basic insights of *Sagesse.*

His interest in Abhishiktananda became much more evident after 1969. In 1973 he contributed an article under the title "The Cosmic Influence of the Holy Spirit and the Gospel Message" (pp. 117-38) to a volume in honor of Fr. Joseph Putz and other professors of St. Mary's College, Kurseong/Vidyajyoti, Delhi, which I edited and entitled *God's Word among Men* (Delhi: Vidyajyoti, 1973 [belated apologies for the exclusive language!]). The Holy Spirit had been one of the main topics of interest to the theologian Dupuis. In this article he proposes that the awareness of the role of the Spirit may be the key to a theological understanding of other religions including their scriptures and sacraments. Towards the conclusion he notes that

> [a]mong the non-Christian religions some appear specially sensitive to the values of interiority and of the person's self-transcendence in God. Such religious traditions, however inadequate, may bear a special witness to the secret presence of the Spirit in men's hearts, and constitute precious stepping-stones for His open recognition in Christ. The religious tradition of Hinduism is a case in point. (136-37)

At this point a footnote cites the article by Abhishiktananda, "An Approach to Hindu Spirituality."[2] While the metaphor of stepping-stones may derive from P. Charles, "interiority" and "self-transcendence" echo the language of Abhishiktananda. More importantly, on the same page the Holy Spirit is alluded to as "the mystery of divine intimacy, of the togetherness or 'non-duality' (*advaita*) of Father and Son, and, consequently, of the 'non-duality' of God and man," and here we have another reference to Dom Le Saux, *Sagesse hindoue, mystique chretienne* (Paris, 1965). The use of the language of *advaita* in connection with the Trinity was bold for a Catholic theologian thirty years ago. It may possibly have been criticized by those to whom the Festschrift was offered, Dupuis's much respected mentors in the Faculty of Kurseong, who had earlier taken a rather cold attitude towards the theological ventures of the French monk. In spite of its ambiguity, Dupuis "receives" this terminology of the mystic and integrates it in a solid theological essay meant to offer a Christian understanding of the mystery of God as communion and of the insertion of humanity into that mystery, both fruits of the operation and action of the Spirit of God. The reflection is enriched by a quotation from the Eastern theologian O. Clement, who says that the Holy Spirit makes Christ present and the cosmos resurrected.

In 1972 the St. Mary's Theological Faculty moved from Kurseong to Delhi where Dupuis met Abhishiktananda a number of times. He even persuaded Abhishiktananda to agree to visit the Faculty and deliver to the students some lectures on Christology and the Trinity from an Indian perspective. It was a sign of the growing trust between the Swami and the Professor that Abhishiktananda, ever reluctant to indulge in public lectures and never comfortable in the academic world he so often criticized, agreed, though reluctantly, to give the lectures. Unfortunately a heart attack in July 1973 and his passing to the "Further Shore" in December of the same year prevented the realization of the plan. After his death, manuscript notes were found among the papers of the Swami written in preparation for those lectures. These notes were incomplete and had not yet taken the form of lectures. They were just jottings of some ideas the Swami intended to put forward. The notes, carefully translated into English and annotated by Fr. James Stuart, were later published in the *Vidyajyoti Journal*.[3]

In the fall of 1977, four years after the death of Swamiji, Dupuis published in *Revue theologique de Louvain* (8 [1977], 448-60) a theological note entitled "Conscience du Christ et experience de l'Advaita." The search into the human consciousness of Jesus had been earlier a point of interest for the professor of Christology. It had led him to pay particular attention to the role of *experience* in the theological task. Thus, in the 1969 meeting of the now defunct Indian Christian Theological Association, he had presented a paper on "Knowing Christ through the Christian Experience."[4] Experience is essential to the Christian faith, the experience of our being children of God in Christ. Experience is not opposed to faith: on the contrary, faith *is* the experience Jesus Christ enables us to have. These rich pages were most probably written before Dupuis met Abhishiktananda later the same year, and do not betray any significant influence from the Swami's writings. Nor do they contain any reference to the Upanishads or the Indian experience. But there is already a point of convergence and the encounter of the two will help to develop Dupuis's understanding of the significance of experience in Christian life.

The 1977 article in *RTL* shows clearly that a dialogue in depth has taken place between the theologian and the monk. Even the title shows it. In the terminology used we find not only the word "experience," but also the more descriptive expression *eveil*, "awakening," which is a typical word in Abhishiktananda's Journal and other writings. "Awakening" translates the Sanskrit verb *budh, bodhati*, whose meaning includes the idea of waking up and that of awareness, noticing, or understanding. The passive participle *buddha* designates the one who under a *ficus religiosa* was *awakened* (at times translated as *illumined*) to an understanding of reality formulated in the "four noble truths." *Eveil* has now entered explicitly into Dupuis's theological vocabulary to denote the result of grace, the action of God in and through Christ. The word seems to suggest a process of bringing to consciousness rather than creating a different reality or a new relationship. However, one could also say that this consciousness itself is a new creation.

This article has four sections. The first analyzes the pre-Easter consciousness of the historical Jesus as far as we can perceive it through the post-Easter records of his disciples. For Dupuis the central element of this consciousness was that Jesus related to God as Father: the Abba consciousness. Sonship involves both distance or a relationship of difference—*"I and the Father"*—and closeness and intimacy, which John expresses as oneness—*"are one."* Dupuis does not think that in Jesus this oneness indicates merely that Jesus shares in the mission of the Father; for if "never has any one spoken like this" (Jn 7:46), it is because no one had the same intimate relation with God. This oneness thus involves "a mutual immanence" and therefore mutual knowledge and mutual love, and finds expression in the total obedience of the man Jesus to the Father's will. The roots of this human consciousness of Jesus are sought in the eternal begetting of the Word. Jesus' "sense of a total dependence on the Father is a human echo of a deeper origin" (452). It is because of this deep union of Jesus with the Father that he not only speaks the words of God to us but also *is* the Word of God with us, the total revelation. Yet, being human, Jesus' revelation cannot exhaust the mystery of the Father: it must remain "limited, incomplete and imperfect."

From this Dupuis passes on to analyze the Advaita experience of the Upanishads, specially expressed in the "great sayings" *aham brahma asmi* and *tat tvam asi* ("I am Brahman" and "Thou art That") of the Brhad Aranyaka and the Chandogya, respectively, sayings that can be dated around the seventh or sixth century BCE. He also alludes to the teaching of the modern sage Ramana Maharshi as reported by Abhishiktananda. Here Dupuis indicates that the intention of the Indian *advaita* is to reach the divine consciousness itself, to know as the Absolute alone can experience Itself, and in that absolute experience to realize the vacuity of all created existence. The third section of the article compares the experiences of the Upanishads and the Gospels and shows how they differ and yet how one enables us to better understand the other. Paradoxically, he says, it is in Jesus that the Upanishadic experience finds its truest application. No one can affirm more truly that "I am Brahman" than he who shares the same nature with the Father from all eternity. Here again Dupuis quotes abundantly from *Sagesse* and from *La rencontre*, the two theological works which Swamiji would partially disown in his later life. (However, a closer reading of *Sannyasa* shows that this level of reflection does not totally disappear even in the later years, in spite of Abhishiktananda's frequent critique of the *nama-rupa* level of conceptual theology.)

The last section of this study shows how the Christian too is called to share in the experience of the sonship of Jesus and therefore can also in a way make his or her own Jesus' *advaita* experience. There is here a "Christian *advaita*" which surely differs from the *advaita* described in the Upanishads. But this does not mean that Christians do not learn anything from the teachings of the Upanishads. They can

> learn from the religious experience of the Hindu sages—and from the self-manifestation of God to them—that communion in and with the Divine Reality cannot be understood after the model of finite communion. When in Jesus the Christian says "Thou" to the Father, the influence of the Upanishadic experience of Brahman-Atman helps him to be conscious that the "Father" is also the "Ground of being," the Self (*Soi*) at the centre of me. (64)

Clearly in this reflection Dupuis draws much from the mature works of Abhishiktananda, exposes it with the clarity of thought so characteristic of him, and enriches the teaching by references to the ancient Christian tradition.

Fr. Dupuis's most serious study of Abhishiktananda is probably his "Introduction" to *Interiorité et revelation. Essais theologiques* par Henri Le Saux, Swami Abhishiktananda.[5] The Introduction, signed Vidyajyoti, March 1980, is found on pp. 11-34 of the book. Much of this serious study is also found as chapter 3 of *Jesus Christ a la rencontre des religions,*[6] in English, *Jesus Christ at the Encounter of World Religions.*[7] Here I shall first give a short account of the 1980 "Introduction" taking into consideration its use in Dupuis's later books. After this I shall glance at other references to the Indian tradition which Dupuis makes in his books of 1989/1991 and which collect some material he had used in his early teaching career in Kurseong and Delhi.

Dupuis introduces Abhishiktananda as the man who came to India with a contemplative vocation and after his visits to Ramana Maharshi developed a desire to enter personally, and not merely by study, into the religious experience of India. Abhishiktananda wants not merely to inculturate Christian monasticism or even Christian theology in India. He wants to share in and be transformed by Indian spirituality. A Benedictine monk, he has been in search of God and is ready to be "shocked" by the Hindu mystical experience. He must feel it directly, in himself. An authentic experience of the Divine must be self-validating; and if there is a variety of such experiences, since they all touch the Real, they must be compatible. India called Abhishiktananda to the special vocation of being a Hindu-Christian monk, with a renunciation at least similar to that of the authentic sadhus in India, who voluntarily live in total detachment from material comforts and endeavor to empty their minds of all content in order to directly realize the Absolute that is beyond all name and form. This experience must occupy the place invaded by theology. For Abhishiktananda dialogue meant experimenting with *advaita.*

Following the pages of Abhishiktananda's Journal, at that time still unpublished, Dupuis speaks of the deeper light emerging from his double experience and of the "immense joy" that the Swami feels. However, there is a crucifying tension and conflict between his Christian upbringing which he loves so much and the Upanishads about which also he has a total conviction: "The experience of the Upanishads is true. I know it!," he writes in his Diary toward the end of his life (May 11, 1972). If Brahman alone is really true, does the Christian relegate the whole history of salvation, including the Lord Jesus himself, to the realm of the merely historical, a lesser truth than the Truth of the Absolute Self? The inner struggle is intense and lasting: "I cannot be a Hindu and Christian at the same time, nor can I be simply a Hindu or simply a Christian," he wrote already in 1957. In 1970 he will note: "[Between] Christianity and *advaita,* neither opposition nor incompatibility. Two different planes. *Advaita* is opposed to nothing whatsoever." Yet then he reduces the Christian *darsana* (vision) to the order of the empirical world, not to the Absolute. In the year of his death he will note: "Trying to come up with a new [Vedantic] Trinitarian theology [as he had attempted in *Sagesse*] leads us down blind alleys. It is replacing *theos* with *theologia,* and confusing the notion of God with God. My whole *Sagesse* theme crumbles, and in this total crumbling—the awakening." His faith leads him through dark valleys. But he continues trusting experience, though always ready to critique any formulation of it. In *Jesus Christ* Dupuis quotes here from the Swami's small book *Prayer*:[8]

> Nothing can . . . content [the soul] apart from God in himself. Yet it is incapable of attaining to this until it has become willing to pass beyond itself and to plunge and be lost in the very abyss of God. Then it is that it understands that silence is the loftiest and truest praise: *Silentium tibi laus.* [The soul] itself is now but silence, a silence to which it has been introduced by recollection in its remotest depths and the calming of its inner activity, but a silence that the Spirit now causes to ring with the echo of the eternal Word, a silence all expectancy, a simple regard toward the One who is there, simple attention, simple awakening.

Dupuis shows that at this stage *advaita* does not mean monism or denial of the world. But the world of rites and of theology, even the world of adoration of the personal God, is not the Absolute truth: it is only a reflection of the Truth. The sage must live in both worlds but each at its level. This is Abhishiktananda's living *advaita.* As a living spirituality, it did not seem to produce any fissure in him—he was a very wholesome personality; as an intellectual search the integration of both planes always remained a problem. It was even a drama, as it seemed to belittle what was the core of his faith life: the Eucharist, to which he was faithful till the end in spite of the inner tension he felt between it and the *advaita* spirituality. "His whole life was marked by a search of an ever elusive synthesis, never completed except in the 'discovery of the Grail' which took him away" (18). His spiritual adventure was his theology: he did not need to elaborate a mental synthesis—this was not his vocation. His was a vocation of liminality, of crossing frontiers: "It is still best, I think, to hold, even in extreme tension, these two forms of a single 'faith', until the dawn appears," he wrote to his great friend Odette Baumer on December 12, 1970. In a recent article Amaladoss wants us to look at the world with bifocals, so that we see Reality both as historically true and as transcendent, analogous to some teachings of the Buddhist and Hindu traditions.[9]

Clearly Abhishiktananda goes beyond inculturation. He aims at sharing both the Hindu and the Christian experiences, at being himself the furnace where these two great traditions melt and perhaps even fuse with one another. The way there is not by theological synthesis but by mystical depth.

Dupuis classifies Abhishiktananda's reflections into some clear stages:

1. At the level of *Sagesse, Advaita* and Trinity are harmonised. *Advaita* teaches us that the Trinitarian relations are well beyond our concepts, and the Trinity reveals the fullness of life of the One without a second. "Advaita simplifies

the Trinity; the Trinity enlarges Advaita," Dupuis wrote pithily in his preface to the second French edition of *Sagesse*.[10] He says Trinity and Advaita lived here in a symbiosis rather than as a synthesis. No threat to the Christian faith. Assimilation of some aspects of the Hindu tradition which conform to it. The later Abhishiktananda will find this work too intellectual, too "Greek."

2. There is a contrast between *nama-rupa* or the world of appearances and multiplicity and the Absolute Reality of the Eternal. To the former belong all history, with its truth, its dogmas, its liturgies, its adoration (based on dualism). Advaita belongs to the other level, the *paramarthika*, the Absolute, to which no dogma can belong, not even the Trinity. Jesus of history belongs to the *nama-rupa*. However, he does not disappear or become inconsequential: he is "an ephemeral, phenomenal manifestation of the real Christ of faith" (78).

3. The Christ of faith is revealed in the religious psychology of Jesus: his Abba and his "I am" sayings. His Abba consciousness is interpreted as the Hebrew expression of total nearness which can only be identity. "Jesus discovered that Yahweh's 'I am' belonged to him." Inversely, in discovering the meaning of his existence, "I am" (reminiscences of Ramana Maharshi!), he "discovered the true, total, unimaginable sense of the name of Yahweh." That is *advaita*. Jesus had the *advaita* experience.

4. How then is Jesus Savior? By being paradigmatic. He shows the way every human being must go. He is the symbol and every symbol is unique and universal. "He is the guru who proclaims the mystery." He is the mirror I adore, love and consecrate myself to, and in doing so "I have recognized myself." Jesus' uniqueness is a false problem. He is the manifestation of the eternal mystery of awakening, the "ignition point" where the non-manifest becomes manifest, realized. His universality is based precisely on his very non-duality with every human being, and each one must discover the "I am."

Dupuis, the Critic of Abhishiktananda

Dupuis does more than summarize and interpret the reflections of the mystic. In a "critical evaluation" he enters into a dialogue with him, after noting Abhishiktananda's acknowledgment of the provisional character of his reflections and his denial of having formulated a theology. By definition *advaita* is not a theology.

Dupuis first questions the dichotomy the Swamiji makes between experience and expression. While accepting that conceptual understanding is never adequate to the experience, Dupuis asks whether any experience is ever totally dissociated from a conceptual apparatus. Have we to say that there is only one experience of God, and that all differences derive from conceptual interpretations? Or can there be different experiences of the Divine? And is any of them totally dissociated from concepts, mental or verbal, with which they are present to our consciousness? A psychology of knowledge is at stake in this double question.

Secondly, is Jesus' consciousness really the *advaita* of Abhishiktananda? The "I am" of Jesus, is it the "I am" of a solipsistic God the Father *reflected* in Jesus but leaving no space for the creature Jesus? Or is it an "I am" of the Son who affirms an identity of being with the Father and yet remains *related* to Him as Son?

The final question regards God's own affirmation of history. Compared to the eternity of God, historical existence seems to be weak and almost unworthy of consideration. But if a divine revelation affirms history and the material universe, are we not to embrace and accept history with the passion with which God has embraced it—a passion indeed in the double sense of the word? One could add that this divine affirmation of Jesus and, with him, of all history and even of all material existence seems to be implied in the mystery of the Ascension, wherein the human Jesus becomes the risen Lord "sitting at the right hand of the Father." The language is crudely symbolic, even mythological. The faith it communicates is the faith in a God who lovingly affirms the human expression of his Son and gives it eternal, *paramarthika,* validity (the "right hand")—and with it the whole of history is redeemed from its vanity, its *maya.*

Dupuis gives witness to the "glimmers of [the] dawn" beyond the night of the spirit that transformed Abhishiktananda in his last years. Abhishiktananda seems to recover the taste and joys of ritual and symbolism, specially in the *diksha* (rite of renunciation) of his disciple Marc which he concelebrated with a Hindu monk Swami Cidananda. There seemed to be a new balance in his life, manifested even in the radiance of his countenance. Dupuis quotes an unpublished section of a letter Abhishiktananda wrote from Gyansu to his old friend Dom Emile Landry, O.S.B., at Kerganon:

> Joy abides, grows, deepens in ever more intimate discovery of the essential. . . . The approaches are intoxicating. They cut you off from everything, but they reveal everything, like the nights of St John of the Cross. Overleaping limits—night for the mental only, when it seeks to understand and report its categories of the Real. Heady wine, that you fear to share. It overthrows everything. . . . Here, in solitude without and within, the solitude of the Only [One], in the transcendence of all uttering and all thinking, you understand *eimi,* "I am"—the name under which Yahweh revealed himself. Then Easter becomes awakening to nothing new, but to what is—to that reality that has neither origin nor end. (April 21, 1973)

In the last important book by Fr. Dupuis, *Toward a Christian Theology of Religious Pluralism,*[11] the explicit presence of Abhishiktanada is more discreet. Dupuis seeks here a theology of pluralism for our planet. The Christological question is of course central to it. Here eleven pages are devoted to "Hindu Mysticism and Christian Mystery" wherein Dupuis discusses the question of Advaita, Saccidananda and the complementarity or even convergence of the various expressions of the face of the Divine found in the religious traditions of humanity. In his explanation of the Indian tradition he continues in the line of Abhishiktananda, but is not confined to him.

Dupuis and India

This essay is not meant to be a theological critique of Fr. Dupuis or of Swami Abhishiktananda. It wants only to point out that the theologian and the monk, whose careers in India largely overlapped, had a certain spiritual symbiosis and complemented one another. It is true that we have looked at the matter mostly from the writings of Fr. Dupuis. In vain we would search for explicit references to the theology of Dupuis in the writings of Abhishiktananda. Only one letter (and one postcard) from him to Fr. Dupuis have been preserved in the Archives of the Abhishiktananda Society. In vain will we search for Dupuis's name in the published selections of Abhishiktananda's Journal, who at any rate does not refer much to contemporary theologians. The relation between the two may have been asymmetrical. But it did exist, both at the personal level and at the level of theological reflection. Abhishiktananda was not a theologian, but a contemplative in search of inner silence and the experience of the Divine. He professed to care little for ideas, though he was constantly wrestling with them. The theologian on the other hand had to root his reflection in the experience of India. For Dupuis, for nearly forty years a teacher (1959-98), the Indian theological and mystical tradition was of great importance, a theological source. Abhishiktananda, who lived as a Hindu-Christian and was intellectually very alive, had precious insights into Indian spirituality. Dupuis became his interpreter in various ways—at the personal level, in his didactic work, in his writings.

We must not, however, think that Abhishiktananda was the only source from which Dupuis drew on the Indian tradition. We have mentioned in passing his personal Indian experience and his wide reading in Hinduism, specially in what has been termed "The Renaissance of Hinduism" of the last two centuries. His chapter on Abhishiktananda in *Jesus Christ a la rencontre des religions* (26 pp.) is preceded by two significant chapters. The first, "The 'Unbound' Christ Acknowledged in Hinduism" (37 pp.), is quite insightful in presenting the Hindu understandings of Jesus Christ. The other on "Hindu and Christian Christologies: Doctrines in Dialogue" (21 pp.) reflects on the role of Yoga and Advaita in our understanding of Christ. These are important contributions. As mentioned above, Dupuis is at present one of the few theologians in the West sufficiently trained to establish a serious dialogue between the Hindu theological tradition and the Christian faith, as well as a dialogue between Indian Christian theology where he has been present for a long time and western theology, including that of Rome.

However, not all aspects of Indian theology are sufficiently reflected in his work. Many in India may regret that there is little evidence of, appreciation for and reflection on Dalit and Tribal theologies. No one can of course be equally competent in all spheres of theology. These last trends of theology have developed in India mostly after the departure of Dupuis to teach at the Gregorian University. His training has not been in the sociology of religions, which is so important as a basis for understanding such peoples' theologies. Nor has Dupuis been particularly interested in the Latin American liberation theology, although he is certainly well informed about it. The focus of his publications has been the encounter of religions rather than the conflict of classes.

A New Alexandria

In 1877 the University of Cambridge started what was called "The Cambridge Mission in Delhi" under the inspiration of a biblical scholar, Dr. Brooke Foss Westcott, later Bishop of Durham. Westcott conceived the idea of a mission in Delhi whose focus would be education and dialogue. Dialogue meant interpreting the faith of the West to the East. But equally important was the conviction that "the West has much to learn from the East, and the lesson will not be taught till we hear the truth as it is apprehended by Eastern minds."[12] Westcott's vision was that of a "New Alexandria" in Delhi: "At Alexandria in the first ages the Faith found its widest and most philosophic expression through Origen and Athanasius; as we are encouraged to do, we therefore welcome the past as the omen of the future," said Westcott. For him the Cambridge Mission, now known as The Brotherhood of the Ascended Christ, "should not just be a center of learning, but also the means whereby Christianity could be interpreted into the terms of Indian philosophy and thought."[13] This could be done only through education.

For a century and a quarter of its presence in Delhi the Brotherhood has been faithful to that initial inspiration. It has indeed engaged in pastoral work as the circumstances of the time demanded. But it also served with much dedication St. Stephen's College, a leading academic institution in what had been the capital of the Mughal empire, and was from 1912 the capital of British and Independent India. The Brotherhood was also involved with the Indian Society for Promoting Christian Knowledge (ISPCK) which has published much material on Indian Christian thinking and dialogue, including the English works of Swami Abhishiktananda. People of the caliber of G. A. Lefroy (later Bishop of Lahore and eventually Bishop of Calcutta and Metropolitan of India) and C. F. Andrews, the close confidant of Mahatma Gandhi, did serious work of dialogue with the Indian religions and reinterpretation of Christianity for the Indian context. Even today Fr. James Stuart is still at this task, largely through his dedication to the life and work of Abhishiktananda.

It is significant, I think, that during his stay in the mountains of North India Swami Abhishiktananda found in the Brotherhood of the "New Alexandria" a great support for his vocation and for his writing. In a sense the "New Alexandria" was fulfilling its original mission specially through him, in an ecumenical context that overcame the parochialism of the past and enlarged its horizons to the whole of humanity. When Jacques Dupuis came to Delhi he was for thirteen years a next-door neighbor and friend of the Brotherhood, and maintained a close contact with the work of Abhishiktananda, while he himself was also busy in the task of interpreting the Christian faith to the world of the East. Not surprisingly, this dialogue between faith and culture ran into many problems in the old and the new Alexandria. As Bishop Lefroy said a century ago, "there is still a heavily

Western biased agenda dictating what is, and what is not, correct. . . ."

Not in vain, therefore, had Dupuis done his doctoral studies on Origen, the theologian and mystic of the "old" Alexandria. His contribution to fulfilling the "Alexandrian" vocation is precisely to facilitate this dialogue of faith and culture. His task demanded a contact with the mystical tradition. Dupuis was helped in this role by his respect for and friendship with Swami.

It would be wrong, however, to see Dupuis as a mere commentator of Abhishiktananda. On his own he brought a wealth of understanding and knowledge of the Christian and the Indian traditions to his dialogue with the Swami and to his own theological enterprise. Called to be a theologian in the Church, it has not been his vocation to experiment with the mode of life of Indian *sannyasis* or to wander through the numberless holy places of India. His role is different. But theology must keep contact with the mystical tradition, whether in Rome or in Asia. Like Origen, Dupuis too moved elsewhere in his later life, but continues in a different academic context the same work of interpreting the Christian faith for our new culture of pluralism. He draws from the mysticism of the East to formulate his theology in the West, always open to the way in which the presence of God has been manifested in the human spirit.

References

[1] James Stuart, *Swami Abhishiktananda.: His life told through his letters* (Delhi: ISPCK 1995 [1989]), 220.

[2] Abhishiktananda, "An Approach to Hindu Spirituality," *The Clergy Review* 54 (1969), 163-74.

[3] Abhishiktananda, "Notes for Lectures on Christology and the Trinity," trans. James Stuart, *Vidyajyoti Journal* 64 (2000), 598-612.

[4] Dupuis, "Knowing Christ through the Christian Experience," *The Indian Journal of Theology* 18 (1969), 54-64.

[5] Dupuis, "Introduction," in Henri Le Saux, Swami Abhishiktananda, *Essais theologiques*, published in the collection edited by M.-M. Davy, "Le Soleil dans le Coeur" (Sisteron: Editions Presence, 1982), 11-34.

[6] Dupuis, *Jesus-Christ à la recontre des religions* (Paris: Desclée, 1989).

[7] Dupuis, *Jesus Christ at the Encounter of World Religions* (Maryknoll, N. Y.: Orbis, 1991).

[8] Abhishiktananda, *Prayer* (Delhi: ISPCK, 1967); French, significantly, *Eveil a soi— Eveil a Dieu* (Paris: Centurion, 1971).

[9] See M. Amaladoss, "Abhishiktananda, 'Peace and Transcendence,' " *VJTR* 66 (2002), 292-94.

[10] Dupuis, Preface to second edition of *Sagesse* (Paris: Centurion, 1991).

[11] Dupuis, *Toward a Christian Theology of Religious Pluralism* (Maryknoll, N.Y.: Orbis, 1997).

[12] C. M. Millington, *"Whether We Be Many or Few," A History of the Cambridge/Delhi Brotherhood* (Bangalore: Asian Trading Corporation, 1999), at 10 and, 12.

[13] As quoted by Paul Hedges, *Preparation and Fulfilment* (Frankfurt: Peter Lang, 2001), 195, 196.

13

Transfiguration and the Gospel of John

Dorothy Lee

The work of Jacques Dupuis shows, among other things, a keen regard for New Testament theology and a sensitivity to the complexity of the biblical text. While giving due weight to the Christian tradition, his method of engaging theology explores a diversity of perspectives, both within and beyond the bounds of Christian theological thinking. The Fourth Gospel is central to his Christology, although he is aware also of other New Testament ways of understanding the person and work of Christ. Dupuis's work in discerning parallels across different religious and theological "worlds" aids in building bridges between disciplines (as well as religious traditions) that belong together and need to remain in dialogue.

The current essay, in the spirit of Jacques Dupuis, explores parallels between a specific Synoptic theme and the very different world of the Fourth Gospel. One of the puzzling features of the relationship between John and the Synoptics is the absence of the transfiguration from the Johannine narrative (Mk 9:2-10/Matt 17:1-9/Lk 9:28-36). The transfiguration story is concerned with the manifestation of Jesus' glory (*doxa*), a theme hardly alien to the Fourth Gospel. Why then its absence from the narrative of this Gospel? Whether or not John knew the Synoptics has been the subject of debate for well over a century. If a consensus exists at all, it is that John is largely independent of the Synoptic Gospels.[1] However, this view need not deny Johannine knowledge of Synoptic-like traditions. If Luke's divergent account of the transfiguration has features that suggest the use of an independent source (alongside that of Mark),[2] and if references to the transfiguration are found elsewhere in the New Testament (2 Pet 1:16-18; cf. 2 Cor 3:18), it is likely that John was aware of some form of the transfiguration story.

The Synoptic account of the transfiguration describes the revelation of glory in the person of Jesus[3]—a glory suggested by the whiteness of Jesus' garments, the presence of Moses and Elijah, the enveloping cloud, and the divine voice attesting to his identity. The story lies at, or near, the literary and theological center of each Gospel, especially the revelation of the way of the cross (Mk 8:27-9:1/pars.). Although *a theologia crucis* is more characteristic of Mark (and possibly Matthew) than of Luke, in all three Gospels the transfiguration marks the beginning of Jesus' fateful journey to Jerusalem. Luke's narrative also has features that are unique to his Gospel: like a number of significant events throughout Luke-Acts, the transfiguration is set within the context of prayer (Lk 9:28b-29) and Jesus is depicted as discussing his "departure" in Jerusalem with Moses and Elijah (*exodos*, Lk 9:31).

The transfiguration can be interpreted in apocalyptic terms. For Howard Clark Kee, the Markan account is "a proleptic vision of the exaltation of Jesus as kingly Son of man granted to the disciples as eschatological witnesses."[4] Yet the transfiguration has also an epiphanic quality. According to J. P. Heil, an epiphany is a literary genre that narrates the advent of a divine or heavenly being in visible form, with a message or revelation pertaining to faith and salvation.[5] In this sense, the transfiguration is an epiphany, a revelation of Jesus' divine identity in bodily form. It parallels his baptism by John the Baptist (Mk 1:9-11/pars.) and is a story in which "the divine being assumes visible form and appears before the eyes of human beings."[6] In these terms, what we see of Jesus is his "external, proleptic, and temporary transformation by God into a heavenly being while still on earth."[7] Epiphany and apocalyptic vision need not be seen as mutually exclusive; both make sense of the transfiguration.

Is it possible that John's Gospel betrays an awareness of the transfiguration? Vernon H. Kooy has argued that it does.[8] He sees the motif as woven "into the warp and woof of [the Gospel's] tapestry,"[9] regardless of whether the fourth evangelist knew the actual story. Arguing on the basis of Johannine "glory" language, Kooy sees the transfiguration as underlying the Prologue to the Gospel (Jn 1:1-18), the first and last of the Johannine "signs" (the wedding at Cana, 2:11, and the raising of Lazarus, 11:4, 40), the episode of the Greeks coming to "see" Jesus (12:20-47)—which Kooy regards as the climax of the Gospel—and the imagery that pervades Jesus' last meal and farewell discourse (13:1-17:26).[10]

The whole of the Fourth Gospel might thus be described as a "transfiguration" narrative. John's Gospel throughout is concerned with the revelation of divine glory in Jesus, and the transforming response of faith in him as the divine Son and Word of the Father. It is an epiphany from beginning to end, with apocalyptic dimensions that are given a present orientation, very different from the Gospel of Mark.[11] There are elements that we might expect to see in a Johannine re-working of the transfiguration tradition:

- geographical elements, such as the mountain-top,[12] the radiating light and the enveloping cloud;
- the presence of Moses and Elijah, reinforcing Jesus' Christological identity;
- a change in bodily form, in which Jesus' divine glory is unveiled and radiates through his physical presence;
- the confirmation of the divine voice, attesting to Jesus' identity and teaching;
- the presence of the disciples and the theme of faith.[13]

There are a number of Johannine passages that contain these elements, suggesting the influence of transfiguration traditions. These passages overlap with, but are not identical to, those discussed by Kooy.

The Prologue (John 1:1-18)

The five elements are present, however partially, in the Prologue to the Gospel. Although the geographical references are largely absent, the theme of light is a dominant symbol (Jn 1:4-9). The images of mountain and cloud—symbols of divine presence—are missing, but the heightened language and imagery of the Prologue conveys a similar impression of lofty transcendence and mystery, with overtones of Moses' experience on Mt. Sinai.[14] The Prologue is an example of "barrier penetration" in which the divine world opens its gates to disclose light and life to creation.[15]

Although Elijah is not mentioned, Moses is referred to in the Prologue in positive terms (Jn 1:17). The inclusion of Moses and Elijah in the Synoptic accounts—which is not easy to interpret—conveys a sense of the presence of God's ancient people and the Old Testament Scriptures (Mk 9:4/pars.).[16] Moses plays a similar role in the Fourth Gospel, the law pointing symbolically to the "grace and truth" of Jesus' advent.[17] Like Moses, the law throughout John's Gospel is thus on Jesus' side (e.g. Jn 5:45-47) and discloses his identity to the eyes of faith. The figure of Elijah in the Synoptic tradition hardly features in the Johannine account (cf. Jn 1:21, 25).[18]

Most importantly, the language of glory becomes explicit in describing the incarnation: "And the Word become flesh and dwelt [lit. 'tabernacled'/'pitched his tent'] among us. And we beheld his glory, the glory of the Father's only Son, full of grace and truth" (Jn 1:14). As Jesus is transfigured in the Synoptic Gospels to reveal his true identity and his definitive eschatological role, so in the Prologue Jesus' fleshly reality is the manifestation of divine *doxa* (glory). In his flesh Jesus reveals his identity as the divine Logos/Son, who abides in intimate and eternal union with the Father.[19] C. K. Barrett sees 1:14 as expressing "the paradox which runs through the whole gospel: the *doxa* is not to be seen *alongside* the *sarx* [flesh], nor *through* the *sarx* as through a window; it is to be seen in the *sarx* and nowhere else."[20] The transfigured flesh of Jesus radiates God's loving and life-giving glory.[21] While there is no explicit divine voice, the omniscient author of the Gospel presents what is, for John, the divine perspective on Jesus' identity: the voice of the Father is uttered in the being of the Son, who is the divine Word from all eternity, perpetually abiding in love and intimacy with the Father ("turned toward" the Father, 1:1-2;[22] "in the bosom of the Father," 1:18).

The focus on Christological identity is significant also for its bearing on faith and salvation. The "we" of 1:14c defines those who have received new birth (Jn 1:12-13; cf. 3:1-8), conveying a sense of intimacy and belonging that points to the community of faith.[23] Unlike the Synoptics, there is no misunderstanding at this point; the community of disciples sees and identifies the divine glory, responding in faith. Indeed, the dynamic between the first reference to "flesh" at 1:13 and the second at 1:14 is a transforming one: believers come to share in the divine nature, just as—and indeed solely because—the Logos/Son comes to share in human nature. While remaining transcendent, he takes human form and trans-figures humanity to become "children of God" (*tekna tou theou*, 1:12), resplen-dent with divine glory. The incarnation parallels the tabernacle [*skênê*] as the dwelling-place of God's glory: "O Lord, I have loved the beauty of your house, and the place of the dwelling of your glory [*skênômatos doxês sou*]" (Ps 25:8 LXX; see also Wisd 7:25, 9:8-11; Sir 24:8). Peter's desire in the Synoptics to build three tents (Mk 9:5-6/pars.) is paralleled in John by the believing response of the community of faith and its recognition that God's presence abides in the sacred "tent"/temple which is Jesus himself (*eskênôsen*, Jn 1:14b). The three "tents," rejected by the Synoptic Father, are here manifest as the one divine "Tent" in whom the Father's presence resides.[24] For John, the divine indwelling is sym-bolized Christologically in the One whose flesh reveals God's glory. Despite re-jection, there are those who accept joyfully the revelation.

Transfiguration in the Fourth Gospel differs from the Synoptics in at least one important respect. In John it is enunciated, not as the change from an ordinary humanity that veils divine identity to a transcendent humanity that radiates the divine, but rather as the change from spirit to flesh, from divine to human—from a transcendent divinity that is the Source of life to a divinity that displays itself, now for the first time, within the material world. The early Fathers understand this as a fundamental transformation in the manifestation of God to the world, which has as its goal the corresponding transfiguration of human beings to divine glory, thus restoring the divine image:

> The one who is, becomes. The uncreated is created. . . . The one who enriches becomes a beggar; for he begs for my own flesh, so that I might become rich in his divinity. The one who is full becomes empty; for he empties himself of his glory for a little time so that I might share in his fullness.[25]

The flesh of the Johannine Jesus becomes the icon of divine presence and indwelling. It is not confined to singular moments of epiphany, where the true identity breaks through from time to time, as in the Synoptics. In the Fourth Gospel it is present in every contour of the life and being of Jesus; for the reader, there is no hiddenness to the revelation of glory.

The Wedding at Cana (John 2:1-11)

The same elements associated with the transfiguration are identifiable also in the wedding at Cana. Absent are the geographical references and any explicit reference to Moses or Elijah—although the jars of purification, representing Ju-daism, play a similar role to Moses and Elijah in pointing to Jesus as the fullness of revelation. The evangelist directs the reader's attention to the epiphanic nature of this, the first of the Johannine "signs," giving clues to its meaning in the reference to the "hour," the presence of the mother of Jesus, and the editorial conclusion: "and he revealed his glory and his disciples believed in him" (2:11). The "signs" of Jesus' ministry, and indeed all his words and deeds, are to be interpreted from the lens of glory, already made visible within the flesh of Jesus. The epiphany of glory is the explicit purpose of the Johannine Jesus' life, death and resurrection in its every aspect. The Cana story will lay the ground-work for the reader's interpretation of Jesus' ministry, as will be confirmed again and again throughout the Gospel narrative. The glory of the Johannine Jesus is a permanent manifestation: neither hidden nor momentary in its presentation to the world.

The message of the Cana "epiphany" is a complex one and not easy to decipher, except in the light of what follows.[26] Alongside the theme of the "hour" and the revelation of glory is belief in the efficacious word of Jesus. Of particular importance is the parallel with the divine voice in the Synoptic account of the transfiguration. From within the cloud, God summons the three disciples to "listen to him" (Mk 9:7/pars.), directing their attention to the teaching which Jesus has already begun on the way to Jerusalem, especially as that relates to the cross. The instructions of the mother of Jesus to the stewards parallel the Synoptic heavenly voice: "Do whatever he tells you" (Jn 2:5). The reader is invited to trust implicitly in the words of Jesus, who is himself the divine Word. Listening to, and trusting in, the One who is the definitive revelation of God is a common theme in all four Gospels.

Curiously enough, the wedding at Cana does involve a kind of "transfiguration" in the changing of water into wine.[27] John interprets the symbols Christologically as the contrast between the Jewish traditions (which form the symbolic backbone to the Gospel) and the advent of Jesus himself. His presence signifies the transfiguration of Judaism: from a lesser to a greater revelation, from "signs and shadows" to divine reality (especially Jn 5-10).[28] At the heart of this "transfiguration" is the unveiling of a glory that is somewhat veiled within Israel's past (recognized by Abraham, Moses and Isaiah, according to the evangelist, and portended in the traditions of Judaism), but now lucid and unmistakable in the person of Jesus. It is Judaism therefore that is "transfigured" at Cana: the jars of water for purification are transformed into the wine of the new—epitomized, made visible, incarnated in Jesus Christ. The rituals and feasts of Judaism become the symbolic medium pointing the reader to the presence of the divine, incarnate Son.

The Bread of Life Narrative (John 6)

As we would expect, similar elements are to be found in the Bread of Life narrative. Despite misunderstanding the significance of the feeding, the crowds witness a "sign" or, as John himself often prefers to call it, a "work" (6:2, 14, 26-30). This time the setting is a mountain (6:3), unlike the Synoptic narratives which locate the feeding in the wilderness (*erêmos topos*, Mk 6:32/pars.; *erêmia*, Mk 8:4/par.). Though the *doxa* language is implicit in the Johannine account, transfiguration elements are present. The five barley loaves and two fish are not changed into something different, as with the water at Cana, but rather are multiplied into an astonishing abundance that feeds 5,000 people (6:10) and leaves twelve baskets of left-over scraps (6:12-13). The revelatory nature of this event is heralded in Jesus' epiphany on the water to the frightened disciples immediately after the feeding (6:16-21). It develops in the symbolic and sacramental meaning that the feeding acquires in the dialogue with the crowds/"Jews" (6:22-65). The narrative presents the unfolding revelation of Jesus as the "Bread which has come down from heaven" (*ho katabainôn/ho katabas*, 6:33, 41, 50-51). Jesus is both the giver of the bread and the heavenly food, the host and the repast in one (6:53-58).

Other elements associated with the transfiguration are also evident. Judaism is represented by Moses who is a symbolic figure and by the use of exodus imagery. These Jewish symbols are apparent in the proximity of the feeding to Passover (6:4), in the discussion concerning the manna (6:31-33), in the references to the ancestors (our fathers, 6:31, 49, 58) and in the rebellious mutterings of "the Jews" (6:41-43).[29] Moreover, the divine voice is present in Jesus' testimony to the Father. It is God who "speaks" in the transfiguring revelation of Jesus as the Bread of life, and those who listen to him are hearing no less than the Father's voice: "everyone who hears and learns from the Father comes to me" (6:45). The faith of the disciples is also a Johannine theme in this narrative. At the end when other, potential disciples have left, scandalized by Jesus' words, Peter rightly confesses his faith in Jesus as "the Holy One of God" (6:67-69).

The Coming of the "Hour" (John 12:20-36)

The coming of the Greeks to "see" Jesus signals to the Johannine reader that at last the "hour" of Jesus' departure has come: now, in the words of the hostile Pharisees in the preceding pericope, "the world has gone after him" (12:19). The story is not a Johannine "sign" and there is no overt "transfiguration," but the "hour" is the revelation of glory and requires Jesus' consent. As the eternal Son, he possesses from the Father divine authority over life and death (*exousia*, cf. 5:17-30),[30] so that he can "lay down my life in order that I might take it up again" (10:17-18). The Greeks are not bypassed but shown that to "see" Jesus means believing in him as the revealer. They are called to serve and follow him as he makes his journey through death to life (12:24-26).[31] Faith is an important aspect of this scene, in the presence of Gentile would-be followers whose request is transmitted to Jesus through Philip and Andrew, two of the Johannine inner circle of disciples (12:22; cf. 1:40, 43-45).

None of this would seem particularly reflective of the transfiguration were it not for the verses that follow, which weave together elements from both the transfiguration and the Synoptic Gethsemane (Jn 12:27-33; cf. Mk 14:32-42/pars.).[32] The Johannine Jesus (unlike the Markan Jesus) chooses not to pray for the removal of the cup, despite his distress of soul, but asks instead that the Father's name be glorified (Jn 12:28a; cf. Mk 14:36). This is the only place in the Fourth Gospel where the Father speaks directly: "I glorified it and I will glorify it again" (12:28b). These words confirm Jesus' prayer and disclose the unity of heart and will between Father and Son which undergirds the Passion. Just as the divine voice from the cloud at the Synoptic transfiguration confirms Jesus' identity to the disciples and his destiny in Jerusalem, the place of the Passion, so the voice of the Johannine Father confirms the "hour" of the Passion as the glorification of the divine name. The voice speaks not for the benefit of Jesus but for those standing around (12:30; cf. 11:42) who will witness Jesus' exaltation on the cross when he draws "all people"—or "all things"—to himself (12:32).[33] Using the image of light, Jesus challenges the crowd to believe in the face of their misunderstanding (12:29). As a major symbol of the Gospel, associated with the Feast of Tabernacles, light is a manifestation of divine glory (12:35-36; cf. Jn 1:3-5); indeed, Jesus speaks as the Light of the world (8:12, 9:5). The imagery parallels the whiteness/light symbolism of the Synoptic transfiguration. There are thus a number of elements suggestive of transfiguration in this Johannine narrative, as Kooy notes.[34] The Gethsemane scene, which in the Synoptic tradition depicts Jesus' (successful) struggle to face his impending death and obey the Father's will, becomes in the Johannine tradition a moment of transfiguration, revealing Jesus' true identity and God-ordained destiny in the context of the Passion.[35]

Jesus' Concluding Prayer (John 17)

The "Prayer of the Departing Redeemer" at the end of the Farewell Discourse also has overtones of the transfiguration.[36] C. H. Dodd interprets the prayer as performative: it is an symbolic enactment of Jesus' ascent in an act of mutual glorification.[37] Prayer by definition represents the ascent of the soul to God. In this instance, however, Jesus prays as the fully manifest Son of the Father,[38] his prayer being the symbol of that ascent which is the inner meaning of the Passion. The ascent is at the same time the revelation of glory: both the Father's glory and the glory given to the Son. The Son is fully present to the Father (cf. 1:1-2, 18), revealing the glory which is the meaning of his life and death. He is the true temple in whom the divine glory tabernacles.[39] Just as in the Lukan account, Jesus' prayer is both the context and the means of his transfiguration—the revelation of his divine identity—with a fundamental relationship to the Passion, so too the Johannine Jesus stands in prayer before the Father, disclosing an identity that is uniquely and eternally his. The manifestation of glory is confirmed in the repetition of glory/glorification throughout the prayer: in the opening verses (vv. 1-5) and also later (vv. 10, 22, 24), along with related imagery of sanctification (vv. 17-19), oneness (vv. 21-23) and love (vv. 24, 26). What is "transfiguring" about Jesus' identity is precisely the "anabasis" which the prayer enacts. His return to the Father, through his "exaltation" on the cross, will change the nature of his fleshly presence in the world, as Mary Magdalene discovers in the Easter garden (20:16-18).

John 17 represents also the ingathering of the community of faith, both present and future, which is itself a "transfiguring" event. The "we" of 1:14 are now the subject of Jesus' prayer. The disciples are drawn into the love and unity of Father and Son. Unlike the Synoptics, the disciples are not uncomprehending at this point (see 16:29-30)—though their abandonment of Jesus shows the limits of their comprehension (16:31-32)[40]—nor are they terrified in being drawn into the "bright cloud" of Jesus' glory.[41] The Johannine tradition as a whole has a more optimistic view of the disciples than the Synoptics: not so much for historical reasons but in order to emphasize the unity of the community as it is gathered into the epiphany of divine glory. It is much clearer in the Fourth Gospel that glory is something that Jesus shares with the disciples (17:22). His longing that future disciples "see my glory" (v. 24) makes clear that the sight of the revelation is itself salvific. To see the fleshly Jesus in the stance of prayer, his whole being—and particularly his death—an ascent to the Father, is fundamental to the iconography of the Fourth Gospel; to behold him is itself salvific.

At the same time, there are several features of the Fourth Gospel that make the Synoptic story of the transfiguration difficult to incorporate. John's use of apocalyptic themes is very different from the Synoptics. That which in the Synoptics is eschatological in a futuristic sense, either in relation to the resurrection (itself an apocalyptic event) or the Parousia, in John's Gospel is radically anticipated in the here-and-now of the community's experience. Schnackenburg refers to this as "the magnificent one-sidedness of Johannine eschatology."[42] Whereas glory in the Synoptics is associated with the Parousia and the future Coming of the Son of Man (Mk 13:26/pars.), in the Fourth Gospel it relates primarily to the incarnation (1:14). Apocalyptic symbolism is a largely present reality in the Johannine world.

The same could be said of other themes.[43] The transfiguration in the Synoptics is in part an epiphany, an unveiling of the hidden identity of Jesus. In Mark's Gospel, the secrecy motif, especially in the first half of the Gospel, creates a sense of Jesus' identity as hidden from the eyes of the world. It is manifested in the baptism (Mk 1:11) and at the transfiguration (Mk 9:7), where the divine voice witnesses to Jesus as the Beloved Son;[44] it is also manifest on the cross, where the Roman centurion witnesses to Jesus as Son of God (*huios tou theou,* Mk 15:39). These are moments of epiphany where the veil is torn open (cf. Mk 1:10, 15:38) and the identity of Jesus revealed to the eyes of faith. In the Fourth Gospel, by contrast, the identity of Jesus is more explicit than in the Synoptics; it is transparent from the beginning (1:6-8, 15, 29-36, 41-51, 2:11). Rather than distinguishing the Christologies of Mark and John by the category of humanity or divinity, therefore, it may be more helpful to see the distinction in terms of hiddenness and openness.

Not unrelated is the way Mark's Gospel stresses the blindness of the disciples, a theme also evident (though not as strongly) in Matthew and Luke. In the Synoptic transfiguration, where Jesus manifests his "glory," the three disciples fail to understand (Mk 9:4-6/pars.). The Markan account narrates the transfiguration early in the journey to Jerusalem, and the divine voice enjoining the disciples to "listen to him" (Mk 9:5) underscores the disciples' own need for illumination and "transfiguration." This theme, which will reach its climax in the Markan Passion, is already palpable in the stories of the healing of blind men which bound Mark's travel story (Mk 8:22-26, 10:47-52).[45] By contrast, while the disciples in John have moments of incomprehension, they move more readily to a comprehension of Jesus' identity, although this remains incomplete until Easter.

The Synoptic story of the transfiguration is absent from the Gospel of John for reasons that we can only guess: its seemingly momentary quality, its depiction as a futuristic apocalyptic event, and its portrayal of the disciples as misunderstanding the revelation of divine glory. Nevertheless, a case can be made that John has taken the tradition of the transfiguration, through either direct or indirect knowledge of the Synoptics, and used it in a diffuse way throughout his Gospel. Traces of this tradition can be discerned in the Prologue, which sets the tone for the Gospel, the wedding at Cana, which gives the reader the interpretative clue to the "signs" and works of Jesus' ministry, the Bread of Life narrative on the mountain, the coming of the "hour" at the end of the first half of the Gospel, and the prayer of Jesus which sums up the second half of the Gospel, with its double theme of ascent/glorification and the ingathering of the community into the transfiguring glory of Father and Son.

Yet John's understanding of the meaning of the transfiguration, even in its attenuated Johannine form, is somewhat different from the Synoptics. In all four Gospels, Jesus is portrayed as the unique Son, the one beloved of the Father. In John, Jesus' divine identity is transparent throughout the Gospel which sees one epiphany folding over into another. If there is a sense of metamorphosis, it lies not in a singular moment of self-revelation but rather in the incarnation, as it is enunciated in Jesus' ministry and in his death on the cross, signifying the mutual glorification of Father and Son. The transfiguration takes place in the self-giving life and love of God which crosses the chasm between divine and human, and in which the very being of God—ineffable, invisible, unknowable, intangible (Jn 1:18, 6:46)—stoops to enter the world of speech, sight, perception, touch; extending and in one sense exchanging divine identity for human, immortality for mortality, creator for creation. The effect is to change the nature of Jesus' flesh, displaced across barriers of space and time.[46] The transfiguration of glory to flesh in condescension and grace effects a corresponding transformation of "all flesh" (17:2) to radiate divine glory.

References

[1]See, for example, D. Moody Smith, *Johannine Christianity: Essays on Its Setting, Sources, and Theology* (Edinburgh: T. & T. Clark, 1984), 95-172.

[2]See, for example, Barbara Reid, *The Transfiguration: a Source- and Redaction-Critical Study of Luke 9:28-36* (Paris: J. Gabalda, 1993), 39-94, and J. Murphy-O'Connor, "What Really Happened at the Transfiguration?" *Bible Review* 3 (1987), 14-16.

³In Mark, *doxa* is used not at the transfiguration but at 8:38 (cf. Matt 16:27) where it refers to the Father's glory. The word is mentioned explicitly in the transfiguration only at Luke 9:32-33. Matthew uses the related imagery of light in relation to Jesus' face and clothing (Matt 17:2) and the cloud "full of light" that covers them (Matt 17:5). Mark makes no explicit mention of light in his description of Jesus' clothing, nor does he describe Jesus' face, yet the supernatural whiteness of the clothing suggests both divine light and glory (Mk 9:3). Also in Luke, Jesus' face (*eidos tou prosôpou autou*) changes in prayer and his clothing becomes white (Lk 9:29).

⁴H. C. Kee, "The Transfiguration in Mark: Epiphany or Apocalyptic Vision?," in J. Reumann (ed.), *Understanding the Sacred Text.: Essays in Honor of Morton S. Enslin on the Hebrew Bible and Christian Beginnings* (Valley Forge: Judson Press, 1972), 149. Kee argues against the view that the Markan story is an epiphany. The transfiguration has also been seen, among other things, as a legend that was originally a resurrection story (cf. especially R. Bultmann, *The History of the Synoptic Tradition* [ET Oxford: Blackwell, 1963)], 259-61). For a succinct survey of theories on the form of the story, see A.D.A. Moses, *Matthew's Transfiguration Story and Jewish-Christian Controversy* (Sheffield, England: Sheffield Academic Press, 1996), 20-26.

⁵J. P. Heil, *The Transfiguration of Jesus: Narrative Meaning and Function of Mark 9:2-8, Matt 17:1-8 and Luke 9:28-36* (Roma: Editrice Pontificio Istituto Biblico, 2000), 38-39 (also pp. 35-49).

⁶Heil, *Transfiguration of Jesus*, 39.

⁷Ibid., 314.

⁸Vernon H. Kooy, "The Transfiguration Motif in the Gospel of John," in J. I. Cook (ed.), *Saved by Hope* (Grand Rapids: Eerdmans, 1978), 64-78.

⁹Ibid., 72. G. B. Caird sees the absence of the transfiguration from John's Gospel as the result of John's view that "the whole ministry of Christ, and the Cross in particular, was the revelation of that glory of the Father in which Jesus lived" ("The Transfiguration," *Expository Times* 67 [1955-56], 294).

¹⁰Kooy, "Transfiguration," 69-72.

¹¹John Ashton argues that, although the Fourth Gospel is not an Apocalypse, it does contain a number of characteristic apocalyptic themes and motifs, expressed within John's unique perspective (*Understanding the Fourth Gospel* [Oxford: Clarendon, 1990], 383-406).

¹²The mountain-top, along with the reference to "six days" (Mk 9:2/par.), has overtones of Moses on Mount Sinai beholding the glory of God (Exod 24:15-18, 34:29-35).

¹³Peter's suggestion that three tents be constructed is probably an attempt to imprison the revelation, or make it permanent, thus avoiding the necessity of the *via dolorosa*. It may also be linked to the Feast of Tabernacles; see J. Fitzmyer, *The Gospel According to Luke (I-IX),* (New York: Doubleday, 1979), 801. In any case, Peter mistakenly puts the three figures on an equal level.

¹⁴M. D. Hooker, "'What Doest Thou Here, Elijah?': A Look at St. Mark's Account of the Transfiguration," in L. D. Hurst and N. T. Wright (eds.), *The Glory of Christ in the New Testament* (Oxford: Clarendon, 1987), 61-63.

¹⁵T. E. Schmidt, "The Penetration of Barriers and the Revelation of Christ in the Gospels," *Novum Testamentum* 34 (1992), 245.

¹⁶Most modern commentators do not accept the traditional view that Moses represents the law and Elijah the prophets. Both are Old Testament figures, both are interpreted as eschatological and both are associated with light/glory. For a succinct survey of views of their significance in the transfiguration, see W. D. Davies and D. C. Allison, *The Gospel According*

to Saint Matthew, vol. 2 (Edinburgh: T. & T. Clark, 1991), 697-99. On the reason for Mark's placement of Elijah before Moses, see Hooker, "What Doest Thou Here, Elijah?," 69-70.

[17]As Dupuis points out in his discussion of the Prologue, the law given through Moses is already a "grace," but "Jesus Christ is God's supreme grace" (*Who Do You Say I Am? Introduction to Christology* [Maryknoll, N.Y.: Orbis, 1994], 72-73).

[18]The link between John the Baptist and Elijah, important in Mark and Matthew, is explicitly denied in the Fourth Gospel (1:21).

[19]See Kooy, "Transfiguration Motif," 67-69.

[20]C. K. Barrett, *The Gospel According to St. John*, 2nd ed. (London: SPCK, 1978), 165.

[21]On flesh as the fundamental Johannine symbol of divine glory, see D. Lee, *Flesh and Glory. Symbol, Gender and Theology in the Gospel of John* (New York: Crossroad, 2002), 29-64.

[22]On this translation of the preposition *pros*, see for example X. Léon-Dufour, vol. 1, *Lecture de l'évangile selon Jean* (Paris: Editions du Seuil 1988-1996), 68-72.

[23]Note the use of "we" in 2 Peter 1:16-18; see Kooy, "Transfiguration Motif," 76.

[24]I am indebted for this suggestion to Dr. Grantley McDonald of the University of Melbourne. J. A. McGuckin, on the basis of Jewish tradition, sees the three tents in the Synoptics as "tabernacle-shrines appropriate for heavenly visitors" (*The Transfiguration of Christ in Scripture and Tradition* [Lewiston/Queenston: Edwin Mellen, 1986], 74-75).

[25]Gregory of Nazianzus, "In Sanctum Pascha" in J.-P. Migne (ed.), vol. 36, *Patrologia Cursus Completus. Series Graeca* (Paris: Garnier, 1844-91). For a summary of different Patristic theories of the transfiguration, see McGuckin, *Transfiguration*, especially 99-128.

[26]As Beverley Gaventa points out, "[m]ost of what is needed to understand the story is *not* said" (*Mary. Glimpses of the Mother of Jesus* [Edinburgh: T. & T, Clark, 1999), 88.

[27]On the symbolism of the narrative, see Lee, *Flesh and Glory*, 66-68, 143-47.

[28]See F. J. Moloney, *Signs and Shadows. Reading John 5-12* (Minneapolis: Fortress, 1996), especially 152-53.

[29]On John 6 as a continuous narrative, see D. Lee, *The Symbolic Narratives of the Fourth Gospel: The Interplay of Form and Meaning* (Sheffield, England: Sheffield Academic Press, 1994), 126-160.

[30]As M. M. Thompson puts it, "the unity of the life-giving *work* of Father and Son" . . . also predicates a remarkable status of the Son, one which is not made of any other creature. The Son 'has life in himself' " (*The God of the Gospel of John* [Grand Rapids: Eerdmans, 2001], 78-79).

[31]F. J. Moloney, *The Gospel of John* (Collegeville, Minn.: Liturgical Press, 1998), 351-53.

[32]On the transfiguration elements in this scene, see R. Bultmann, *The Gospel of John* (ET Oxford: Blackwell, 1971), 428, and R. E. Brown, *The Gospel According to John*, vol. 1 (New York: Doubleday, 1966), 476.

[33]"All things" (*panta*) is a well-attested alternative to "all people" (*pantas*) in a number of textual witnesses; further on this, see G. Beasley-Murray, *John* (Waco, Texas: Word Books, 1987), 205.

[34]Kooy, "Transfiguration Motif," 69-70.

[35]Note the peculiar feature of the Lukan disciples' somnolence (Lk 9:32) which resembles their response in Luke's account of Jesus' agony on the Mount of Olives (Lk 22:45-46).

[36]See R. Schnackenburg, *The Gospel According to St. John*, vol. 3 (London: Burns & Oates, 1982), 167-202.

[37]C. H. Dodd, *The Interpretation of the Fourth Gospel* (Cambridge: Cambridge University Press, 1953), 419-20.

[38]Robert W. Jenson describes John 17 as "inner discourse of the Trinity exposed to our overhearing" (*Systematic Theology. Vol. 1: The Triune God* [Oxford: Oxford University Press, 1997], 93).

[39]On the Johannine Jesus as the temple of God, see M. L. Coloe, *God Dwells With Us: Temple Symbolism in the Fourth Gospel* (Collegeville, Minn.: Liturgical Press, 2001).

[40]John plays down the story of the disciples' failure. While retaining the story of Peter's denial (18:15-18, 25-27), he does not actually narrate the disciples' abandonment of Jesus, even though Jesus predicts it (16:32a). Yet Jesus is not abandoned in this Gospel (16:32b). The four holy women and the beloved disciple were present at the foot of the cross (19:25-27), and Jesus' consciousness of his Father's presence never deserts him (19:28-30).

[41]In Mark and Matthew it is not clear who enters the cloud (Mk 9:7/Matt 17:5); for Luke, the three disciples are manifestly drawn into the cloud (and thus terrified, Lk 9:34).

[42]Schnackenburg, *St. John*, vol. 2, 437.

[43]Judgement, for example, is a dimension of present experience (Jn 5:24), unlike the Synoptics where it is eschatological in a future sense (Mk 8:38/pars.).

[44]Note the parallel in the Testament of Levi 18:6-7 (c. 200 BCE): "The heavens will be opened, and from the temple of glory sanctification will come upon him [the new priest which the Lord will raise up after his vengeance is over], with a fatherly voice, as from Abraham to Isaac. And the glory of the Most High shall burst forth upon him"; see Brown, *John*, vol. 1, 468.

[45]M. D. Hooker, *The Gospel According to St. Mark* (London: A. & C. Black, 1991), 251-253.

[46]On the displacement of the physical body of Jesus in events such as the transfiguration, resurrection and ascension, see Graham Ward, "Bodies: the Displaced Body of Jesus Christ," in J. Millbank et al., *Radical Orthodoxy* (London/New York: Routledge, 1999), 163-81.

14

Many Strings, a Single Melody

Samuel Rayan, S.J.

God is Love (1 Jn 4:8, 16). God is a community, a trinity of love; an eternal Self-giving and Intercommunion of the Father, the Word and the Spirit. God is Sat-Cid-Ananda: Reality, Consciousness and Joy.

I

God loves into existence this world and all of us. This world with all its splendor, wonder and beauty; with all its variety, interdependence and complementarity. Existence, life and self are love's gifts. They come from the Father through the Word in the Spirit. We are ourselves their love-gift; and we are a word of love God speaks to us; a call and an invitation to come to God to keep moving closer to share God's life ever more intimately and to live for ever in personal communion with the Divine, as well as with all our sisters and brothers, both human and other. A call am I, then, and an echo of God's word and a touch of God's Spirit. That creative call and touch our hearts can't forget. They remain inscribed deep within us, and keep throbbing at the center of our being and echoing in every fibre that textures us and our cosmos. They ground our existence and constitute our selves.

That means we are rooted in God through the Word in the Spirit, and are radically oriented towards God, the ultimate goal, meaning and wholeness of every created reality. The dynamism of this orientation makes our hearts restless and launches them on a quest which continues till they find God and rest in God. (Augustine;[1] Ps 95:11; Heb 3:11- 4:11). God's choosing to love us into existence constitutes an encounter of the Divine with the human, God taking the initiative to call, invite, challenge and enable us to respond appropriately, adequately, in freedom and love. This encounter, occurring always through God's Word in the Holy Spirit, is the place of God-experience, and the birthplace of religiousness. It is this experience, mediated through various cultures, that find expression as religions. The content of these cultural embodiments, the sense of the Divine, is not mere human effort at self-justification or at control of God. The religions, at their core, are responses provoked by divine interventions. Their human components can be deficient. They are, nevertheless, basically *theanthropic* (to adapt a usage of Raimundo Panikkar).[2] They are not purely natural. All divine interventions are grace, including creation and the gift given us of ourselves and this world.

II

The divine-human encounter occurs at the very center and in the foundations of created reality. It abides there, illumining, inviting, challenging, enabling and gladdening us as long as we endure. It may not always be formally recognized as God-experience; therefore, it may not always get expressed in religious terms and symbols. But it will, unless thwarted, articulate itself as genuine humanity in just and honest dealings, in gentle and compassionate behavior, in a world view where persons come before things and the common good has priority over private gain, where love is central and readiness for selfless service is normal. It is to such cases, perhaps, of anonymous religions that Paul refers when he describes those who, "not having the law (set down in tablets and codices), still through their own innate sense behave as the law commands . . . then they are a law for themselves. They can demonstrate the effects of the law engraved on their hearts, to which their conscience bears witness" (Rom 2:13-15). Such persons may have no "religion," in the sense of creeds, rituals and institutions; but they can have "faith," in the sense of commitment to what humanizes and contributes to justice, peace and the common good. For, even without explicit knowledge of God, they have opted to walk a way which is actually God's, and to live in a realm where God's will holds sway. One cannot help recalling in this context men like Gautama the Buddha and his faithful disciples down the centuries.

Genuine faith does not consist in saying "Lord, Lord" nor in reciting creeds and mouthing dogmas; not even in working miracles and practicing prophecy. It consists rather in doing what God wishes to see done on this earth (Mt 7:21-27; 1 Cor 13:1-3). It is a matter of life and service, of commitment to designs and plans which are God's though not yet known as such. It is not a question of grammar and rhetoric, though these too have their place. That is why Jesus asks with indignation: "Why do you call me, Lord, Lord, and not do what I say?" (Lk 6:46-49): a rebuke which the religion which claims his name would do well to consider. Note how Jesus lays the accent elsewhere than is usual in institutional Christianity. "Any one," says he, "who does the will of God, that person is my brother, and sister and mother" (Mk 3:31-35). Jesus keeps insisting that he himself was sent and had come to do the Father's will, even at great cost to himself (Jn 4:34; 9:4;10:37; 14:11; Mk 14:35-36). In fact Jesus takes true worship and religion past locales, temples, and rituals, and re-founds them in the heart's sincerity, loving mercy and human solidarity (Jn 4: 20-24; Mt 5:20-45; 9:10-13; 12: 1-7; Hos 6:6).

III

The divine-human encounter and exchange are carried on not only in the se-cret recesses of each person's heart; the human community as well is a scene of this exciting dialogue. All the people around us, people the world over, are also a word of love that God is addressing to everyone. They too are called to be light to all eyes, a challenge to every life, and an encouragement to every heart. They are co-listeners with us to what God is saying each day through peoples and events; they are our collaborators in seeking, finding and doing God's will, and co-pil-grims on the way to our final destiny in the One who is Love without end. The people are sacraments of God's presence and God's self-giving. Our neighbors, therefore, and the human community are not foreign to anybody's approach to and experience of God. They belong inwardly to our God-experience and reli-gious/spiritual life. The Word that has called us is a Light "that gives light to everyone" (Jn 1:9; 3:19; 8:12; 12:46). If then we live in the light that God is, "we have a share in each other's life" (1 Jn 1:5-7).

That is why most of the commandments center on justice and love for the neighbor (Ex 20-23; Dt 5; 15:12-18; 24:10-21; 25: 13-16; Lv19:9-18,33-36; 25). And nearly the whole of the Sermon on the Mount, summing up Jesus' message, concerns neighborly relationships (Mt 5-7). The Sermon and the judgement par-able in Matthew 25:31-46, as well as the story Jesus told of the compassionate Samaritan (Lk 10:25-37), convey the critical truth: it is in our neighbor that God is met in responsive faith and love. What the Samaritan did is authentic faith and genuine religious practice—quite a model for all, though no mention of God is made in the story and no creed confessed. A contrast is emphasized with the expressly religious figures of the priest and the Levite, who perhaps were hasten-ing from the temple and had no time to waste on a stranger bleeding to death on a highway. Similarly, peoples of all epochs of history will be assembled before the king and rewarded, not for performing rituals, saying prayers, or supporting priests and sanctuaries, but for the true faith and religion of feeding the hungry, clothing the naked, sheltering the homeless, and visiting the sick and the jailed to comfort them, heal them, and liberate them (Mt 25:31-46).

The disclosure of the God-dimension, the Jesus-dimension, and of what the compassionate people of Matthew 25 did to the victims of human systems comes as a welcome surprise and necessary corrective to the traditional images of the spiritual and the religious. It defines religion's authentic core. Hence a disciple's clear and challenging assertion that anyone who professes to love God but hates or neglects a brother or sister is a liar (1 Jn 4:20-21). Love for God and love for neighbor are inseparably one, and are what religion and salvation are all about. This is especially so, since God's Word became flesh, became one of us, became a suffering neighbor, and dwelt among us (Jn 1:14). Hence anyone who loves neighbors, especially the needy and the despised, "has passed over from death to life" and belongs now to the realm of the resurrection (1 Jn 3:14; 4:7-8). God welcomes us with love and, therefore, also with the question, "where is your brother/sister? And how are they?" Each person and every community should be able to give a reply different from the one Cain gave (Gen 4:8-10).

IV

There is a still wider arena where the Divine meets and addresses the human: our universe, this cosmos. The universe we know, as well as its outreaches beyond our ken, is also reality God has loved into existence through his Word under the auspices of the hovering Spirit (Gen1:1-2; Jn 1:1-3; Heb1:1-3; Col 1:15-20). The entire cosmos and every component of it, big and small, many-splendored and diverse, are an echo of the eternal Word, a breath of the Creator Spirit, and something God is saying to us about God's self and about us. It is a self-disclosure of God, meant to call forth saving, humanizing-divinizing faith in everyone included in the world and involved in its processes; that is why unfaith, ungodliness, and a refusal of justice and service are unacceptable. "For, what can be known about God . . . God has made plain . . . ever since the creation of the world, the invisible existence of God and his everlasting power has been clearly seen by the mind's understanding of created things" (Rom 1:18-20; see Wisd 13:1-9; Is 40:26-29). That has established, for every person and all generations of peoples from the dawn of history, the rich, proximate possibility of faith-commitment, of genuine worship and thanks, of authentic religion.

To this basic conviction about the universe being a faith-provoking divine revelation and a resonance of God's creative Word, Paul gives expression more than once. In a spontaneous utterance, Paul summons a Lycaonian crowd, bent on worshiping him, to turn to "the living God who made sky and earth and the sea and all that these hold"; they should turn to the One who has never left anybody without evidence of his own divine self. And the evidence consists in the good things he does for people, like the rain he sends from heaven, the seasons of fruitfulness, the food he gives, and the joy with which he fills their hearts. The message is that in such seasonal and daily experiences God keeps coming and challenging us to weave with him a lasting relationship of loving communion (Acts 14:8-17). The same truth Paul proclaimed in Athens, calling people's attention to "the God who made the world and everything in it," who also "gives everything, including life and breath, to everyone," and who distributes nations and races across the expanses of time and space, "so that they might seek the Deity, and feel their way toward him and succeed in finding him" (Acts 17:24-31).

Paul is stating the Jewish-Christian faith in the divine plan of offering salvation to everyone and providing everybody with the means to attain it (Acts 17:23-27; 1 Tim 2:4). Paul goes further, and acknowledges the existence among the ancients of a sense of the living God, of a personal relationship to God, and of a joyful sense of security in God's bosom. Paul is glad to cite two poet-seers of old as attesting to God's loving, caring closeness to us humans. Did not a sixth-century (BCE) poet, Epimenides of Cnossos, sing that "it is in him (God) that we live and move and exist"? And did not a third-century (BCE) poet, the Cilician Aratus, intuit God's fatherly love and celebrate the fact that "we are all his children"? (Acts 17:28). A piece of good news all human hearts would rejoice to hear.

The universe bears witness to God. The heavens proclaim God's glory and his handiwork. "Day discourses of it to day, and night to night hands on the knowledge," quietly, silently. (Ps 19). So do every tree and flower, every sporting little animal, every singing bird, every star and grain of sand and every drop of water making its way to the earth, to the stream, to the ocean. The rivers clap their hands and the mountains shout for joy (Pss 96:11-12; 98:7-8; Is 55:12-13). The trees lift up their hands in prayer (Joyce Kilmer).[3] We pause and say to ourselves, "silence, my soul, these trees are prayers !" (Rabindranath Tagore).[4] Generations have experienced the universe as "numinous" because it, or the Spirit through it, has been nodding (*nuo*) and beckoning to us to listen and move closer to God.

V

All this means that from the beginning of human history God has been coming to peoples in many ways, with an offer of love and life; God has been encountering peoples at various levels of reality, showing God's self in numerous symbols and images and speaking in diverse idioms. God has been inviting and challenging people, and enabling them to respond. For God never ceases to love and care for anything God has loved into being. God clothes in beauty and splendor the flowers of the field, feeds the birds in the sky, takes note of every sparrow that falls to the ground, and keeps count of every hair on our head. To God, human persons are of far greater worth than flowers and birds. We can then be sure that God has always walked with his human family and with everyone of its members, amply providing for the light and grace humans need in order to respond to God's initiatives and so reach wholeness. Humans have indeed responded in a variety of ways and measures. They have sought God, worshiped, and prayed. They have sensed God's demands, and tried to be just and kind to one another. They have given shape to symbols and celebrations in God's honor, from within many a concrete historical situation and cultural milieu.

That is how the many religious traditions have come to be, each with an authentic faith-experience of the Transcendent at its core, but differing from others according to differences in gifts received from Above and differences in the cultures of the communities concerned. In all these traditions, in their different ways of conduct and life, in their precepts and teachings, in their minds, hearts, rites, customs and scriptures, there is much that is precious and true, both religious and human. This surely is the fruit of the Word of God who illumines every human heart and questing community (cf. LG 16-17; AG 3,9,11; GS 22,92; NA 2; Jn 1:9). These spiritual gifts and treasures, these God-experiences and religious achievements are in their multiplicity and variety, mutually complementary, meant for exchange, sharing and mutual enrichment in the world-wide family of God, down the centuries, and across all ethnic, political and cultural boundaries.

VI

All this is God's doing, God's work through the Word in the Spirit, in view of the wholeness and happiness of all whom God has loved into existence, and with whom God shares divine reality and life. God's love for the world is so great, indeed, and so faithful and generous, that God gives his Word-Son for its liberation and salvation (Jn 3:16-17; 1 Tm 2: 4). The Word's entry into and participation in cosmic processes and in human history do honor to the whole creation and enhance the divine-human encounter, rendering it deeper, warmer, richer, and more beautiful, intimate and effective. With that, all human traditions—cultural, spiritual and religious—stand challenged to greater openness to God and to one another, to finer commitment to justice and love, as well as to global fraternity and responsibility. The Spirit is now more intimately active in peoples' hearts, cultures and religious heritage. The incarnation of the Word has infused new light and strength into the fabric of the universe and of human history, enabling it to welcome and realize more fully than ever the reign of God, which was inaugurated at creation and has been growing and achieving itself historically in and through every human commitment to justice and solidarity.

It is important to note that the coming of the Word enfleshed in Jesus of Nazareth and the emergence of his faith-community did not cause humanity's centuries-old and divinely led religious experiences and traditions to wither away and become redundant and meaningless. It is not clear that for Paul, "faith, once offered to Christians, abolishes, by virtue of a divine decree, the value of all religions" (J. Dupuis).[5] In Romans 1:18-32, the wrath of God is said to fall not on people's knowledge of God and religions but on their sin, immorality and idolatry; for "they knew God (from God's self-disclosure in creation) and yet they did not honor him as God nor gave thanks." With the knowledge they had of God from creation and from conscience (Rom 1:20-21; 2:14-15), they could have given God due worship. But they, some or many, failed. Even those who profess the Christian faith can sin and even turn idolatrous through greed, for "greed is the same thing as worship of a false God" (Col 3:5; Eph 5:5; Mt 6: 24). Elsewhere too what Paul rejects and wants to see destroyed is sin, and not religious traditions however imperfect (cf. 2 Cor 5:16-19; Eph 4:17-22; Col 3:5-10).

VII

It is true, nevertheless, that many Christian thinkers and even the Christian Churches have entertained for centuries the belief, asserted also officially, that "outside the (Roman Catholic) Church there is no salvation," no saving grace or faith or sacraments. This was a new version of an old Israelite view that the tribes they encountered in Canaan were to be exterminated and their cities given to the flames; these were to be placed under the curse of destruction (*herem*) by order of Israel's God. There was no salvation outside Israel (cf. Josh 6, 8,10 and 11). But that was before Israel came to a proper monotheistic faith. Once that faith was in place, Israel was able to recognize many a saint in the course of history, and to concern itself with bringing God's justice and love to the ends of the earth (Is 42:1-6; Amos 9:7). Even then the old habit of counting Yahweh as Israel's private good, disallowed to everybody else, persisted; and Jonah had to challenge it in a short story replete with exquisitely pungent humor.

Does the axiom, "No salvation outside the Church," purport to damn Israel's patriarchs and prophets along with all human beings who lived before the birth of a baby to Mary of Nazareth? Apparently not, though that would be in the logic of the axiom. The axiom has been applied only to the time after Jesus Christ, who has entrusted to his Church all the means of grace and faith necessary for salvation. It seems somewhat odd that, with such a fresh outpouring of love and grace as the Christ-event, the possibilities of salvation should shrink and God's mind become narrow. One would have expected the possibility of salvation to expand and render it easy for everyone to ride its waves. The axiom makes God small: either he is not the creator of everyone; or he did not call and destine everybody to eternal communion with himself; or, having created and called everyone, God forgot most of them, or arbitrarily excluded many and refused to give them the needed light and grace. In any case he could not be God; the axiom amounts to a confession of atheism. No wonder that today it stands repudiated. The official disowning of it began in 1949 with a letter the Vatican sent to the Archbishop of Boston. The rejection of the axiom was definitively sealed by the Second Vatican Council, (cf. LG 16; GS 22). The axiom itself seems to have been the offspring of extremist notions of original sin, and to have gained in strength through struggles against schisms and heresies, and through the power struggles between East and West and between popes and kings (e.g., the Council of Florence, 1442; and Boniface VIII's *Unam Sanctam* in 1302).

VIII

Today the Church has a more positive view of the religions of the world. She recognizes and respects their openness to the divine and their sense of the beckoning Spirit, all expressed in their worship, prayer and sacred scriptures, no less than in their (often corporate) commitment to human dignity, freedom, justice, and peace. The Church is anxious not only to share her spiritual riches with them, but also to share in their spiritual treasures, to initiate and carry on a dialogue at all levels of thought and life, and to work together to solve pressing human problems, alleviate human suffering, and build a gentle, joyful and beautiful world in tune with the One who is Love and is our common Origin and Destiny.

Jesus' Beatitudes and the entire message presented in the Sermon on the Mount (Mt 5-7) or the Sermon on the Plain (Lk 6:17-49), re-read in our context, could provide a starting point for dialogue between religions. Some corresponding and significant starting points in the spiritual tradition of India could be the following intuitions and aspirations of our ancestors:

The One Real (Truth) the sages call by many names
  ekam sad vipra bahudha vadanti (Rigveda 164.46).
The whole world is indeed a dear and little family
  vasudhaiva kutumbakam.
May all peoples be well and happy
  loka samasta sukhino bhavantu.
Non-injury (non-violence) is the highest religion or duty
  ahimsa paramo dharma.
One ought to work with eyes fixed on the integration
  (unity and well-being) of the whole world
  lokasamgrahamevapisampasyan kartum arhasi
  (Bhagavadgita 3: 20).
Meanwhile this could be our common prayer:
From the unreal (untruth) lead me to the Real (truth);
from darkness lead me to the Light;
and from death lead me to Immortal Life
  asato ma sadgamaya
  tamaso ma jyotir-gamaya
  mrtyor-ma amrtam gamaya (Brhadaronyaka Upanishad
  1. 3. 28).

References

[1]*Confessions*, 1.1.

[2]See "The Jordan, the Tiber, and the Ganges," in John Hick and Paul Knitter (eds.), *The Myth of Christian Uniqueness: Toward a Pluralistic Theology in Religions* (Maryknoll, N.Y.: Orbis, 1987), 89-106.

[3]"Trees," in Ralph L. Woods (ed.), *A Treasury of the Familiar* (New York: MacMillan, 1959), 583.

[4]"Stray Birds," in Sisir Kumar Das (ed.), *The English Writings of Rabindranath Tagore*, vol. 1 (New Delhi: Sahitya Academy, 1994), 408 (vs. 95).

[5]*Toward a Christian Theology of Religious Pluralism* (Maryknoll, N.Y.: Orbis, 1997), 48-49.

Part IV

TWO ROMAN DOCUMENTS

15

"Dialogue and Proclamation"

A Reading in the Perspective
of Christian-Muslim Relations

Archbishop Michael Louis Fitzgerald, M.Afr.

Introduction

Although questions were raised about certain points in Jacques Dupuis's book *Toward a Christian Theology of Religious Pluralism*, it offers a most remarkable synthesis of theological reflection on this important theme and will probably remain for a long time the standard work of reference in this field. When the volume was being presented at the Pontifical Gregorian University, I made the following observation:

> His book is a work of *general* theology. Can it be complemented by works of *contextual* theology? I am not so much thinking here of the geographical as of the religious context. Can the themes treated in this book be taken up in relation to single religions, Buddhism, Hinduism, even Traditional Religions? Would this be a worthwhile enterprise?[1]

The document *Dialogue and Proclamation*, of which Fr. Dupuis was one of the drafters, also remains at a general level. It recognizes nevertheless the need for more particularized approaches: "It is also important that specific studies on the relationship between dialogue and proclamation be undertaken, taking into account each religion within its geographical area and sociocultural context" (88).[2]

The present article will try to respond to this need by reading this document in the light of relations with Muslims. The reflections will still remain general, however, since restrictions of space will not make it possible to pay attention to the different geographical and cultural contexts.

The Relevance of the Theme

In showing a need for reflection on dialogue and proclamation, DP first calls attention to "a new awareness of the fact of religious plurality" (4a). The same paragraph speaks about the "clear evidence of revival" of certain religions. Both these observations apply to Islam. In the last decades the movement of populations has brought large numbers of Muslims into societies that are Christian, at least by tradition. Moreover many of the Muslims who have come to stay in Western societies are claiming the right to practice their religion to the full. This situation calls for renewed reflection on relations between Christians and Muslims.

DP speaks also about hesitation as regards to dialogue (4b), perhaps because of the problems it raises (4c). It could be noted that these hesitations have existed also among Muslims, but are gradually being overcome.[3]

The World Day of Prayer for Peace, in Assisi, October 27, 1986, was seen as having given a great impetus to interreligious relations (5). It is true that there were not many Muslims present at that event. On subsequent occasions, however, as the Prayer for Peace in Europe and especially in the Balkans, held in January 1993, and the Day of Prayer for Peace in the World, on January 24, 2002, Muslims responded much more readily to the invitation. This could be taken as a sign of greater confidence on their part and also of a recognition that they need to engage in dialogue with Christians and others.

All these factors could point to the utility of giving greater consideration to dialogue and proclamation within the context of Christian-Muslim relations.

A Christian Approach to Islam

The section of DP dedicated to interreligious dialogue starts with important reflections of a theological nature. It summarizes the teaching of the Second Vatican Council and of the more recent magisterium, and then suggests some elements for discernment in the attitude to take towards the religions.

Vatican II

The running title before (14) reads "Religious traditions are viewed positively." This could be illustrated by what the Council has to say about Islam.[4] The Muslims are given the "first place" among those who acknowledge the Creator and who adore the one God (LG 16). Thus Islam holds the first rank among the non-biblical monotheistic religions. Moreover it is said that the Church looks upon Muslims "with esteem" (NA 3). When one remembers how contentious the history of relations between Christians and Muslims has been, this declaration acquires added significance. It constitutes moreover a reminder and an exhortation to Christians, when tensions arise, to distinguish between the failures or excesses of some Muslims and the values of Islam. There are also general affirmations of the Declaration *Nostra Aetate* concerning religions in general. Religions provide answers for the fundamental questions of human existence (NA 1). Nothing that is true and holy in religions is rejected by the Church (NA 2). Therefore the members of the Church are encouraged to enter into a dialogue of exchange and collaboration with the members of other religions (ibid.). All this applies to Islam, although this is not stated explicitly.

DP has shown that "the Council has openly acknowledged the presence of positive values not only in the religious life of individual believers of other religious traditions, but also in the religious traditions to which they belong" (17). What are these values insofar as Islam is concerned?

There are matters concerning belief. There is the fact that "together with us [Christians] they [Muslims] adore the one merciful God, mankind's judge on the last day" (LG 16). The fact that Islam is an uncompromisingly monotheistic religion can raise difficulties for the acceptance of the "with us" of the Conciliar statement. Some Christians do not wish to admit that Muslims adore the same God, since the latter do not accept that there is a Trinity of Persons in God. Similarly there are Muslims who refuse to accept Christians as true monotheists. There is need for dialogue to clarify that a different understanding of God does not destroy the unity of belief in one God. Moreover Islam believes in a God "who has spoken to men" (NA 3), though the Council does not give any further details about the way Islam understands how God has communicated with human beings. The idea of prophecy is mentioned implicitly, since it is stated that Muslims venerate Jesus as a prophet, though not acknowledging him to be God, and that they honor Mary, the virgin mother of Jesus. The Council, however, to the disappointment of many Muslims, chose not to say anything about the role of Muhammad.[5] It is obvious that Christians could only at the most attribute to Muhammad a qualified prophetic role, which would be far below the Muslims' belief in his definitive role as the bringer of the final revelation, the seal of the prophets. Silence was therefore preferred.

With regard to the values in the way Muslims live their religion, emphasis is put on faith, with acknowledgment being given to Abraham as a model, and the way this faith is lived out in an upright life. In the practical manner of worshiping God reference is made by the Council to three of the five "pillars" of Islam: prayer, almsgiving and fasting (NA 3). There is silence once again on the first pillar, witness (*shahâda*), presumably because its second element consists in the profession of faith in Muhammad as Messenger of God, and on the last pillar, pilgrimage (*hajj*), probably because the pilgrimage to Mecca was also seen as being too intimately connected with the person of Muhammad. On all these points there is matter for dialogue between Christians and Muslims, examining both the commonalities and the differences.

After outlining the Council's positive attitude towards religions, DP also acknowledges that the Council stresses the continuing necessity of the missionary activity of the Church (18). This has to be remembered in relation to Muslims.

The Church, in announcing Jesus Christ and in proffering an invitation to join the community of believers in Jesus Christ, cannot exclude any category of persons. Yet this proclamation is to be accomplished in accordance with the principle of religious liberty as expressed in the Declaration *Dignitatis Humanae*. Here again there is an opportunity for dialogue, examining the concept and practice of both proclamation of the Gospel and *da'wa* (the call to Islam), a dialogue which may not always be easy but which can be fruitful.[6]

The Recent Magisterium

Since the Vatican Council there has been little development in the official teaching of the Church about Islam, yet the Popes have constantly encouraged an assimilation of the Council's vision. This can be seen from the many addresses concerned with Christian-Muslim dialogue, but also from their own practical example. The impact of Assisi 1986 has already been mentioned. The visit of John Paul II to al-Azhar, Cairo, February 24, 2000, and the warm reception he received there, has led to this day being commemorated annually. The visit to the Umayyad Mosque in Damascus in the Spring of 2001 was also of considerable significance, the first time a Sovereign Pontiff had ever entered a mosque. Important also was the invitation to representatives of the different Muslim communities, Sunni, Shi'ite, and Druze, to attend the Synod for Lebanon in 1995 as official observers.

Paul VI, when visiting Uganda in 1969, celebrated Mass in Namugongo, the place where many of the young Martyrs of Uganda were burned to death. Later, addressing the Islamic communities of Uganda, he stated: "In recalling the Catholic and Anglican Martyrs, We gladly recall also those confessors of the Muslim faith who were the first to suffer death, in the year 1848, for refusing to transgress the precepts of their religion."[7]

It is interesting to notice this acceptance of a "unity of witness" which anticipates, and in some measure even goes beyond, the "ecumenism of martyrdom" which John Paul II has emphasized.

For his part, John Paul II has given a strong impetus to dialogue with Muslims by appealing to Christians "to recognize and develop the spiritual bonds that unite us [Christians and Muslims]."[8] Accordingly John Paul II does not hesitate to speak about "brotherhood" between Christians and Muslims and to emphasize the role of faith. A clear statement in this vein is found in his address to Muslims in the Philippines in February 1981:

> I deliberately address you as brothers; that is certainly what we are, because we are members of the same human family, whose efforts, whether people realize it or not, tend towards God and the truth that comes from him. But we are especially brothers in God who created us and whom we are trying to reach, in our own ways, through faith, prayer and worship, through the keeping of his law and through submission to his designs.[9]

This may seem banal, but in the early Christian tradition the term "brother" was often reserved for fellow Christians, and even today there are some who would not wish to acknowledge the faith of Muslims. Yet the mystery of the unity of humanity, in its origins and destiny, is something to which the present Pope will return again and again. It is the true foundation for dialogue (28).

One further point could be added. DP had already drawn attention to the universal action of the Spirit (17). John Paul II returned to this in an address given during the General Audience on September 9, 1998:

It must be kept in mind that every quest of the human spirit for truth and goodness, and in the last analysis for God, is inspired by the Holy Spirit. The various religions arose precisely from this primordial human openness to God. At their origins we often find founders who, with the help of God's Spirit, achieved a deeper religious experience. Handed on to others, this experience took form in the doctrines, rites and precepts of the various religions.[10]

Though this statement remains general, it is significant since it would appear to be the first reference by the magisterium to the role of founders of religions. Whether and to what extent it applies to Muhammad would remain to be investigated.

Discernment

The fact that the presence of God can be seen in other religious traditions does not mean that everything in them is good. They have their limitations. Consequently

an open and positive approach to other religious traditions cannot overlook the contradictions which may exist between them and Christian revelation. It must, where necessary, recognize that there is incompatibility between some fundamental elements of the Christian religion and some aspects of such traditions (31)

Applying this to Islam, one would have to point to doctrinal differences, regarding the Trinity, the divinity of Christ, the death of Jesus on the cross and the redemptive value of his passion, death and resurrection, not to mention the different understanding of the relationship between human beings and God. There are also other points of contrast, for instance certain qur'anic prescriptions which would imply discrimination against women, or a different concept of religious liberty. Dialogue with Muslims cannot abstract from such. It cannot be mere accommodation but must include a critical stance.

Yet the challenge is not just one way. Our document points out: "Christians too must allow themselves to be questioned. Notwithstanding the fullness of God's revelation in Jesus Christ, the way Christians sometimes understand their religion and practice it may be in need of purification" (32).

Many Christians living among Muslims have experienced the purifying effect of contact with Islam. It is as if their faith is being scoured of accretions and brought back to its essential content. There can be a greater appreciation of the divine transcendence, but also of that great love which leads God to become man. There is less of a tendency to take the Incarnation for granted. Christians can be challenged too by the firmness of faith of Muslims and their readiness to express their faith in public. Though he did not mention Islam by name, John Paul II probably had Muslims in mind when he wrote:

> It sometimes happens that the firm belief of the followers of non-Christian religions—a belief that is also an effect of the Spirit of truth operating outside the visible confines of the Mystical Body—can make Christians ashamed at being often themselves disposed to doubt concerning the truths revealed by God and proclaimed by the Church, and prone to relax moral principles and open the way to ethical permissiveness (*Redemptor Hominis,* 6).

Nor did the Pope hesitate to suggest, in a talk to the parish priests of Rome at the beginning of Lent one year, that Muslims tend to take fasting more seriously than Christians.

Conversion

This section of DP ends with some reflections on the dialogue of salvation. It is because God has been in dialogue with humankind that the Church, and individual Christians, must be in dialogue with all (38). So the aim of dialogue is not merely mutual understanding and friendly relations (39). These should not be minimized, and remain a legitimate goal of dialogue. This is particularly so where Christian-Muslim relations are concerned, since these are so often fraught with tension. One of the tasks of dialogue will be to try to discover the causes of the tension, which quite often are not religious but rather economic, social and political, and then to build up confidence in order to remedy the situation.

Dialogue, however, can go deeper, leading to a strengthening of each one's religious commitment and a more generous response to God's personal call. This should not be understood as "helping Muslims to be better Muslims." It is rather an encouragement to a process of conversion to God. Of this a previous document had spoken: "In biblical language, and that of the Christian tradition, conversion is the humble and penitent return of the heart to God in the desire to submit one's life more generously to him. All persons are constantly called to this conversion."[11]

It must be said that within the Islamic tradition there is a wealth of spiritual writings which emphasize this constant process of conversion, in the search for sincerity, in the elimination of anything that might threaten single-minded devotion to God. In fact the need for on-going conversion could itself be a fruitful theme for Christian-Muslim dialogue.

The document just quoted continues, nevertheless: "In the course of this process, the decision may be made to leave one's previous spiritual or religious situation in order to direct oneself toward another" (ibid.).

It is important to keep open this possibility of conversion understood in this other sense as a change of religious allegiance. This is not something that Islam readily accepts. Apostasy (*ridda*), defined as "an act of rejection of faith committed by a Muslim whose Islam has been affirmed without any coercion," has serious legal consequences such as dissolving a marriage or annulling inheritance rights, and can even put the life of the convert from Islam in danger.[12] Of course the Catholic Church does not acquiesce easily to departure from the Church, and applies the canonical sanction of excommunication to the apostate, i.e. to one who totally repudiates the Christian faith.[13] Yet this does not entail civil consequences. The right to change one's religion, as part of the right to religious liberty, is one of the thorny questions that will keep returning in conversations between Christians and Muslims.

The Forms of Dialogue

The various forms of dialogue, dialogue of life, dialogue of action, dialogue of theological exchange, dialogue of religious experience (42), all exist in Christian-Muslim relations. It is hardly necessary to insist upon this. It should perhaps be said that theological dialogue is difficult, given the fundamental differences in belief which have already been mentioned. There is a danger of descending into polemics, defending one's own position and attacking that of the other by any means. Theological dialogue between Christians and Muslims will only be fruitful if it aims at clarification rather than refutation, and includes a real attempt to appreciate the logic of the other's position. In fact, however, formal dialogue between Christians and Muslims will often be concerned with social questions, such as the use of the earth's resources, the role of women in society, religious education, to mention only some of the topics discussed in colloquia in which the Pontifical Council for Interreligious Dialogue has been involved.

There is indeed a need "to join together in trying to solve the great problems facing society and the world" (44). There are examples of common action, such as a joining of forces to defend family values during the 1994 UN Cairo Conference on Population and Development. There have been joint statements condemning terrorism, put out by the Islamic-Catholic Liaison Committee and by the Joint Committee of Al-Azhar and the Pontifical Council for Interreligious Dialogue, following the events of September 11, 2001. There would be room for more cooperation to promote integral development, social justice and human liberation.

A further context calling for interreligious cooperation is that of culture (45). There is much to be done in the field of education, particularly since the increased religious plurality in society presents new challenges. There is a need to create a culture of dialogue, in order to prevent what might be the self-fulfilling prophecy of the "clash of civilizations." It is interesting to note that it was an Islamic country, Iran, that persuaded the United Nations to declare the Year 2001 to be the Year of the Dialogue of Civilizations.

Here it might be possible to point to something missing from the document *Dialogue and Proclamation*. When dealing with the different forms of dialogue the impression is given that it is always a question of *bilateral* dialogue, Buddhist/Christian, Hindu/Christian, Jewish/Christian, Muslim/Christian, though this is not said explicitly. There could have been some mention of *trilateral* and *multilateral* dialogue. Trilateral dialogue, Jews/Christians/Muslims, or the dialogue of the Abrahamic faiths, is not new, but is perhaps growing. The political realities of the Middle East render this type of dialogue difficult, but also underline how necessary it is, since understanding has to be created and respect and confidence restored. Because of the antagonisms that can be aroused in bilateral or trilateral dialogue, multilateral dialogue can prove useful by helping to soften the points of conflict. Here too there is a growth of interreligious organizations, responding to a felt need in today's society.

Dispositions for Dialogue

All the dispositions for dialogue indicated by DP (47-49) apply to relations with Muslims. A balanced attitude is required. On the one hand there is the need to overcome prejudices: that Islam is fatalistic, legalistic, morally lax, fanatical; that it is opposed to change, a religion of fear;[14] or that all Muslims are terrorists. Muslims are very sensitive to what they term *islamophobia*. On the other hand ingenuity is to be avoided. As has been said above, there are aspects of Islam which are incompatible with Christianity. Moreover there are radical elements in Muslim societies, from which Muslims themselves suffer, and these should not be ignored.

A further condition for fruitful dialogue is religious conviction. Christians entering into dialogue with Muslims should not be afraid to give witness to their faith in Jesus Christ. Dialogue leads to mutual witness, but this cannot come about if one of the partners is unwilling to share that which is held to be most precious. Of course, as Peter says, this witness needs to be given in the right manner: "have your answer ready for people who ask you for the reason for the hope that you all have. But give it with courtesy and respect and with a clear conscience" (1 Pet 3:15-16).

The third condition is openness to truth. Because of their belief in Jesus Christ as the Son of God, Lord and Savior of the whole of humankind, Christians may be inclined towards a sense of superiority. They should remember that "the fullness of truth received in Jesus Christ does not give individual Christians the guarantee that they have grasped that truth. In the last analysis truth is not a thing we possess, but a person by whom we must allow ourselves to be possessed" (49).

It can be useful to try to convey this conviction to Muslims. They like to classify Christians as " People of the Book," yet, as our name implies, we are followers of a person, Jesus Christ, who is the Way, the Truth and the Life. Now Muslims too can develop a sense of superiority, based on their conviction that to them the final revelation has been given. Perhaps they would need to be encouraged to accept the radical meaning of their frequent invocation *Allâhu akbar*, God is always greater that anything we can ever conceive, and it is He who is calling us to Himself. That is why dialogue can be described as a process in which we "walk together toward truth."[15]

Obstacles

DP is a realistic document and has no hesitation in mentioning difficulties that can arise in dialogue (51-54). It is not necessary to deal at length with all these, but some have particular relevance to Christian-Muslim relations. There is mention of sociopolitical factors. These could include majority-minority relations. It is difficult to engage in dialogue if being in a minority situation leads to the adoption of a defensive attitude. Such a difficulty can only be overcome by ensuring freedom and respect for each person's rights. There is also mention of burdens of the past. These would include not only the Crusades, which still have the capacity for rankling Muslims, and colonialism, but also the practice of slavery which has aroused negative feelings toward Islam, especially among many peoples of Africa. The Declaration *Nostra Aetate* took cognizance of this: "Over the centuries many quarrels and dissensions have arisen between Christians and Muslims. The sacred Council now pleads with all to forget the past, and urges that a sincere effort be made to achieve mutual understanding" (NA 3).

It may not be possible to forget the past; there could be an attempt to re-read the past together and so come to a better understanding and even to a " purification of memories."

Another obstacle mentioned is suspicion about the other's motives in dialogue. On the one hand, some Muslims tend to think that Christians enter into dialogue as a covert way of trying to bring about conversions to Christianity, just as they entertain the same suspicions regarding the charitable activity of the Church, its *diakonia*. From the Christian side there is a certain diffidence with regard to Muslims, the feeling that they are only entering into dialogue in order to strengthen the position of the Muslim minorities and bring about the eventual domination of Islam. This can be compounded when there is seen to be a lack of reciprocity, religious freedom demanded for Muslims in Western countries but not granted to Christians in certain Muslim majority countries. These questions themselves have to be tackled in dialogue. As is stated very clearly: "Many of these obstacles arise from a lack of understanding of the true nature and goal of interreligious dialogue. These need therefore to be constantly explained" (53).

Yet certainly progress has been made. Muslims have set up their own structures for dialogue, such as the International Islamic Forum for Dialogue, or the

Permanent Committee of Al-Azhar for Dialogue with Monotheistic Religions. With the help of these structures it has been possible, as has been mentioned above, to make joint statements of Catholics and Muslims about such issues as terrorism, or the situation in the Holy Land. This is a sign of growing confidence.

Proclaiming Jesus Christ

The second section of the document *Dialogue and Proclamation* gives a summary presentation of the mandate given to the Church to proclaim Jesus Christ as Lord and Savior. Much of this does not require any particular commentary from the point of view of Christian-Muslim relations, but some observations can be made.

There is an insistence on the urgency of proclamation (66). However difficult it may be for Muslims to accept Jesus Christ as Son of God, Lord and Savior, this does not dispense Christians from bearing witness to their faith, and inviting Muslims to embrace that faith if and when, in the Spirit, they discern that it is the moment to do this. As is made clear, the Church is to follow the lead of the Spirit (68). This will give a particular quality to the manner in which the Gospel is proclaimed: with confidence in the power of the Spirit, but also with humility and respect; in a dialogical and inculturated manner (70), recognizing and making use of the values which those who are being addressed have received from Islam.

So obstacles to proclaiming the Gospel to Muslims could be created by a lack of appreciation for their religious background and an attitude of superiority (73). On the other hand, some difficulties may arise from outside the Christian community (74), such as the circumstances obtaining in some majority Muslim countries. These could be restrictions with regard to religious freedom, limiting the possibility of presenting the Christian message or putting restrictions on the possibility of conversion to Christianity. There is in certain places an identification of belonging to a particular nationality or ethnic group and being a Muslim. In the light of this it is recalled that proclamation is not the only element of the Church's mission, and that

> in situations where, for political or other reasons, proclamation as such is practically impossible, the Church is already carrying out her evangelizing mission not only through presence and witness but also through such activities as work for integral human development and dialogue (76).

It must be repeated that these activities, the social outreach of the Church and its commitment to dialogue, are not geared to proclamation but are ways in which the Church tries to express the respectful love of God for all people. Nevertheless, the duty of proclamation remains: "in other situations where people are disposed to hear the message of the Gospel and have the possibility of responding to it, the Church is in duty bound to meet their expectations" (ibid.).

Dialogue and Proclamation Taken Together

The document ends with some reflections on the relationship between dialogue and proclamation. They are closely linked, for dialogue contains an element of witness to one's own faith, and proclamation is to be carried out in a dialogical manner. Yet they remain distinct, for the goal of each is different. They are both authentic elements of the Church's evangelizing mission, and in fact " one and the same local Church, one and the same person, can be diversely engaged in both" (77). This was my own personal experience in Northern Sudan, where the Catholic parish was at one and the same time running a catechumenate, providing adult education with the help of Muslim teachers for all who wished to avail of the opportunity, and generally cultivating good relations with the Muslim population. The need to attend to "the particular circumstances of each local Church" (78) is very relevant with regard to Christian-Muslim relations.

A reference is made to a "spirit of emulation" (79), encouragement given to all religious institutions and movements "to meet, to enter into collaboration, and to purify themselves in order to promote truth and life, holiness, justice, love and peace" (80). In today's increasingly pluralistic world there is a growth in multi-religious movements. Christians and Muslims find themselves side by side, and together with people of other religious traditions, in trying to face up to common problems. They stimulate one another to greater efforts. John Paul II has included interreligious dialogue in his "charter of action" for the Church in the current millennium:

> In the climate of increased cultural and religious pluralism, which is expected to mark the society of the new millennium, it is obvious that this dialogue will be especially important in establishing a sure basis for peace and warding off the dread spectre of those wars of religions which have so often bloodied human history. The name of the one God must become increasingly what it is: *a name of peace and a summons to peace* (*Novo Millennio Ineunte*, 55).

These reflections end with a brief meditation on Jesus as the model of dialogue (85-86). These paragraphs need to be expanded, and this is in part at least the aim of a further document being prepared by the Pontifical Council for Interreligious Dialogue on the spirituality of dialogue. Christians who are engaged in relations with Muslims can find a stimulus to their meditation in the Islamic view of Jesus, not only according to the Qur'an and classical tradition, but also in the approach of certain contemporary Muslims.[16] Moreover the mystery of Jesus, though understood differently by Christians and Muslims, invites to further dialogue:

> Why did God wish to speak to humankind? What did he wish to say? How has he said it? How is his word to be received? Whatever may be the final

identity that Muslims and Christians attribute to and recognize in Jesus, Son of Mary—and on this point, as has been noticed, there are profound differences—it remains true that he appears to both groups as someone who has a particular relationship with the mystery of the Word and the process of its transmission: he belongs to their spiritual patrimony and therefore cannot remain foreign to them. It is consequently desirable that, while respecting the final identity which each attributes to him, they may derive mutual enrichment from the values of faith and submission, of love and sacrifice, of which he remains for many the symbol, the witness and the model.[17]

Conclusion

Dialogue and Proclamation called for specific studies with regard to the different religions (87-88). The present essay has been one attempt to heed this call. It has tried to show that, although this document remains at a general level, the principles it announces and the guidance it gives are fully relevant to relations between Christians and Muslims. It can be considered a faithful reflection on and application of the Conciliar Declaration *Nostra Aetate*. The events of the last decade and the entry into a new millennium have in no way diminished its importance. Those who helped to draft it, including Jacques Dupuis, are deserving of gratitude.

References

[1]Michael L. Fitzgerald, "Toward a Christian Theology of Religious Pluralism by Fr. Jacques Dupuis," in *Pro Dialogo* 108 (2001/3), 336.

[2]Pontifical Council for Interreligious Dialogue, Congregation for the Evangelization of Peoples, *Dialogue and Proclamation*, Vatican City, 1991, no. 88. This document will be referred to as DP; the numbers given between parentheses in the text refer to its paragraphs. On the relationship of DP to the encyclical *Redemptoris Missio*, which preceded it by a few months, see Jacques Dupuis, "Dialogue and Proclamation in Two Recent Documents," in *Bulletin. Pontificium Consilium pro Dialogo inter Religiones* 80 (1992),165-72.

[3]See Ataullah Siddiqui, *Christian-Muslim Dialogue in the Twentieth Century* (London, Macmillan, 1997), 50-56.

[4]R. Caspar, "Islam according to Vatican II," in Michael L. Fitzgerald and Robert Caspar, *Signs of Dialogue. Christian Encounter with Muslims* (Zamboanga City, Philippines: Silsilah Publications, 1992), 233-45.

[5]See Siddiqui, *Christian-Muslim Dialogue*, 35.

[6]See Khurshid Ahmad and David Kerr (eds.), *Christian Mission and Islamic Da'wah*, a special issue of the *International Review of Mission* 65 (1976), and also J.-M. Gaudeul and M. L. Fitzgerald, "A Difficult Dialogue: Chambésy 1976," in *Encounter. Documents for Muslim-Christian Understanding* 36 (Rome: Pontifical Institute of Arabic and Islamic Studies, June-July 1977).

[7]Francesco Gioia (ed.), *Interreligious Dialogue. The Official Teaching of the Catholic Church (1963-1995)* (Boston: Pauline Books & Media, 1997), no. 263.

[8]"Address to the Catholic Community of Ankara," November 29, 1979, in Gioia, *Interreligious Dialogue*, no. 339.

[9]In Gioia, *Interreligious Dialogue*, no. 363.

[10]See *Insegnamenti di Giovanni Paolo II*, vol. 21/2 (Vatican: Libreria Editrice Vaticana, [1998], 250); English translation: "Journeying Together: The Catholic Church in Dialogue with the Religious Traditions of the World," in the *Pontifical Council for Interreligious Dialogue* (Vatican: Libreria Editrice Vaticana, 1999), 13.

[11]"The Attitude of the Church toward Followers of other Religions," Secretariat for Non-Christians, no. 37.

[12]See the various articles on this topic by Mahmoud Ayoub and Sami A. Aldeeb Abu-Sahlieh in *Islamochristiana* 20 (1994).

[13]This refers to canons nos. 751 and 1364 of the *Codex Iuris Canonici* (Vatican: Libreria Editrice Vaticana, 1983).

[14]On the elimination of these prejudices, see Maurice Borrmans, *Guidelines for Dialogue between Christians and Muslims* (New York/Mahwah, N.J.: Paulist Press, 1990), 70-77.

[15]"Attitude of the Church," no. 13.

[16]See Maurice Borrmans, *Jésus et les musulmans d'aujourd'hui* (Paris, Desclée, 1996).

[17]Ibid., 2377 (my translation).

16

"Ecclesia in Asia"

Hans Waldenfels, S.J.

Retrospect and Prospect

On November 9, 1999, Pope John Paul II published the Post-Synodal Apostolic Exhortation *Ecclesia in Asia*, which provided the results of the Special Asian Synod that took place in the Vatican from April 18 to May 14, 1998. In the following year, 2000, on August 6, the letter found its continuation in the declaration *Dominus Iesus* authored by the Congregation for the Doctrine of the Faith. The connection between these two Roman documents[1] became evident through the *notification* published on February 26, 2001, by the same Congregation dealing with *Toward a Christian Theology of Religious Pluralism* by Father Jacques Dupuis, S.J., a teacher of dogmatic theology who deserves our high respect and gratitude. Men like him, who honestly and at the same time prudently reflect upon grave problems of our times, do not call for warnings but invite endorsement and encouragement. The various Roman documents, however, manifest a certain attitude in dealing with both the local Asian Churches and theological reflection. Therefore, they should be critically re-read and reconsidered—and that all the more, because often enough people get the feeling that discourse inside the *communio Ecclesiarum* calls for improvement and the development of truly dialogical intra-church structures. Such changes are required because they would give witness to the credibility and seriousness of the Church in her request for a dialogue between both the Church and world and the Church and other religions. Therefore, I would like to examine the ways of arguing in *Ecclesia in Asia*, to direct attention to some crucial issues in the Asian context, and, finally, to mention some focal points which are highly important for the development of the local churches in Asia. That will lead to a retrospective view of the Roman document becoming a prospective view opening up the future of the apostolic work in Asia.

Perception

On the Structure of Ecclesia in Asia

The document consists of seven chapters, from which chapter 1 (*The Asian Context*) calls for our special attention. Chapters 2-4 deal with fundamental positions of the Christian faith and its proclamation: chapters 2 and 4 with Jesus the Redeemer as a gift to Asia, especially Jesus the Savior as he has to be proclaimed; chapter 3 with the Holy Spirit as Lord and giver of life. Chapters 5-7 treat more practical issues from various perspectives: chapter 5 (*Community and Dialogue for Mission*) describes the fields of partnership in dialogue: communion within the Church, solidarity among the Christian churches, and ecumenical and interreligious dialogue. Chapter 6 (*The Service of Human Promotion*) has as its keywords: social doctrine of the Church, the dignity of the human person, the preferential option for the poor, the gospel of life, health care, education, peace-making, the problems of globalization and foreign debts, and the environment. Chapter 7 (*Witnesses to the Gospel*) deals with the different groups involved in the proclamation of faith: pastors and pastoral workers, lay-people, families, youth, those working with the mass media, and martyrs.

The enumeration of the various topics shows that the document is mainly occupied with problems which are common to all people throughout the world and not really specific to Asians. That leads to the conclusion that the face of Asia has to be looked for in chapter 1 and its description of the Asian context. In a certain way it becomes evident how Asia is seen through the eyes of those who prepared the papal document; their points of interest explain the basis for "trans-lating" the Christian message into the Asian context.

The Asian Context

For the authors of *Ecclesia in Asia* it must have been highly important that Jesus the Savior "took flesh as an Asian" (1) and that the Near East with Palestine is considered part of Asia (see, for instance, 5, 6, and 9). Certainly things can be seen like that. However, that Indians, Chinese, Koreans, Japanese and other Asians judge things in the same way, is not at all sure. No doubt, it might flatter people to know that their continent can be considered the native soil for all the great world religions. And yet, that does not prevent them from calling Christianity a religion of the "Far West" and a "foreign religion."

The outline of the Asian context starts with a short account of the "Religious and Cultural Realities," the "Economic and Social Realities," and the "Political Realities;" it is followed by a comparatively lengthy sketch about "the Church in Asia: Past and Present." Curiously, in the whole outline modern Japan is not mentioned once.[2]

There are two front lines in Asia, as many observers agree: the multiplicity of religions and the social inequality including the problem of the poor. That leads to two theological mainstreams which, however, do not oppose but complement each other:[3] the theology of religions or—as Jacques Dupuis puts it—of religious pluralism,[4] and the theology of liberation in view of the various social fields of constraint and oppression. Strangely the two mainstreams of theological thought are treated in the Roman document only in a rather superficial and vague manner.

The Religions

The religions in Asia are enumerated in the following way:

> Asia is also the cradle of the world's major religions—Judaism, Christianity, Islam and Hinduism. It is the birthplace of many other spiritual traditions such as Buddhism, Taoism, Confucianism, Zoroastrianism, Jainism, Sikhism and Shintoism. Millions also espouse traditional or tribal religions, with varying degrees of structured ritual and formal religious teaching. The Church has the deepest respect for these traditions and seeks to engage in sincere dialogue with their followers. The religious values they teach wait their fulfilment in Jesus Christ. (6)

At the beginning the reader is not invited to look at the Indian subcontinent, at Central Asia with China, at the Far East with Japan and Korea but at the marginal regions of the Near East (from the Western point of view): with Palestine and the Arabic countries. The quotation calls on the one hand for a sincere dialogue, but ends on the other hand with a traditional theological judgment.

In a second paragraph a good number of cultural and religious values are enumerated, among them "the spirit of religious tolerance and peaceful co-existence," "a remarkable capacity for accommodation and a natural openness to the mutual enrichment of peoples," "signs of great vitality and a capacity for renewal," and "a deep thirst for spiritual values":

> All of this indicates an innate spiritual insight and moral wisdom in the Asian soul, and it is the core around which a growing sense of "being Asian" is built. This "being Asian" is best discovered and affirmed not in confrontation and opposition, but in the spirit of complementarity and harmony. In this framework of complementarity and harmony, the Church can communicate the Gospel in a way which is faithful both to her own Tradition and to the Asian soul. (6)

Unfortunately this point of view has little impact upon the arguments which follow. But how can an interreligious dialogue take place when the gifts and talents of the others are not taken into account anymore?

The Social Realities

Evidently it is easier for Church circles to analyze the social realities and to perceive the various features of the process of urbanization and the impacts and consequences of modern civilization (cf. 7): exploitation of the weaker sectors of society, the emergence of urban conglomerations which lead to organized crime, terrorism, prostitution, degradation and exploitation of women, abuse of children, unsurmountable poverty, illiteracy, lack of education, and the denial of basic human rights and fundamental freedoms. In perceiving these realities the Church does not compete with other religions. However, the Church cannot be indifferent in situations like these, because to a large extent present social realities result from the technological transfer coming from the West, from the invasion of *"globalization"* with all its opportunities and dangers.

Globalization refers to the many net-works connecting the different regions of the world by way of communications, mass media and trade, by interdependence in the supply of petroleum and water, by scientific transfers in the fields of biology, medicine, physics and chemistry, and by space exploration and space travel. All of this, on the one hand, leads to new insights and possible uses in daily social life; on the negative side, however, globalization involves many items which can endanger humankind, even in its very existence. *Ecclesia in Asia* mentions the eye-catching negative phenomena in the process of modernization, without, however, giving reasons for them. Reasons should be produced on the basis of anthropological research and the findings of cultural sciences.

Here we should not overlook the fact that the process of globalization levels down many differences and thus destroys multiplicity in favor of uniformity. The tension between universality and particularity is reduced, to the disadvantage of the latter. Notwithstanding the positive side of global net-works, in many cases they lead to a reduction of space for freedom and create new dependencies. Even if solidarity and a sense of community are emphasized and the notion of *"inter"* (between nations, religions, cultures etc.) emerges strongly, identity can be lost, and new centralizations produced, and that not only in the field of economics. Serious reflection on the reasons for these developments is missing in *Ecclesia in Asia*. Probably a review of developments inside the Church—moving away from the importance of the local churches toward a restoration of a centralized universal Church—would have invited a critical view of church developments as well. What *Ecclesia in Asia* explains about local Churches and the universal Church in nos. 25-27 remains rather abstract and along the lines of formal considerations; at its best it recalls facts but does not open new horizons for the future.

In the overall description of the economic-social-political realities we come to the point that—as with the paragraph on religions and cultures—the conclusions remain rather general and cannot be distinguished from advice given to other continents and cultures in the world. We have to add that the given advice follows more or less the "dogmatic" self-understanding of the editors. This is all the more regrettable because for decades the Federation of Asian Bishops' Conferences (FABC) has been engaged in seeking solutions to all the questions at issue, and many proposals have been published by the FABC secretariat. The series *FABC Papers* is a rich mine for anybody who wants to know about pastoral and ecclesio-sociological issues in Asia. I wonder why *Ecclesia in Asia* does not mention this series at all and evidently does not make use of it.[5]

Dialogue

In our times we do not have to call for dialogue; we have to establish and enter into conversations.[6] That cannot be difficult for a Church which believes in the triune God. *Dialogue,* however, always implies both listening and speaking—*listening* because dialogue presupposes partnership between several (at least two) equivalent (not equal) participants, *speaking* because everyone expresses himself and acts from his/her own standpoint. *Interreligious dialogue* means that the different participants introduce their own particular solutions to the basic questions of humankind. In a document like *Ecclesia in Asia* it is not enough to enumerate the other religions or list a series of well-known virtues and attitudes. It has to be asked how the religions of Asia reply to the questions posed in *Nostra Aetate* no. 1:

> What is the human being? What is the meaning and the purpose of life? What is the good, what sin? Where does suffering come from? What is its significance? What is the way to true happiness? What is death, the judgment and the reward after death? And finally: What is the ultimate and unspeakable mystery of our existence from which we come and to which we go?

All the basic terms mentioned here—human being, meaning, purpose, good and evil, suffering, way, happiness, death, reward, "beyond (death)," and mystery—can be found also in Asian religions. Therefore these religions are obviously able to dialogue with Christianity. These are common questions that we must take up.

One might argue that such a project is beyond the scope of the Roman document, and to a certain extent that is true. And yet: did not the local Asian Churches and their theologians deserve that their efforts be appreciated or at least recognized? *Ecclesia in Asia* does not show any appreciation for the work done by theologians, foreign and native. Their endeavors cannot be restricted to the education of ecclesial leaders, as mentioned in 43. If there is a continent where men and women are engaged in finding access to spiritual traditions outside Christianity and in testing how they could be applied to the traditional Christian context, it is Asia. It is in Asia that people have learnt that all dialogues in words begin in dialogues of silence. Because of the incomprehensibility of silence, non-verbalized dialogues in silence are exposed to risks and dangers. Nevertheless, it makes sense to follow the traces of the Spirit wherever he works, and to search—in the words of Hans Urs von Balthasar—for "the Unknown beyond the Word." This theologian, who remains highly respectable in official ecclesial circles, wrote in an essay on "the Unknown beyond the Word":[7]

> As Christian contemplation in the dimensions of divine silence of love cannot and will not be detached from the Word manifested in the flesh, from the human being who succeeded to be the pure expression of God, so Christian action of love will not and cannot be able to get detached from the

visibility of the Church as brotherhood and vessel of the sacraments and the word. (At the same time) even while transcending into the freedom of encountering *every* fellow-creature . . . every worldly beauty in nature and art, every human good and even sin, ugliness, and lie in every situation unforeseen,—it will not be kept on leading-strings by the word and not be directed by receipts and time-tables which can be consulted, it is rather exposed to the dimension of creative invention. Only by faith we are enabled to let go the word as a kind of railing and to walk free from giddiness in the space of freedom; only in faithful hope we can dare ourselves with Peter out of the boat into the wavy infinity of God's Spirit. All of sudden there exist no formulas anymore, the other standing before us would neither understand it nor could he/she use it; he/she demands something else, unknown to him/her, unknown also to us, something which to both of us only the Creator Spirit of Love can give.

Perspectives

The daring phrases of Hans Urs von Balthasar open up a future which nobody can measure. Since, however, even the "Unknown beyond the Word" is mediated by words, even in a stammering manner it is appropriate—as a second step—to deal with some perspectives which, in interreligious encounter between Christianity and other Asian religions, will be important for a cooperative effort toward peace and justice in the world. We consider mainly three points: (1) the image of the world and the human being with its linguistic substrata (*philosophical-anthropological*), (2) the genuine Christian point of view (*theological-Christological*), (3) the Church and the ways of following Christ (*ecclesiological-pneumatological*).

Image of the World and Humankind (**Weltbild** *and* **Menschenbild**).

The plurality in the ways of being human we experience, first of all, in the multiplicity of languages.[8] In Christian understanding, we swing between the message about the confusion of languages at Babel (which entails a negative view of plurality) and the Pentecostal miracle of languages—people understand each other in various languages and experience that as an enrichment (which leads to a positive view of plurality). In Asia, the experience of multiplicity seems to prevail in anthropological and cosmological approaches as well. That does not mean that the unity of all things is not seen; actually unity seems to act in the background as an incomprehensible and inconceivable point of convergence, and that to the extent that wherever it imposes itself in its full power and might, daily life tends to become an illusion. Obviously individuals by no means enjoy the importance and dignity which they possess in Western history with all its demands for human self-determination and self-reflection.

Here we cannot speak for all Asian languages. However, we cannot overlook the fact that the texture of human relationships is highly developed in the Chinese language and all the languages it has influenced. These relations and structures can also be observed in the Indian religions and many tribal religions as well. They even go beyond the limits of death. Here we find the intersection of two phenomena. On the one hand, people still cultivate and keep contact with the dead; ancestor worship is very much alive. On the other hand, belief in reincarnation touches upon the wide fields of suffering where people become aware of the many ways they endure unfreedom and constraint. In this sense relational textures and net-works are not only a blessing; in many instances they are experienced as fateful and call for liberation.

Existing relational net-works are carried away by the many side-effects of modern "civilization" which comes from the West and brings with it many destructive powers. Traditions are destroyed; country life changes to urban life; innumerable people are uprooted and lose their roots in family and village life. At the same time they lose sight of their faith and their religion; they do not believe anymore in the traditional religious answers about the beginning and end of human life and the world.

As regards Asian world religions, their power of renewal partly comes from their growing resistance to Western impulses and their most important religious basis, Christianity. As long as Western inventions were considered profitable for civilizing processes, Christianity, too, was given a chance; for in countries oriented to Christianity, Christian religion seemed to be at the root of their success. A good example of this comes from the Polynesian countries with their various forms of the cargo cult. However, wherever Western influences, colonialism, modern technologies and globalization are viewed critically, opposition to Christianity as a Western, foreign religion grows. At the same time the inspiration for the local religions is reconsidered, and these religions begin once again to exercise their fascination even beyond their home bases. In the Western world of today Hinduism, Buddhism, and Taoism, for instance, have become religious alternatives.

The Unique Christ

Dominus Iesus, as well as *Ecclesia in Asia,* emphasizes Jesus of Nazareth as unique; at the same time they announce him as the universal mediator of salvation. *Ecclesia in Asia* explicitly calls him "the only Savior" (no. 11; see also, for instance, nos. 13, 14, 18, and 20), though without discussing the teachings of the Asian religions. Rightly Jesus Christ is said to be a "gift to Asia." But the question, what kind of gifts the Asian religions—in the sense of the wise men from the East—bring to the crib in adoration of the Lord remains unanswered. Here we cannot repeat what Jacques Dupuis in his landmark volume of 1997 expounded about the history of Christian approaches to and dealings with religious pluralism. We cannot discuss the answers of Christian doctrine concerning the ways toward salvation and the overcoming of suffering, guilt, death and eternal damnation. Our purpose here is more modest. We want to point to some barriers which oppose the Christian doctrine of the uniqueness of Christ.

We recalled above the multiplicity of languages. We called attention to the fact that Asian thought is strongly shaped by relations, connections, and networks, as well as by polarities and oppositions—with the consequence that, at first glance, whatever is single does not connect but remains isolated. However, wherever unity and unicity exercise a one-sided effect, it results in an immense absorption which makes any plurality vanish—as the ocean hides all drops of water and waves which the rivers collect, and no drop of water, no wave, and no river exists anymore.

There is one more point: the uniqueness of Christ refers to the singularity of a human person in history whose life-span runs from conception and birth to the time of inevitable death. However, where history is considered a process which can be repeated and in which the ordinary individual usually leaves behind only some few tiny traces, people brought up in thought patterns which do not highly value individuality and singularity have to gain, first of all, a basic understanding of uniqueness and singularity in general. To get the facts straight: Western people, also Western Christian thinkers, cannot and should not simply presuppose that Asian people easily understand the important role which individuality, singularity and uniqueness play in Occidental thought and life. Besides, Lessing's famous saying ("Accidental truths of history never can become the proof of necessary truths of reason")[9] shows that even the European enlightenment was not ready to ascribe universal significance to single historical events or occurrences; we cannot expect Asians to understand at once the positive meaning of singularity. The difficulty of valuing personality positively can be seen by referring to the late Japanese philosopher Keiji Nishitani.[10] He is one of the few Asian thinkers who rather early realized that for Western people "being a person" contains a very strong positive meaning, which for Asians is difficult to grasp. Where people do not understand the meaning of uniqueness, obviously it must be difficult to introduce them to the uniqueness of Christ and the universality of salvation offered by him alone.

Here we have to pay attention to the concepts which are chosen for translation. To give one example: in order to translate the radical way of God's incarnation as it took place in Jesus of Nazareth, Indians use the Sanskrit term *"avatāra."* In its basic meaning the term refers to various descents of the deity *Vishnu* and proves to be only relatively suitable to explain God's unique incarnation in Jesus Christ. Unfortunately for Indian theologians it seems to be extremely difficult to discuss this situation with Roman authorities.[11]

There are other instances. Do Western theologians imagine what it means to a local church when the national episcopal conference changes the term for God? Just that happened in Japan after the Pacific War, when for various reasons the conference decided to adopt as the term for God the native *kami* instead of the originally Chinese *ten-shu* (Lord of Heaven). Both terms have their own root meaning, which only after long reflection becomes compatible with the Judeo-

Christian concept of God. It was the late Japanese bishop of Hiroshima, Dominicus Yoshimatsu Noguchi, who reckoned the decision in favor of *kami* among the outstanding events in the history of Japanese thought, because in many circles of the population the term provoked a monotheistic view of God instead of the traditional polytheism.

Since the Chalcedonian formula *"vere Deus, vere homo"* stands behind the Christian conviction of the uniqueness of Christ and classically expresses this uniqueness, it must be clear that without a thorough-going discussion of the concept of God the doctrine of the unique Christ and the universality of his salvific work will remain a closed book.

The same proves to be true regarding the doctrine of the Holy Spirit. Here again it would be very helpful to study the possibilities which a language offers for speaking about spirit, and especially about the Holy Spirit. We know about the differences between the Latin *spiritus,* the Greek *pneuma* and the Hebrew *ruach*. Moving to the English language—unlike German where we have only the term *Geist* which can be used in singular and plural—we find two terms, *spirit* and *ghost*. Without entering into a more detailed discussion, we have to notice that in the Sino-Japanese context, including Korean, we discover several terms referring to "spirit." This brings up the question: which of them is the most qualified to express the reality of the Holy Spirit? I mention only four terms in Japanese: *ki, rei, kokoro, sei-shin.* Japanese Christians translate Holy Spirit with *sei-rei,* but we should know that the meaning of *rei* comes close to the English *ghost.* For Chinese theology Aloysius Chang, S.J., has suggested adopting the Chinese term *ch'i* (Japanese *ki*), a basic term which implies atmosphere, air, breath, breathing, and energy.[12] These examples show that it is not enough to argue in favor of the uniqueness of Christ and his salvific work simply through theses and their explanations; we need to prepare the linguistic and conceptual ground in which God's action through Jesus Christ in the Spirit can take root.

Church and Following Jesus

The Post-Synodal Exhortation is entitled *Ecclesia in Asia.* That brings us to the Church and its appearance in Asia. Strangely enough the Church is not a major topic in the document. The relationship of unity and plurality, the universal Church and local churches, is not elaborated with a view to the concrete forms which the Church has developed on the Asian continent. In the foreground is the unity of the Church which finds its strongest expression in Papal Primacy (see 24-25). As the text states, "The Synod Fathers acknowledged the service which the Dicasteries of the Roman Curia and the Holy See's Diplomatic Service rendered to the local Churches, in the spirit of communion and collegiality" (25). The Catholic Eastern Churches are mentioned in particular (27), as well as the suffering Churches in the territories of the former Soviet Union, in China, in Korea, and in Jerusalem (28).

What is missing becomes clear when the "Key Areas of Inculturation" are treated and encouraging words are expected. With regard to the liturgy we read:

The national and regional Bishops' Conferences need to work more closely with the Congregation for Divine Worship and the Discipline of the Sacraments in the search for effective ways of fostering appropriate forms of worship in the Asian context. Such cooperation is essential because the Sacred Liturgy expresses and celebrates the one faith professed by all and, being the heritage of the whole Church, cannot be determined by local Churches in isolation from the universal Church. (22)

Here we ask: What are the rights of the bishops, the bishops' conferences, the local churches, the pastors, and the lay-people? Which processes of learning are supported? And again: which language is competent and decisive? And who judges whether translations are faithful to the matters at stake, and whether they serve the people who speak the language and are supposed to understand the texts? After all, the proclamation of the Gospel is not only a theological affair, but a linguistic matter as well, with all the consequences that involves.

The task of interreligious dialogue is beautifully stated:

Interreligious relations are best developed in a context of openness to other believers, a willingness to listen and the desire to respect and understand others in their differences. For all this, love of others is indispensable. This should result in collaboration, harmony and mutual enrichment. (31)

However, what is valid in external contacts, must, first of all, stand the test inside the *Una sancta*. Hence we expect a mutual listening between the local churches, a recognition of their characteristic features and an affirmation of mutual enrich-ments. After all, how can the Church "take from the various cultures the positive elements already found in them" (21), unless she experiences them beforehand?

The statements about inculturation are to be found in chapter 4: *Jesus the Savior: Proclaiming the Gift*. However, since Jesus belongs to the history of hu-mankind, following Christ is explained by narratives. Here we come across a very interesting observation which should be applied wherever structures, men-tal as well as organizational and social, threaten to hinder the activity of the Spirit:

In general, narrative methods akin to Asian cultural forms are to be preferred. In fact, the proclamation can most effectively be made by narrating his story, as the Gospels do. The ontological notions involved, which must always be presupposed and expressed in presenting Jesus, can be complemented by more relational, historical and even cosmic perspec-tives. The Church . . . must be open to the new and surprising ways in which the face of Jesus might be presented in Asia. (20)

What is stated here, requires space for freedom which, once it is granted and opened, should not be quickly closed again out of fear. Unfortunately the docu-ment coming from the center of the Church, is not encouraging and instills a fearful silence.

Focal Points

We finish with some references to focal points which might be decisive for the future of the Church in Asia. We mention four: (1) the worldwide (and that includes Asia) pre-occupation with Islam; (2) the challenges of the Indian subcontinent; (3) the religious afflictions of China; (4) the religious competition in Asia.

The Islamic Challenge

The events of September 11, 2001 changed throughout the world the focal points of concern. All of a sudden, worldwide attention began focusing again on the Middle East, Afghanistan, Kashmir, Pakistan, India, Iran and Iraq—all countries with a predominantly Muslim population. The largest Islamic communities live in Asia—in Indonesia, as well as in the countries just mentioned. An awakened consciousness in Islamic populations has led to new conflicts and struggles. Still rather unknown is the fact that, like Christianity, Islam is also less monolithic than has been thought. Besides, Islam and Islamism not only have their religious nature, but also heavily influence the political and public life of peoples.

Islam is also a religion where the principles of interreligious dialogue have to be re-examined. It is not sufficient that Christians are ready to dialogue and religious leaders occasionally exchange courtesies. First, we should be sure about the fundamental readiness and ability on both sides to enter dialogue. Then again we should bring to mind the various levels of understanding, languages, ways of thinking, standpoints, and ability to think from the standpoint of the other. It is correct to demand that in view of the variety of possible standpoints Christians ensure their own standpoint, as it is stated in 31 of *Ecclesia in Asia*: "Only those with a mature and convinced Christian faith are qualified to engage in genuine interreligious dialogue."

Indian Diversity

Up to the present India remains the classical country of religious and cultural diversity and co-existence. It has the reputation of being one of the countries with the oldest religious and literary sources. Reflective philosophical thought and religious practices of meditative immersion belong together. Secularism as supported by the Indian State expresses tolerance towards the various religious pillars of India. This remains true even if at the present time clashes between Muslim and Hindu groups often occur and in many places Christians suffer persecution and suppression.

As regards the Catholic Church, she participates in the Indian diversity in her own way. There is no country on earth where so many different Catholic rites exist as in India—with the consequence that India enjoys three bishops' conferences. Spreading faith among non-Christians is no longer the monopoly of the

Latin-rite local churches. The Church in India is one of the most dynamic in the world. That the Indian Church and her theologians are struggling for forms of liturgy and rites which are more appropriate to the mind of the Indian population, is a well-known fact. However, it is also true that these efforts are often watched with suspicion, so that much of what is thought about and done occurs in secret and does not enter inner-Church discourse. If anywhere bishops' conferences need more competence in decision-making, India's Conferences must be mentioned.

In this context experience in the field of spirituality should be gratefully recalled. It cannot convince anybody when Western circles, who themselves do not convincingly practice spiritual exercises, religious life and methods of prayer, try to intervene in a theoretical way and judge spiritual journeys undertaken in a continent like India. Certainly a discernment of spirits is called for. But can there be a discernment of spirits where no spirits are blowing and felt? Only people who themselves are moved by spirits are able to search and to call for the true Spirit, so that they can join in the conversation about this matter. We have to realize, too, that spiritual authorities and the authority grounded in the hierarchical order of the Church are by no means identical. That calls attention to a further point which must be considered with regard to India: namely, the ways of popular devotion which are still often mixed with pre- or non-Christian forms of devotion. As mentioned before, India is a sub-continent where, like Korea, two theological tendencies are combined: the theology of religions which includes a theology of spiritual practices, and the theology of liberation concerned with the public social life. Both tendencies are engaged in finding the proper ways of communicating the Christian faith to India.

If anywhere the incarnation of God in Jesus of Nazareth as the decisive gift of the Lord to humankind calls for an appropriate translation into the intellectual horizon and the languages of the people, it is India. However, it is of utmost importance for the bridge-building that, first of all, the Indian bridge-supports are sufficiently taken into account. It is not enough to repeat again and again what Christians want to bring across the bridge, unless the bridge itself is built.

China and the Church in Distress

China is the most populous country in the world. *Ecclesia in Asia* mentions it several times (nos. 3, 8, 9, 28). And yet it is not enough to recall the situation with sympathy and hope. The central question concerns the relationship between the identity given by belonging to a nation and the identity founded in the following of Christ, between patriotism and a religion which tries to combine nations and cultures. Therefore, we are concerned with the relation not only between state and religion, or State and Church, but also between the universal Church and local churches. It is generally known that the Church in China is deeply divided: there is a church which thinks it better to make arrangements with the government and party in order to survive, and a church which is opposed to all that, notwithstanding the consequences which include persecution, prison, labor camps, and even death. The problem is in itself both ecclesiological-juridical and spiritual. The tragedy of the division in the Church becomes manifest when we see how many State-approved bishops immediately or later ask for recognition from the Holy See, and how many communities belonging to the "Patriotic Church" remember the Holy Father openly in their liturgy.

The question where to draw the line between *ius divinum* and *ius humanum* (especially *ecclesiasticum*), between unchangeable rights, because founded in the will of God, and changeable rights, which have developed in history and, therefore, are open to be changed again, has to be discussed with regard to China more energetically. In fact, the domain of the *ius divinum* should be restricted and become less extensive. On the one hand, it is true that in politically difficult situations external influences and decisions are apt to strengthen people in distress. On the other hand, however, is it not in accordance with the following of Christ to give freedom to the Spirit precisely in the community formed by the imitation of Christ, namely the Church? Since the Vatican has the character of a sovereign state, the true authority of the Pope, which basically is a spiritual authority directed by the Holy Spirit, is often concealed outside the Church. The authority of Pope John Paul II is not grounded on his rights as a political sovereign, but upon his immense spiritual radiance which is rivaled only by the influence of the Dalai Lama.

Religious Competition

We do not have to deny the Christian confession of Jesus Christ as the universal Savior, in order to realize that this confession alone does not solve the problem of religious plurality. The various religions have left too many positive traces during the history of humanity. On the other hand, Christianity cannot criticize the negative and even depraved traits in other religions without admitting the dark spots and shadow side in its own history. In a purely human approach it is difficult to defend one side against the other. In the meantime the Church discovers and admits what is also holy, true and good in other religions. However, the Church unfortunately still finds it hard to discover in all that we perceive the activity of the triune God.

Wherever Christian faith is announced, this is mostly done in a way that the basic truths are not handed over to people but are rather presupposed as being already known. In a time where in the Western world belief in God is vanishing and people are searching for appropriate ways of finding God, undoubtedly it would be of great help to learn about the ways to God in the religions and cultures of other parts of the world. In view of Asia we reach a twofold conclusion.

• As regards Islam it seems that for Muslims the majority of Christians are not convincing in their belief in God. Many converts from Christianity to Islam claim that for the first time as Muslims they attained true belief in God. God incarnate in Jesus turns out to be a big dilemma, and that all the more because the confession of Christ's divinity seems to disappear more and more in the confession of his humanity. On this point the arguments in *Ecclesia in Asia* offer no real reply to the question of Christ's divinity and the question of God in general.

- In Buddhism and other non-theistic religions like the Chinese religions, Confucianism and Taoism, we encounter people who, if they do so at all, do not pose the question of God as the Western traditions do. Without doubt these religions fit in with people who have lost their belief in God or did not possess it at all. With some reason Buddhism has even been called an "atheistic religion." That brings us to a different question: what, after all, makes Buddhism a religion?

One idea, which for some time was quite common in the Western world, proves to be false. Modern Western intellectuals considered Buddhism a radical form of ultimate self-realization, an independently self-obtained liberation, a radically humanist-autonomous religion—over against all kinds of heteronomy and external determination. However, what appears to be anthropocentric, contradicts completely Asian self-understanding. Asian thinkers do not set an anthropocentric, but a non-anthropocentric view, over against a theocentric view. This is combined with an attitude which—in the terms of German Christian mysticism—is characterized by "letting (things) go" (German *"loslassen"* or simply *"lassen"*) and radical abandonment. Moreover, the human is embedded in the world of all the living and in the whole cosmos. For good reasons, we query Asians over their view of a human being and their understanding of history, society, individuality, and the difference between man and animals.

There is another feature which brings non-theistic religions together: the call for the Beyond or the Other-World. Enclosed by this-worldliness and driven by the wheel of re-births, human beings, wherever they live, yearn for a life-beyond. In the meantime, practices for finding and achieving happiness, the pursuit of salvation as integral health and all-embracing freedom, and new ways of consciousness for the total human being, soul and body, are spreading to the Western world and create a new experience of religious pluralism.

In this context of questions and answers Christianity has to find its place with its own liberating message. It possesses a new chance to develop and demonstrate its own forms of liberated life. This becomes difficult only when the message does not meet people in places where they live and feel unsaved, threatened, and in distress, and when the message is announced in a self-assured dogmatic manner. *Ecclesia in Asia* repeatedly speaks about *"sharing"* and about the communication of a precious "gift." This inviting language reaches the heart of people who are searching. But what is wrong if other people and other religions also feel inclined to offer what they consider precious and to share it with others? According to St. Paul, we are all athletes running in the stadium but only one can win (1 Cor 9:24-27). In German, a competition is called a *"Kon-kurrenz,"* or "running together" in a competition that aims at reaching the goal. Is it not true that all believers—Christians and believers in other religions—are companions in the running-match and that they race against each other? In this race we have to overcome and to come off victorious.

References

[1]Undoubtedly there are links between *Ecclesia in Asia* and *Dominus Iesus*, yet the latter explicitly refers to the former only once and that in a footnote: *Dominus Iesus*, n. 73. Could the reason be that *Ecclesia in Asia* speaks of "a framework and spirit of complementarity," whereas *Dominus Iesus* objects to the use of the language of complementarity (nos. 6, 9)?—eds.

[2]Could this silence about modern Japan be an official reaction to the strong line taken by the Japanese bishops before the Asian Synod met? See the London *Tablet,* April 25, 1998, 507 (eds.)

[3]See A. Pieris, *An Asian Theology of Liberation* (Maryknoll, N.Y.: Orbis, 1988); also F. Wilfred (ed.), *Verlaß den Tempel. : Antyodaya—indischer Weg zur Befreiung* (Freiburg: Herder, 1988).

[4]See J. Dupuis, *Toward a Christian Theology of Religious Pluralism* (Maryknoll, N.Y.: Orbis, 1997).

[5]For the quotations from *Ecclesia in Asia,* I use *FABC Papers* No. 94, published January, 2001.

[6]For the following see also H. Waldenfels, *Christus und die Religionen* (Regensburg: F. Pustet, 2002).

[7]See H. U. von Balthasar, *Creator Spirit: Explorations in Theology III* (San Francisco: Ignatius Press, 1993), 110-11; also H. Waldenfels, *Kontextuelle Fundamentaltheologie* (Paderborn: F. Schöningh, 2000), 339-40; idem, *Gottes Wort in der Fremde: Theologische Versuche II* (Bonn: Borengässer, 1997), 183-84.

[8]For the following section, see H. Waldenfels, *Gottes Wort in der Fremde* (see note 7); Part I, *Languages as Bridges into the Alien.*

[9]See G. E. Lessing, *On the Proof of the Spirit and of Power: Lessing's Theological Writings,* trans. H. Chadwick (Stanford, Calif.: Stanford University Press, 1957), 53.

[10]See K. Nishitani, *Religion and Nothingness,* trans. J. Van Bragt (Berkeley: University of California Press, 1982), 46-76; also H. Waldenfels, *Absolute Nothingness. Foundations for a Buddhist-Christian Dialogue,* trans. J. W. Heisig (New York/Ramsey, N.J.: Paulist Press, 1980), 79-92.

[11]One attempt undertaken under the guidance of W. Kasper is by G. Augustin, *Gott eint—trennt Christus? Die Einmaligkeit und Universalität Jesu Christi als Grundlage einer christlichen Theologie der Religionen——ausgehend vom Ansatz Wolfhart Pannenbergs* (Paderborn, Germany: Bonifatius, 1993).

[12]See A. B. Chang Chún-shen, *Dann sind Himmel und Mensch in Einheit. Bausteine chinesischer Theologie* (Freiburg, Germany: Herder, 1984), 103-37.

Part V

AN EDITOR AND A JOURNALIST

17

Creating Space to Rethink the Mission of Christians

The Contributions of Jacques Dupuis

William R. Burrows

Among the many controversies that have dogged the Catholic Church and the rest of the Christian world in the past fifty years, two closely related questions are especially important for Christian identity. The first comes in the modern form of answers to the Christological question: "Who do *you* say I am?" (Mk 8:29; Mt 16:15). The second concerns Christian evaluation of religious pluralism and asks, "If Jesus the Christ is the universal final savior, what relationship do other religious Ways have to the Christian Way?"

Both questions have been at the heart of Jacques Dupuis's long and fruitful career as teacher, editor, and theologian. Few if any theologians have been as careful and thorough in grappling with these questions as Father Dupuis. It is a great honor to contribute to this volume that celebrates his eightieth birthday by bringing into relief his many contributions to the Church and interreligious understanding.

I hope to show that Jacques Dupuis's work provides space in which the Gospel can be interpreted in a multidimensional, wholistic way that respects other traditions and allows the followers of Jesus to remain true to the core truths of their faith.

A Personal Overview of the Achievement of Jacques Dupuis

As I was preparing this essay, I found myself reading a wonderful article by Anne Carr. In an instant I realized that Jacques Dupuis provides a bridge of solid, craftsmanlike interpretations of the *vetera* of Scripture and Tradition to the *nova* of insights from both feminist and process thought about the nature of human existence in a multireligious world. That bridge takes readers who study his work carefully into a world where they can enter wholeheartedly into interreligious interchange among the world's great and small religious traditions.

While not utilizing process theological language, Dupuis's work reveals God's Holy Spirit as God-present, luring and enabling humans to move beyond depression and fatalism in the face of evil, and beyond the temptation to anesthetize ourselves to find private respite from a tempestuous world. What Anne Carr did dramatically for me was remind me of the power of certain feminist and process insights into God and the world. Carr reminds us that one overarching issue for contemporary theology is the need to move beyond images of divine power and providence taken from regal potentates exercising domination over their subjects. Instead, she says, "Jesus is no longer seen simply as mediator but as the eschatological prophet who sends the Holy Spirit."[1] And here the world of "Spirit Christology" offers us the possibility of a doctrine of Christ's "Lordship" that is not taken from the experience of subjects relating to all-powerful kings.

One of the underlying problems that the traditional theology of religion bequeathed to the modern era, I believe, is that titles such as "Lord"—as commonly ascribed to Jesus—have long been interpreted within an interlocking set of analogies and metaphors envisioning divine saving power as exerted solely inside Christianity. Feminist theology has revealed this set of analogies as shot through with indefensible patriarchalism. Process thought has shown it to be inconsistent with what we know about the nature of God's relationship to the world in the so-called "New Universe Story." The primary hermeneutic key for articulating the exercise of Lordship by Jesus as the Christ in classical theology was borrowed from the exercise of an imperial juridical decree. In the West especially, fastening upon Pauline metaphors of salvation as justification by forgiveness of sins, this outlook came to dominate the theological imagination. And to be sure there is plenty of warrant in the Christian Testament to interpret justification as a decree that only Christians would be saved. What happens, though, if the power that providentially moves the world toward the Kingdom is not coercive but "educive"? By which I mean empowerment that "leads one out" of imprisonment? The Latin roots of course are *e* ("out of " or "from") and *ducere* ("lead"), the same roots as the word "educate."

What if the work of Jesus and the Spirit interlocks to reveal to all the world God as the future of humankind? A God who seeks to liberate us and empower our attempts to transcend the limits and illusions that imprison us? And what if the vocation of Israel and Christians is to bear witness in a particular way to both the divine depths of cosmic and human life, on the one hand, and the means to "realize" consciously the depths of the life God breathes into the entire universe, on the other hand? In helping Christians see their tradition's conviction that Jesus the Christ is the alpha and the omega point in an historical process where religious pluralism is an aspect of the "relational unity" of humanity's deepest reality, Dupuis shows that the world religions can best be considered as *complementary* yet *asymmetrical* in revealing aspects of the divine and human mystery in history.[2] In addition, he asks us to consider whether the apparent relational convergence of religious traditions has implications for the shape of the eschaton. He brings the work of a lifetime together in the poetic final pages of his *Toward a*

Christian Theology of Religious Pluralism, where he asks us to consider a new way of construing the claims of the "high" Christology of First Corinthians. His entire work, I think, is dedicated to suggesting ways in which it can it be "good news" to all humans in all their religious variety that at the eschaton all will be subject to Christ, as Christ is subject to the Father, so that "God may be all in all" (1 Cor 15:26-29). If God's manner of relating to the world is coercive, it is hard to see how such news can be "good," yet Dupuis asks us to think new thoughts about this, one of the hardest of New Testament teachings.

In the First Letter to the Corinthians, Paul says, "No one says 'Jesus is Lord' except by the Holy Spirit" (12:3). He makes this statement after a long disquisition on how God's wisdom is foolishness to the wise and is epitomized in salvation coming through the crucifixion of Jesus (1:18-2:16). This little text stands as shorthand for Christian teaching that faith is a gift produced by the inner testimony of the Holy Spirit, who is the link between the heart and mind of a potential believer, and the fundamental, objective tenets of a tradition summed up in the statement, "Jesus is Lord." "Lord" (*kyrios*), as used by Paul, is shorthand for universal, final savior and ruler of all that is and will be. But this lordship is defined in terms of kenosis and the death of Jesus on the cross, suggesting that our understanding of Jesus as *kyrios* needs always to be informed by the paradox of the cross. I doubt that such an understanding will sit easily in the minds of those for whom ideas about the Church's shape and governance owe at least as much to the image of the divine Caesar as to the Crucified Jesus.

As I worked on the central texts of the contemporary Catholic magisterium on other religions in the mid-1970s through the 1980s at the University of Chicago, I was aware that neither the so-called "pluralist" and "exclusivist" positions could be squared with Vatican II or subsequent papal teaching.[3] I also concluded that conciliar and papal teachings were the most plausible interpretation of the Bible and subsequent tradition for our day. Nevertheless, I was not able to say yet, "I believe them to be *true*."

Working as Orbis's editor on two books by Jacques Dupuis between 1990 and 1994,[4] however, made me think and pray about the intertwining of Christological and interreligious issues in ways that began to change me. When I began to see the refinements that Dupuis introduced in his third book,[5] he moved me beyond my own prior skepticism in regard to the official Catholic position, because I saw Dupuis articulating convincingly a theological position that

1. was faithful to Scripture, tradition, and contemporary experience of religious truth and power in other religious Ways;
2. proved that nothing hindered Christians from entering into honest, mutual relations and dialogue with followers of other traditions nor barred expecting to learn really significant things about the mystery of God and creation in such interchanges;
3. articulated a view of the final revelation of Christ's universal salvific role that was consonant with the re-creation foreshadowed at Easter and Pentecost and testified to in the experience of the Church;

4. showed that the advent of God's eschatological Kingdom could be a genuinely surprising miracle of grace that would be truly Good News to *all* persons
   of good will who had lived sincere lives following genuine religious and human Ways; and finally
5. moved beyond older theological stalemates to propose that religious plurality
   itself was an aspect of world process in which the several traditions had complementary, asymmetrical, and convergent roles to play in the emergence of the
   eschatological Whole that is the same for all religious Ways.

These five points are my way of drawing out and stating in my own words
what Dupuis is about in chapters 13 through 15 and in the conclusion of *Toward
a Christian Theology of Religious Pluralism*. They underpin what I mean when I
say that his theology of religious pluralism creates a space in which both Christians and others can converse and bring into relief their fundamental intuitions
and perspectives on the origin, meaning, and destiny of creation. On that foundation, the world's great religious and humanistic traditions can join in dialogue on
the nature of the Holy and its relationship to us, as well as collaborate to help
overcome suffering and evil. I write this essay as Phillip Berryman has finished
the translation of Dupuis's fourth book and as we at Orbis put it into production.[6]
Looking at all four books, I believe that no one has done a better job than Father
Dupuis in retrieving the *vetera* of Scripture and its interpretation in the Patristic
era. That retrieval is matched by his ability to bring the great Tradition forward in
the light of the *nova* of contemporary insights into the riches, the power, the
grace, and the truth he believes are to be found in other religious traditions. Jacques
Dupuis's achievement makes it possible for Christians today to rethink our mission in the world without denigrating other religious ways and traditions and to
carry that mission to the ends of the earth in integral witness to Jesus of Nazareth,
whom the Christian Testament calls "the Christ."

The Christological Question

It is important to recall that the Christological question has been raised for the
past one hundred and fifty years in the context of post-Enlightenment *skepticism*
about whether either Scripture or second order theological language *can* speak
reliably about anything "real" transcending the world we see about us. In addition, the theology of religion question has been raised in the context of post-
Enlightenment *relativism*, which regards religious traditions as roughly equal,
culturally conditioned expressions of common human experience.

The answer to the question of Christian identity in a religiously plural world
depends on the answer given to the Matthean and Marcan question on who Jesus
is. If I agree that Peter's answer in Matthew 16:16 is correct—that Jesus is "the
Messiah, the Son of the living God"—a second set of questions arises. Is the
Christology of St. Paul in his Letter to the Romans correct in asserting in chapter
8 that the messiahship of Jesus is of universal and final significance for all the

world? Bear in mind that Paul probably wrote Romans around the years 57 or 58 of the Common Era and that the date of the final redaction of Matthew's Gospel was probably thirty years later.[7] It is therefore likely that the circles in which Matthew and the other two synoptic gospels were being brought together were aware that the Hebrew word *messiah*, translated into the Greek *christos*, was being given universal, cosmic significance. At the very least, we cannot escape the fact that the Church that finally assembled the various strata of the New Testament in the presently accepted canon did so knowing that, taken as an *ensemble*, the books of the Christian Testament were making such a claim. Thus, whether one wishes to take clues from the so-called "ascending" Christological perspective of the first three Gospels or from the so-called "descending" Christological perspective of Paul, John's Gospel, and much of the rest of the New Testament, Jacques Dupuis is certainly right to say:

> God's formal intent in Jesus Christ is to inject the divine gift of self into humanity as deeply as can be, into the very stuff of the humanity that is called to share the divine life. In other words, to make the divine self-bestowal as immanent as possible. The plenary insertion of God's self-communication into the human race . . . consists precisely in God's personal self-insertion into the human family and its history, that is, in the mystery of the Incarnation of the Son of God in Jesus Christ. This can be called the principle of God's creative and restorative "immanent self-communication."[8]

What began to be clearer to me as I wrestled with the matters Dupuis was proposing became inescapable when I realized that chapter 6 of *Who Do You Say I Am?*, where he was dealing with the universal claims of the New Testament, made me look at the *purpose* of the New Testament *as testimony*. Either the New Testament as-a-whole meant to testify to the primitive community's belief that Jesus the Christ is the universal and final Savior of the cosmos or it is a fraud. A fraud because, although there is, for example, an important ethical element in the teaching of Jesus, the Christian Testament is not held together by that. Indeed, there is little in the ethical teaching or even the ethical example of Jesus that cannot be found in the Pentateuch, the Prophets, or the Writings of the Hebrew Testament or in Jewish and gnostic intertestamental literature. Thus no matter how historical scholars resolved the question whether Jesus was a wandering cynic intent on bringing about a new "brokerless" relationship to God, upsetting Jewish and Roman power, and seeking to usher in an egalitarian society between the shores of the Mediterranean and the Dead Sea,[9] either the Christian Testament means to testify to the uniqueness of Jesus as the Christ, or it perpetrates a fraud.

Rather than embrace traditional Christological orthodoxy, theologians following critical-historical studies since the mid-nineteenth century have delivered three major interpretations of Jesus: (1) the preacher of an eschatological kingdom; (2) the teacher of a higher ethic of love; and, (3) the inciter of social revolution and a liberationist ethic. Undoubtedly there are strong cases to be made for each. Embarrassed by the first as unacceptable for contemporary Westerners, however, most scholars focus on the second two. Yet it is the person of Jesus as eschatological prophet identified totally with God and God's design to save the world around which the Christian Testament as-a-whole (*kath' hólu*, whence the word *katholikós* and the English word "catholic") coalesces. For the Greeks of the first century, according to the apostle Paul in the earliest strata of the New Testament down through John, the scandal of Jesus was that God's way of dealing with the world was taught as revealed not in philosophy but the death of Jesus.

For the people of our own age, the cross has lost none of its power to confound. To that paradox is added the notion that, despite what we know about the riches of other religions, the Christ-event—with the cross as *axis mundi* between the life and the resurrection of Jesus—is, according to the Church, decisive for the salvation of *all* the world.[10] To that we must add that the Lukan scheme of the Gospel as volume one and the Acts of the Apostles as volume two brings into relief a teaching that is equally important to the whole New Testament—Jesus, the one guided by the Holy Spirit during his life to reveal and further the advent of the Reign of God as the world's goal, imparts the Holy Spirit to his followers so they may be guided by her in their lives to do the same.

Contemporary academia offers no support for judging on the basis of experience that *any* religious or philosophical tradition can articulate the meaning and destiny of the Whole. Working within the limits of the documentary record, archeology, and testimony of contemporaries and near-contemporaries, Jesus *is* a teacher like Confucius and a prophet like Moses and Muhammad. He is also something more, an enigmatic, multi-dimensional figure like Siddhartha Gautama. The followers of both Jesus and Siddhartha gave titles that ascribe cosmic significance to them, "the Christ" on the one hand, "the Buddha" on the other.[11] One may *believe* that Jesus is more, even uniquely the once-for-all incarnation of the very divine *Logos*, the "principle" that creates the world, guides universal process, and through whom God is saving the entire world. But one cannot *demonstrate* any of these eschatological claims on the basis of historical evidence. Alas, Troeltsch is right, historical studies reach "truth" only on the basis of analogy and probability.[12] As he says, the historical method "relativizes each and every thing . . . not nihilistically" but by considering the objects of its study as data, "parts of a Whole . . . whose ultimate principles cannot be known on the basis of historical research . . . in the way dogmatic theology seeks to speak about the Whole."[13]

Knowing all this, however, Dupuis deals wholistically with the Church's Christological tradition, articulating, for instance the uniqueness of Jesus "not as the 'relative' uniqueness" that Troeltsch knew so well. Rather, he does so on the basis of "the theology that rests on faith," and in which, "in the order of salvation as traditionally understood by Christian faith, there is an absolute uniqueness."[14] In that faith, Troeltsch knew, Jesus was portrayed as universal savior and constitutive of the salvation of all human beings.

In that context the question, "If this is so, how can a Christian find anything salvific in other religious Ways?" is itself ineluctable, and to its development in Dupuis's theology we turn.

Theology of "Religious Pluralism"
and the Mission of Christians Today

Because of the length limits imposed on a single essay, I will not attempt to articulate the symphonic movement of Dupuis's theology of "religion" or his developing theology of "religious pluralism." It is, though, important to see the distinction between the two as crucial to grasp what his work means for understanding the mission of Christians today in a world where it is impossible—on either philosophical or historical grounds—to maintain the superiority of Christianity or any other tradition over other religious Ways.

The first step is to realize that neither a *theology of religion* nor a *theology of religious pluralism* can be universally acceptable. Theology makes its ultimate recourse to its founder and the central texts of a given tradition. It construes the world from that point of view, and when it does so, it is ultimately self-referential, caught in a "hermeneutic circle." Of this Dupuis is fully aware.[15] To the extent that such a claim is *theology*, it makes statements about the shape of the Whole or the world process that will eventuate in an eschatological Whole. Thus one can have a *Christian* theology of religion or—although such terminology would not be fully commensurate—a *Hindu* or a *Taoist* theology of religion. But there is today, and as far as we can see into the future, no *universal* theology of religion. That is to say, there is no universally acceptable interpretation of ultimate reality. De facto, perhaps because of the clarity with which the New Testament claims absoluteness for the Christ, troubled Christians have, since the late nineteenth century led the world in working on theology "of religion," to explain how followers of other traditions can or cannot be saved without becoming Christian. Many did so, thinking that they were articulating a theory that would gain universal acceptance.[16] Dupuis has always known he is articulating a *Christian* solution to a Christian problem.[17] Theology of religion (or "of religions") is thus primarily an intra-Christian dialogue that has tried either to justify exclusivist texts in the Bible or to square exclusivist texts with sentiments that such texts are unworthy of a loving God's self-revelation in Jesus and the Holy Spirit.

In any case, in chapters entitled "Salvation without the Gospel" and "Economy of the Spirit, Word of God, and Holy Scriptures" in *Jesus Christ at the Encounter of World Religions*, Dupuis tries to show that Catholicism has moved from holding that salvation occurs only in explicit, formal, conscious relationship to Christ to a position that respects other traditions and that teaches that sincere followers of other traditions will be saved by a loving God even without becoming Christian. The theological warrant for this is the judgment that the Holy Spirit is active in a distinct manner on a cosmic scale outside visible Christianity.[18] The Spirit and Christ, Dupuis says, are not "in mutual opposition, as if they functioned in two distinct economies. They are actually two inseparable aspects of one economy of salvation."[19] He proposes that we understand the Holy Spirit as giving life to the cosmos and transforming the world, in Teilhardian language, guiding the world process toward the omega point. He takes great care to show that the work of the

Spirit outside visible Christianity is both real and cannot produce fruits opposed to the *Logos* or the Christic principle that providentially lures the world process onward to its destiny in the Kingdom. In my own dissertation research, I concluded that the Catholic position at and since Vatican II is one of "irenic ambivalence" toward other religious Ways—*irenic* in recognizing genuine truth and power in them; *ambivalent* in retaining commitment to the person and revelation of Jesus as God's ultimate self-disclosure. In the very convolution of his language, I sense that Dupuis is struggling with this irenic ambivalence to clarify how what occurs in visible Christianity does not exhaust the divine care for humanity and the cosmos, while holding fast also to the Christian tradition's teaching on the uniqueness of Christ and the historical mission of his Church in mediating and visibly manifesting the reality of salvation.

In the introduction *Toward a Christian Theology of Religious Pluralism*, Dupuis brings into relief the move beyond theology of religions to articulating a constructive theology of religious *pluralism*. Put in simple language, if the Spirit is active in other religious traditions, and if, as seems the case, religious pluralism is not going to disappear from the world, what is the significance of the pluralism itself? What Dupuis seeks to do in this book is search for,

> in the light of Christian faith . . . the meaning in God's design for the plurality of living faiths and religious traditions with which we are surrounded. Are all the religious traditions of the world destined, in God's plan, to converge? [If so,] where, when, and how?[20]

Father Dupuis's answer to that question requires him to reread the Scriptures, early Christian literature, the history of Christian doctrine, and contemporary theologians. He seeks guidance from conciliar and papal teaching, and the result is an awesome accomplishment. Reading and rereading his early books yields new insights on every page. One gets to the same place more quickly in his most recent book, *Christianity and the Religions: From Confrontation to Dialogue*. Still, it is in the conclusions reached in *Toward a Christian Theology of Religious Pluralism* that I find the most important principles for a renewed theology of mission. Here he observes that the humanity of Jesus Christ is the sacrament of God's will to save, but he says also in this book that one is "led to viewing the mystery of God's self-disclosure in Jesus Christ as essentially relational to what God has done and continues to do to humankind through history, from beginning to end."[21]

To put flesh on the bones of that insight, I return to Anne Carr's overview of God's providence and power. She notes that there is hunger today for the twelfth-century's "symbolic, narrative, metaphorical . . . monastic-mystical tradition."[22] She also notes that this tradition is joined organically in Christian tradition to what Edward Schillebeeckx has called the "Christian constant," a "mystical-political polarity."[23] And here I believe the mission of Christians in the contemporary world begins to assume great clarity.

Christian mission since 1492 has been defined as a function of the Church's efforts to proclaim the Gospel to persons of other traditions and to expand the membership of the Church. By any measure that "mission" has been spectacularly successful; yet its link to the colonial enterprise has weakened its usefulness for describing what the Church is about in our own day. Minimally, I think, it is time to claim deeper dimensions for the word "mission," a word that was first popularized by Father Dupuis's Jesuit forebears. Although inviting interested persons into the Church is an essential aspect of Christianity's open table fellowship, clarity is needed on an essential point. Namely, that a wholistic manifestation of the love of God *among* the nations (*missio inter gentes*) should—in our age of consumer advertising—take priority over proclaiming the Gospel *to* the nations (*missio ad gentes*) with an aim to gain converts.

In an age of consumerism with advertising claim and counter-claim, on the one hand, and lingering resentment of Christian mission's ties to the colonial era, on the other, service, witness, and the dialogue of life are far better signs of God's mission than seeking converts. But such activities depend upon the authenticity of the people who bear the name of Christ, and this authenticity depends upon the seriousness with which Christians are in dialogue with Jesus in the communion with the Spirit. In that connection, the greatest gift of the Jesuits to the modern world is *The Spiritual Exercises* of Saint Ignatius. The *Exercises* are in essence a means of guiding an individual seeking to bring his or her life into unity with God's purposes. Not "God's purposes" as if there were a blueprint an individual must discover, but helping one participate in the theonomous depths of cosmic life as they can be realized by one's own authenticity.

At one level, Father Dupuis explicates the Christian tradition of radical dialogue in the light of what sensitive Christians such as Bede Griffiths and Henri Le Saux (Abhishiktananda)—both of whom he knew—have *experienced* in intense lives of dialogue.[24] Such lives, he knows, are examples of how Christians and followers of other religious Ways can enter into the deepest possible communion and help us all partake more deeply in the historical convergence of all religious traditions on what Christians call God's Kingdom. From his many years in India, Dupuis knows that the path of authentic dialogue-in-depth is arduous but rewarding. His theology shows that the practice of dialogue is our entrée not into something exotic but into the dynamics of God's own self-communication. He justifies this practice by a careful, conservative revisioning of the Christian tradition, clearing a space in which followers of Christ can open themselves up to persons of other traditions. Every other aspect, program, and plan that goes on under the rubric of "mission" needs to be subordinated to that reality. Mission must be dialogic and dialogue is an end in itself, for the communion brought about by dialogue is the deepest dimension of God's own mission in our midst luring us into self-giving love. The mission of Christians, accordingly, is to carry on the work of Christ in dialogue with the followers of other ways, and theology must begin to realize it is best construed as a wisdom that will lead people deeper into a contemporary equivalent of what Carr refers to in recalling the medieval "symbolic, narrative, metaphorical . . . monastic-mystical tradition." While the theology of Jacques Dupuis is nothing if it is not rigorously intellectual and critical, its purposes, I believe, are best brought into relief by saying he has cleared a space in which a new generation of Christians can enter into dialogue with a new generation of followers of other religious Ways. He has freed Christians from the burden of thinking they must always be proclaiming a message and shown us it is all right to listen.

References

[1]Anne E. Carr, "Providence, Power, and the Holy Spirit," *Horizons* 29 (2002), 82.

[2]I am summarizing swathes of Jacques Dupuis's thought, found most accessibly in *Christianity and the Religions* (Maryknoll, N.Y.: Orbis, 2002), chapters 5 through 8.

[3]William R. Burrows, "The Roman Catholic Magisterium on 'Other' Religious Ways: Analysis and Critique from a Postmodern Perspective," (Unpublished dissertation, University of Chicago Divinity School, 1987).

[4]Jacques Dupuis, *Jesus Christ at the Encounter of World Religions* (Maryknoll, N.Y.: Orbis , 1991); id., *Who Do You Say I Am?: Introduction to Christology* (Maryknoll, N.Y.: Orbis, 1994).

[5]Jacques Dupuis, *Toward a Christian Theology of Religious Pluralism* (Maryknoll, N.Y.: Orbis, 1997).

[6]Jacques Dupuis, *Christianity and the Religions: From Confrontation to Dialogue*, trans. Phillip Berryman (Maryknoll, N.Y.: Orbis, 2002).

[7]Raymond E. Brown, *An Introduction to the New Testament* (New York: Doubleday, 1997), 560, 171.

[8]Dupuis, *Who Do You Say*, 146-47.

[9]I write these words as shorthand for what John Dominic Crossan argues in *The Historical Jesus: The Life of a Mediterranean Jewish Peasant* (San Francisco: HarperSanFrancisco, 1991); see 416-26, especially 421-22.

[10]Many documents could be cited, but Pope John Paul's encyclical on mission (*Redemptoris Missio*, December 7, 1990), arts. 4-11, is an excellent summary of conciliar and papal teaching on the decisiveness and universal finality of the Christ-event.

[11]See Leo D. Lefebure, *The Buddha and the Christ* (Maryknoll, N.Y.: Orbis, 1993) for an up-to-date and incisive laying out of how Jesus the Christ and Siddhartha the Buddha are similar and different.

[12]Ernst Troeltsch, "Über historische und dogmatische Methode in der Theologie," *Gesammelte Schriften*, vol. 2, *Zur religiösen Lage, Religionsphilosophie, und Ethik* (Tübingen: J. C. B. Mohr [Paul Siebeck], 1922), 731-33.

[13]Ibid., 737, 745.

[14]Dupuis, *Jesus Christ*, 191.

[15]In ibid., Dupuis has one of the most lucid accounts of the hermeneutical circle I know; see 245-47.

[16]See, for example, Paul F. Knitter, *Introducing Theologies of Religion* (Maryknoll, N.Y.: Orbis, 2002), 2-3.

[17]Dupuis, *Religious Pluralism*, 8-10.

[18]See John Paul II, *Redemptoris Missio,* no. 28.

[19]Dupuis, *Jesus Christ*, 153.

[20]Dupuis, *Religious Pluralism,* 10.

[21]Ibid., 385.

[22]Carr, "Providence, Power, and the Holy Spirit," 86.

[23]Ibid., 87, citing Schillebeeckx, *Christ: The Experience of Jesus as Lord* (New York: Seabury, 1980).

[24]See Jacques Dupuis, "Christianity and the Religions: Complementarity and Convergence," in Catherine Cornille (ed.), *Many Mansions? : Multiple Religious Belonging and Christian Identity* (Maryknoll, N.Y.: Orbis, 2002), 61-75.

18

Dupuis Profile

Robert Blair Kaiser

My assignment is to give a personal portrait of the man we honor in this volume. It wasn't easy to persuade Dupuis to talk about himself. "People have been following your troubles with the Holy Office," I told him, "but they know nothing about you. They need to know who you are, where you come from."

He shrugged, not quite understanding why that mattered. He said his work spoke for itself. I think he only agreed to let me get as close to him as I did, because I had shared meals with him since I had returned to Rome in the fall of 1999. I had become a friend who knew how to listen to his stories, draw him out, laugh at his sardonic humor, and not betray him.

Only then could I come even close to breaking through his everyday persona, which, to most of the faculty and students at the Gregorian University where he still lives, is "gruff and grum." Most of his fellow Jesuits on the faculty keep their distance. Which is probably the way he likes it. He is a serious theologian, given to heavy reading and thinking and writing—he writes most of his articles in English—and he is not at all interested in small talk that will take him away from his work.

"In the community here at the Gregorian University," one senior professor told me, "Dupuis is considered something of a curmudgeon. Nice enough, mind you, but he doesn't talk about the weather, or Italian football, and he doesn't gossip. He doesn't even give you a nod in the hallway."

I

To understand why Dupuis is such a no-nonsense guy, you have to go back to his roots. He was born into a pious, middle-class Catholic family (his father was an engineer) in most-Catholic Belgium, in 1923. He had an older sister (Monique, who ended up marrying an engineer) and two younger brothers, who both became engineers. But Frère Jacques seemed born for higher things. He got the best possible start when his parents enrolled him at a Jesuit elementary school in the first grade. "In a sense," Dupuis told me, "I entered the Jesuits at the age of five."

He passed six formative years in that Jesuit grammar school (where he started to learn English), and then spent six more years in a Jesuit secondary school, where he found "four memorable Jesuit teachers." No one was surprised when he followed in their footsteps by entering the Jesuits at the age of 17, along with four of his classmates.

He got the education that was standard in those pre-conciliar days for all the Jesuits in the world: two years Novitiate (or boot camp), two years Juniorate (classical studies), three years of Philosophy, and then three years of Regency—with a slight twist. Instead of teaching in a Jesuit high school in Belgium, he volunteered for the missions in India. At Vatican II, which I covered for *Time* magazine, I had met some marvelous Belgian bishops, but few of them actually lived in Belgium. A great many zealous Belgians had gone off to Africa and Asia as missionaries, and became the kind of bishops who were beginning to understand that they were not Roman legates, bearers of a colonial European culture, but men seeking ways to plant an indigenous Gospel. Dupuis was that kind of Belgian missionary.

It was in India, at St. Xavier's College, Calcutta, that Dupuis made his first acquaintance with young men who, though they were not Catholics, impressed him with their goodness, and with a kind of attractive piety they had learned from their (mostly) Hindu mothers and Hindu fathers. To Dupuis, it seemed clear that God had revealed himself in and through their Hindu faith. And so now Dupuis began to think harder about the variety of religions in the world. It was now much more obvious to him than ever: these religions weren't bogus. What were they then? Well, he wouldn't presume to say what God had in mind when these religions took shape. "I don't know," Dupuis once told me. "And I don't think Ratzinger knows either." Here, I think, Dupuis may have been thinking of a famous statement from Karl Rahner: "God is and always will be incomprehensible mystery." History itself, for Dupuis, is something of a mystery, too. But it is also a *locus theologicus* for him, a jumping off place for further theological reflection that can promote more realistic (and more peace-making) dialogue between Christians and . . . everyone else.

In any event, Dupuis had no other choice than to start thinking new thoughts about the providence of God—in a world where the majority of its people have never heard the name of Jesus. Was the major part of humankind then, to be denied the "salvation" that comes only through Jesus? He didn't think so. This was Dupuis's first exposure to what he has called "the concrete experience [that] opens one's eyes to reality."

Dupuis's life in India forced him to examine "the interaction between text and context." He did his theological studies in India, was ordained in India, and was assigned to teach theology in India. He wrote a doctorate on Origen for which he studied one year in India and eighteen months at the Gregorian. He re-entered India on the very day the permit expired for his permanent residence there. In all, he lived 36 years in India, and even took his vacations in India, exploring the country alone on a motorcycle. "I never dreamed I would ever leave India, or even ask to go anywhere else," he told me. "I thought I'd live in India, work in India, and die in India."

For a time, before, during and after Vatican II, he was also the official theologian for the Indian Bishops' Conference, where he helped effect a tighter collaboration between the many religious order priests in India and the nation's bishops. Dupuis also helped the Indian bishops implement the Council's Constitution on the Sacred Liturgy. Dupuis told me that a high point of his life as a priest came soon after the Council when he was able to celebrate one of India's first Masses facing the people.

Then, one day in 1984, Father General Kolvenbach told Dupuis he was being transferred to Rome to teach "other religions" at the Gregorian, something that the General believed Dupuis was uniquely qualified to do. Some Indian Jesuits were glad to see him go. A high-ranking Italian Jesuit told me, "Dupuis was too conservative for them."

Ironic. Dupuis was too conservative in India, surrounded as he was by pioneering, sometimes even radical, theologians like the Jesuit, Samuel Rayan, who had been making some devastating critiques of the theologies that were brought to India by missionaries from Europe. According to Rayan, those missionaries "stressed hierarchy, power, submission, resignation and other-worldly salvation, rather than community, friendship, obedience to truth, pursuit of justice and the Reign of God on earth." I have the text of a talk Rayan delivered a few years ago to a missionary group. It was strong stuff.

> Jesus made it a point [Rayan wrote] to decolonize the religion and the theology of the people, which had been occupied by royal, priestly and wealthy settlers from the time of Solomon. Religion became priest-ridden and expensive, legalistic and burdensome. It had its outcastes and untouchables. It also had its ways of fleecing the poor. Jesus marginalized the temple and all priestly pretensions. The temple is destined to disappear. Worship shall be in spirit and truth. Mercy not sacrifice. People, not Sabbath.

The difference between Rayan and Dupuis? My guess is that Rayan has worked all his life in the relative obscurity of his native India. But Dupuis was brought to Rome to perform a high-wire act—without a net, too close to the Gregorian University's official overseers inside the Vatican.

Fourteen years later, Dupuis found himself sidelined as a professor, as long as he was under investigation. For Dupuis, then 74, it seemed like an irreparable blow to his standing as a scholar—in an important new branch of theology that might help humankind veer away from the kind of arrogant arguments that had triggered religious wars through much of human history.

Had Dupuis run up against one of the Curia's favorite bugaboos—"irenicism," the notion that one religion is as good as another? Not really. Rather, Dupuis had been trying to find in the magisterial documents of his own Church a more open way of evaluating other faith traditions. He had said he was "aiming at a change of mind—and of heart—in my own constituency." In this, Dupuis had thought that he was following a mandate from the pope himself, John Paul II, who told the professors at the Gregorian University on December 15, 1979 that they should "endeavor to be creative, without allowing yourselves to be too easily satisfied with what has proved useful in the past." The pope told the professors that they should "have the courage to explore new ways, though with prudence."

That's exactly what Dupuis was doing. Given the current history that had come to a focus with the most recent revival of fundamentalism among a militant minority in all religions, I had thought Dupuis's prudent presence on the interreligious scene was a fine example of providence at work in human affairs. In the dialogue between the major religions that most thinking people believe necessary today, many believed that the Church needs scholars who are constitutionally attuned to find the good and the true and the beautiful in every religion. Dupuis, said his supporters, was one of those scholars, one of the best, and if he did not exist, the Church would have to invent him.

Once ensconced in Rome, some Vatican offices enlisted Jim Dupuis—to help write position papers on how the Church could engage in interreligious dialogue. In 1991, he helped with parts of a document published jointly by the Pontifical Council for Interreligious Dialogue and the Congregation for the Evangelization of Peoples. It was called "Dialogue and Proclamation." One passage (29) said, "It is in the sincere practice of what is good in their own religious tradition and following the dictates of their conscience that the members of other religious traditions respond positively to God's invitation and receive salvation in Jesus Christ." Dupuis said that, "however guarded the affirmation of the document may be, it meant to say exactly what it says." He vividly recalled an intervention by Cardinal Decourtray of Lyons at the time the text was under discussion. Decourtray said, somewhat angrily, "If we are not willing to affirm that much, we had better go home and forget about publishing a document."

Dupuis's new life in Rome, both at the Gregorian and in high-level discussions inside the Vatican, launched Dupuis into deeper waters. He wondered whether the arrogance of Roman theologians was any great help in the general push for religious peace in the world. In what sense did Christ already represent "the fullness of revelation"? And did the Church possess that fullness? Anyone who had studied Church history knew the answer to the second question; the Church has always been somewhat short of the mark. In answer to the first question, Dupuis knew that Jesus made a good beginning with his life, death and resurrection. But what about the end times? Won't Christ complete his revelation then, when we will see "face to face" and no longer "dimly" (1 Cor 13:12)?

"Asking questions like these," Dupuis told me, "is what finally got me into trouble." But when Dupuis talked about his "trouble," he said the word with a kind of lilt in his voice. If it was trouble, even trouble that gave him an ulcer, I thought it was also a kind of happy trouble, for it put Dupuis into the ranks of those (admittedly few) pioneering theologians (many of them in Asia) who help give Catholic theology what little vitality it has today. There were more theologians like Dupuis around during Vatican II, and the Church has never been more vital, more alive, more exciting—and more relevant to the needs of people who want to live cheek by jowl with people of many faiths who share the same earnest wishes to make a better world, together.

II

At the Gregorian today, Dupuis has time for perhaps one very loyal friend, the Australian Jesuit Gerald O'Collins. It was O'Collins who took on the task of serving as Dupuis's advocate in his dealings with the Congregation for the Doctrine of the Faith (CDF). A member of the Gregorian's theology faculty for almost 30 years (and for six years its dean), O'Collins had never been anyone's legal advisor. It was O'Collins who introduced me to Jim Dupuis, who took a liking to me because, as O'Collins put it, I was "a jolly fellow." I think he meant that I knew how to listen to Dupuis and draw him out—like, maybe, a good therapist. I did learn how to laugh at Dupuis's jokes. I was one of the few laymen at a celebration of Dupuis's sixty years as a Jesuit in the spring of 2001, and honored to sit at Dupuis's small table in the refectory of the Gregorian, along with O'Collins and two Indian Jesuits, Herbie Alphonso, who teaches at the Greg, and Gaston Roberge, who had come to the party as a special delegate of the Calcutta Province to which Dupuis still belongs. And it was O'Collins who suggested that I might be the one who could write a profile of Dupuis. "Find out more," O'Collins suggested, "about Dupuis's life in India."

In this, I only had modest success. I did discover that Dupuis had once spent a golden month in Kashmir in 1954. When I asked him about it, his eyes flashed and he smiled at the memory of it. "For me," said Dupuis, "Kashmir was Venice in Switzerland."

I was interviewing Dupuis in his room on an upper floor of the Gregorian University, a very small room that served as his bedroom and his office. It was the cell of a man vowed to poverty, but I couldn't help feel that Dupuis was rich, too. He had the morning sun streaming in on him through a window that looked out on the garden of the Colonna Palace; he was surrounded by hundreds and hundreds of books, and he had a big, oversized desk and a computer perched at its side. What more could a scholar want?

A little more space? Perhaps. Before Christmas 2000, I had sent Dupuis a large poinsettia plant to brighten up his room where he lay recuperating from minor stomach surgery. "How'd you like the plant?" I asked. "I took it to the infirmary," he said, without remembering to say thanks. "I had no place for it in my room."

I urged Dupuis to tell me more about Kashmir. His description of it made me understand (as the international news stories about Kashmir in the spring of 2002 never quite explained) why India and Pakistan had been squabbling over the region for decades. Kashmir—as Dupuis remembered it—was one of the most beautiful spots on earth. It was a land linked by lake after lake after lake, all of them lined with lotus blossoms, all of their glassy blue surfaces reflecting the snows of the surrounding peaks.

In the 1950s, one could travel around Kashmir for a month on a few hundred dollars—which is just what Dupuis was able to do the month after he was ordained in November 1954 as a member of the Calcutta Province of the Society of Jesus. "My parents couldn't come to my ordination. Not all the way from Belgium," said Dupuis. "They couldn't afford it. But my sister, Monique, and my cousin, Cecile, could. And so, these two single young ladies came to see me become a priest. And then my superiors gave me permission to take this trip with them on a houseboat through the lake region not far from Srinagar."

Other than that excursion to Kashmir, Dupuis took me on no other intimate journeys. He didn't seem to have any hobbies, or favorite foods, or favorite movies. I wanted to ask him more about his favorite students in India, but I didn't have time. I would have been surprised if he had told me he didn't have any favorite students, for his eyes had brightened when I had asked him good questions about his favorite thing, theology. And I can imagine him in some fast-paced theological discussions with his brightest students.

But I cannot imagine him resonating very much with theologians less conservative than he. He made a sour face when I asked him to comment on what I thought was a brilliant piece on Christology written by the Sri Lankan Jesuit, Aloysius Pieris. Yet some of Dupuis's writing sounds a little like Pieris's own brand of liberation theology—which is something you *do* as well as study.

"The primacy of orthopraxy seems to be plain gospel truth," Dupuis wrote in *Louvain Studies* (in a 1999 piece called " 'The Truth Will Make You Free'—The Theology of Religious Pluralism Revisited," (pp. 211-263). "In John's Gospel Jesus says: 'He who does what is true comes to the light.' Discipleship leads to the knowledge of Jesus. . . . Only then can theology become truly relevant to the human condition."

Or, as the bishops attending the Asian Synod affirmed in 1998 (I am offering a paraphrase crafted by Dupuis): "The discovery of the person of Jesus is more important than teaching doctrines about him, and must in any case come first in a context where experience is paramount in religious endeavor."

III

A curious footnote to the Dupuis case: I learned that as Dupuis was fighting his battle with the CDF, he found a good deal of help—and opposition—from his brothers in the Society of Jesus. Father General Kolvenbach led the forces supporting Dupuis, with strong help from Gerald O'Collins, the Australian Jesuit who served as Dupuis's advocate. On September 4, 2000, Kolvenbach and O'Collins accompanied Dupuis on Dupuis's first and only visit to the Palazzo Sant' Ufficio. The encounter eventually led to Dupuis's final compromise with the CDF on February 26, 2001.

But, while Dupuis was being defended by Kolvenbach and O'Collins, he was also being attacked by other Jesuits. The man who delated Dupuis to the CDF was a Jesuit. I have the man's name, but his name is not important, nor is he. When I asked Dupuis the man's area of expertise, Dupuis growled, "Any damn thing." It was another Jesuit, an editor of the Italian Jesuits' bimonthly *Civiltà Cattolica*, who wrote a severe assessment of Dupuis's book in *Civiltà* that ended by calling the theology of religious pluralism proposed in the book "problematic and provocative." That review didn't help Dupuis much at the Holy Office, where yet a third Jesuit, a German, was working on the Dupuis case.

In an interesting parallel, the French Dominicans were split over Dupuis. The Dominican community at Montpellier spent weeks reading his controversial book, and then invited Dupuis to lead them in discussing it. Claude Geffré, O.P., spoke at the 1997 presentation of the book in Paris, and has continued his valuable dialogue with Dupuis (see the "Select Bibliography" below). But the Dominicans of Toulouse, through articles in the *Revue thomiste* for 1998, 2001 and 2002, maintained a vigorous, but sub-standard, theological attack on Dupuis's thought. Among other things, they forgot the teaching of John Paul II in *Redemptor Hominis*: all human beings, without exception, share in the grace of Christ's redemption, from the first moment of their existence (13).

For a year, Dupuis hardly did anything else but answer questions from the CDF. On December 25, 1998, Dupuis responded to the Congregation's first set of questions—with a 200-page reply. He waited more than six months for the CDF verdict on that reply. Another letter came from Cardinal Ratzinger, who was not satisfied with Dupuis's answers; he appended a text of eleven pages containing a doctrinal judgment on Dupuis's book, with a new set of questions to be answered, again in complete secrecy, in three months. Dupuis complied. On November 1, 1999, he sent his replies—60 more pages. After that, silence from the CDF. Dupuis stewed, and puzzled over papal statements that might give him a clue to his fate.

Then came his meeting with Cardinal Ratzinger on September 4, 2000, and on the following day, he got an answer of sorts with the publication of *Dominus Iesus*. Finally, six months later, on February 26, 2001, the CDF issued a "Notification" regarding Dupuis that was surprisingly mild. It reported that Dupuis had acknowledged "ambiguities and difficulties" that might lead readers of his work to some wrong conclusions. But Ratzinger demanded no changes in Dupuis's book—only that Ratzinger's critique of Dupuis's book be included in subsequent editions.

Within hours, Father Kolvenbach issued a press release that put a benign spin on the story. He said the Notification "recognized" Dupuis's book "for the seriousness of its methodological research, the richness of the scientific documentation, and the originality of its exploration." Kolvenbach also said that the Notification "helps the reader to interpret the book according to the doctrine of the Church. On this solidly established dogmatic basis we hope that Father Jacques Dupuis can continue his pioneer research."

Dupuis did continue his pioneering work. At the age of 78, he is now officially retired from teaching. But he continues to write and give conferences—around the world. He is now much better known and more esteemed for surviving attacks on his theology. He has as many invitations as ever to lecture and contribute articles.

But how explain that Dupuis's staunchest supporters—and most severe critics—were all Jesuits? What it demonstrates is this: that twenty-first century Jesuits are no longer in lock-step. They are an advance guard of a Church that is growing up in a new kind of freedom, where almost everything will soon be up for grabs, and where the future will be determined by those who do not necessarily have the power of power, but the power of reason.

A Bibliography of the Writings
of Jacques Dupuis, S.J.

1960

Book Reviews

Jean Daniélou, *The Christian Today* (Tournai: Desclée, 1960), *The Clergy Monthly* 24/8: 317-318.

1961

Book Reviews

A. H. Armstrong - R. A. Markus, *Christian Faith and Greek Philosophy* (London: Darton, Longman & Todd, 1960), *The Clergy Monthly* 25/2: 75-76.

M. Raymond, *Our Life, Our Sweetness, Our Hope* (Dublin: Clonmore & Reynolds, 1960), *The Clergy Monthly* 25/2: 77.

Son and Saviour. The Divinity of Jesus Christ in the Scriptures. A Symposium by A. Gelin, J. Schmitt, P. Benoit, M. E. Boismard and D. Mollat (London: Geoffrey Chapman, 1960), *The Clergy Monthly* 25/6: 236-237.

Léon Cristiani - Jean Rilliet, *Catholics and Protestants: Separated Brothers* (London: Sands & Co., 1960), *The Clergy Monthly* 25/10: 395.

Henri Crouzel, *Origène et la "connaissance mystique"* (Bruges: Desclée de Brouwer, 1961), *The Clergy Monthly* 25/10: 396-397.

1962

Book Reviews

Jean Abelé, *Christianity and Science* (London: Burns & Oates, 1961), *The Clergy Monthly* 26/4: 155.

François Taymans d'Eypernon, *The Blessed Trinity and the Sacraments* (Dublin: Clonmore & Reynolds, 1961), *The Clergy Monthly* 26/5: 190-191.

1963

Book Reviews

Emile Mersch, *Le Christ, l'homme et l'univers. Prolégomènes à la théologie du corps mystique* (Bruges: Desclée de Brouwer, 1962), *The Clergy Monthly* 27/5: 200.

Claude Olivier, *Jerôme* (Paris: Les éditions ouvrières, 1963), *The Clergy Monthly* 27/8: 324.

Herbert Musurillo, *Symbolism and the Christian Imagination* (Dublin: Helicon Press, 1962), *The Clergy Monthly* 27/9: 362-363.

1964

Book Reviews

Karl Rahner, *The Church and the Sacraments* (Edinburgh/London: Nelson, 1963), *The Clergy Monthly* 28/9: 355.

Claude Tresmontant, *Toward the Knowledge of God* (Dublin: Helicon, 1961), *The Clergy Monthly* 28/9: 357.

Robert L. Richard, *The Problem of an Apologetical Perspective in the Trinitarian Theology of St. Thomas Aquinas* (Rome: Analecta Gregoriana, 1963), *The Clergy Monthly* 28/9: 357-358.

William D. Lynn, *Christ's Redemptive Merit. The Nature of Its Causality According to St.Thomas* (Rome: Analecta Gregoriana, 1962), *The Clergy Monthly* 28/9: 358.

Baptism in the New Testament. A Symposium by A. George, J. Delorme, D. Mollat, J. Guillet, M.E. Boismard, J. Duplacy, J. Giblet and Y.B. Tremel (London: Geoffrey Chapman, 1964), *The Clergy Monthly* 28/9: 360.

Romano Guardini, *The Humanity of Christ. Contributions to a Psychology of Jesus* (London: Burns & Oates, 1964), *The Clergy Monthly* 28/10: 396.

Jean Daniélou, *Primitive Christian Symbols* (London: Burns & Oates, 1964), *The Clergy Monthly* 28/10: 396-397.

1965

"Aids for the Liturgy of the Word," *The Clergy Monthly* 29/10: 386-388.
"A Personalistic Theology," *The Clergy Monthly* 29/11: 431-433.
"The Unknown Christ of Hinduism," *The Clergy Monthly Supplement* 7/7: 278-283.

Book Reviews

Jean Daniélou, *A History of Early Christian Doctrine Before the Council of Nicaea*. Vol..1: *The Theology of Jewish Christianity* (London: Darton, Longman & Todd, 1964) *The Clergy Monthly* 29/4: 158-159.

Burkhard Neunheuser, *Baptism and Confirmation* (London: Burns & Oates, 1964), *The Clergy Monthly* 29/4: 161-162.

Jean Mouroux, *The Mystery of Time. A Theological Inquiry* (New York: Desclée, 1964), *The Clergy Monthly* 29/7: 276.

R. Marlé, *Le problème théologique de l'herméneutique* (Paris: Editions de l'Orante, 1963), *The Clergy Monthly* 29/12: 472-473.

H. Barré, *Trinité que j'adore. Perspectives théologiques* (Paris: P. Lethiclleux, 1965), *The Clergy Monthly* 29/12: 475.

Godfrey Diekmann, *Come, Let Us Worship* (London: Darton, Longman & Todd, 1962), *The Clergy Monthly* 29/12: 476.

1966

"The Cosmic Christ in the Early Fathers," *The Indian Journal of Theology* 15/3: 106-120.

Book Reviews

Aloys Grillmeier, *Christ in the Christian Tradition. From the Apostolic Age to Chalcedon (451)* (New York: Sheed & Ward, 1965), *The Clergy Monthly* 30/3: 77.

Jean Galot, *La rédemption, mystère d'alliance* (Paris / Bruges: Desclée de Brouwer, 1965), *The Clergy Monthly* 30/2: 77-78.

1967

L'"esprit de l'homme". Etude sur l'anthropologie religieuse d'Origène (Bruges: Desclée de Brouwer).

The Mystery of Christ, Incarnate Word and Redeemer. Part I: *The Person of Christ*; Part II: *The Work of Christ* (Kurseong: St. Mary's Theological College).

The Sacraments, Personal Encounter of Christ and Men in the Church (Kurseong: St. Mary's Theological College).

"The Christocentrism of Vatican II, I," *The Clergy Monthly* 31/10:361-370.

Book Reviews

H. Bouëssé - J. J. Latour (eds.), *Problèmes actuels de christologie* (Bruges: Desclée de Brouwer, 1965), *The Clergy Monthly* 31/2: 75-76.

Yves Congar, *Jésus-Christ* (London: Geoffrey Chapman, 1966), *The Clergy Monthly* 31/2: 76.

J. M. Carmody - T. E. Clarke, *Sources of Christian Theology.* Volume III: *Christ and His Mission: Christology and Soteriology* (Westminster, Md: The Newman Press, 1966), *The Clergy Monthly* 31/6: 233-234.

J. M. Carmody - T. E. Clarke, *Word and Redeemer. Christology in the Fathers* (Glen Rock, N.J.: Paulist Press, 1966), *The Clergy Monthly* 31/7: 275.

Leopold Sabourin, *The Names and Titles of Jesus. Themes of Biblical Theology* (New York: Macmillan, 1967), *The Clergy Monthly* 31/7: 275.

1968

The Eucharistic Mystery (Kurseong: St. Mary's Theological College).

"The Christocentrism of Vatican II, II," *The Clergy Monthly* 32/6: 245-257.

"Towards a Communal Eucharistic Celebration," *The Clergy Monthly* 32/9: 401-417.

Book Reviews

Edward Schillebeeckx, *Revelation and Theology. Theological Soundings I,* 1 (London: Sheed & Ward, 1967), *The Clergy Monthly* 32/5: 235.

Louis Bouyer, *Eucharistie. Théologie et spiritualité de la prière eucharistique* (Tournai: Desclée, 1966), *The Clergy Monthly* 32/5: 235-236.

C. Vagaggini, *The Canon of the Mass and Liturgical Reform* (London: Geoffrey Chapman, 1967), *The Clergy Monthly* 32/5: 236.

Raymond Panikkar, *Māyā e Apocalisse. L'incontro dell'Induismo e del Cristianesimo* (Roma: Edizioni Abete, 1966), *The Clergy Monthly* 32/5: 242.

Karl Rahner - A. Häussling, *The Celebration of the Eucharist* (London: Burns & Oates/ Herder & Herder, 1967), *The Clergy Monthly* 32/6: 285-286.

Karl Rahner - A. Häussling, *Die Vielen Messen und das Eine Opfer. Eine Untersuchung über die rechte Norm der Messhäufigkeit* (Freiburg: Herder Verlag, 1966), *The Clergy Monthly* 32/6: 285-286.

Lucien Deiss, *Early Sources of the Liturgy* (London: Geoffrey Chapman, 1967), *The Clergy Monthly* 32/6: 287-288.

Thierry Maertens, *A Feast in Honour of Yahweh. A Study of the Meaning of Worship* (London: Geoffrey Chapman, 1967), *The Clergy Monthly* 32/6: 288.

Thierry Maertens - Jean Frisque, *Guide for the Christian Assembly. A Background Book of the Mass Day by Day*, 5 volumes (London: Darton, Longman & Todd, 1967) *The Clergy Monthly* 32/6: 288-289.

1969

"Second All-India Liturgical Meeting," *The Clergy Monthly* 33/5: 219-223.

"Some New Thinking on the Eucharist," *The Clergy Monthly* 33/9: 381-392.

"The New Ordo Missae," *The Clergy Monthly* 33/10: 448-457.

"The New Eucharistic Prayers," *The Clergy Monthly* 33/11: 490-495.

"Knowing Christ through the Christian Experience," *Indian Journal of Theology* 18/1: 54-64.

Book Reviews

Lucien Cerfaux, *The Christian in the Theology of Saint Paul* (London: Geoffrey Chapman, 1967), *The Clergy Monthly* 33/5: 230-231.

Edward Schillebeeckx, *Le monde et l'Eglise. Approches théologiques III* (Bruxelles: Editions du Cep, 1967), *The Clergy Monthly* 33/5: 231-232.

Gabriel Marcel, *Problematic Man* (New York: Herder & Herder, 1967), *The Clergy Monthly* 33/5: 232.

Raymond E. Brown, *Jesus God and Man. Modern Biblical Reflections* (London: Geoffrey Chapman, 1968), *The Clergy Monthly* 33/9: 421-422.

Jacques Maritain, *De la grâce et de l'humanité de Jésus* (Bruges: Desclée de Brouwer, 1967), *The Clergy Monthly* 33/9: 422-423.

L. Boros, *God Is with Us* (London: Burns & Oates, 1967), *The Clergy Monthly* 33/9: 423.

Christian Duquoc, *Que dites vous du Christ? De Saint Marc à Bonhoeffer* (Paris: Editions du Cerf, 1969), *The Clergy Monthly* 33/9: 423-424.

J. P. Jossua, *Le salut, Incarnation ou Mystère Paschal chez les Pères de l'Eglise de Saint Irénée à Saint Léon le Grand* (Paris: Editions du Cerf, 1968), *The Clergy Monthly* 33/10: 469-470.

P. De Rosa, *God our Saviour, A Study of the Atonement* (London: Geoffrey Chapman, 1968), *The Clergy Monthly* 33/10: 470.

1970

"The Presence of Christ in Hinduism," *The Clergy Monthly* 34/4: 141-148.

Book Reviews

R. H. Fuller, *The Foundations of New Testament Christology* (London: Fontana Library, Collins, 1969), *The Clergy Monthly* 34/9: 413-414.

A. Hamman, *The Paschal Mystery. Ancient Liturgies and Patristic Texts* (Staten Island: Alba House, 1969), *The Clergy Monthly* 34/9: 415-416.

Karl Rahner, *The Trinity* (London: Burns & Oates/ Herder & Herder, 1969), *The Clergy Monthly* 34/10: 459.

G. Bonnet, *Jésus est ressuscité. Les effets d'une parole* (Tournai: Desclée, 1969), *The Clergy Monthly* 34/10: 460.

G. McCauley, *Sacraments for Secular Man* (New York: Herder & Herder, 1969), *The Clergy Monthly* 34/10: 460-461.

Ronald A. Sarno, *Let Us Proclaim the Mystery of Faith* (Denville, N.J.: Dimension Books, 1970), *The Clergy Monthly* 34/11: 502.

1971

God Three and One (Kurseong: St. Mary's Theological College).

J. Dupuis-I. M. Echaniz-J. Volckaert, *Community Prayer Book*, I-II (Gandi-Anand: Anand Press).

"Trinity and World Religions," *The Clergy Monthly* 35/ 2: 77-81.

"Western Christocentrism and Eastern Pneumatology," *The Clergy Monthly* 35/ 5: 190-198.

"The Christian Priesthood," *The Clergy Monthly* 35/5: 204-211.

"Christ and the Holy Spirit in Liturgical Worship," *The Clergy Monthly* 35/6: 248-257.

"Towards a New Image of the Priest," *The Clergy Monthly* 35/8: 326-337; 35/9 : 380-391.

"Nagpur International Theological Conference," *The Clergy Monthly* 35/11: 458-471.

"Jesus God and Man. Some Reflections on W. Pannenberg's Christology," *The Indian Journal of Theology* 20/4: 213-220.

"The Presence of Christ in Hinduism," *Religion and Society* 18/1: 33-45.

"The Salvific Value of Non-Christian Religions," *The Living Word* 78/4: 228-255.

Book Reviews

Fernando Vittorino Joannes (ed.), *Rethinking the Priesthood* (Dublin: Gill & Macmillan, 1970), *The Clergy Monthly* 35/2: 87-88.

Michèle Aumont, *400 prêtres parlent du sacerdoce* (Tournai: Desclée, 1970), *The Clergy Monthly* 35/2: 88-89.

Lancelot Sheppard (ed.), *The New Liturgy. A Comprehensive Introduction* (London: Darton, Longman & Todd, 1970), *The Clergy Monthly* 35/ 4: 183-184.

Thierry Maertens, *Assembly for Christ. From Biblical Theology to Pastoral Theology in the Twentieth Century* (London: Darton, Longman & Todd, 1970), *The Clergy Monthly* 35/4: 184-185.

A. G. Hogg, *Karma and Redemption. An Essay toward the Interpretation of Hinduism and the Re-statement of Christianity* (Madras: The Christian Literature Society, 1970), *The Clergy Monthly* 35/4: 186-187.

N. Lash - J. Rhymer (eds.), *The Christian Priesthood* (London: Darton, Longman & Todd/ Denville, N.J.: Dimension Books, 1970), *The Clergy Monthly* 35/ 6: 268-270.

John Jay Hughes, *Man for Others. Reflections on Christian Priesthood* (London: Sheed & Ward, 1970), *The Clergy Monthly* 35/6: 270-271.

A. Vergote, - A. Descamps - A. Houssiau, *L'eucharistie, Symbole et Realité* (Gembloux: Duculot, 1970), *The Clergy Monthly* 35/6: 271-272.

Le prêtre, hier, aujourd'hui, demain. Congrès d'Ottawa (24-28 Août 1969) (Paris: Editions du Cerf, 1970), *The Clergy Monthly* 35/7: 309-310.

Michel Dortel-Claudot, *Etat de vie et rôle du prêtre* (Paris: Le Centurion, 1971), *The Clergy Monthly* 35/7: 312-313.

Pedro C. Sevilla, *God as Person in the Writings of Martin Buber* (Manila: Loyola House of Studies, 1970), *The Clergy Monthly* 35/8: 356-357.

1972

"The Salvific Value of Non-Christian Religions," in *Documenta Missionalia 5: Evangelization, Dialogue and Development* (Roma: Università Gregoriana Editrice), 169-193.

"Planning the Liturgy of Tomorrow: Third All-India Liturgical Meeting," *The Clergy Monthly* 36/3: 93-105.

Book Reviews

D. Bonhoeffer, *Christology* (London: Collins, 1971), *The Clergy Monthly* 36/1: 42-43.

G. Meagher (ed.), *Priest: Person and Ministry* (Dublin: Gill & Macmillan, 1970), *The Clergy Monthly* 36/1: 44-45.

1973

The Christian Faith in the Doctrinal Documents of the Catholic Church, J. Neuner - J. Dupuis (eds.), (Bangalore: Theological Publications in India; subsequent revised and enlarged editions: 1975, 1979; also Christian Classics: Westminster, 1975).

"The Cosmic Influence of the Holy Spirit and the Gospel Message," in G. Gispert-Sauch (ed.), *God's Word among Men* (Delhi: Vidyajyoti Institute of Religious Studies) 117-138.

"The Salvific Value of Non-Christian Religions," in J. Pathrapankal (ed.), *Service and Salvation. Nagpur Theological Conference on Evangelization* (Bangalore: Theological Publications in India), 207-233.

"Foreword" to: I. Vempenny, *Inspiration in the non-Biblical Scriptures* (Bangalore: Theological Publications in India), xiii-xv.

"Teilhard's Theology," *The Clergy Monthly* 37/3: 117-120.

"The Christology of P. Schoonenberg," *The Clergy Monthly* 37/6: 227-242.

"The Christ-Event in Salvation History," *The Clergy Monthly* 37/7: 275-280.

"The Declaration *Mysterium Ecclesiae*," *The Clergy Monthly* 37/ 319-326.

"Towards a Convergence of Ministries," *The Clergy Monthly* 37/9: 337-353; 37/10: 391-400.

"On the New Eucharistic Prayers," *The Clergy Monthly* 37/ 10: 401-405.

Book Reviews

A. Manaranche, *Je crois en Jésus-Christ aujourd'hui* (Paris: Le Seuil, 1972), *The Clergy Monthly* 37/4: 161-163.

A. Rouillé, *Prêtres d'aujourd'hui pour demain* (Paris: P. Lethielleux, 1971), *The Clergy Monthly* 37/4: 165-166.

Hans Küng, *Why Priests?* (Glasgow: Collins, 1971), *The Clergy Monthly* 37/5: 209-210.

Karl Rahner - W. Thüsing, *Christologie — systematisch und exegetisch. Arbeitsgrundlagen für eine interdisziplinäre Vorlesung* (Freiburg/ Basel/ Wien: Herder, 1972), *The Clergy Monthly* 37/6: 246-247.

N. Crusz, *Bells of Silence. Story of an Ex-priest* (Colombo: N.C. Publications, 1972), *The Clergy Monthly* 37/6: 249-250.

Jean Daniélou, *Gospel Message and Hellenistic Culture. A History of Early Christian Doctrine before the Council of Nicaea* (London: Darton, Longman & Todd, 1973), *The Clergy Monthly* 37/7: 287-288.

A. M. Greeley, *The Jesus Myth* (London: Search Press, 1972), *The Clergy Monthly* 37/7: 288-289.

Dom Bernard Billet, *Bernadette. Une vocation "comme tout le monde"* (Paris: P. Lethielleux, 1971), *The Clergy Monthly* 37/7: 291-292.

G. Delarue, *L'évangile, livre des pauvres* (Paris: P. Lethielleux, 1972), *The Clergy Monthly* 37/7: 292.

Raymond Panikkar, *Worship and Secular Man* (London: Darton, Longman & Todd, 1973), *The Clergy Monthly* 37/7: 293-294.

Pierre Benoit, *Jesus and the Gospel*, Volume I (London: Darton, Longman & Todd, 1973), *The Clergy Monthly* 37/8: 331.

Horst Bürkle - Wolfgang M.W. Roth (eds.), *Indian Voices in Today's Theological Debate* (Delhi: ISPCK/ Madras, CLS, 1972), *The Clergy Monthly* 37/8: 331-332.

H. Desroche, *Les dieux rêvés. Théisme et athéisme en utopie* (Tournai: Desclée, 1972), *The Clergy Monthly* 37/8: 333-334.

Wilfrid J. Harrington, *The Path to Biblical Theology* (Dublin: Gill & Macmillan 1973), *The Clergy Monthly* 37/9: 369-370.

A. G. Martimort (ed.), *The Church at Prayer* (Shannon: Irish University Press, 1973), *The Clergy Monthly* 37/9: 371-372.

F. McLean (ed.), *Religion in Contemporary Thought* (Staten Island, N.Y.: Alba House, 1973), *The Clergy Monthly* 37/ 10: 409-410.

L. Boros, *Hidden God* (London: Search Press, 1973), *The Clergy Monthly* 37/10: 411-412.

Marcus Braybrooke, *The Undiscovered Christ* (Madras: The Christian Literature Society, 1973), *The Clergy Monthly* 37/10: 412-413.

Hans Urs von Balthasar and Joseph Ratzinger, *Two Say Why* (London: Search Press, 1973), *The Clergy Monthly* 37/10: 414-415.

Joseph Pathrapankal (ed.), *Service and Salvation* (Nagpur Theological Conference on Evangelization) (Bangalore: Theological Publications in India, 1973), *The Clergy Monthly* 37/11: 449.

1974

"The Cosmic Economy of the Spirit and the Sacred Scriptures of Religious Traditions," in D.S. Amalorpavadass (ed.), *Research Seminar on Non-Biblical Scriptures* (Bangalore: National Biblical, Catechetical and Liturgical Centre), 117-135.

"Unity of Faith and Dogmatic Pluralism," *The Clergy Monthly* 38/ 9: 378-390; 38/10: 442-450.

"The Use of non-Christian Scriptures in Christian Worship in India," *Studia Missionalia* 23: *Worship and Ritual* (Roma: Università Gregoriana Editrice), 127-143.

"Synod of Bishops 1974," *Doctrine and Life* 25/5: 323-348.

Book Reviews

Thomas Merton, *Contemplative Prayer* (London: Darton, Longman & Todd, 1973), *The Clergy Monthly* 38/1: 42-43.

Henri J. M. Nouwen, *Pray to Live. Thomas Merton: A Contemplative Critic* (Notre Dame, Indiana: Fides Publications, 1972), *The Clergy Monthly* 38/1: 43-45.

Gerhard Ebeling, *Introduction to a Theological Theory of Language* (London: Collins, 1973), *The Clergy Monthly* 38/2: 90-91.

David Cairns, *The Image of God in Man* (London: Collins, 1973), *The Clergy Monthly* 38/ 2: 91-93.

J. A. T. Robinson, *The Human Face of God* (London: SCM Press, 1973), *The Clergy Monthly* 38/6: 275-277.

Raymond Panikkar, *The Trinity and the Religious Experience of Man* (London: Darton, Longman & Todd, 1973), *The Clergy Monthly* 38/7: 322-323.

L. Boros, *Meditations* (London: Search Press, 1973), *The Clergy Monthly* 38/7: 323.

R. Bouchard - M. Lejeune, *Eucharist and Community* (Kampala: Pastoral Institute of Eastern Africa, 1973), *The Clergy Monthly* 38/7: 323-324.

Towards Adult Christian Community. Report of the AMECEA Catechetical Congress, 1973 (Kampala: Pastoral Institute of Eastern Africa, 1973), *The Clergy Monthly* 38/7: 323-324.

C. Nyamiti, *The Scope of African Theology* (Kampala: Pastoral Institute of Eastern Africa, 1973), *The Clergy Monthly* 38/7: 323-324.

"Be Reconciled with God and with One Another," (Bombay: Saint Paul Press, 1973), *The Clergy Monthly* 38/7: 327-328.

F. X. Durrwell, *The Apostolate and the Church* (London: Sheed & Ward, 1973), *The Clergy Monthly* 38/8: 371-372.

J. Aixala, *Saints in the Liturgy* (Ranchi: Catholic Press, 1974), *The Clergy Monthly* 38/8: 372-373.

1975

"Religion and the Quality of Life. Second World Conference on Religion and Peace," *Vidyajyoti Journal of Theological Reflection* 39/3 : 98-110.

"Priestly Vocation After Vatican II," in Thomas Thyparampil (ed.), *Vocation: God's Call to Man* (Poona: National Vocation Service Centre), 145-157.

"Synod of Bishops 1974," *Vidyajyoti* 39/4: 146-169.

"Reflections on Church Structures and Ministries," *Vidyajyoti* 39/11: 478-490.

"Le mouvement théologique en Inde*," Revue théologique de Louvain* 6/3: 324-331.

"The Religious in the Particular Church," in *Religious and the Local Church* (Delhi: CRI Permanent Secretariat) 1-16.

"The Mission of Inculturation of Religious in the Church," in *Religious and the Local Church* (Delhi: CRI Permanent Secretariat) 17-30.

"Promotion and Formation of Vocations for Evangelization in India," *The Search* 3/2: 4-9; 3/3: 12-18.

"La rencontre des religions. Dialogue et théologie," *Revue théologique de Louvain* 6/2: 194-204.

Book Reviews

Karl Rahner, *Theological Investigations*, Volume XI: *Confrontations 1* (London: Darton, Longman & Todd, 1974), *Vidyajyoti* 39/5: 235-236.

Raymond E. Brown, *The Virginal Conception and the Bodily Resurrection of Jesus* (London: Geoffrey Chapman, 1973), *Vidyajyoti* 39/8: 332-333.

Pierre Benoit, *Jesus and the Gospel*, Volume II (London: Darton, Longman & Todd, 1974), *Vidyajyoti* 39/8: 333-334.

René De Haes, *Pour une théologie du prophétique. Lecture thématique de la théologie de Karl Rahner* (Louvain: Editions Nauwelaerts, 1972), *Vidyajyoti* 39/8:334-335.

J. Delorme (ed.), *Le ministère et les ministères selon le Nouveau Testament* (Paris: Le Seuil, 1974), *Vidyajyoti* 39/9: 417-418.

G. Philips et al., *Théologie. Le service théologique dans l'Eglise*. Mélanges offers à Yves Congar pour ses soixante-dix ans (Paris: Editions du Cerf, 1974), *Vidyajyoti* 39/9: 419-420.

Bruce Vawter, *This Man Jesus. An Essay towards a New Testament Christology* (London: Geoffrey Chapman, 1975), *Vidyajyoti* 39/10: 467.

Anthony Tyrrell Hanson, *Grace and Truth. A Study in the Doctrine of the Incarnation* (London: SPCK, 1975), *Vidyajyoti* 39/10: 467-468.

Piet Schoonenberg, *The Christ* (London: Sheed & Ward, 1974), *Vidyajyoti* 39/10: 468.

Alan Richardson, *The Political Christ* (London: SCM Press, 1973), *Vidyajyoti* 39/10: 469.

Nicholas Lash, *His Presence in the World. A Study in Eucharistic Worship and Theology* (London: Sheed & Ward, 1974), *Vidyajyoti* 39/10: 471.

A. E. Harvey, *Priest or President?* (London: SPCK, 1975), *Vidyajyoti* 39/10: 471-472.

Xavier Léon-Dufour, *Resurrection and the Message of Easter* (London: Geoffrey Chapman, 1974), *Vidtajyoti* 39/11: 515.

Charles Kannengiesser, *Foi en la résurrection, résurrection de la foi* (Paris: Beauchesne, 1974), *Vidyajyoti* 39/11: 515-516.

Gerald O'Collins, *Has Dogma a Future?* (London: Darton, Longman & Todd, 1975), *Vidyajyoti* 39/11: 514.

John Coventry, *Christian Truth* (London, Darton: Longman & Todd, 1974), *Vidyajyoti* 39/11: 516.

1976

"Ministry and Ministries in the Church," in D. S. Amalorpavadass (ed.), *Ministries in the Church in India. Research Seminar and Pastoral Consultation* (New Delhi: CBCI Centre), 72-87.

"Ecumenical Collaboration at the Regional National and Local Levels," *Vidyajyoti* 40/1: 35-45.

"The Religious in the Particular Church," *Vidyajyoti* 40/3: 97-111.

"The Religious in the Particular Church," *Report of the CBCI General Meeting, Hyderabad, January 4-14, 1976* (New Delhi: CBCI Centre) 1-18.

"The Religious in the Particular Church," *In Christo* 14/2: 63-73.

"Apostolic Exhortation *Evangelii Nuntiandi*," *Vidyajyoti* 40/5: 218-230.

"New Ministries: A Pastoral Approach," *Vidyajyoti* 40/ 9: 398-412.

"The Mission of Inculturation of Religious in the Local Church," *In Christo* 14/3: 116-124.

"L'économie cosmique de l'Esprit et les Saintes Ecritures des traditions religieuses," *La vie spirituelle* 616, 58: 729-746.

Book Reviews

Ladislas Boros, *The Cosmic Christ* (London: Search Press, 1975), *Vidyajyoti* 40/1: 48.

Bernard Basset, *Let's Start Praying Again* (London: Sheed & Ward, 1974), *Vidyajyoti* 40/ 1: 48.

Karl Rahner, *Theological Investigations*. Volume XII: *Confrontations 2* (London: Darton, Longman & Todd, 1974), *Vidyajyoti* 40/2: 86-87.

Karl Rahner, *Theological Investigations*, Volume XIII (London: Darton, Longman & Todd, 1975), *Vidyajyoti* 40/2: 86-87.

Edward Schillebeeckx, *The Understanding of Faith. Interpretation and Criticism* (London: Sheed & Ward, 1974), *Vidyajyoti* 40/2: 88.

J. Jomier, *Jesus. The Life of the Messiah* (Madras: The Christian Literature Society, 1974), *Vidyajyoti* 40/2: 95.

Karl Rahner (ed.), *Encyclopedia of Theology. A Concise Sacramentum Mundi* (London: Burns & Oates, 1975), *Vidyajyoti* 40/3: 134-135.

André Manaranche, *Ceci est mon corps* (Paris, Le Seuil, 1975), *Vidyajyoti* 40/3: 137.

A Critique of Eucharistic Agreement (London: SPCK, 1975), *Vidyajyoti* 40/3: 137-138.

The Agreed Statements: Eucharistic Doctrine (1971); Ministry and Ordination (1973) (London: SPCK, 1975), *Vidyajyoti* 40/3: 138.

Charles Kannengiesser (ed.), *Politique et théologie chez Athanase d'Alexandrie* (Paris: Beauchesne, 1974), *Vidyajyoti* 40/3: 142-143.

Raymond E. Brown, *Biblical Reflections on Crises Facing the Church* (London: Darton, Longman & Todd, 1975), *Vidyajyoti* 40/5: 231.

Peter Hebblethwaite, *The Runaway Church* (London: Collins, 1975), *Vidyajyoti* 40/5: 232.

John Macquarrie, *Christian Unity and Christian Diversity* (London: SCM Press, 1975), *Vidyajyoti* 40/5: 232-233.

Jacques Rollet, *Libération sociale et salut chrétien* (Paris: Editions du Cerf, 1974), *Vidyajyoti* 40/5: 235.

Wolfhart Pannenberg, *The Apostles' Creed. In the Light of Today's Questions* (London: SCM Press, 1975), *Vidyajyoti* 40/6: 283.

Walbert Bühlmann, *The Coming of the Third Church. An Analysis of the Present and Future of the Church* (Slough: St. Paul Publications, 1976), *Vidyajyoti* 40/7: 329.

René Laurentin, *L'évangélisation après le quatrième synode* (Paris: Le Seuil, 1975), *Vidyajyoti* 40/7: 329-330.

Qui portera l'évangile aux nations? XLIVème semaine de missiologie de Louvain (Bruges: Desclée de Brouwer, 1974), *Vidyajyoti* 40/7: 330-331.

Report of the General Meeting of the Catholic Bishops' Conference of India, Hyderabad, January 4-13, 1976 (Delhi: CBCI Centre, 1976), *Vidyajyoti* 40/7: 336.

Bertrand de Margerie, *Christ for the World. The Heart of the Lamb: A Treatise on Christology* (Chicago: Franciscan Herald Press, 1974), *Vidyajyoti* 40/8: 382-383.

Wilfrid J. Harrington, *Christ and Life* (Dublin: Gill & McMillan, 1975), *Vidyajyoti* 40/8: 383.

Gerald A. McCool (ed.), *A Rahner Reader* (London: Darton, Longman & Todd, 1975), *Vidyajyoti* 40/8: 383-384.

Karl Rahner, *Christian at the Crossroads* (London: Burns & Oates, 1975), *Vidyajyoti* 40/8: 384.

Karl Rahner, *Encounters with Silence* (Bangalore: St. Paul Publications, 1975), *Vidyajyoti* 40/8: 384.

William Johnston, *Silent Music. The Science of Meditation* (London: Collins, 1976), *Vidyajyoti* 40/9: 428.

Bede Griffiths, *Return to the Centre* (London: Collins, 1976), *Vidyajyoti* 40/10: 479.

H. J. Steben et al., *Koinônia. Communauté-Communion* (Paris: Beauchesne, 1975), *Vidyajyoti* 40/11: 516.

1977

Jesus Christ and His Spirit. Theological Approaches (Bangalore: Theological Publications in India).

"Community and Ministry," in Pedro S. de Achtegui (ed.), *Asian Colloquium on Ministries in the Church (Hong Kong, February 27 - March 5, 1977)* (Hong Kong: FABC), 223-243.

"Ministries in the Church: An Asian Colloquium," *Vidyajyoti* 41/ 6: 242-260.

"Colloque d'Asie: Ministères dans l'Eglise," *Spiritus* 69/18: 365-385.

"Christus und die indische Advaita-Erfahrung," *Orientierung* 41/15-16: 168-172.

"Conscience du Christ et expérience de l'Advaita," *Revue théologique de Louvain* 8/4: 448-460.

"Bulletin: Five Years of Theological Reflection in India," *Indian Theological Studies* 14/ 1: 91-114.

"The Church's Response to the Present Needs of India," *General Meeting of the Catholic Bishops' Conference of India (Bombay, January 9-15, 1977)* (New Delhi: CBCI Centre), 3-36.

Book Reviews

Karl Rahner, *Theological Investigations*. Volume XIV (London: Darton, Longman & Todd, 1976), *Vidyajyoti* 41/10: 471-472.

Report of the General Meeting of the Catholic Bishops' Conference of India (Bombay, January 9-15, 1977) (New Delhi: CBCI Centre, 1977), *Vidyajyoti* 41/10: 475.

1978

"A National Consultation on Conciliar Unity," *Vidyajyoti* 42/5: 233.

"A New Theological Collection," *Vidyajyoti* 42/6: 280-284.

"Theological Foundation for the Interpretation of Man," *The Indian Journal of Theology* 27/3-4: 160-170.

"A Commentary on the Mass of Christ the Light," *Word and Worship* 11/9: 379-382.

"The Uniqueness of Jesus Christ in the Early Christian Tradition," *Jeevadhara* 47/ 8: 393-408.

"The Symbol of the Apostles," *Word and Worship* 15/3: 87-93.

"The Spiritual Theology of Origen," in Mayeul de Druille (ed.), *Christian Spirituality for India* (Bangalore: Asirvanam Benedictine Monastery) 56-70.

Book Reviews

James D. G. Dunn, *Jesus and the Spirit. A Study of the Religious and Charismatic Experience of Jesus and the First Christians as Reflected in the New Testament* (London: SCM Press, 1975), *Vidyajyoti* 42/3: 140-141.

Geza Vermes, *Jesus the Jew. A Historian's Reading of the Gospel* (London: Collins, 1976), *Vidyajyoti* 42/3: 141-142.

Milan Machovec, *A Marxist Looks at Jesus* (London: Darton, Longman & Todd, 1976), *Vidyajyoti* 42/3: 142-143.

Yves Congar, *Un peuple messianique* (Paris: Editions du Cerf, 1975), *Vidyajyoti* 42/4: 190-191.

Bernard Lonergan, *The Way to Nicea, The Dialectical Development of Trinitarian Theology* (London: Darton, Longman & Todd, 1976), *Vidyajyoti* 42/4: 191-192.

Bernard Basset, *And Would You Believe It? The Story of the Nicene Creed* (London: Sheed & Ward, 1976), *Vidyajyoti* 42/4: 192.

Yves le Gal, *Question(s) à la théologie chrétienne* (Paris: Editions du Cerf, 1975), *Vidyajyoti* 42/4: 192-193.

John Wilcken, *The Priest Today. Theological and Spiritual Reflections* (Melbourne: The Polding Press, 1976), *Vidyajyoti* 42/4: 193.

Hans Küng, *On Being a Christian* (London: Collins, 1977), *Vidyajyoti* 42/5: 236-238.

Walter Kasper, *Jesus the Christ* (London: Burns & Oates, 1976), *Vidyajyoti* 42/5: 238-239.

Peter de Rosa, *Jesus Who Became Christ* (London: Collins, 1977), *Vidyajyoti* 42/5: 239-240.

Jürgen Moltmann, *The Crucified God* (London: SCM Press, 1976), *Vidyajyoti* 42/5: 240-241.

Thomas F. Torrance, *Theology in Reconciliation. Essays towards Evangelical and Catholic Unity in East and West* (London: Geoffrey Chapman, 1975), *Vidyajyoti* 42/5: 241-242.

Report of the General Meeting of the Catholic Bishops' Conference of India (Mangalore, January 9-17, 1978) (New Delhi: CBCI Centre 1978), *Vidyajyoti* 42/5: 279.

Avery Dulles, *The Resilient Church. The Necessity and Limits of Adaptation* (Dublin: Gill & Macmillan, 1978), *Vidyajyoti* 42/7: 336-337.

Dermot A. Lane, *The Reality of Jesus. An Essay in Christology* (New York: Paulist Press, 1975), *Vidyajyoti* 42/ 9: 430-431.

Gerald O'Collins, *What Are They Saying about Jesus?* (New York: Paulist Press, 1977), *Vidyajyoti* 42/9: 431.

Michael B. McGarry, *Christology after Auschwitz* (New York: Paulist Press, 1977), *Vidyajyoti* 42/9: 431-432.

Peter Kelly, *Searching for Truth. A Personal View of Roman Catholicism* (London: Collins, 1978), *Vidyajyoti* 42/9: 434-435.

Karl Rahner, *Grundkurs des Glaubens. Einführung in den Begriff des Christentums* (Freiburg im Breisgau: Herder, 1976), *Vidyajyoti* 42/11: 528-529.
Karl Rahner, *Foundations of Christian Faith* (London: Darton, Longman & Todd, 1978), *Vidyajyoti* 42/11: 528-529.

1979

"Reflections on Recent Trends in Christology," in *Theological Miscellanea. A Volume Published in Honour of Monsignor Agapito Lourenco* (Goa), 25-32.
"Bishop-Religious Relationship," *Vidyajyoti* 43/1: 25-36.
"Authority in the Church: Towards an Ecumenical Convergence on Papacy," *Vidyajyoti* 43/3: 98-11; 43/4: 151-168.
"First Encyclical Letter of Pope John Paul II," *Vidyajyoti* 43/7: 325-335.
"A Letter of Pope John Paul II to All the Priests of the Church on the Occasion of the Holy Thursday 1979," *Vidyajyoti* 43/7: 335-339.
"Letter on Certain Questions Regarding Eschatology," *Vidyajyoti* 43/12: 527-534.

Book Reviews

Ignacio Ellacuría, *Freedom Made Flesh. The Mission of Christ and His Church* (Maryknoll, N.Y.: Orbis Books, 1976), *Vidyajyoti* 43/1: 43-44.
José Porfirio Miranda, *Being and the Messiah* (Maryknoll, N.Y.: Orbis Books 1977), *Vidyajyoti* 43/1: 44-45.
Michael H. Crosby, *Thy Will Be Done. Praying the Our Father as Subversive Activity* (Maryknoll: N.Y., Orbis Books, 1977), *Vidyajyoti* 43/1: 45.
Sebastian Kappen, *Jesus and Freedom* (Maryknoll, N.Y.: Orbis Books, 1977), *Vidyajyoti* 43/1: 45-46.
John Desrochers, *Christ the Liberator* (Bangalore: The Centre for Social Action, 1977), *Vidyajyoti* 43/1:46.
Tissa Balasuriya, *Jesus Christ and Human Liberation* (Colombo: Centre for Society and Religion), *Vidyajyoti* 43/1: 46-47.
————, *Eucharist and Human Liberation* (Colombo: Centre for Society and Religion, 1977), *Vidyajyoti* 43/1: 46-47.
Norman Perrin, *The Resurrection Narratives, A New Approach* (London: SCM Press, 1977), *Vidyajyoti* 43/2: 91-92.
Martin Hengel, *The Son of God. The Origin of Christology and the History of Jewish-Hellenistic Religion* (London: SCM Press, 1976), *Vidyajyoti* 43/2: 92-93.
Angelo Amato (ed.), *Problemi attuali di Cristologia* (Roma: LAS, 1975), *Vidyajyoti* 43/2: 93.
Bernard Bro, *Jésus Christ ou rien* (Paris: Editions du Cerf, 1977), *Vidyajyoti* 43/2: 93-94.
Henri Cormier, *The Humor of Jesus* (New York: Alba House, 1977), *Vidyajyoti* 43/2: 94.
Malachi Martin, *Jesus Now* (London: Collins, 1977), *Vidyajyoti* 43/2: 94-95.
Gerald O'Collins, *The Calvary Christ* (London: SCM Press, 1977), *Vidyajyoti* 43/2:95.
Robert J. Daly, *The Origins of the Christian Doctrine of Sacrifice* (London: Darton, Longman & Todd, 1978), *Vidyajyoti* 43/2: 95-96.
Frances M. Young, *Sacrifice and the Death of Christ* (London: SPCK, 1975), *Vidyajyoti* 43/2: 96.
Jürgen Moltmann, *The Church in the Power of the Spirit. A Contribution to Messianic*

Ecclesiology (London: SCM Press, 1977), *Vidyajyoti* 43/3: 138-139.

George T. Montague, *The Holy Spirit. Growth of a Biblical Tradition* (New York: Paulist Press, 1976), *Vidyajyoti* 43/3: 139-140.

Heribert Mühlen, *A Charismatic Theology. Initiation in the Spirit* (London: Burns & Oates, 1978), *Vidiajyoti* 43/3: 140.

Donal Dorr, *Remove the Heart of Stone. Charismatic Renewal and the Experience of Grace* (Dublin: Gill & Macmillan, 1978), *Vidyajyoti* 43/3: 140-141.

Michael Ramsey—Léon-Joseph Cardinal Suenens, *Come, Holy Spirit* (London: Darton, Longman & Todd, 1977), *Vidyajyoti* 43/3: 141.

Edward D. O'Connor (ed.), *Charismatic Renewal* (London: SPCK, 1978), *Vidyajyoti* 43/3: 141-142.

Jon Sobrino, *Christology at the Crossroads. A Latin American Approach* (London: SCM Press, 1976), *Vidyajyoti* 43/4: 194-195.

Ignatius Echaniz, *Biblical Prayer-Book and Missal* (Anand, Gujarat: Sahitya Prakash, 1978), *Vidyajyoti* 43/4: 195-196.

James D. G. Dunn, *Unity and Diversity in the New Testament. An Inquiry into the Character of Earliest Christianity* (London: SCM Press, 1977), *Vidyajyoti* 43/5: 236-237.

John Hick, *God and the Universe of Faiths* (London: Collins, 1977), *Vidyajyoti* 43/5: 237-238.

Choan-Seng Song (ed.), *Growing Together into Unity. Texts of the Faith and Order Commission on Conciliar Fellowship* (Madras: The Christian Literature Society, 1978), *Vidyajyoti* 43/5: 240.

Louis Bouyer, *Le Père invisible. Approches du mystère de la divinité* (Paris: Editions du Cerf, 1976), *Vidyajyoti* 43/7: 342

Léon-Joseph Cardinal Suenens, *Your God? The Oxford University Mission 1977* (London: Darton, Longman & Todd, 1978), *Vidyajyoti* 43/7: 342.

Keith Ward, *The Concept of God* (Glasgow: Collins, 1977), *Vidyajyoti* 43/7: 342-343.

Andrew M. Greeley, *The Great Mysteries. An Essential Catechism* (Dublin: Gill & Macmillan, 1977), *Vidyajyoti* 43/7: 343-344.

Donald Coggan, *The Heart of the Christian Faith* (Glasgow: Collins, 1978), *Vidyajyoti* 43/7: 344.

David E. Jenkins, *The Contradiction of Christianity* (London: SCM Press, 1976), *Vidyajyoti* 43/7: 344.

David Tracy - Hans Küng - Johann B. Metz (eds.), *Toward Vatican III. The Work that Needs to Be Done* (Dublin: Gill & Macmillan, 1978), *Vidyajyoti* 43/8: 385-386.

Sergio Torres - Virginia Fabella (eds.), *The Emergent Gospel. Theology from the Underside of History* (Maryknoll, N.Y.: Orbis Books, 1978), *Vidyajyoti* 43/8: 386.

Léon-Joseph Cardinal Suenens, *Ecumenism and Charismatic Renewal: Theological and Pastoral Orientations* (London: Darton, Longman & Todd, 1978), *Vidyajyoti* 43/8: 386-387.

Kilian McDonnell, *Charismatic Renewal and Ecumenism* (Ramsey, N.J.: Paulist Press, 1978), *Vidyajyoti* 43/8: 387.

Raymond Panikkar, *The Intra-Religious Dialogue* (New York/ Ramsey: Paulist Press, 1978), *Vidyajyoti* 43/10: 537.

Kenneth Cragg, *The Christian and Other Religions* (London/ Oxford: Mowbrays, 1977), *Vidyajyoti* 43/10: 537-538.

Donald G. Dawe - John B. Carman (eds.), *Christian Faith in a Religiously Plural World* (Maryknoll, N.Y.: Orbis Books, 1978), *Vidyajyoti* 43/10: 538.

Patrick Sookhdeo (ed.), *Jesus Christ the Only Way.Christian Responsibility in a Multicultural Society* (Exeter: The Paternoster Press, 1978), *Vidyajyoti* 43/10: 538-539.

1980

"A Report on Liturgical Renewal," *Vidyajyoti* 44/1: 31-36.
"John Paul II in Istanbul," *Vidyajyoti* 44/2: 83-86.

Book Reviews

Jürgen Moltmann, *The Open Church. Invitation to a Messianic Life-Style* (London: SCM Press, 1978), *Vidyajyoti* 44/1: 37.

Michael Winter, *Mission Resumed?* (London: Darton, Longman & Todd, 1979), *Vidyajyoti* 44/1: 37-38.

Juan Luis Segundo, *The Hidden Motives of Pastoral Action. Latin American Reflections* (Maryknoll N.Y.: Orbis Books, 1978), *Vidyajyoti* 44/1: 38.

J. D. Crichton, *The Once and the Future Liturgy* (Dublin: Veritas Publications, 1977), *Vidyajyoti* 44/1: 39-40.

J. D. Crichton, *The Prayer of the Church* (London: Geoffrey Chapman, 1978), *Vidyajyoti* 44/1: 39-40.

M. Amaladoss, *Do Sacraments Change?* (Bangalore: Theological Publications in India, 1979), *Vidyajyoti* 44/1: 40.

Ernest Lucier, *The Eucharist: The Bread of Life* (New York: Alba House, 1977), *Vidyajyoti* 44/1: 40.

New Catholic Encyclopedia. Volume XVII: Supplement: *Change in the Church* (Publishers Guild, in Association with the McGraw-Hill Book Company, Washington, D.C., New York, N.Y., 1979), *Vidyajyoti* 44/2: 87.

Karl Rahner, *Theological Investigations,* Volume XVI (London: Darton, Longman & Todd, 1979), *Vidyajyoti* 44/2: 87-88.

Karl Rahner, *The Spirit in the Church* (London: Burns & Oates, 1979), *Vidyajyoti* 44/2: 88.

M. Malinski, *Pope John Paul II. The Life of My Friend Karol Wojtyla* (London: Burns & Oates, 1979), *Vidyajyoti* 44/2: 92-93.

Peter Hebblethwaite, *The Year of Three Popes* (London/ Glasgow: Collins, 1979), *Vidyajyoti* 44/2: 93.

Albino Luciani, *Illustrissimi. The Letters of Pope John Paul I* (London: Collins, 1979), *Vidyajyoti* 44/2: 93.

Report of the General Meeting of the Catholic Bishops' Conference of India (Ranchi, October 17-25, 1979), (New Delhi: CBCI Centre, 1980), *Vidyajyoti* 44/3: 113.

John A. T. Robinson, *Truth Is Two-Eyed* (London: SCM Press, 1979), *Vidyajyoti* 44/5: 248.

Choan-Seng Song, *Third-Eye Theology. Theology in Formation in Asian Settings* (Maryknoll, N.Y.: Orbis Books, 1979), *Vidyajyoti* 44/5: 249.

Yves M. J. Congar, *Je crois en l'Esprit Saint*. Tome I: *L'Esprit Saint dans l'"Economie": Révélation et expérience de l'Esprit*. Tome II: *"Il est Seigneur et il donne la vie"* (Paris: Editions du Cerf, 1979), *Vidyajyoti* 44/6: 297-298.

C. F. D. Moule, *The Holy Spirit* (Oxford: Mowbray, 1978), *Vidyajyoti* 44/6: 298.

Billy Graham, *The Holy Spirit. Activating God's Power in Your Life* (London: Collins, 1979), *Vidyajyoti* 44/6: 298.

Charles E. Hummel, *Fire in the Fireplace* (Oxford: Mowbray, 1979), *Vidyajyoti* 44/6: 298-299.

Simon Tugwell, *Did You Receive the Spirit?* (London: Darton, Longman & Todd, 1979), *Vidyajyoti* 44/6: 299.

Raymond E. Brown - Karl P. Donfried - Joseph Fitzmyer - John Reumann (eds.), *Mary in the New Testament. A Collaborative Assessment by Protestant and Roman Catholic Scholars* (Bangalore: Theological Publications in India, 1979), *Vidyajyoti* 44/7: 346.

Leonardo Boff, *Jesus Christ Liberator. A Critical Christology for Our Time* (Maryknoll, N.Y.: Orbis Books, 1978), *Vidyajyoti* 44/7: 346-347.

Albert Nolan, *Jesus Before Christianity* (Maryknoll, N.Y.: Orbis Books, 1978), *Vidyajyoti* 44/7: 347.

Charles Massabki, *Christ: Liberation of the World Today* (New York: Alba House, 1978), *Vidyajyoti* 44/7: 347-348.

José Comblin, *Jesus of Nazareth* (Maryknoll, N.Y.: Orbis Books, 1979), *Vidyajyoti* 44/7: 348.

José Comblin, *Sent from the Father* (Maryknoll, N.Y.: Orbis Books, 1979), *Vidyajyoti* 44/7: 348.

Joseph G. Donders, *Jesus the Stranger* (Dublin: Gill & Macmillan, 1979), *Vidyajyoti* 44/7: 348.

Paul Kevin Meagher - Thomas C. O'Brien - Consuelo Maria Aherne (eds.), *Encyclopedic Dictionary of Religion* (Washington, D.C.: Corpus Publications, 1979). Three Volumes. *Vidyajyoti* 44/8: 391.

Walbert Bühlmann, *Courage Church!* (Maryknoll, N.Y.: Orbis Books, 1978), *Vidyajyoti* 44/10: 539.

Joseph Comblin. *The Meaning of Mission* (Maryknoll, N.Y.: Orbis Books, 1978), *Vidyajyoti* 44/10: 539-540.

Herbert E. Hoefer (ed.), *Debate on Mission* (Madras: Gurukal Lutheran Theological College and Research Institute, 1979), *Vidyajyoti* 44/10: 540.

1981

"Evangelising Communities for South Asia," *Vidyajyoti* 45/2: 72-78.
"New Norms for Laicisation," *Vidyajyoti* 45/3: 138-142.
"A Catechetical Series for East Africa," *Vidyajyoti* 45/ 4: 191-192.
"Commemorating Two Councils," *Vidyajyoti* 45/6: 256-257.
"The Classics of Western Spirituality," *Vidyajyoti* 45/10: 503-507.

Book Reviews

Raymond E. Brown, *The Community of the Beloved Disciple* (New York/ Ramsey, Paulist Press: 1979), *Vidyajyoti* 45/ 3: 144.

Cecil Hargreaves, *Asian Christian Thinking. Studies in a Metaphor and its Message* (Delhi: ISPCK, 1979), *Vidyajyoti* 45/3: 148.

M. Davy, *Henri Le Saux: Swami Abhishiktananda. Le passeur entre deux rives* (Paris: Editions du Cerf, 1981), *Vidyajyoti* 45/5: 248.

Raymond Panikkar, *Myth, Faith and Hermeneutics* (New York/ Ramsey, Paulist Press: 1979), *Vidyajyoti* 45/5: 249.

John Hick - Peter Hebblethwaite (eds.), *Christianity and Other Religions* (London: Collins, 1980), *Vidyajyoti* 45/5: 250-251.

Paul Hacker, *Theological Foundations of Evangelization* (St. Augustine: Steyler Verlag, 1980), *Vidyajyoti* 45/5: 251.

John Eagleson - Philip Scharper (eds.), *Puebla and Beyond. Documentation and Commentary* (Maryknoll N.Y.: Orbis Books, 1979), *Vidyajyoti* 45/7: 348.

Kosuke Koyama, *50 Meditations* (Maryknoll, N.Y.: Orbis Books, 1979), *Vidyajyoti* 45/7: 349-350.

René Latourelle, *Finding Jesus through the Gospels. History and Hermeneutics* (New York: Alba House, 1979), *Vidyajyoti* 45/8: 401-402.

Karl Rahner - Wilhelm Thüsing, *A New Christology* (London: Burns & Oates, 1980), *Vidyajyoti* 45/8: 402-403.

James P. Mackey, *Jesus, the Man and the Myth. A Contemporary Christology* (New York/ Ramsey: Paulist Press, 1979), *Vidyajyoti* 45/8: 403.

Leonard Swidler (ed.), *Consensus in Theology. A Dialogue with Hans Küng and Edward Schillebeeckx* (Philadelphia: The Westminster Press, 1980), *Vidyajyoti* 45/8/ 403-404.

J. R. Armogate (ed.), *Comment être chrétien. La réponse de Hans Küng* (Paris: Desclée de Brouwer, 1979), *Vidyajyoti* 45/8: 404.

B. C. Butler, *The Church and Unity. An Essay* (London: Geoffrey Chapman, 1979), *Vidyajyoti* 45/8: 404-405.

Anthony Mookenthottam, *Towards a Theology in the Indian Context* (Bangalore: Asian Trading Corporation, 1980), *Vidyajyoti* 45/8: 405-406.

Peter Fernando, *Inculturation in Seminary Formation* (Pune: Ishvani Kendra, 1980), *Vidyajyoti* 45/8: 405-406.

S. M. Michael, *The Cultural Context of Evangelization in India* (Pune: Ishvani Kendra, 1980), *Vidyajyoti* 45/8: 405-406.

Sundar Clarke, *Let the Indian Church Be Indian* (Madras: The Christian Literature Society, 1980), *Vidyajyoti* 45/8: 405-406.

Bruce J. Nicholls, *Contextualisation: A Theology of Gospel and Culture* (Exeter: The Paternoster Press, 1979), *Vidyajyoti* 45/8: 405-406.

Leopold Sabourin, *The Bible and Christ. The Unity of the Two Testaments* (New York: Alba House, 1980), *Vidyajyoti* 45/9: 449-450.

Christopher Butler, *The Theology of Vatican II* (London: Darton, Longman & Todd, 1981), *Vidyajyoti* 45/9: 450.

A. Schilson - Walter Kasper, *Théologies du Christ aujourd'hui* (Paris: Desclée, 1978), *Vidyajyoti* 45/9: 450-451.

Jean-Noël Bezançon, *Le Christ de Dieu* (Paris: Desclée de Brouwer, 1979), *Vidyajyoti* 45/ 9: 451.

Jacques Guillet, *Jesus Christ in Our World* (Wheathampstead, Hertfordshire: Anthony Clarke Books, 1977), *Vidyajyoti* 45/9: 451-452.

Jacques Guillet, *The Religious Experience of Jesus and His Disciples* (Wheathampstead, Hertfordshire: Anthony Clarke Books, 1979), *Vidyajyoti* 45/9: 451-452.

John Coventry, *Faith in Jesus Christ* (London: Darton, Longman & Todd, 1980), *Vidyajyoti* 45/9: 452.

Rudolf Schnackenburg, *Christ Present and Coming* (London: SPCK, 1978), *Vidyajyoti* 45/9: 452.

Dietrich Wiederkehr, *Belief in Redemption. Concepts of Salvation from the New Testament to the Present Time* (London: SPCK, 1979), *Vidyajyoti* 45/9: 453.

L. Lochet, *Jésus descendu aux enfers* (Paris: Editions du Cerf, 1979), *Vidyajyoti* 45/9: 453.
William R. Burrows, *New Ministries: The Global Context* (Maryknoll, N.Y.: Orbis Books, 1980), *Vidyajyoti* 45/9: 453-454.

1982

The Christian Faith in the Doctrinal Documents of the Catholic Church. Fourth Revised and Enlarged Edition. J. Neuner - J. Dupuis (eds.), (Bangalore: Theological Publications in India, 1982/ London, Collins, 1983).
"Restructuring the CBCI Activities," *Vidyajyoti* 46/ 3: 151-152.
"The Indian Church in the Struggle for a New Society," *Vidyajyoti* 46/7: 352-363.
"More 'Classics of Western Spirituality,' " *Vidyajyoti* 46/10: 509-510.

Book Reviews

Gustave Martelet, *Oser croire en l'Eglise* (Paris: Editions du Cerf, 1979), *Vidyajyoti* 46/4: 201.
Geoffrey Preston, *Hallowing the Time. Meditations on the Cycle of the Christian Liturgy* (London: Darton, Longman & Todd, 1980), *Vidyajyoti* 46/4:201-202.
Juan Luis Segundo, *Theologies in Conflict* (Maryknoll, N.Y.: Orbis Books, 1979), *Vidyajyoti* 46/4: 202.
Gerald H. Anderson - Thomas Stransky (eds.), *Liberation Theologies in North America and Europe* (New York/ Ramsey: Paulist Press, 1979), *Vidyajyoti* 46/4: 202-203.
Placidio Ezdozain, *Archbishop Romero: Martyr of Salvador* (Maryknoll, N.Y.: Orbis Books, 1981), *Vidyajyoti* 46/4: 203.
Teofilo Cabestreto, *Mystic of Liberation. A Portrait of Pedro Casaldáliga* (Maryknoll, N.Y.: Orbis Books, 1981), *Vidyajyoti* 46/4: 203.
Pierre Teilhard de Chardin, *The Heart of the Matter* (London: Collins, 1978), *Vidyajyoti* 46/4: 203-204.
Brahmachari Amaldas, *Yoga and Contemplation* (London: Darton, Longman & Todd, 1981), *Vidyajyoti* 46/4: 205.
Homer A. Jack (ed.), *World Religion/ World Peace* (New York: World Conference on Religion and Peace, 1979), *Vidyajyoti* 46/4: 205206.
Homer A. Jack (ed.), *Religion in the Struggle for World Community* (New York: World Conference on Religion and Peace, 1980), *Vidyajyoti* 46/4: 205-206.
Karl Rahner, *Theological Investigations* Volume XVII: *Jesus, Man and the Church* (London: Darton, Longman & Todd, 1981), *Vidyajyoti* 46/5: 255.
Raimundo Panikkar, *The Unknown Christ of Hinduism. Towards an Ecumenical Christophany*, Revised and Enlarged Edition (London: Darton, Longman & Todd, 1981), *Vidyajyoti* 46/5: 256-257.
Yves M.-J. Congar, *Je crois en l'Esprit Saint.* Tome III: *Le fleuve de vie coule en Orient et en Occident* (Paris: Editions du Cerf, 1980), *Vidyajyoti* 46/ 6: 306-307.
Spirit of God, Spirit of Christ. Ecumenical Reflections on the Filioque Controversy (London, SPCK/ Geneva: World Council of Churches, 1981), *Vidyajyoti* 46/6: 307-308.
Lukas Vischer (ed.), *La théologie du Saint Esprit dans le dialogue entre l'Orient et l'Occident* (Paris: Le Centurion, 1981), *Vidyajyoti* 46/6: 307-308.
Sergio Torres - John Eagleson (eds.), *The Challenge of Basic Christian Communities* (Maryknoll, N.Y.: Orbis Books, 1981), *Vidyajyoti* 46/6: 308.

Albert Vanhoye, *Prêtres anciens, prêtre nouveau selon le Nouveau Testament* (Paris: Le Seuil, 1980), *Vidyajyoti* 46/6: 308-309.

Edward Schillebeeckx, *Le ministère dans l'Eglise* (Paris: Editions du Cerf, 1981) *Vidyajyoti* 46/6: 309-310.

1983

"Editorial: What Do Our Readers Think?," *Vidyajyoti* 47/7: 307-319.

Book Reviews

Karl Rahner, *Theological Investigations*, Volume XX (London: Darton, Longman & Todd, 1981), *Vidyajyoti* 47/3: 153.

Padraig Flanagan (ed.), *A New Missionary Era* (Maryknoll, N.Y.: Orbis Books, 1982), *Vidyajyoti* 47/ 7: 353.

Towards a New Age in Mission. The Good News of God's Kingdom to the Peoples of Asia (Manila: Theological Conference Office, 1981), *Vidyajyoti* 47/7: 353-354.

Your Kingdom Come. Mission Perspectives. Report on the World Conference on Mission and Evangelism (Melbourne, Australia, 12-25 May, 1980) (Geneva: World Council of Churches, 1981), *Vidyajyoti* 47/7: 354.

Gerald H. Anderson (ed.), *Witnessing to the Kingdom: Melbourne and Beyond* (Maryknoll, N.Y.: Orbis Books, 1982), *Vidyajyoti* 47/7: 354-355.

Orlando Costas, *Christ Outside the Gate. Mission Beyond Christendom* (Maryknoll, N.Y.: Orbis Books, 1982), *Vidyajyoti* 47/7: 354-355.

M. V. Cyriac, *Meeting of Religions. A Reappraisal of the Christian Vision* (Madras/ Madurai: Dialogue Series, 1982), *Vidyajyoti* 47/7: 355-356.

S. J. Samartha, *Courage for Dialogue. Ecumenical Issues in Inter-Religious Relationships* (Geneva: World Council of Churches, 1981), *Vidyajyoti* 47/7: 356.

Gerald H. Anderson - Thomas Stransky (eds.), *Christ's Lordship and Religious Pluralism* (Maryknoll, N.Y.: Orbis Books, 1981), *Vidyajyoti* 47/7: 356-357.

Bernard Rey, *Jésus Christ, chemin de notre foi* (Paris: Editions du Cerf, 1981), *Vidyajyoti* 47/8: 412.

E. L. Mascall, *Whatever Happened to the Human Mind?* (London: SPCK, 1980), *Vidyajyoti* 47/8: 412-413.

A. E. Harvey (ed.), *God Incarnate: Story and Belief* (London: SPCK, 1981), *Vidyajyoti* 47/8: 413.

Ursula King, *Towards a New Mysticism. Teilhard de Chardin and Eastern Religion* (London: Collins, 1980), *Vidyajyoti* 47/8: 413-414.

Robert Faricy, *All Things in Christ. Teilhard de Chardin's Spirituality* (London: Collins, 1981), *Vidyajyoti* 47/8: 414.

J. A. Lyons, *The Cosmic Christ in Origen and Teilhard de Chardin* (Oxford: Oxford University Press, 1982), *Vidyajyoti* 47/8: 414-415.

Lucas Grollenberg et al., *Minister? Pastor? Prophet? Grassroot Leadership in the Churches* (London: SCM Press, 1980), *Vidyajyoti* 47/8: 415.

Brian Mahan - L. Dale Richesin (eds.), *The Challenge of Liberation Theology* (Maryknoll, N.Y.: Orbis Books, 1981), *Vidyajyoti* 47/8: 415-416.

Kunceria Pathil (ed.), *Reconciliation in India* (Bombay: St. Paul Publications, 1982), *Vidyajyoti* 47/8: 382.

Ralph Martin, *A Crisis of Truth* (Ann Arbor, Mich.: Servant Books, 1982), *Vidyajyoti* 47/9: 466.

Yves Congar, *Diversités et communion. Dossier historique et conclusion théologique* (Paris: Editions du Cerf, 1982), *Vidyajyoti* 47/10: 522-523.

J. M. R. Tillard, *L'évêque de Rome* (Paris: Editions du Cerf, 1982), *Vidyajyoti* 47/10: 524.

Bernard Barzel, *Mystique de l'ineffable dans l'hindouisme et le christianisme : Cankara et Eckhart* (Paris; Editions du Cerf, 1982), *Vidyajyoti* 47/11: 560.

Bede Griffiths, *The Marriage of East and West* (London: Collins, 1982), *Vidyajyoti* 47/11: 560-561.

Emmanuel Vattakuzhy, *Indian Christian Sannyāsa and Swami Abhishiktananda* (Bangalore: Theological Publications in India, 1981), *Vidyajyoti* 47/11: 561.

1984

"Editorial: The Editor Takes Leave," *Vidyajyoti* 48/6: 269.

Book Reviews

James D. G. Dunn, *Christology in the Making. Inquiry into the Origins of the Doctrine of the Incarnation* (London: SCM Press, 1980), *Vidyajyoti* 88/3: 163-164.

Frans Jozef van Beeck, *Christ Proclaimed: Christology as Rhetoric* (New York/ Ramsey: Paulist Press, 1979), *Vidyajyoti* 48/3: 164.

Bernard Sesboüé, *Jésus-Christ dans la tradition de l'Eglise* (Paris: Desclée, 1982), *Vidyajyoti* 48/3: 164.

Joseph Bernard, *Le Christ de Dieu pour Ignace de Loyola* (Paris: Desclée, 1981), *Vidyajyoti* 48/3: 156.

Gerald Anderson - Thomas Stransky (eds.), *Faith Meets Faith* (New York/ Ramsey: Paulist Press, 1981), *Vidyajyoti* 83/4: 216.

Paul Maroky (ed.), *Convergence. A Study on Pierre Teilhard de Chardin and Other Eminent Thinkers* (Kottayam: Oriental Institute of Religious Studies, 1981), *Vidyajyoti* 83/4: 216.

Joseph G. Donders, *The Jesus Option. Reflections on the Gospels for the C-Cycle* (Maryknoll, N.Y.: Orbis Books, 1982), *Vidyajyoti* 83/5: 268.

Joseph G. Donders, *The Peace of Jesus. Reflections on the Gospels for the A-Cycle* (Maryknoll, N.Y.: Orbis Books, 1983), *Vidyajyoti* 83/5: 268.

1985

"Forms of Interreligious Dialogue," in *Portare Cristo all'uomo*. I: *Dialogo* (Roma: Università Urbaniana, 1985) 175-183.

"Forms of Interreligious Dialogue," *Bulletin* 59, 20/2: 164-171.

"The Practice of Agapè is the Reality of Salvation: A Response to P. Starkey," *International Review of Mission* 296, 74: 472-477.

Book Reviews

Julien Ries, *Le sacré comme approche de Dieu et comme resource de l'homme* (Louvain - la-Neuve: Centre d'histoire des religions, 1983), *Gregorianum* 66/3: 562.

George Chemparathy, *L'autorité du Veda selon les Nyāya-Vaisésikas* (Louvain-la-Neuve: Centre d'histoire des religions, 1983), *Gregorianum* 66/3: 562.

Giuseppina Scalabrino Borsani, *Aspects et évolutions du système Vedanta au cours des siècles du Moyen Age* (Louvain-la-Neuve: Centre d'histoire des religions, 1983), *Gregorianum* 66/3: 562.

Joseh Hajjar, *Bible et témoignage chrétien en pays d'Islam* (Louvain-la-Neuve: Centre d'histoire des religions), *Gregorianum* 66/3: 562.

Robert Smet, *Le problème d'une théologie hindoue-chrétienne selon Raymond Panikkar* (Louvain-la-Neuve: Centre d'histoire des religions, 1983), *Gregorianum* 66/3: 562.

Jean-Claude Polet, *Mythe de création et création poétique* (Louvain-la-Neuve: Centre d'histoire des religions, 1984), *Gregorianum* 66/3: 562.

René Lebrun, *Ebla et les civilisations du Proche-Orient ancien* (Louvain-la-Neuve: Centre d'histoire des religions, 1984), *Gregorianum* 66/3: 562.

Ted Schoof (ed.), *The Schillebeeckx Case* (New York/ Ramsey: Paulist Press, 1984), *Gregorianum* 66/3: 563.

Joseph E. Monti, *Who Do You Say that I Am? The Christian Understanding of Christ and Antisemitism* (New York/ Ramsey: Paulist Press, 1984), *Gregorianum* 66/3: 589-590.

1986

"Un decennio di riflessione nelle chiese dell'Asia. Il mutato ruolo della chiesa nei problemi socioeconomici," *Civiltà cattolica* 3262; 137, II: 326-339.

Book Reviews

The New Jerusalem Bible (London: Darton, Longman & Todd, 1985), *Gregorianum* 67/1: 149-150.

Donato Valentini, *Il nuovo popolo di Dio in cammino* (Roma: LAS, 1984), *Gregorianum* 67/1:154.

Luigi Sartori (ed.), *Papato e istanze ecumeniche* (Bologna: Edizioni Dehoniane, 1984), *Gregorianum* 67/1: 154-155.

Chris Saldanha, *Divine Pedagogy. A Patristic View of Non-Christian Religions* (Roma: LAS, 1984), *Gregorianum* 67/1: 167-168.

Hans Staffner, *The Significance of Jesus Christ in Asia* (Anand, Gujarat: Sahitya Prakash, 1985), *Gregorianum* 67/2: 382-383.

Virginia Fabella - Sergio Torres (eds.), *Doing Theology in a Divided World* (Maryknoll, N.Y.: Orbis Books, 1985), *Gregorianum* 67/2: 383-384.

Joseph A. Grassi, *Broken Bread and Broken Bodies. The Lord's Supper and World Hunger* (Maryknoll, N.Y.: Orbis Books, 1985), *Gregorianum* 67/2: 395.

Thomas Matus, *Yoga and the Jesus Prayer Tradition. An Experiment in Faith* (New York/ Ramsey: Paulist Press, 1984), *Gregorianum* 67/2: 396.

A. Mathias Mundadan, *Indian Christians: Search for Identity and Struggle for Autonomy* (Bangalore: Dharmaram Publications, 1984), *Gregorianum* 67/2:396.

Carolyn Osiek, *What Are They Saying about the Social Setting of the New Testament?* (New York/Ramsey: Paulist Press, 1984), *Gregorianum* 67/2: 397.

Jon Sobrino - Juan Hernandez Pico, *Theology of Christian Solidarity* (Maryknoll, N.Y.: Orbis Books, 1985), *Gregorianum* 67/2: 397.

William M. Thompson, *The Jesus Debate. A Survey and Synthesis* (New York/ Mahwah:

Paulist Press, 1985), *Gregorianum* 67/3: 547-549.
Thomas N. Hart, *To Know and Follow Jesus. Comparative Christology* (New York/ Ramsey: Paulist Press, 1984), *Gregorianum* 67/3: 549-550.
Claus Bussmann, *Who Do You Say? Jesus Christ in Latin American Theology* (Maryknoll, N.Y.: Orbis Books, 1985), *Gregorianum* 67/3: 550-551.
Juan Luis Segundo, *The Historical Jesus of the Synoptics* (Maryknoll, N.Y.: Orbis Books, 1985), *Gregorianum* 67/3: 551-553.
Christian Duquoc, *Messianisme de Jésus et discrétion de Dieu. Essai sur la limite de la christologie* (Genève: Labor et Fides, 1984), *Gregorianum* 67/3: 553.
Glenn F. Chestnut, *Images of Christ. An Introduction to Christology* (Minneapolis: The Seabury Press, 1984), *Gregorianum* 67/3: 554.
Jacques Guillet, *Entre Jésus et l'Eglise* (Paris: Editions du Seuil, 1985), *Gregorianum* 67/ 3: 554-555.
La théologie à l'épreuve de la vérité. Travaux du CERIT dirigés par Marc Michel (Paris: Editions du Cerf, 1984), *Gregorianum* 67/4: 770-771.
Deane William Ferm, *Third World Liberation Theologies. An Introductory Survey* (Maryknoll, N.Y.: Orbis Books, 1986), *Gregorianum* 67/4: 771-772.
Deane William Ferm (ed.), *Third World Liberation Theologies. A Reader* (Maryknoll, N.Y.: Orbis Books, 1986), *Gregorianum* 67/4: 771-772.
Theo Witvliet, *A Place in the Sun. Liberation Theology in the Third World* (Maryknoll, N.Y.: Orbis Books, 1985), *Gregorianum* 67/4: 772-773.
Julien Ries, *L'expression du sacré dans les grandes religions.* Tome II: *Peuples indo-européens et asiatiques, Hindouisme, Bouddhisme, Religion égyptienne, Gnosticisme, Islam* (Louvain-la-Neuve: Centre d'histoire des religions, 1983), *Gregorianum* 67/4: 788-789.
Julien Ries, *Les chemins du sacré dans l'histoire* (Paris: Aubier, 1985), *Gregorianum* 67/ 4: 789-790.
Santità a confronto. Ebraismo-Taoismo-Shintoismo-Induismo-Islamismo-Cristianesimo (Milano: Centro Interreligioso Henri Le Saux, 1985), *Gregorianum* 67/4: 790.
Richard Henry Drummond, *Toward a New Age in Christian Theology* (Maryknoll, N.Y.: Orbis Books, 1985), *Gregorianum* 67/4: 791-792.
Clifford G. Hospital, *Breakthrough. Insights of the Great Religious Discoverers* (Maryknoll, N.Y.: Orbis Books, 1985), *Gregorianum* 67/4: 792.
Cheriyan Menacherry, *An Indian Philosophical Approach to the Personality of Jesus Christ* (Roma: Urbaniana University Press, 1986), *Gregorianum* 67/4: 801.

1987

"The Kingdom of God and World Religions," *Vidyajyoti* 51/11: 530-544.
"Dialogo interreligioso nella missione evangelizzatrice della chiesa," in *Vaticano Secondo. Bilancio e prospettive.* A cura di R. Latourelle, Vol.2 (Assisi: Cittadella), 1234-1256.
"Lay People in Church and World. The Contribution of Recent Literature to a Synodal Theme," *Gregorianum* 68/1-2: 347-390.
"World Religions in God's Salvific Design in Pope John Paul II's Discourse to the Roman Curia (22 December 1969)," *Seminarium* 37/1-2: 29-41.
"Il ruolo della chiesa nei problemi socioeconomici secondo la riflessione teological asiatica," *Civiltà cattolica* 3293; 138, III: 355-368.
"Auf dem Wege zu ortsgebundenen Theologien," *Internazionale katholische Zeitschrift Communio* 16/5: 409-419.

Book Reviews

Alexandre Faivre, *Les laïcs aux origines de l'"Eglise* (Paris: Le Centurion, 1984), *Gregorianum* 68/1-2: 348-352.

Yves Congar, *Lay People in the Church. A Study for a Theology of the Laity* (London: Geoffrey Chapman, 1985), *Gregorianum* 68/1-2: 352-355.

Yves Congar, *Ministères et communion ecclésiale.* (Paris: Editions du Cerf, 1971), *Gregorianum* 68/1-2: 355-358.

Alberic Stacpoole, *Vatican II by Those Who Were There* (London: Geoffrey Chapman, 1986), *Gregorianum* 68/1-2: 358-360.

Les laïcs: Leur mission dans l'Eglise et dans le monde (Paris: Le Centurion, 1985), *Gregorianum* 68/ 1-2: 360-361.

Leonard Doohan, *The Lay-Centred Church* (Minneapolis: Winston Press, 1984), *Gregorianum* 68/1-2: 363-366.

Cormac Murphy-O'Connor, *The Family of God* (London: Darton, Longman & Todd, 1984), *Gregorianum* 68/1-2: 366-367.

Anton Houtepen, *People of God. A Plea for the Church* (London: SCM Press, 1984) *Gregorianum* 68/1-2: 367-369.

Leonardo Boff, *Ecclesiogenesis. The Base Communities Reinvent the Church* (Maryknoll, N.Y.: Orbis Books, 1986), *Gregorianum* 68/1-2: 369-373.

Marcello de Carvalho Azevedo, *Communautés ecclésiales de base. L'enjeu d'une nouvelle manière d'être Eglise* (Paris: Le Centurion, 1986), *Gregorianum* 68/1-2: 373-376.

Guy Régnier, *L'apostolat des laïcs* (Paris: Desclée, 1985), *Gregorianum* 68/1-2: 376-377.

David N. Power, *Gifts that Differ: Lay Ministries Established and Unestablished* (New York: Pueblo Publishing Company, 1980), *Gregorianum* 68/1-2: 377-381.

Mitverantwortung aller in die Kirche. Hrsg. v. F. Courth - A. Weiser (Limburg: Lahn-Verlag, 1985), *Gregorianum* 68/ 1-2: 381-382.

AA.VV., *Il laici nella chiesa,* (Torino: Elle Di Ci, 1986), *Gregorianum* 68/1-2: 382-385.

B. Forte, *Laicato e laicità* (Genova: Marietti, 1986), *Gregorianum* 68/1-2: 385-386.

De vocatione et missione laicorum in Ecclesia et in mondo viginti annis a Concilio Vaticano II elapsis. Lineamenta (Libreria Editrice Vaticana, 1985), *Gregorianum* 68/1-2: 386-390.

1988

"Christ, sauveur universel: scandale pour les religions orientales," *Communio* 13/4: 76-86.

"Il dialogo con l'Induismo nella missione della chiesa in India," *Civiltà cattolica* 3322; 139, IV: 336-347.

"On Some Recent Christological Literature," *Gregorianum* 69/4: 713-740.

"Christus, der Erlöser, als Argernis der Ost-religionen," *Internazionale katholische Zeitschrift Communio* 17/4: 312-316.

"Cristo, salvatore universale: Scandalo per le religioni orientali," *Communio* 13/4: 15-27.

Book Reviews

Yves M. J. Congar, *The Word and the Spirit* (London, Geoffrey Chapman/ San Francisco: Harper and Row, 1986), *Gregorianum* 69/1: 152-153.

François-Xavier Durrwell, *Holy Spirit of God. An Essay in Biblical Theology* (London: Geoffrey Chapman, 1986), *Gregorianum* 69/1: 153-154.

Julien Ries (ed.), *L'expression du sacré dans les grandes religions*. III. *Mazdéisme, Cultes isiaques, Religion grecque, Manichéisme, Nouveau Testament, Vie de l'homo religiosus* (Louvain-la-Neuve: Centre d'histoire des religions, 1986), *Gregorianum* 69/1: 177-178.

Julien Ries (ed.), *Les rites d'initiation* (Louvain-la-Neuve: Centre d'histoire des religions, 1986), *Gregorianum* 69/1: 178-179.

Kenneth Kramer, *World Scriptures. An Introduction in Comparative Religions* (New York/ Mahwah: Paulist Press, 1986), *Gregorianum* 69/1: 180.

Frank Whaling, *Christian Theology and World Religions. A Global Approach* (Basingstoke: Marshall Morgan and Scott, 1986), *Gregorianum* 69/1: 180-181.

Thomas A. Kochumuttom, *Comparative Theology. Christian Thinking and Spirituality in Indian Perspective* (Bangalore: Dharmaram Publications, 1985), *Gregorianum* 69/1: 181-182.

Denis Edwards, *What Are They Saying about Salvation?* (New York/ Mahwah: Paulist Press, 1986), *Gregorianum* 69/1: 185.

Joseph A. Fitzmyer, *Scripture and Christology. A Statement of the Biblical Commission with a Commentary* (New York/ Mahwah: Paulist Press, 1986), *Gregorianum* 69/1: 185-186.

Monique Verheecke, *Dieu et l'homme. Dialogue et combat* (Louvain-la-Neuve: Centre d'histoire des religions, 1986), *Gregorianum* 69/1: 186.

The New Testament. New International Version. An Ecumenical Bible Study Edition (New York/ Mahwah: Paulist Press, 1986), *Gregorianum* 69/2: 354-355.

Walbert Bühlmann, *The Church of the Future. A Model for the Year 2001* (Maryknoll, N.Y.: Orbis Books, 1986), *Gregorianum* 69/2: 358-359.

Commission théologique internationale, *Textes et documents (1969-1985)* (Paris: Editions du Cerf, 1988), *Gregorianum* 69/3: 563-564.

Enchiridion Vaticanum 9: Documenti Ufficiali della Santa Sede 25.1.1983 - 14.12.1985. A cura di Bruno Testacchi e Guido Mocellin (Bologna: Edizioni Dehoniane, 1987), *Gregorianum* 69/3: 565.

Oscar Cullmann, *L'unité par la diversité. Son fondement et le problème de sa réalisation* (Paris: Editions du Cerf, 1986), *Gregorianum* 69/3: 588-590.

_____, *L'unità attraverso la diversità. Il suo fondamento e il problema della sua realizzazione* (Brescia: Queriniana, 1987), *Gregorianum* 69/3: 588-590.

Leonard Swidler (ed.), *Toward a Universal Theology of Religion* (Maryknoll, N.Y.: Orbis Books, 1987), *Gregorianum* 69/3: 590-592.

Leonardo Boff - Clodovis Boff, *Introducing Liberation Theology* (Maryknoll, N.Y.: Orbis Books, 1987), *Gregorianum* 69/3: 601.

Dermot A. Lane, *Foundations for a Social Theology. Praxis, Process and Salvation* (New York/ Ramsey: Paulist Press, 1984), *Gregorianum* 69/3: 601-602.

William Reiser, *An Unlikely Catechism. Some Challenges for the Creedless Catholic* (New York/ Mahwah: Paulist Press, 1985), *Gregorianum* 69/3: 602.

V. Lawrence Sundaram, *A Great Indian Jesuit, Father Jerome D'Souza (1897-1977)* (Anand, Gujarat: Sahitya Prakash, 1986), *Gregorianum* 69/3: 602-603.

Rembert G. Weakland, *All God's People. Catholic Identity after the Second Vatican Council* (New York/ Mahwah: Paulist Press, 1985), *Gregorianum* 69/3: 603.

Donald Juel, *Messianic Exegesis. Christological Interpretation of the Old Testament in Early Christianity* (Philadelphia: Fortress Press, 1988), *Gregorianum* 69/4: 713-714.

Arland J. Hultgren, *Christ and His Benefits. Christology and Redemption in the New Tes-

tament (Philadelphia: Fortress Press, 1987), *Gregorianum* 69/4: 714-717.

Luise Schottroff - Wolfgang Stegemann, *Jesus and the Hope of the Poor* (Maryknoll, N.Y.: Orbis Books, 1985), *Gregorianum* 69/4: 717-719.

Jacques Schlosser, *Le Dieu de Jésus. Etude exégétique* (Paris: Editions du Cerf, 1987), *Gregorianum* 69/4: 719-721.

Aloys Grillmeier, *Christ in Christian Tradition*. Volume II: *From the Council of Chalcedon (451) to Gregory the Great (590-602)*. Part I: *Reception and Contradiction. The Development of the Discussion about Chalcedon from 451 to the Beginning of the Reign of Justinian* (London/ Oxford: Mowbray, 1987), *Gregorianum* 69/4: 721-724.

Juniper B. Carol, *Why Jesus Christ? Thomistic, Scotist and Conciliatory Perspectives* (Manassas: Trinity Communications, 1986), *Gregorianum* 69/4: 724-726.

Mario Serentha, *Gesù Cristo ieri, oggi e sempre. Saggio di cristologia* (Leumann: Torino, Elle Di Ci, 1986), *Gregorianum* 69/4: 726-728.

Hans Küng, *The Incarnation of God. An Introduction to Hegel's Theological Thought as Prolegomena to a Future Christology* (Edinburgh: T. & T. Clark, 1987), *Gregorianum* 69/4: 728-731.

Thomas Sheehan, *The First Coming. How the Kingdom of God Became Christianity* (New York: Random House, 1986), *Gregorianum* 69/4: 731-734.

Jon Sobrino, *Jésus en Amérique Latine. Sa signification pour la foi et la christologie* (Paris: Editions du Cerf, 1986), *Gregorianum* 69/4: 734-735.

Jon Sobrino, *Jesus in Latin America* (Maryknoll, N.Y.: Orbis Books, 1987), *Gregorianum* 69/4: 734-735.

Leonardo Boff, *Passion of Christ, Passion of the World. The Facts, Their Interpretation, and Their Meaning Yesterday and Today* (Maryknoll, N.Y.: Orbis Books, 1987), *Gregorianum* 69/4: 735-737.

Juan Luis Segundo, *The Christ of the Spiritual Exercises* (Maryknoll, N.Y.: Orbis Books, 1987), *Gregorianum* 69/4: 737-740.

1989

Jésus-Christ à la rencontre des religions (Paris: Desclée; reprint: 1994).

Gesù Cristo incontro alle religioni (Assisi: Cittadella; reprint:1991)

"Awakening to Self — Awakening to God in the Spiritual Experience of Abhishiktananda," in A. Thottakara (ed.), *Self and Consciousness: Indian Interpretations* (Bangalore: Dharmaram), 61-78.

"Eveil à soi — eveil à Dieu dans l'expérience spirituelle d'Henri Le Saux," *Nouvelle revue théologique* 111/6: 866-878.

"Le dialogue avec l'hindouisme dans la mission évangélisatrice de l'Eglise," *Bulletin* 24/2: 257-269.

"Interreligious Dialogue in the Church's Evangelizing Mission. Twenty Years of Evolution of a Theological Concept," in R. Latourelle (ed.), *Vatican II: Assessment and Perspectives*, vol. 2 (New York/Mahwah: Paulist Press), 237-263.

Book Reviews

Gavin D'Costa, *Theology and Religious Pluralism. The Challenge of Other Religions* (Oxford: Basil Blackwell, 1986), *Gregorianum* 70/1: 179-182.

1990

"Le dialogue avec l'hindouisme dans la mission de l'Eglise en Inde," *La documentation catholique* 2006, 72: 516-521.

"Dialogo interreligioso," "Evangelizzazione e missione," "Reincarnazione," "Scritture Sacre," "Teologia della liberazione," "Unicità e universalità" in *Dizionario di teologia fondamentale*. Diretto da René Latourelle - Rino Fisichella (Assisi: Cittadella) 310-317; 406-415; 915-917; 1083-1088; 1281-1288; 1382-1391.

Book Reviews

C. S. Song, *Theology from the Womb of Asia* (Maryknoll, N.Y.: Orbis Books, 1986), *Gregorianum* 71/2: 394-395.

Julien Ries, *Les chrétiens parmi les religions. Des Actes des Apôtres à Vatican II* (Paris: Desclée, 1987), *Gregorianum* 71/2: 395-396.

Ignatius Jesudasan, *A Gandhian Theology of Liberation* (Anand, Gujarat: Sahitya Prakash, 1987), *Gregorianum* 71/2: 396.

Bernard Sesboüé, *Jésus-Christ, l'unique médiateur. Essai sur la rédemption et le salut.* Tome I: *Problématique et relecture doctrinale* (Paris: Desclée, 1988), *Gregorianum* 71/2: 397.

La salvezza oggi (Roma: Università Urbaniana, 1989), *Gregorianum* 71/2: 412-413.

Generoso Florez, *An Appeal to the Church. The Mission of the Church in Asia* (Anand, Gujarat: Sahitya Prakash, 1986), *Gregorianum* 71/2: 413-414.

Hans Staffner, *Jesus Christ and the Hindu Community. Is a Synthesis of Hinduism and Christianity Possible?* (Anand, Gujarat: Sahitya Prakash, 1988), *Gregorianum* 71/2: 414.

S. Arokiasamy - G. Gispert-Sauch (eds.), *Liberation in Asia. Theological Perspectives* (Anand, Gujarat: Sahitya Prakash, 1987), *Gregorianum* 71/2: 425.

1991

Jesus Christ at the Encounter of World Religions (Maryknoll, N.Y.: Orbis Books; reprint: 1993).

Jesucristo al encuentro de las religiones (Madrid: Paulinas).

The Christian Faith in the Doctrinal Documents of the Catholic Church. Fifth Revised and Enlarged Edition. J. Neuner - J. Dupuis (eds.) (Bangalore: Theological Publications in India).

"Theology of Religions: Christian or Universal?," in S. Arokiasamy (ed.), *Responding to Communalism: The Task of Religions and Theology* (Anand, Gujarat: Sahitya Prakash), 271-281.

"Christian Revelation and Christian Theology. Theocentrism and Christocentrism," in Paul Puthanangady (ed.), *Emerging India and the Word of God* (Bangalore: National Biblical, Catechetical and Liturgical Centre), 183-202.

"La missione in Asia negli anni novanta. Un nuovo punto focale dell'evangelizzazione?" *Civiltà Cattolica* 3393; 142, IV: 228-243.

"Le débat christologique dans le contexte du pluralisme religieux," *Nouvelle revue théologique* 113/6: 853-863.

"The Christological Debate in the Context of Religious Plurality," *Current Dialogue* 19:18-31.

"The Christological Debate in the Context of Religious Plurality," *Catholic International* 2/11: 539-544.

"Pluralisme religieux et mission évangélisatrice de l'Eglise," *Spiritus* 122; 32: 63-76.

"Preface," Henri Le Saux, *Sagesse hindoue, mystique chrétienne* (Paris: Centurion), 7-9.

Book Reviews

Robert Kress, *The Church: Communion, Sacrament, Communication* (New York/ Mahwah: Paulist Press, 1985), *Gregorianum* 72/1: 148-149.

Robin Scroggs, *The Reality and Revelation of God. Christology in Paul and John* (Philadelphia: Fortress Press, 1988), *Gregorianum* 72/1: 154.

Marcello Bordoni, *Gesù di Nazaret. Presenza, memoria, attesa* (Brescia: Queriniana, 1988), *Gregorianum* 72/1: 155-157.

Lucien Richard - Daniel T. Harrington (eds.), *Vatican II: The Unfinished Agenda. A Look to the Future* (New York/ Mahwah: Paulist Press, 1987), *Gregorianum* 72/1: 169-170.

Jerald Gort - Hendrik Vroom - Rein Fernhout - Anton Wessels (eds.), *Dialogue and Syncretism. An Interdisciplinary Approach* (Grand Rapids: W. B. Eerdmans, 1989), *Gregorianum* 72/1: 185-186.

Le salut aujourd'hui (Roma: Università Urbaniana, 1990), *Gregorianum* 72/1: 193.

N. P. Tanner (ed.), *Decrees of the Ecumenical Councils.* Volume I: *Nicea I to Lateran V*; Volume II: *Trent to Vatican II* (London: Sheed and Ward/ Washington: Georgetown University Press, 1990), *Gregorianum* 72/4: 771-772.

K. C. Abraham (ed.), *Third World Theologies. Commonalities and Divergences* (Maryknoll, N.Y.: Orbis Books, 1990), *Gregorianum* 72/4: 775-776.

Paul J. Griffiths (ed.), *Christianity through Non-Christian Eyes* (Maryknoll, N.Y.: Orbis Books, 1990), *Gregorianum* 72/4: 786-787.

Gavin D'Costa (ed.), *Christian Uniqueness Reconsidered. The Myth of a Pluralistic Theology of Religions* (Maryknoll, N.Y.: Orbis Books, 1990), *Gregorianum* 72/4: 787-788.

Marcello Zago, *Volti della chiesa in Asia* (Cinisello Balsamo: Paoline, 1990), *Gregorianum* 72/4: 803-804.

1992

The Christian Faith in the Doctrinal Documents of the Catholic Church. Fifth Revised and Enlarged Edition. J. Neuner - J. Dupuis (eds.) (London: Harper-Collins).

"FABC Focus on the Church's Evangelising Mission in Asia Today," *Vidyajyoti* 56/9: 449-468.

"Méthode théologique et théologies locales: Adaptation, inculturation, contextualisation," *Seminarium* 32/1: 61-74.

"Dialogo e annuncio in due recenti documenti," *Civiltà Cattolica,* 3405, 143 II: 221-236.

"Cristianesimo e religioni," *Civiltà cattolica*, 3411-3412, 143 III: 272-278.

"La missione in Asia negli anni '90: Un nuovo punto focale dell'evangelizzazione?" In *Dal nuovo mondo al mondo nuovo* (Roma: Rogate, CISM - USMI - CIMI) 203-233.

"Inculturation and Interreligious Dialogue in India Today," in C. Cornille - V. Neckebrouck (eds.), *A Universal Faith? Peoples, Cultures, Religions, and the Christ* (Louvain: W. B. Eerdmans), 21-47.

"Dialogue and Proclamation in Two Recent Documents," *Bulletin* 80, 17/2: 165-172.

"Evangelization and KingdomValues: The Church and the 'Others,' " *Indian Missiological Review* 14/2: 4-22.

"Vie di salvezza o espressioni dell'uomo religioso? L'interpretazione teologica delle religioni mondiali dal Concilio Vaticano II ad oggi," in *Cristianesimo e religione* (Milano: Glossa), 100-134.

"La cristologia contemporanea nell'area anglofona" in *La cristologia contemporanea*. A cura di Giovanni Iammarrone (Padova: Edizioni Messaggero), 330-382.

"Les religions comme voies de salut?," *Spiritus* 126, 33: 5-15.

"Parole de Dieu et Ecritures sacrées," *Spiritus* 126, 33: 59-65.

Book Reviews

Marc Ellis - Otto Maduro (eds.), *Expanding the View. Gustavo Gutiérrez and the Future of Liberation Theology* (Maryknoll, N.Y.: Orbis Books, 1990), *Gregorianum* 73/1: 156-157.

Walbert Bühlmann, *With Eyes To See. Church and Word in the Third Millennium* (Maryknoll, N.Y.: Orbis Books, 1990), *Gregorianum* 73/1: 157-158.

Norbert Lohfink, *The Covenant Never Revoked. Biblical Reflections on Christian-Jewish Dialogue* (New York/ Mahwah: Paulist Press, 1991), *Gregorianum* 73/4: 750.

Bernard J. Lee, *The Galilean Jewishness of Jesus. Retrieving the Jewish Origins of Christianity* (New York/ Mahwah: Paulist Press, 1988), *Gregorianum* 73/4:757-758.

Dermot A. Lane, *Christ at the Centre. Selected Issues in Christology* (Dublin: Veritas Publications, 1900), *Gregorianum* 73/4: 758.

1993

Introduzione alla cristologia (Casale Monferrato: Piemme; reprints: 1994, 1996).

La fede cristiana in Gesù Cristo in dialogo con le grandi religioni asiatiche (Padova: Portogruaro).

"L'Eglise, le Règne de Dieu et les 'autres' " in *Penser la foi. Recherches en théologie aujourd'hui. Mélanges offerts à Joseph Moingt*. Sous la direction de Joseph Doré et Christoph Theobald (Paris: Cerf/ Assas), 327-349.

"L'Eglise, le Règne de Dieu et les 'autres'," *Revue de l'Institut Catholique de Paris* 46: 95-119.

"FABC Focus on the Church's Evangelising Mission in Asia," *FABC Papers* 64: 1-19.

"Portrait: Henri Le Saux, moine hindou-chrétien," *Unité des chrétiens* 91: 28-29.

"Il cristianesimo e le religioni del mondo," *Popoli* 5: 8-11.

"O debate cristológico no contexto do pluralismo religioso," in F. Luiz Couto Teixeira (organizador), *Diálogo de passaros. Nos caminhos do diálogo interreligioso* (São Paulo: Paulinas), 75-88.

"Dialogue and Proclamation. Reflection on the Relationship between *Redemptoris Missio* and *Dialogue and Proclamation*," *Catholic International* 4/3: 141-144.

"Le tradizioni religiose vie di salvezza?," *Mondo e missione* 122/6: 373.

"Dialogo e missione," *Mondo e missione* 122/7: 446.

"Dialogo e annuncio," *Mondo e missione* 122/9: 604.

Book Reviews

Joseph Fitzmyer, *A Christological Catechism. New Testament Answers* (New York/Mahwah: Paulist Press, 1991), *Gregorianum* 74/1: 158-159.

Robert J. Schreiter (ed.), *Faces of Jesus in Africa* (Maryknoll, N.Y.: Orbis Books, 1991), *Gregorianum* 74/1: 159-160.

Gerard F. O'Hanlon, *The Immutability of God in the Theology of Hans Urs von Balthasar* (Cambridge: Cambridge University Press, 1990), *Gregorianum* 74/1: 160-161.

Paul J. Griffiths, *An Apology for Apologetics. A Study in the Logic of Interreligious Dialogue* (Maryknoll, N.Y.: Orbis Books, 1991), *Gregorianum* 74/1: 175.

Paul Knitter, *Nessun Altro Nome? Un esame critico degli atteggiamenti cristiani verso le religioni mondiali* (Brescia: Queriniana, 1991), *Gregorianum* 74/1: 175-176.

James H. Kroeger (ed.), *Knowing Christ Jesus. A Christological Sourcebook* (Quezon City: Claretian Publications, 1989), *Gregorianum* 74/1: 192.

Eamonn Bredin, *Rediscovering Jesus. Challenge of Discipleship* (Quezon City: Claretian Publications, 1990), *Gregorianum* 74/1: 192.

James H. Kroeger (ed.), *Interreligious Dialogue. Catholic Perspectives* (Davao City: Mission Studies Institute, 1990), *Gregorianum* 74/1: 192-193.

Robert Ellsberg, *Gandhi on Christianity* (Maryknoll, N.Y.: Orbis Books, 1991), *Gregorianum* 74/1: 193.

Leonard Swidler - Lewis John Eron - Gerard Sloyan - Lester Dean, *Bursting the Bond? A Jewish-Christian Dialogue on Jesus and Paul* (Maryknoll, N.Y.: Orbis Books, 1990), *Gregorianum* 74/2: 367-369.

Ronaldo Muñoz, *The God of Christians* (Maryknoll, N.Y.: Orbis Books, 1990), *Gregorianum* 74/2: 382-383.

Leonardo Boff, *New Evangelization. Good News to the Poor* (Maryknoll, N.Y.: Orbis Books, 1992), *Gregorianum* 74/2: 383-384.

Dan Cohn-Sherbok (ed.), *World Religions and Human Liberation* (Maryknoll, N.Y.: Orbis Books, 1992), *Gregorianum* 74/2: 384-385.

William Jenkinson - Helene O'Sullivan (eds.), *Trends in Mission. Toward the Third Millennium. Essays in Celebration of Twenty-Five Years of SEDOS* (Maryknoll, N.Y.: Orbis Books, 1991), *Gregorianum* 74/2: 397-398.

R. S. Sugirtharajah (ed.), *Voices from the Margin. Interpreting the Bible in the Third World* (Maryknoll, N.Y.: Orbis Books, 1991), *Gregorianum* 74/3: 566-567.

Virginia Fabella - Peter K. L. Lee - David Kwang-sun Suh (eds.), *Asian Christian Spirituality. Reclaiming Traditions* (Maryknoll, N.Y.: Orbis Books, 1992), *Gregorianum* 74/3: 589-590.

Chi Dite che Io Sia? Gesù interpella l'ecumenismo e il dialogo interreligioso (Roma: Edizioni Dehoniane, 1992), *Civiltà Cattolica* 3433, III: 103.

Karl Müller, *Teologia della missione* (Bologna: EMI, 1991), *Civiltà Cattolica* 3434, III: 206-207.

Louis J. Luzbetak, *Chiesa e cultura. Nuove prospettive di antropologia della missione* (Bologna: EMI, 1991), *Civiltà Cattolica* 3434, III: 208.

1994

Who Do You Say I Am? Introduction to Christology (Maryknoll, N.Y.: Orbis Books; reprints: 1997, 2000, 2001).

Introducción a la Cristología (Estella, Navarra: Verbo Divino; reprint: 1998).

"Théologie du dialogue interreligieux," in *Les nouveaux appels de la mission.* Actes du colloque international de missiologie, Kinshasa, 20-26 février 1994, *Revue africaine des sciences de la mission* 1/1: 145-174.

"La teologia nel contesto del pluralismo religioso. Metodo, problemi e prospettive," in *Trinità in contesto.* A cura di A. Amato (Roma: LAS), 127-150.

"La fede cristiana in Gesù Cristo in dialogo con le grandi religioni asiatiche," *Gregorianum* 75/2: 217-240.

"Alleanza e salvezza," *Rassegna di teologia* 35/2: 148-171.

"The Church, the Reign of God and the "Others'," *Pro Dialogo*, n.85-86; 1:107-130.

"The Church, the Reign of God and the "Others'," *FABC Papers* 67: 1-47.

"L'universalità del Cristianesimo di fronte alle religioni," *Synaxis* 12/1:133-165.

"Dialogue and Proclamation: A Theological Commentary," in William R. Burrows (ed.), *Redemption and Dialogue* (Maryknoll, N.Y.: Orbis Books), 119-158.

"The Incarnation of the Son of God," in M. J. Walsh (ed.), *Commentary on the Catechism of the Catholic Church* (London: Geoffrey Chapman), 112-126.

"Dialogue and Proclamation in Two Recent Roman Documents," in Augustine Thottakkara (ed.), *Dialogical Dynamics of Religions* (Rome: Centre for Indian and Inter-religious Studies), 110-131.

"FABC Focus on the Church's Evangelising Mission in Asia Today," in Augustine Thottakkara (ed.), *Dialogical Dynamics of Religions* (Rome: Centre for Indian and Inter-religious Studies), 132-156.

Book Reviews

Gabriel Moran, *Uniqueness. Problem and Paradox in Jewish and Christian Traditions* (Maryknoll, N.Y.: Orbis Books, 1992), *Gregorianum* 75/2:353-354.

Stephen B. Bevans, *Models of Contextual Theology* (Maryknoll, N.Y.: Orbis Books, 1992), *Gregorianum* 75/2: 354-356.

Choan-Seng Song, *Jesus and the Reign of God* (Minneapolis: Fortress Press, 1993), *Gregorianum* 75/2: 362-363.

John O'Brien, *Theology and the Option for the Poor* (Collegeville: Liturgical Press 1992), *Gregorianum* 75/2: 363-364.

Curt Cadorette - Marie Giblin - Marilyn J. Legge - Mary Hembrow Snyder (eds.), *Liberation Theology. An Introductory Reader* (Maryknoll, N.Y.: Orbis Books, 1992), *Gregorianum* 75/2: 364.

Choan-Seng Song, *La teologia del terzo occhio. Teologia in formazione nel contesto asiatico* (Padova: Edizioni Messaggero 1993), *Gregorianum* 75/3: 566-567.

André Seumois, *Teologia missionaria* (Bologna: Edizioni Dehoniane, 1993). *Civiltà Cattolica* 3467, IV: 517-519.

La missione del redentore. Studi sull'enciclica missionaria di Giovanni Paolo II. A cura di Enrico Dal Covolo - Achille M. Triacca (Leumann: Elle Di Ci, 1992), *Civiltà Cattolica* 3443, IV: 521-522.

1995

Homme de Dieu Dieu des hommes. Introduction à la christologie (Paris: Editions du Cerf).

Who Do You Say I Am? Introduction to Christology (Manila: Claretian Publications).

"Les religions et la mission," *Gregorianum* 76/3: 585-592.

"Pluralismo religioso e missão evangelizadora da Igreja," *Desafios da Missão* (São Paulo: Mondo e Missão), 119-141.

"Religious Plurality and the Christological Debate," *Focus* 15/2-3: 88-97.

"Il cristianesimo di fronte alle sfide del pluralismo religioso," *Studia Patavina* 42/2: 135-145.

"Communion universelle. Eglises chrétiennes et religions mondiales," *Cristianesimo nella storia* 16/2: 361-381.

"Universalité du christianisme: Jésus-Christ, le Règne de Dieu et l'Eglise," *Revue Africaine des sciences de la mission* 2/2: 125-170.

Book Reviews

Enda Lyons, *Jesus: Self-portait by God* (Dublin: Colomba Press, 1994), *Gregorianum* 76/1: 166.

Nils Alstrup Dahl, *Jesus the Christ. The Historical Origins of Christological Doctrine* (Minneapolis: Fortress Press, 1991), *Gregorianum* 76/1: 166-167.

Claude Sarrasin, *Plein de grâce et de vérité. Théologie de l'âme du Christ selon Saint Thomas d'Aquin* (Venaque: Editions du Carmel, 1992), *Gregorianum* 76/1: 167-168.

Cristianesimo, religione e religioni. A cura del Seminario di Bergamo (Milano: Glossa, 1993), *Gregorianum* 76/1: 195-196.

Caterina Conio, *Abhishiktānanda. Sulle frontiere dell'incontro cristiano-indù* (Assisi: Cittadella, 1994), *Gregorianum* 76/1: 198.

Hans Staffner, *Dialogue, Stimulating Contacts with Hindus* (Anand, Gujarat: Sahitya Prakash, 1993), *Gregorianum* 76/1: 199.

James M. Byrne (ed.), *The Christian Understanding of God Today.* Theological Colloquium on the Occasion of the 400th Anniversary of the Foundation of Trinity College (Dublin: Trinity College, 1993), *Gregorianum* 76/2: 395.

Michael E. Lodahl, *Shekhinah/ Spirit. Divine Presence in Jewish and Christian Religion* (New York/ Mahwah: Paulist Press, 1992), *Gregorianum* 76/2: 424-425.

Leo D. Lefcburc, *The Buddha and the Christ. Explorations in Buddhist and Christian Dialogue* (Maryknoll, N.Y.: Orbis Books, 1993), *Gregorianum* 76/2: 425-426.

Brian O. McDermott, *Word Become Flesh. Dimensions of Christology* (Collegeville: Liturgical Press, 1993), *Gregorianum* 76/3: 606-607.

William J. Lunny, *The Jesus Option* (New York/ Mahwah: Paulist Press, 1994), *Gregorianum* 76/3: 607-608.

John F. O'Grady, *Models of Jesus Revisited* (New York/ Mahwah: Paulist Press, 1994), *Gregorianum* 76/3: 608-609.

Hugo Bianchi (ed.), *The Notion of "Religion"in Comparative Research.* Selected Proceedings of the XVIth Congress of the International Association of the History of Religions, Rome 3rd-8th September 1990 (Roma: "L'erma" di Bretschneider, 1994), *Gregorianum* 76/4: 774.

Cristianesimo e religioni in dialogo. Quaderni del Seminario di Brescia (Brescia: Morcelliana, 1994), *Gregorianum* 76/4: 774-775.

1996

Jesus Christ at the Encounter of World Religions (New Delhi: Intercultural Publications). *The Christian Faith in the Doctrinal Documents of the Catholic Church.* Sixth Revised and Enlarged Edition. J. Neuner - J. Dupuis (eds.) (Bangalore: Theological Publications in India / New York: Alba House).

"Universalità del cristianesimo: Gesù Cristo, il Regno di Dio e la chiesa," in *Universalità del cristianesimo. In dialogo con Jacques Dupuis.* A cura di M. Farrugia (Roma: San Paolo), 19-57; "Dibattito e conclusioni": 297-338.

"Teologia del dialogo interreligioso," in AA.VV., *Le sfide del nostro tempo* (Bologna: EMI), 125-159.

"Teologia della croce e dialogo interreligioso: Dimensione kenotica di Gesù Cristo e della chiesa," in *La croce di Gesù Cristo unica speranza*, Atti del III Congresso Internazionale *"La sapienza della croce oggi(Roma 9-13 Gennaio 1995)"* (Roma: Cippi), 143-166.

Book Reviews

R. S. Sugirtharajah (ed.), *Frontiers in Asian Christian Theology. Emerging Trends* (Maryknoll, N.Y.: Orbis Books, 1994), *Gregorianum* 77/1: 168-169.

Alfred T. Hennelly (ed.), *Santo Domingo and Beyond. Documents and Commentaries from the Fourth General Conference of Latin American Bishops* (Maryknoll, N.Y.: Orbis Books, 1993), *Gregorianum* 77/1: 190-191.

1997

Toward a Christian Theology of Religious Pluralism (Maryknoll, N.Y.: Orbis Books; reprints: 1998, 1999, 2000, 2001, 2002).

Verso una teologia cristiana del pluralismo religioso (Brescia: Queriniana; reprints: 1998, 2000).

Vers une théologie chrétienne du pluralisme religieux (Paris: Editions du Cerf; reprint: 1999).

"Cristianesimo e religioni: una sfida teologica," *Rivista di scienze religiose* 11/2: 411-422.

"Vers une théologie chrétienne du pluralisme religieux," *La vie spirituelle*, 724: 573-580.

"Forum ATI: Una sinfonia incompiuta," *Rassegna di teologia* 38/6: 831-833.

"Dialogo interreligioso per una responsabilità mondiale," in *Medio Oriente e matrici culturali dell'Europa* (Vicenza: Rezzara) 190-199.

"Cristo universale e vie di salvezza," *Angelicum* 74/2: 193-218.

"Alleanza e salvezza," in *Testi di meditazione* 75 (Magnano: Monastero di Bose), 1-30.

"La comunicación en el dialogo interconfessional," in Centro Estudios Teológicos, *Actas del IV Congresso Diálogo "fe-cultura,"* La Laguna, "La communicación humana y sus multiples manifestationes artisticas," 118-138.

Book Reviews

Jon Sobrino, *The Principle of Mercy. Taking the Crucified People from the Cross* (Maryknoll, N.Y.: Orbis Books, 1994), *Gregorianum* 78/1: 168-169.

James H. Charlesworth, *Gesù nel giudaismo del suo tempo alla luce delle più recenti scoperte* (Torino: Claudiana, 1994), *Gregorianum* 78/1: 176.

Anthony J, Godzieba, *Bernhard Welte's Fundamental Theological Appproach to Christology* (New York: Peter Lang, 1994), *Gregorianum* 78/1: 177.

Jürgen Moltmann, *Chi è Cristo per noi oggi* (Brescia: Queriniana, 1995), *Gregorianum* 78/1: 177-178.

Abraham J. Malherbe - Wayne A. Meeks (eds.), *The Future of Christology. Essays in Honor of Leander E. Keck* (Minneapolis: Fortress Press, 1993), *Gregorianum* 78/1: 178.

Terrance L. Tiessen, *Irenaeus on the Salvation of the Unevangelized* (London: The Scarecrow Press, 1993), *Gregorianum* 78/1: 187.

Gerhard Schneider, *Cristologia del Nuovo Testamento* (Brescia: Paideia, 1994), *Gregorianum* 78/2: 390.

Joachim Gnilka, *Gesù di Nazareth. Annuncio e storia* (Brescia: Paideia, 1993), *Gregorianum* 78/2: 390-391.

Evelyne Maurice, *La christologie de Karl Rahner* (Paris: Desclée, 1995), *Gregorianum* 78/2: 391.

Rudolf Schnackenburg, *La persona di Gesù Cristo nei quattro vangeli* (Brescia: Paideia, 1995), *Gregorianum* 78/3: 562-563.

Carlo Porro, *Chiesa, mondo e religioni. Prospettive di ecclesiologia* (Torino: Elle Di Ci, 1995), *Gregorianum* 78/3: 567.

Hans Waldenfelds, *Il fenomeno del cristianesimo. Una religione mondiale nel mondo delle religioni* (Brescia: Queriniana, 1995), *Gregorianum* 78/3: 577.

Donald J. Goergen, *Jesus, Son of God, Son of Mary, Immanuel* (Collegeville: Liturgical Press, 1995), *Gregorianum* 78/4: 779-780.

Eduard Schweizer, *Gesù. La parabola di Dio. Il punto sulla vita di Gesù* (Brescia: Queriniana, 1996), *Gregorianum* 78/4: 780-781.

Aldo Moda, *Religione e religioni oggi* (Cosenza: Lionello Giordano, 1996), *Gregorianum* 78/4: 795-796.

1998

"Gesù Cristo, Salvatore universale e le altre religioni, cammini di salvezza," *Religione e scuola* 26/4: 64-70; 26/5: 40-45.

"L'Esprit-Saint répandu sur le monde: Fondement du dialogue interreligieux," *Lumen Vitae* 53/1: 57-66.

"Insieme per pregare o pregare insieme?" *Studi ecumenici* 16/1: 11-30.

"Premiers échos du Synode pour l'Asie," *Etudes* 3893: 215-227.

"La novidad de Jesucristo frente a las religiones mundiales," *Estudios trinitarios* 32/1-2: 3-37.

"Le dialogue interreligieux à l'heure du pluralisme," *Nouvelle revue théologique* 120/4: 544-563.

"Le pluralisme religieux dans le plan divin de salut," *Revue théologique de Louvain* 29/4: 484-505.

"La presencia universal del Espiritu y la Misión de la Iglesia," *Misiones extranjeras* 163:61-71.

"La universalidad de Jesucristo en el pluralismo actual," *Misiones extranjeras* 168: 485-502.

"First Echoes of the Synod for Asia," *Landas* 12/2: 13-28.

"Congar, Yves," "Daniélou, Jean," "Lubac, Henri de," in G. H.Anderson (ed.), *Biographical Dictionary of Christian Mission* (New York: Macmillan), 148, 168, 413.

"Les chrétiens à la rencontre des 'autres'," *Horizons* 29: 5-7.

Book Reviews

Thomas P. Rausch, *Catholicism at the Dawn of the Third Millennium* (Collegeville: Liturgical Press, 1996), *Gregorianum* 79/1: 188-189.

Thomas J. Reese, *Inside the Vatican. The Politics and Organization of the Catholic Church* (London: Harvard University Press, 1996), *Gregorianum* 79/1: 193-194.

Karl-Josef Kuschel, *La controversia su Abramo. Ciò che divide — e ciò che unisce ebrei, cristiani e musulmani* (Brescia: Queriniana, 1996), *Gregorianum* 79/1: 203-204.

Giovanni Iammarrone, *La cristologia francescana. Impulsi per il presente* (Padova: Edizioni Messaggero, 1997), *Gregorianum* 79/2: 395-396.

Giovanni Marchesi, *La cristologia trinitaria di Hans Urs von Balthasar. Gesù Cristo pienezza della rivelazione e della salvezza* (Brescia: Queriniana, 1997), *Gregorianum* 79/2: 396-398.

La fede in un'epoca di pluralismo. A cura di Scaria Thuruthiyil (Roma: LAS, 1997), *Gregorianum* 79/2: 412-413.

Erich Zenger, *Il Primo Testamento. La Bibbia ebraica e i cristiani* (Brescia: Queriniana, 1997), *Gregorianum* 79/3: 568-569.

Pierre Grelot, *Jésus de Nazareth, Christ et Seigneur. Une lecture de l'Evangile.* Tome I (Paris: Editions du Cerf, 1997), *Gregorianum* 79/3: 583-584.

Michael L. Cook, *Christology as Narrative Quest* (Collegeville: Liturgical Press, 1997), *Gregorianum* 79/3: 584-585.

Severino Dianich, *Il Messia sconfitto. L'enigma della morte di Gesù* (Casale Monferrato: Piemme, 1997), *Gregorianum* 79/3: 597.

Roch A. Kereszty, *Jesus Christ: Fundamentals of Christology.* Edited by J. Stephen Maddux (New York: Alba House, 1991), *Gregorianum* 79/4:769-770.

Roch A. Kereszty, *A Supplement to Jesus Christ: Fundamentals of Christology* (New York: Alba House, 1997), *Gregorianum* 79/4: 769-770.

M. John Farrelly, *Faith in God through Jesus Christ. Fundamental Theology* (Collegeville: Liturgical Press, 1997), *Gregorianum* 79/4: 770-771.

Francis D'Sa (ed.), *The Dharma of Jesus. Interdisciplinary Essays in Memory of George M. Soares-Prabhu* (Pune: Institute for the Study of Religion / Anand, Gujarat: Sahitya Prakash, 1997), *Gregorianum* 79/4: 771.

Francis D'Sa, *Dio, l'Uno e Trino e l'Uno-Tutto. Introduzione all'incontro tra Cristianesimo e Induismo* (Brescia: Queriniana, 1996), *Gregorianum* 79/4: 774-775.

1999

Introduçao à cristología (São Paulo: Ed. Loyola).

Wprowadzenie do chrystologii (Krakow: Widawnictwo WAM).

Rumo a uma teología crista del pluralismo religioso (São Paulo: Paulinas).

"Preface": Henri Le Saux, *Lettres d'un sanyasi chrétien à Joseph Lemarié* (Paris: Les Editions du Cerf): 7-1.

"Salvezza universale in Gesù Cristo e vie di salvezza," in *Le Religioni come esperienza e attesa della salvezza* (Milano: Segretariato Attività Ecumeniche): 55-77.

"El pluralismo religioso en el plan divino de la salvacíon," in *Selecciones de teología* 151, 38/3: 241-253.

"La novedad de Jesucristo frente a las religiones mundiales," in *Encarnacíon redentora,* Seminas de Estudios Trinitarios 33 (Salamanca: Secretariado Trinitario): 13-47.

"The Christian Meaning of Salvation," in *Tenrikyo-Christian Dialogue* (Tenri: Tenri University Press): 373-389.

"The Spirit, Basis for Interreligious Dialogue," *Theology Digest* 46/1: 27-31.

"Un Dio vale l'altro?" *Servizio della parola* 305 (Feb.-Marzo): 11-15.

"Jesus with an Asian Face," *Third Millennium* 2/1 :6-17.

"Un Dio Padre di Gesù Cristo per la salvezza del mondo," *Rivista di scienze religiose* 13/ 1: 31-47.

"Il Regno di Dio e la missione evangelizzatrice della chiesa," *Ad Gentes* 3/2: 133-155.

"La teologia del pluralismo religioso revisitata," *Rassegna di teologia* 40/5: 667-693.

" 'The Truth Will Make You Free'. The Theology of Religious Pluralism Revisited," *Louvain Studies* 24/3: 211-263.

"Jesus with an Asian Face," *Sedos Bulletin* 8/9: 211-216.

"Il volto asiatico di Gesù," *Il Regno-Documenti* 19: 648-652.

"L'Eglise face au pluralisme religieux d'aujourd'hui," *Amitiés* 23: 3-5.

Book Reviews

Anne Hunt, *The Trinity and the Paschal Mystery. A Development in Recent Catholic Theology* (Collegeville: Liturgical Press, 1997), *Gregorianum* 80/1: 180-181.

Jerome Crowe, *From Jerusalem to Antioch. The Gospel across Cultures* (Collegeville: Liturgical Press, 1997), *Gregorianum* 80/1: 189.

Pierre Grelot, *Jésus de Nazareth, Christ et Seigneur. Une lecture de l'Evangile*, Tome 2 (Paris: Editions du Cerf, 1998), *Gregorianum* 80/1: 191-192.

Basil Studer, *The Grace of Christ and the Grace of God in Augustine of Hippo. Christocentrism or Theocentrism* (Collegeville: Liturgical Press, 1997), *Gregorianum* 80/1: 192.

Karl Barth, *L'umanità di Gesù. L'attualità del messaggio cristiano* (Torino: Claudiana, 1997), *Gregorianum* 80/1: 210.

Peter C. Phan, *Responses to 101 Questions on Death and Eternal Life* (New York/ Mahwah: Paulist Press, 1997), *Gregorianum* 80/2: 375.

Bernard Senécal, *Le Christ à la rencontre de Gautama le Bouddha. Identité chrétienne et bouddhisme* (Paris: Editions du Cerf, 1998), *Gregorianum* 80/2: 382.

Giancarlo Rinaldi, *La Bibbia dei pagani*. Vol.1: *Quadro storico*; Vol. 2: *Testi e documenti* (Bologna: Edizioni Dehoniane, 1998), *Gregorianum* 80/3: 556-557.

James D. G. Dunn, *The Christ and the Spirit*. Vol. 1: *Christology*; Vol. 2: *Pneumatology* (Edinburgh: T. & T. Clark, 1998), *Gregorianum* 80/3: 565-566.

Renzo Lavatori, *Lo Spirito Santo, dono del Padre e del Figlio. Ricerca sull'identità dello Spirito come dono* (Bologna: Edizioni Dehoniane, 1998), *Gregorianum* 80/3: 576-577.

Pier Giorgio Gianazza, *Lo Spirito Santo. Summa pneumatologica di Yves Congar* (Roma: LAS, 1998), *Gregorianum* 80/3: 577-578.

Pierre Nautin, *L'Evangile retrouvé. Jésus et l'Evangile primitif* (Paris: Beauchesne, 1998), *Gregorianum* 80/4: 771-772.

Religione e religioni. Metodologia e prospettive ermeneutiche. A cura di Giuseppe Lorizio (Padova: Edizioni Messaggero, 1998), *Gregorianum* 80/4: 774-775.

Geneviève Comeau, *Catholicisme et judaïsme dans la modernité. Une comparaison* (Paris: Editions du Cerf, 1998), *Gregorianum* 80/4: 775-776.

Raimon Panikkar, *L'esperienza di Dio* (Brescia, Queriniana, 1998), *Gregorianum* 80/4: 776-777.

2000

Hacia una teología cristiana del pluralismo religioso (Santander: Sal Terrae).

"Pregare insieme: perché? come?," in *La preghiera respiro delle religioni*. Atti della XXXVI sessione di formazione ecumenica (Chianciano Terme, 24-31 Luglio 1999). A cura del Segretariato Attività ecumeniche (Ancora), 19-47.

"Cristianesimo e religioni nel terzo millennio: Identità e comunione," in *L'immaginario contemporaneo*, Atti del Convegno Letterario Internazionale (Ferrara, 21-23 Maggio 1999). A cura di Roberto Pazzi (Ferrara: Leo S. Olschki), 63-77.

"Hindou-chrétien et chrétien-hindou," in D. Chira - J. Scheuer (eds), *Vivre de plusieurs religions: Promesse ou illusion?* (Paris: Editions de l'atelier) 54-64.

"Il cristianesimo e le religioni nella teologia cattolica degli anni recenti," in *Religione e religioni. A partire dai "Discorsi" di Schleiermacher.* A cura di Sergio Sorrentino (Assisi: Cittadella), 295-324.

"El dialogo interreligioso en época de pluralismo," in *Selecciones de teología* 153; 39/1: 11-23.

"Un Dios, Padre di Jesucristo, para la salvacíon del mondo," in *Selecciones de teología*, 155; 39/3: 177-188.

"Trinitarian Christology as a Model for a Theology of Religions," in T. Merrigan - J. Haers (eds.), *The Myriad Christ. Plurality and the Quest for Unity in Contemporary Christology* (Leuven: University Press), 83-97.

"One God, One Christ, Convergent Ways," *Theology Digest* 47/3: 211-218.

"Il Verbo di Dio, Gesù Cristo e le religioni del mondo," *Studia Patavina*: 47/2: 461-484.

"Pour le Règne de Dieu: Quelle Eglise? Quelle mission," *Spiritus* 159: 227-240.

Book Reviews

Michel Fédou, *Regards asiatiques sur le Christ* (Paris: Desclée, 1998), *Gregorianum* 81/ 1: 186-187.

Hans Waldenfels, *Rivelazione, Bibbia, tradizione, teologia e pluralismo religioso* (Cinisello Balsamo: San Paolo, 1999), *Gregorianum* 81/1: 195-196.

Antoine Vergote, *Modernité et christianisme. Interrogations critiques réciproques* (Paris: Editions du Cerf, 1999), *Gregorianum* 81/2: 373.

Gerhard Lohfink, *Does God Need the Church? Toward a Theology of the People of God* (Collegeville: Liturgical Press, 1999), *Gregorianum* 81/2: 374-375.

Philip Cunningham, *A Believer's Search for the Jesus of History* (New York/ Mahwah: Paulist Press, 1999), *Gregorianum* 81/2: 379.

Jean-Pierre Torrell, *Le Christ et ses mystères. La vie et l'oeuvre de Jésus selon Saint Thomas d'Aquin*, Tome I (Paris: Desclée, 1999), *Gregorianum* 81/2: 380-381.

Jean Grootaers, *Actes et Acteurs à Vatican II* (Leuven University Press, Peeters, 1998), *Gregorianum* 81/2: 388-389.

Harding Meyer, *That All May Be One. Perceptions and Models of Ecumenicity* (Cambridge: William B. Eerdmans 1999), *Gregorianum* 81/2: 395.

Philip A. Cunningham - Arthur F. Starr (eds.), *Sharing Shalom. A Process for Local Interfaith Dialogue Between Christians and Jews* (New York/ Mahwah: Paulist Press, 1998), *Gregorianum* 81/2:396.

James L. Fredericks, *Faith among Faiths. Christian Theology and Non-Christian Religions* (New York/ Mahwah: Paulist Press, 1999), *Gregorianum* 81/2: 396-398.

Consiglio Episcopale Latinoamericano, *Teologia al plurale. Il caso dell'America Latina* (Bologna: Edizione Dehoniane, 1999), *Gregorianum* 81/2: 403-404.

Wilfrid J. Harrington, *John: Spiritual Theologian. The Jesus of John* (Dublin: The Columba Press, 1999), *Gregorianum* 81/2: 404.

Jean-François Chiron, *L'infaillibilité et son objet. L'autorité du magistère infaillible de l'Eglise s'étend-elle sur les vérités non révélées?* (Paris: Editions du Cerf, 1999), *Gregorianum* 81/3: 790-791.

Charles Perrot, *Gesù* (Brescia: Queriniana, 1999), *Gregorianum* 81/4: 793.

Gerd Theissen - Annette Merz, *Il Gesù storico* (Brescia: Queriniana, 1999), *Gregorianum* 81/4: 793-795.

2001

The Christian Faith in the Doctrinal Documents of the Catholic Church. Seventh Revised and Enlarged Edition. J. Neuner - J. Dupuis, (eds.) (Bangalore: Theological Publications in India / New York, Alba House).

Toward a Christian Theology of Religious Pluralism (Anand, Gujarat: Sahitya Prakash).

Il cristianesimo e le religioni: Dallo scontro all'incontro (Brescia: Queriniana).

"L'unità e il pluralismo: Il Cristianesimo e le religioni," in *Chrzescijanstwo Jutra (Lublin 18-21 September).* Acts of the International Congress of Fundamental Theology. Ed. Institute of Fundamental Theology, 722-742.

"Universality of the Word and Particularity of Jesus Christ," in Daniel Kendall - Stephen T. Davis (eds.), *The Convergence of Theology. A Festschrift Honoring Gerald O'Collins, S.J.* (Mahwah: Paulist Press), 320-342.

"Il dialogo interreligioso in una società multireligiosa," in *Impariamo a dialogare* (Parma: Benedittina Editrice), 40-61.

"La missione evangelizzatrice della chiesa nel contesto del pluralismo religioso," in *Ricerca.* A cura della Federazione Italiana Universitaria 2-3, *Il prossimo lontano:* 26-28.

"Comunione e condivizione nel dialogo interreligioso: La fede personale e l'esperienza dell'altro," in *Teologia delle religioni e liturgia.* A cura di Sergio Ubbiali (Padova: Edizioni Mesaggero), 170-194.

"Il dialogo interreligioso in una società multireligiosa," *Odegitra,* A cura dell'Istituto Superiore di Scienze religiose "Odegitra" di Bari, 7:35-51.

"Une vocation commune d'enfants de Dieu," *Louvain* 121: 19-22.

"Christianity and Other Religions: From Confrontation to Encounter," *The Tablet,* 20 October: 1484-1485; 27 October: 1520-1521; 3 November: 1560-1561.

"Le Verbe de Dieu, Jésus-Christ et les religions du monde," *Nouvelle revue théologique* 123/4: 529-546.

"Christianity and Other Religions: From Confrontation to Encounter," *Sedos Bulletin* 33: 12 (December), 320-25.

"Le Verbe de Dieu, Jésus-Christ et les religions du monde," *Cedrus Libani* 64/4, 99-107.

Bernard Sesboüé, *Tout récapituler dans le Christ. Christologie et sotériologie d'Irénée de Lyon* (Paris: Desclée, 2000), *Gregorianum* 82/1: 180-181.

David J. Bosch, *La transformazione della missione. Mutamenti di paradigma in missiologia* (Brescia: Queriniana, 2000), *Gregorianum* 82/1: 184-185.

Remi Gounelle, *La descente du Christ aux enfers. Institutionalisation d'une croyance* (Paris: Institut des études augustinennes, 2000), *Gregorianum* 82/3: 597-599.

Raymond Winling, *La résurrection et l'exaltation du Christ dans la littérature de l'ère patristique* (Paris: Editions du Cerf, 2000), *Gregorianum* 82/4: 794-795.

2002

Le rencontre du christianisme et des religions: De la confrontation au dialogue (Paris: Editions du Cerf).

Christianity and the Religions. From Confrontation to Dialogue (Maryknoll, N.Y.: Orbis Books/London: Darton, Longman & Todd; reprint 2003).

El cristianesmo y las religiones. Del Desencuentro al diálogo (Santander: Sal Terrae).

La fede cristiana nei documenti dottrinali della chiesa cattolica, A cura di Jacques Dupuis (Roma: Paoline).

"From Religious Confrontation to Encounter," *Theology Digest* 49/2: 103-108.

"Gesù, la chiesa apostolica e le religoni," in Juan José Tamayo Acosta, ed. *10 parole chiave su Gesù di Nazareth. Dalle 'vite' su Gesù* (Assisi: Cittadella Editrice), 379-422.

"Christianity and Religions: Complementarity and Convergence," in Catherine Cornille (ed.), *Many Mansions? Multiple Religious Belonging and Christian Identity* (Maryknoll, N.Y.: Orbis Books), 61-75.

"Insieme per pregare," *Viator*, 1:7-9.

"El Verbo di Dios, Jesucristo, y las religiones del mundo," *Selecciones de teología*, n. 162, 41 (Abril-Junio): 93-104.

"Le dialogue interreligieux dans une société pluraliste," *Archaeus* (Bucarest) 6/2-2: 55-67.

"From Religious Confrontation to Encounters," *Theology Digest* 49/2: 103-108.

"Abbiamo tutti lo stesso Dio," *Credere oggi* 129/3: 155-168.

"Le dialogue interreligieux dans une société pluraliste," *Wydawca* (Cracovia) 1/2: 53-67.

"Religiones (Diálogo de)," in Jesús Conill (ed.), *Glosario para una sociedad intercultural* (Bancaja, Valencia): 320-327.

"Culture, inculturation et eucharistie," in Maurice Brouard (ed.), *Eucharistia. Encyclopédie de l'Eucharistie* (Paris: Editions du Cerf): 337-348.

"O diálogo inter-religioso numa sociedade pluralista," *Didaskalia* 32/1: 69-81.

"Synod for Asia: First Echoes," in J. H. Kroeger and Peter C. Phan (eds.), *The Future of Asian Churches: The Asian Synod and Ecclesia in Asia* (Quezon City: Claretian Publications), 20-29.

"Le dialogue interreligieux dans une société pluraliste," *Wydawca* (Krakow) 1/2: 53-67.

Book Reviews

La fede di Gesù. A cura di Giacomo Canobbio (Bologna: Ed. Dehoniane, 2000), *Gregorianum* 83/1: 179-180.

La théologie en Europe. Sous la direction de de Christhof Theobald (Paris: Editions du Cerf, 2000), *Gregorianum* 83/1: 190.

J. R. Quinn, *Per una riforma del papato. L'impegnativo appello all'unità dei cristiani* (Brescia: Queriniana, 2000), *Gregorianum* 83/1: 192-192.

Changer la papauté? Sous la direction de Paul Tihon (Paris: Editions du Cerf, 2000), *Greorianum* 83/1: 193-194.

M. C. Boys, *Has God Only One Blessing? Judaism as a Source of Christian Self-Understanding* (New York/Mahwah: Paulist Press, 2000), *Gregorianum* 83/1: 200-201.

Marcello Bordoni-Nicola Ciola, *Gesù Nostra Speranza. Saggio di escatologia in prospettiva trinitaria* (Bologna: Edizioni Dehoniane, 2000), *Gregorianum* 83/3: 574.

Claude Geffré, *Croire et interpréter. Le tournant herméneutique de la théologie* (Paris: Editions du Cerf, 2001), *Gregorianum* 83/3: 578-579.

Gisbert Greshake, *Il Dio unitrino. Teologia trinitaria* (Brescia: Queriniana, 2000), *Gregorianum* 83/3: 571-572.

Bernard Sesboüé, *Le magistère a l'épreuve. Autorité, vérité et liberté dans l'Eglise* (Paris: Desclée de Brouwer, 2001), *Gregorianum* 83/3: 573-574.

Christian Duquoc, *Christianisme mémoire pour l'avenir* (Paris: Editions de Cerf, 2000), *Gregorianum* 83/3: 581.

Bernard Sesboüé, *Karl Rahner* (Paris: Editions du Cerf, 2001), *Gregorianum* 83/3: 579.

Robert A. Burns, *Roman Catholicism after Vatican II* (Washington, D.C.: Georgetown University Press, 2001), *Gregorianum* 83/4: 790-791.

Adrian Graffy, *Trustworthy and True. The Gospels Beyond 2000* (Dublin: The Columba Press, 2001), *Gregorianum* 83/4: 781.

Christopher M. Bellitto, *Renewing Christianity. A History of Church Reform from Day One to Vatican II* (New York/ Mahwah: Paulist Press, 2001), *Gregorianum* 83/4: 789-790.

Luiz Carlos Susin, *Così umano, così divino. Gesù nella cristologia narrativa* (Milano: Paoline, 2001), *Gregorianum* 83/4: 800-801.

Bernard de Margerie, *Newman face aux religions de l'humanité* (Paris: Parole et Silence, 2001), *Gregorianum* 83/4: 799-800.

Christian Duquoc, *"Credo la chiesa," Precarietà istituzionale e Regno di Dio* (Brescia: Queriniana, 2001), *Gregorianum* 83/4: 791.

Enzo Bianchi, *Si tu savais le don de Dieu. La vie religieuse dans l'Eglise* (Bruxelles: Editions Lessius, 2001), *Gregorianum* 83/4: 797.

Maurice Hogan, *Seeking Jesus of Nazareth* (Dublin: The Colomba Press, 2001), *Gregorianum* 83/4: 785.

Thomas H. West, *Jesus and the Quest for Meaning. Entering Theology* (Minneapolis: Fortress Press, 2001), *Gregorianum* 83/4: 786.

Hermann J. Pottmeyer, *Il ruolo del papato nel terzo millennio* (Brescia: Queriniana, 2002), *Gregorianum* 83/4: 791-792.

Francis Cardinal Arinze, *Religions for Peace. A Call for Solidarity to the Religions of the World* (London: Darton Longman & Todd, 2002), *The Tablet* 8 June: 16-17.

Alan Race, *Interfaith Encounter* (London: SCM Press, 2001), *The Tablet* 8 June: 16-17.

Francis X. Clooney, *Hindu God, Christian God* (Oxford University Press, 2001), *The Tablet* 8 June: 16-17.

Michael Barnes, *Theology and the Dialogue of Religions* (Cambridge University Press, 2002), *The Tablet* 8 June: 16-17.

2003

"O Diálogo Inter-Religioso numa sociedade pluralista," in *Religioes: Identidade e Violencia. XXIII Semana de Estudios Teológicos (4-6 de Fecereiro do 2002)* (Alcala: Faculdade de teologia, 2003).

"Universality of the Word and Particularity of Jesus Christ" in: Secretariat for Interreligious Dialogue, Society of Jesus, *"Toward a Theology of Interreligious Dialogue."* The 15th International Congress of Jesuit Ecumenists, 15-20 August 1999: 18-32; 39-43.

"Le Saux, un mystique qui a fait l'expérience de ce dont il temoigne," *Actualité des religions* 49, Mai-Juin 2003, 17.

A Bibliography of Materials on
Toward a Christian Theology
of Religious Pluralism

I. Official Documents

Congregation for the Doctrine of the Faith, *Letter of Cardinal Joseph Ratzinger to Rev. Father Peter-Hans Kolvenbach,* announcing the decision taken by the CDF of a "Contestation" against the book *Toward a Christian Theology of Religious Pluralism.* (26 September 1998).
> Annexe 1: Text of the decision.
> Annexe 2: nine pages of questions to be answered.

J. Dupuis, *Answer to the Contestation of the Congregation for the Doctrine of the Faith* (25 December, 1998) (187 pp).

Congregation for the Doctrine of the Faith, *Second Letter of Cardinal J. Ratzinger to Rev. Father Peter-Hans Kolvenbach,* stating the inadequacy of the *Answer* (27 July 1999).
> Annexe: "*Giudizio dottrinale*" of the *Answer* by the Congregation, with eleven pages of new questions to be answered.

J. Dupuis, *Answer to the Doctrinal Judgement of the Congregation for the Doctrine of the Faith* (1 November 1999) (59 pp).

Congregation for the Doctrine of the Faith, *Declaration "Dominus Iesus" on the Unicity and Salvific Universality of Jesus Christ and the Church* (Libreria Editrice Vaticana, 2000) (Signed 6 August 2000; published 5 September, 2000).

Congregation for the Doctrine of the Faith, *Notification on the Book of Jacques Dupuis, "Toward a Christian Theology of Religious Pluralism."*
> First draft: 25 August 2000 (not published).
> Second draft: 24 November 2000 (not published).
> Final text dated 24 January 2001 (published in *Osservatore Romano,* 26 February 2001).
> Annexe: *Commentary on the Congregation's Notification* (published in *Osservatore Romano,* 26 Febbraio 2001); text and commentary in *Origins* 30 (8 March 2001): 605-608.

Public Statement of Rev. Fr. Peter-Hans Kolvenbach (26 February 2001) (*Origins* 30: 8 March 2001).

Congregation for the Doctrine of the Faith, *Third Letter of Cardinal J. Ratzinger to Rev. Father Peter-Hans Kolvenbach* (8 January 2002).
> Annexe: Evaluation of affirmations and theological theses maintained by Father Jacques Dupuis after the publication of the Declaration *Dominus Iesus* and of the Notification on the Book *Toward a Christian Theology of Religious Pluralism.*

Congregazione per la dottrina della fede, *Dichiarazione "Dominus Jesus" (6 Agosto 2000),* Documenti e studi (Libreria Editrice Vaticana 2002). (Includes the Italian text of the

Notification by the CDF and of the Article commenting on it, published in *Osservatore Romano*).

II. Presentations of the Book in Paris (27 October 1997) and Rome (22 November 1997)

G. Canobbio, "Note a margine dell'opera di J. Dupuis," *Rassegna di teologia* 38 (1997/6) 829-838.

J. Doré, "Autour de l'ouvrage de Jacques Dupuis," *Revue de l'Institut Catholique de Paris, Transversalités,* Octobre-Décembre, 1998, 159-167.

J. Dupuis, "Vers une théologie chrétienne du pluralisme religieux," *La vie spirituelle*, Septembre 1997, 573-580.

Cl. Geffré, "Le pluralisme religieux comme question théologique," *La vie spirituelle*, Septembre 1997, 580-586.

Mgr. M. Fitzgerald, "Jacques Dupuis, Toward a Christian Theology of Religious Pluralism." *Pro Dialogo*, n.108 (2001/3): 334-341.

III. Book Reviews, Articles and Studies

1995-1996

J. Kuttianimattatil, *Practice and Theology of Interreligious Dialogue* (Bangalore: Kristu Jyoti Publications, 1995), 242-248; 354-360.

F. Teixeira, *Teologia das Religiôes. Uman Visâo Panorâmica* (São Paulo: Paulinas, 1995), 81-91.

M. Farrugia (ed.), *Universalità del cristianesimo. In dialogo con Jacques Dupuis* (Cinisello Balsamo: San Paolo, 1996).

1997

"Al di fuori della chiesa non c'è salvezza? P. Jacques Dupuis risponde alla teologia del pluralismo," *Adista,* 18 Ottobre, 7.

E. Bianchi, "Il Cristo cosmico," *Avvenire*, 22 Novembre.

B. G., Book Review, *Divinitas* 1997/3, 100.

G. Cereti, "Mario Farugia, Universalità del cristianesimo," *Rassegna di teologia* 38: 707-718.

Carli di Cicco, "Da cristiani nel pluralismo religioso," *Asca,* 12 December, 5.

J.-P. Guetny, "Toutes les religions se valent?," *L'actualité religieuse* n. 160, 15 Novembre, 2-3.

D. P. Huang, "Christ, the One Savior of the World: Reflections on Our Emerging Christological Question," *East Asian Pastoral Review* 34: 187-209.

J. H. Kroeger, Book Review, *Bibliografia Missionalia* 61: 331-332.

L'écho, 13 Décembre, 6, Book Review

V. Lobet, "Les chrétiens et les autres: théologie et dialogue," *Le monde*, 26 Décembre.

M. Neusch, "Les religions des autres: Un nouveau chantier pour le théologien," *La Croix,* 9-10 Novembre.

———, "La théologie s'interroge sur les autres religions," *Le Monde,* 21 Décembre.

Rivista Ecclesiástica Brasileira, Dicembre, Book Review.
C. Seravella, Book Review, *Labor* 4, 181.

1998

J.-J. Alemany, Book Review, *Estudios eclesiásticos* 73: 522-524.
J.-M. A., Book Review, *Ecritures,* 1 Juin, 6.
D. G. André, Book Review, *Repsa,* 2, 135.
Fr. Ard., "Dio Salvatore assoluto," *Jesus,* Aprile, 95.
Cl. Barthe, "Dérive dans la théologie des religions. A propos d'un livre de Jacques Dupuis," *Catholica,* Printemps, 80-83.
I. Biffi, "Il monopolio della grazia," *Avvenire*, 14 April, 20.
J. Dupuis, "Appunti alla critica del libro di Jacques Dupuis," firmata da Inos Biffi nell'*Avvvenire*, 14 Aprile (unpublished).
G. Bonnet, "Un grand livre: Notes de lecture," *Esprit et vie,* 19 Mars: 130-131.
Bulletin critique du livre français, Juillet-Aout, 1560, Book Review.
G. Comeau, Book Review, *Mission de l'Eglise*, n.120, Supplément, Juillet, 71-74.
Comité de rédaction, " 'Tout récapituler dans le Christ.' A propos de l'ouvrage de J. Dupuis, *Vers une théologie chrétienne du pluralisme religieux*," *Revue thomiste* 98/4: 591-630.
L. S. Cunningham, Book Review, *Commonweal,* 5 June, 28-29.
G. D'Costa, Book Review, *Journal of Theological Studies* 59/2: 910-914.
————, Book Review, *The Expository Times,* June, 285.
M. de Giorgi, "Jacques Dupuis: un uomo, un pensiero," *Ad Gentes* 2/1: 104-109.
G. De Paoli, "Fede e pluralismo religioso. Una proposta di percorso," *Note Mazziane* 33/2: 81-87.
G. De Rosa, "Una teologia problematica del pluralismo religioso," *La Civiltà Cattolica*, III 129-143.
J. Doré, "Du nouveau sur les religions," *Etudes*, Novembre, 561-564.
L. Elders, *Jacques Dupuis, SJ. Toward a Christian Theology of Religious Pluralism*, 300-334.
————, "Les théories nouvelles de la signification des religions non-chrétiennes," *Nova et Vetera*, 3, 97-117.
P. Emonet, Book Review, *Choisir*, 8 Janvier, 40.
F. Ferrario, "Cristo e il pluralismo religioso," *Riforma,* 27 Febbraio, 6.
B. J. Francis, Book-Review, *Indian Theological Studies,* 2: 192-193.
J. Gadille, "L'exigence missionaire doit porter la foi," *La Croix*, 11 Février.
F. Gaiffi, "Il pluralismo religioso nella riflessione teologica recente: appendice bibliografico," in A. Fabris - M. Gronchi (eds.), *Il pluralismo religioso, Una prospettiva interdisciplinare* (Cinisello Balsamo: San Paolo), 208-210.
D. Gira, "De la tolérance au dialogue," *L'actualité religieuse*, n.166; 15 Mai, 46-47.
M. Grandjean, Book Review, *Journal de Genève*, 14-15 Février.
P. J. Griffiths, Book Review, *The Thomist* 62/2: 316-319.
M. Gronchi, "Il pluralismo religioso e la teologia," in A. Fabris - M. Gronchi (eds.), *Il pluralismo religioso. Una prospettiva interdisciplinare* (Cinisello Balsamo, San Paolo): 172-175.
R. Haight, Book Review, *Theological Studies* 59/2: 347-349.
J. H. Kroeger, Book Review, *Landas,* 12/2: 120-123.
————, Book Review, *Verbum SVD*, 4, 411-413.
————, Book Review, *Indian Missiological Review* 20/4: 98-99.

————, Book Review, *Missiology: An International Review*, 26/3: 372-373.

R. H. Lesser, Book Review, *Vidyajyoti Journal of Theological Reflection,* April, 289-292.

G. Lindbeck, Book Review, *International Bulletin of Missionary Research*, January, 34.

P. M., Book Review, *Unité chrétienne,* 129, Février, 57-58.

N. Madonia, "Unicità e singolarità di Gesù Cristo. Alcune chiavi di lettura," *Rassegna di teologia* 39/2: 233-235.

J. M. Maldamé, Book Review, *Bulletin de littérature ecclésiastique*, 4, 471-474.

T. Merrigan, " 'Pour nous et pour notre salut'. L'action de Dieu selon la théologie des religions," *Lumen Vitae* 53/4: 415-425.

————, "Exploring the Frontiers: Toward a Christian Theology of Religious Pluralism," *Louvain Studies* 23: 338-359.

C. Molari, "Cristo e le altre religioni," *Rocca,* n.15; 1 Agosto, 54-55.

————, "Ascoltare altri nomi di Dio," *Nigrizia,* 7, Luglio-Agosto, 24-28.

N. Nkanza, Book Review, *Telema 4*: 75-89.

G. O'Collins, Book Review, *The Tablet,* 24 January, 110-111.

G. Odasso, *Bibbia e religioni* (Roma, UUP), 52-55.

P. Pallath, Book Review, *Ephrem's Theological Journal* 2/2, October: 185-187.

A. Pellegrini, Book Review, *Vivens Homo,* Gennaio-Giugno, 224-226.

R. Perroud, "Mondialisation: les chrétiens et les autres," *L'ami du peuple,* 11 Janvier.

M. Pivot, Book Review, *Chemins du dialogue,* 11 Avril, 190-193.

A. Race, Book Review, *Theology,* 6, 449-450.

Regno-Attualità, n.22, 669, Book Review.

J. Rigaud, Book Review, *Libre-Sens,* Février.

L. Sartori, Book Review, *Studia Patavina* 45/1: 220-221.

P. Selvadagi, "Il cammino della teologia delle religioni in Italia," *Lateranum* 64/ 2-3: 577-594; at 590-594.

P. Stefani, "Cristo e le religioni. Una teologia cristiana del pluralismo religioso. Il libro di Jacques Dupuis," *Il Regno-Attualità,* 4, 101-105.

L. Steffen, Book Review, *Christian Century,* 8 April, 379-381.

Ch. Tauchner, Book Review, *Mission Studies* 19/2: 178-179.

F. Teixeira, Book Review, *Revista Ecclesiástica Brasileira* 57/4.

————, "Panorâmicas das Abordagens Cristâs sobre as Religiôes. A propósito de un libro I," *Perspectiva Teológica* n.80; 30/1: 57-84.

————, "Para una teologia cristã do pluralismo religioso. A propósito de un libro II," *Perspectiva Teológica* n.81; 30/2: 211-250.

Theology Digest, 45/1: 47, Book Review.

A. Toniolo, "Teologia cristiana delle religioni. Considerazione a partire della recente pubblicazione di Jacques Dupuis," *Rassegna di teologia* 39/2: 285-293.

M. van Parys, Book Review, *Irenikon* 71: 2-3, 426-427.

1999

B. Amato, Book Review, *Salesianum* 61/2: 392-393.

E. Brito, Book Review, *Ephemerides Theologicae Lovanienses,* Decembre, 520-522.

N. Charrière, Book Review, *Revue de théologie et de philosophie* 131/1: 87-88.

A. Couture, Book Review, *Studies in Religion / Sciences Religieuses* 28/1: 109-111.

C. Delhez, "La foi chrétienne et les autres religions," *Dimanche,* 17 Octobre, 2.

J.-P. Denis, "Un dialogue dans le sens de l'histoire," *La vie,* 28 Octobre, 66-68.

L. Elders, "Vers une théologie chrétienne du pluralisme religieux," *Sedes Sapientiae* 68/2: 64-100.

A. Fuentes, Book Review, *Teología,* July-December, 647-649.

J. H. Kroeger, Book Review, *Studies in Interreligious Dialogue,* 9/2: 250-252.

————, Book Review, *Pacifica,* 12, February, 106-108.

————, Book Review, *Spiritus* n.155 (Juin): 225-226.

————, Book Review, *Prodipon* 22/2: 113-116.

————, Book Review, *Asian Journal of Theology,* 13/1: 218-221.

A. Lande, Book Review, *Svennsk Teologisk Kvartalskrift* 1, 39-41.

D. A. Lane, "Vatican II, Christology and the World Religions," *Louvain Studies* 24: 147-170; at 148-149.

R. M., Book Review, *Revue des sciences religieuses,* 2, 244-245.

A, K. Min, Book Review, *Cistercian Studies Quarterly* 34/3: 415-416.

Missiology, 29 July, Book Review: 382.

H. Netland, Book Review, *Trinity Journal* 20, NS 1: 105-111.

T. L. Nichols, "Christocentrism," *Cross Currents*, Summer, 274-276.

————, "Authentic Covenants," *Cross Currents*, Fall, 411-414.

J. Scheuer, "Foi chrétienne et pluralité des religions," *Revue théologique de Louvain* 30: 204-207.

————, Book Review, *Nouvelle revue théologique* 121/4: 679-680.

G. Siegwalt, Book Review, *Revue d'histoire et de philosophie religieuses* 79/4: 524-525.

A. Stagliano, "L'impegno teologico per la "Singolarità" di Gesù Cristo nel contesto del pluralismo religioso," in G. Coffele (ed.), *Dilexit ecclesiam* (Roma: LAS), 319-349; at 329-340.

C. F. Starkloff, Book Review, *Toronto Journal of Theology,* 15/1: 109-111.

S. Zeghidour, "Dieu bénit la multiplicité," *La vie,* 28 Octobre, 69-71.

2000

Ch. Duquoc, Book Review, *Lumière et vie* 1: 104-105.

A. Gounelle, Book Review, *Etudes théologiques et religieuses* 1, 148.

S. Kamath, Book Review, *Dominican Ashram* 17/1: 46-47.

Peter C. Phan, Book-Review, *Dialogue and Alliance,* 14/1: 121-123.

2001

P. M. Bouman, Book Review, *Metanoia* 11, 1-2 (Spring - Summer): 92-93.

R. McClory, Book Review, *U. S. Catholic,* September, 18.

J. L. Sánchez Nogales, "Audaces lineas para la reflexión," *Vida nueva,* 10 Marzo, 43.

2002

G. Hall, "Jacques Dupuis' Christian Theology of Religious Pluralism," *Pacifica* 15:37-50.

IV. *The Doctrinal Controversy: Documents, Comments and Studies*

1998

A. Amato, "L'assolutezza salvifica del Cristianesimo: Prospettive sistematiche," *Seminarium* 38/4, 771-809; at 781-809.

"Another theologian under investigation," *Indian Currents,* 30 November - 6 December, 50-51.

"Another theologian under investigation," *The Tablet,* 21 November, 1550.

M. Crociata, "Verso quale teologia cristiana del pluralismo religioso?" *Ho theológos* 16/1: 87-116.

J. P. Denis, "Faut-il brûler Dupuis?" *La vie,* 19 Novembre, 76.

"Don't Wall up the Faith," *The Tablet,* 21 November, 1531.

"E anche padre Dupuis va davanti al Sant'Ufficio," *Repubblica,* 7 Novembre, 41.

"Editorial: The Human Face of the Church," *Vidyajyoti Journal of Theological Reflection,* 62/12: 887-889.

M. Fédou, "Les religions, chemins de salut?," *Croire aujourd'hui,* 53, Juillet-Août, 24-26

A. Galli, "Pluralismo convergente," *Nigrizia,* Novembre , 6-7.

F. Gentiloni, "I tanti corpi di Cristo," *Il Manifesto,* 15 Novembre, 23.

G. Goubert, "Le Saint Siège conteste un livre du Père Dupuis," *La Croix,* 13 Novembre.

"Inquisizione incruenta: Teologo Gesuita 'estramosso' per deviazioni interreligiose," *Adista,* 7 Novembre, 2-4.

B. Johnston, "Rome censors two more theologians," *The Catholic Herald* 15 November, 1.

"La chiesa processa il Gesuita Dupuis," *Il Gazettino* 8 Novembre, 7.

"Las religiones son iguales: Hinduismo, Buddhismo y Zen sustituyen al Evangelio," in *Los Nuevos Jesuitas,* 85-88.

Letter of Archbishop Henri D'Souza, Archbishop of Calcutta (13 November 1998), *Jivan,* January 1999, 8.

G. O'Collins, "In Defense of Fr Dupuis," *The Tablet,* 12 December, 1650.

"Padre Dupuis finisce sotto processo," *Jesus,* 20 Decembre, 19.

"Shock as popular theologian is put under investigation," *The Universe,* 22 November, 27. 87-116.

A. Yong, "The Turn to Pneumatology in Christian Theology of Religions: Conduit or Detour?" *Journal of Ecumenical Studies* 35/3-4: 437-454; at 447-454.

1999

J. J. Alemany, "Teologia cristiana de las religiones," *Miscelánea Comillas* 57, 290-297.

J. Allen, "Doubts about Dialogue. Encounter with other Religions Runs up against the Vatican's Hard Doctrinal Realities," *National Catholic Reporter,* 27 August, 14-16.

S. Allievi, "Pluralismo religioso e società multietniche," *Filosofia e teologia* 15: 449-451.

"An Indirect Warning to the Bishops of Asia?" *Jivan,* January, 6-8.

T. Balasuriya, "P. Dupuis, 'missionario alla rovescia,' " *Adista,* 11 Ottobre, 4-5.

J. E. Biechler, "A Prospective Review: Horizons at Twenty-Five," *Horizons,* 26/2 (Fall), 262-265.

M. Cagin, "Tout récapituler dans le Christ. A propos d'un ouvrage de J. Dupuis," *Nova et Vetera,* 2, 87-90.

Cardinal Franz König, "En défense du Père Jacques Dupuis," *Choisir,* Mars, 17-19.

Cardinal Franz König, "In Defense of Father Dupuis," *The Tablet,* 16 January, 76-77 (*Adista,* 1 Febbraio, 2-4).

Cardinal Joseph Ratzinger, "Reply to Cardinal König," *The Tablet,* 13 March, 385 (*Adista,* 29 Marzo, 4-5).

"Cardinal Ratzinger's Response," *The Tablet,* 3/10 April, 484.

"Cardinals Take Sides in Battle of the Book," *The Universe,* 28 March, 18-19.

C. M. Cherian, "The Scandal of East Being East," *Jivan*, April, 3.

G. Comeau, "Présence universelle de l'Esprit et pluralisme religieux," in *Au présent de l'Esprit. Colloque du Centre Sèvres* (16 et 17 Octobre, 1998), Médiasèvres, 77-84.

"Cultura e religione," *L'Espresso*, 1 Aprile.

"Declaration of the Jesuit Provincials of South Asia in Defense of their Theologians," *Adista*, 29 Marzo, 2-4.

Documentación. Cardinale Franz König, "En defensa del Padre Dupuis," *Sal Terrae*, February, 167-171.

Documentación. "Los provinciales jesuitas de la India apoyan a sus teólogos," *Sal Terrae*, April, 341-342.

P. Emonet, "Dialogue interreligieux: état de la question," *Choisir*, Novembre, 20-23.

D. Gabrielli, "Il pluralismo religioso tra incubo e grazia," *Confronti*, Febbraio, 23-24.

———, "Duello cardinalizio sul pluralismo religioso," *Confronti*, Maggio, 19-22.

Cl. Geffré, "Babel et Pentecôte," in *Profession Théologien* (Paris, Albin Michel), 196-218.

M. Hauke, "L'unicità di Gesù Cristo e l'universalità della salvezza. Tentativo di sintesi," *Revue théologique de Lugano*, 2, 315-323; at 321.

"I Gesuiti Indiani difendono P. Dupuis e P. De Mello dalle accuse della Congregazione di Ratzinger. La loro dichiarazione," *Adista*, 29 Marzo, 4-5.

"Il Cardinale Franz König prende le difese di Padre Dupuis," *Jesus*, Febbraio, 18.

"Il Cardinale König interviene in difesa del teologo Dupuis," *Adista*, 1 Febbraio , 2-4.

"Jesuit Leaders Critical of Vatican Suspicion," *The Tablet*, 20 March, 411.

"König e Dupuis: Non posso tacere," *Il Regno - Attualità*, Aprile, 87.

"L'Eglise en Inde. Epreuves et controverses," *La Libre Belgique*, 12 Janvier.

S. Karotemprel, "Theological Debate on Religious Pluralism," *Journal of Missiological and Ecumenical Research*, January-September, 49-60.

Y. Khoury, "Les religions en sommet," *Actualité des religions*, Octobre, 8-10.

Paul F. Knitter, "Catholics and Other Religions. Bridging the Gap between Dialogue and Theology," *Louvain Studies* 24: 319-354.

G. Leclerc, "Questions autour du dialogue interreligieux," *France Catholique* n. 26/5 (15 janvier).

C. Longley, "Pluralism Stirs Vatican 'Police'," *Daily Telegraph*, 12 March, 31.

M. N., "Caso Dupuis: domande e stupore," *Il Regno-Attualità*, Agosto, 265.

S. Magister, "Gesuita, non fare l'indiano," *L'Espresso*, 1 Aprile, 101-104.

C. Molari, "Il Verbo di Dio è più grande di Gesù," *Confronti*, Febbraio, 25-26.

"More Questions for Jacques Dupuis," *The Tablet*, 21 August, 1148.

Ch. Morerod, "Eglise et Royaume I: Le débat théologique," *Nova et vetera* 3, 5-36.

J. M. Odero, Book Review, *Boletín de la Secr*, 12, 65-70.

D. O'Grady, "The Dupuis Case" (unpublished).

L. Orsy, "Justice Begins at Home," *The Tablet*, 16 January, 78-81. (*Adista* 1 Febbraio, 4-8).

"Polemica tra cardinali sul teologo censurato. Ratzinger bistratta König," *Adista*, 29 Marzo, 3-4.

C. Porro, "Il cristianesimo e le religioni. Riflessioni sul documento della Commissione Teologica Internazionale," *Revue théologique de Lugano*, 2, 165-177; cfr. 176.

J. R. Quinn, *The Reform of the Papacy. The Costly Call to Christian Unity* (New York, Crossroad), 160-161.

J. Raymaker, "Discussing J. Dupuis's Book," *The Japan Mission Journal*, Summer, 140-144.

J. Rose, "An Indirect Warning to the Bishops of India," *Jivan*, January, 6-9.

L. Sartori, "Il dibattito sul pluralismo religioso. Considerazioni sul caso Dupuis," *Rassegna di teologia* 40/2: 289-292.

"South Asian Jesuit Provincials Support their Theologians," *Jivan*, April 1999, 5.

T. W. Tilley, "Christianity and the World Religions: A Recent Vatican Document," *Theological Studies* 60: 318-337.

"Trop de chemins vers le salut," *L'actualité des religions*, Janvier, 10.

"Tutti gli errori della Congregazione per la dottrina della fede," *Adista*, 1 Febbraio , 4-8.

G. Valente, " 'Se la rivelazione è l'accadere d'un incontro, la libertà dell'uomo è pienamente rispettata'. Il Cardinale König interviene sul 'caso Dupuis' ". Intervista, *30 Giorni*, Gennaio, 76-79.

"Vatican Concerned about Publicity on Dupuis Case," *The Tablet*, 27 March, 448.

H. Waldenfels, "Unterwegs zur einer christlichen Theologie des religiöses Pluralismus. Anmerkungen zum 'Fall Dupuis'," *Stimmen der Zeit*, 9, September, 597-610.

2000

J. L. Allen, *Cardinal Ratzinger: the Vatican's Enforcer of the Faith* (New York, Continuum), 246-250.

A. Amato, "Unicità e universalità del mistero salvifico di Cristo," *Osservatore Romano*, 30 Settembre, 4.

I. Biffi, "Gesù Figlio di Dio, unico Salvatore: una verità da riproporre con forza," *Avvenire*, 19 Marzo (pagina di Bologna).

————, "Il vero e definitivo monoteismo è trinitario. E Gesù è l'autorivelazione del Dio che salva," *Avvenire*, 2 Aprile (pagina di Bologna).

G. L. Brena, "Dialogo interreligioso: Riflessioni filosofiche," *Rassegna di teologia* 41/3: 431-441.

N. Bux, "Noi adoriamo quello che conosciamo (Gv, 4,22). Verità, chiesa, salvezza," *Osservatore Romano*, 4 Ottobre, 10.

F. Clark, *Godfaring* (Washington, Catholic University of America Press), 75-95.

H. Coward, *Pluralism and World Religions. A Short Introduction* (Oxford, Oneworld), 49-50.

M. Crociata (ed.), Gesù Cristo e l'unicità della mediazione (Milano: Paoline).

M. Dhavamony, "La chiesa e le religioni in rapporto alla salvezza," *Osservatore Romano*, 7 Ottobre, 4.

G. E., Book review, *Theology in Context* 1: 112.

R. Fisichella, "Pienezza e definitività della rivelazione di Gesù Cristo," *Osservatore Romano*, 27 Settembre, 6.

P. Gamberini, "La cristologia del pluralismo religioso in un libro recente di Jacques Dupuis," *Filosofia e teologia* 14: 131-144.

J. Dupuis, "Some Observations on the Response of Paolo Gamberini at the Congress of Jesuit Ecumenists (Kottayam, 15-20 August 1999) (unpublished).

G. Iammarrone, "La dottrina del primato assoluto e della Signoria universale di Gesù Cristo nel dibattito attuale sul valore salvifico delle religioni," in I. Sanna (ed.), *Gesù Cristo speranza del mondo. Miscellanea in onore di M. Bordoni* (Roma: Pontificia Università Lateranense): 339-408; at 389-394.

L. Ladaria, "Il Logos incarnato e lo Spirito Santo nell'opera della salvezza," *Osservatore Romano*, 20 Settembre, 4-5.

M. Masashi, "Dominus Iesus: A Plea for Vatican III," *Japan Missionary Journal*, Winter, 274-283.

"Rome and Relativism. Dominus Iesus and the Congregation for the Doctrine of the Faith," *Commonweal*, 20 October, 12-15.

D. Valentini, "Unicità e unità della chiesa," *Osservatore Romano*, 11 Ottobre 2000, 4.

2001

M. Aebischer-Crettol, *Vers un oecuménisme interreligieux* (Paris: Editions du Cerf): 332-346.

J. Allen, "Theologian Dupuis Says he is free at last," *National Catholic Reporter*, 9 March, 11.

J. J. Alemany, *El diálogo interreligioso en el magisterio del la Iglesia* (Madrid, Comillas).

M. Amaladoss, "Pluralism of Religions is not merely Complementary but Convergent," *Jivan*, September, 25.

T. Balasuriya, "Due paradigmi di missione," *Adista* 35 (16 Aprile): 12-13.

J. G. Bedoya, "Marejada entre teólogos por la salvación," *El Pais*, 12 April, 19.

R. Boudreaux, "Vatican has 'difficulties' with Jesuit's book on Pluralism," *Los Angeles Times*, 27 February.

P. Briel, "Le dialogue interreligieux doit être une évangélisation mutuelle," *Le temps*, 12 Avril, 52.

H. St John Broadbent, "The Truth in the Other," *The Tablet*, 27 October, 1527.

————, "Christ the Yardstick," *The Tablet*, 17 November, 1637.

"Case Settled," *Inside the Vatican*, March-April, 16.

"Chiuso il 'processo' a Dupuis: il teologo 'assolto' dalle accuse," *Jesus* 23 (Aprile): 22-23.

F. X. Clooney, *Hindu God, Christian God* (Oxford University Press): 21-23.

J. Coleman, "The Truth in the Other," *The Tablet*, 27 October, 1526-1527.

"Communicato del SAE sulla vicenda di p. Dupuis," *SAE Notizie*, 4, 2 Giugno: 8.

G. Cottier, "Sur la mystique naturelle," *Revue thomiste*, Janvier-Juin, 287-311; at 287-297.

M. Crociata, "Per uno statuto della teologia delle religioni," in *Teologia delle religioni. Bilanci e prospettive,* A cura di M. Crociata (Milano, Paoline): 325-370.

C. Delhez, "Le Père Dupuis a signé," *Dimanche*, 18 Mars.

J.-P. Denis, A.-M. Izoard, "En liberté surveillée," *La vie*, 8 Mars.

M. Dhavamony, "The Uniqueness and Universality of Jesus Christ," *Studia Missionalia*, 50: 193-196.

Archbishop H. D'Souza, " 'Foreword' to J. Dupuis, *Toward a Christian Theology of Religious Pluralism"* (Anand, Gujarat: Sahitya Prakash): xii-xiv.

"Dupuis inquiry ends with honour satisfied," *The Tablet*, 3 March, 319.

"Editorial: The Church and the Other Faiths," *The Tablet*, 3 March, 295.

"Editorial: Due Process in the Church," *America* 184 (9 April): 3.

"Father Dupuis Cleared of Doctrinal Error," *Jivan*, April, 9.

M. Fitzgerald, "The Pontifical Gregorian University and Interreligious Dialogue," *Pro Dialogo*, n.107, 2: 246-247.

I. Francq, "Amère victoire," *Actualité des religions*, Avril, 14-15.

"Fuori del Santo Ufficio non c'è salvezza," *Adista* 35, 10 Marzo, 3.

"Grida di paura del Cardinale Ratzinger. Il pluralismo religioso uccide la teologia cattolica," *Adista* 35, 10 Marzo, 3-4.

Cl. Geffré, *Croire et interpréter. Le tournant herméneutique de la théologie* (Paris: Editions du Cerf), 128-130.

J. Genest (ed.), *Penseurs et apôtres du XXe siècle* (Quebec: Fides), 197-212.

G. Goubert, "Le P. Dupuis entend continuer son travail," *La Croix*, 28 Février, 19.

———, "Jacques Dupuis: Denegada la justicia, la verdad si disvela con retraso," *Iglesia viva*, octubre-diciembre, 73-84.

International Review of Mission, 90/356-357: 197-198.

D. Jackson, "The Truth in the Other," *The Tablet*, 27 October, 1527.

J. Jay, "Justice Denied, Delayed. Truth Exposed," *Indian Currents*, 15 April, 10-16.

Cardinal Franz König, "Let the Spirit Breathe," *The Tablet*, 7 April , 483-484.

G. Leonard-J. Thavis, "Theologian's relief as book is cleared by Vatican probe," *Universe*, 11 March.

J. D'Arcy May, "Catholic Fundamentalism? Some Implications of *Dominus Iesus* for Dialogue and Peacemaking," in M. J. Rainer (ed.), *"Dominus Iesus". Anstössige Wahrheit oder anstössige Kirche?* (Münster: Lit Verlag): 112-133.

"Jesuit theologian explains with relief how Vatican relented," *The Tablet*, 10 March, 352.

R. P. McBrien, "Dominus Iesus: An Ecclesiological Critique," *Centro pro unione*, n. 59 (Spring): 14-22, at 18-19.

J. Mercier, "Christ the Yardstick," *The Tablet*, 17 November, 1637-1638.

José Morales, *Teología de las religiones* (Madrid: Rialp), 110-147; 222-225.

M. N., "La teologia e i suoi lettori," *Il Regno-Attualità*, 46 /6: 148-149.

J. Norton, "Theologian Calls Vatican Investigation a 'Great Suffering'," *National Jesuit News* 30/5: 4, 19.

"Notificazione a p. Dupuis," *Il Regno - Documenti* 46 (1 Marzo), 143-147.

G. O'Connell, "Free to speak at last, Dupuis tells of his ordeal," *Ucan*, 28 February.

L. Orsy, "A Matter of Justice. Was the Trial of Jacques Dupuis Really Necessary?," *America*, 184 (April): 20-22.

S. Peters, "In good company," *The Tablet*, 7 April, 487.

B. Pottier, "Note sur la mission invisible du Verbe chez saint Thomas d'Aquin," *Nouvelle revue théologique*, 123/6: 547-557.

V. Prisciandaro, "Dupuis, nessun errore ma solo 'ambiguità'," *Famiglia cristiana*, 11 Marzo.

———, "Una chiesa a porte aperte," *Jesus* 23 (May): 51.

A. Race, *Interfaith Encounter* (London: SCM Press).

"Card. Ratzinger: Sono teologo e guardiano. Non criticatemi se faccio il mio mestiere," *Adista* 35, 10 Marzo, 5-6.

S. Rayan, "Sulle Ambiguità della 'Notificazione' Vaticana," *Adista* 35 (16 Aprile):10-11.

G. Rota, "Unicità di Gesù Cristo e pluralità delle religioni: per una teologia cristiana delle religioni," *Teologia* 26/3: 256-275.

L. Sandri, "The Vatican delivers warning to Jesuit on religious pluralism," *Ecumenical News International*, 28 February.

L. Sartori, "Riflessioni confidenziali di un amico." Prefazione a J. Dupuis, *Il cristianesimo e le religioni: Dallo scontro all'incontro* (Brescia: Queriniana): 7-13.

J. A. Sayés, *Cristianismo y religiones. La salvacion fuera de la Iglesia* (Madrid: San Pablo): 30-37; 214-231.

E. Scognamiglio, *Il volto di Dio nelle religioni. Un indagine storica, filosofica e teologica* (Milano: Paoline): 141-159.

Th. Seiterich-Kreuzkamp, "Bricht das weiche Wasser den harten Stein?" *Publik-Forum* 7 (6 April): 27-28.

M. Serretti (ed.), *Unicità e universalità di Gesù Cristo. In dialogo con le religioni* (Cinisello Balsamo, San Paolo).

"Signs of the Times," *America*, 12 March, 4-5.

"Sotto esame la Notificazione di Ratzinger," *Adista* 35 (16 Aprile): 7-13.

A. Stanley, "After Vatican Rebuke, a Jesuit finds new but limited freedom," *International Herald Tribune*, 28 February.

F. A. Sullivan, "Ways of Salvation? On the Investigation of Jacques Dupuis," *America* 184 (9 April): 28-31.

F. Teixeira, "Forzature e fraintendimenti sono alla base della 'Notificazione'," *Adista* 35 (16 Aprile): 8-10.

"Theologian's Work merits encouragement, not censure," *National Catholic Reporter*, 9 March.

"Una sola via alla salvezza," *Avvenire*, 27 Febbraio.

"Vatican Rebukes a Theologian, but he says he can work on," *The New York Times International*, 1 March.

"Vatican Reins in Jesuit Theologian," *Indian Currents* 13 (11 March): 37-38.

"Vatican 'Notification' Ambiguous about Ambiguities," *Asia Focus*, 16 March, 3-4.

N. Venturini, "Un Gesuita dall'India al Sant'Ufficio," *Vita pastorale*, 5 Maggio, 96-98.

———, "Risolto il "caso" Dupuis," *Popoli*, Giugno-Luglio, 54-55.

Swami Vikrant, "Inquisition in New Avatar," *Indian Currents*, 6 May, 13-15.

H. Waldenfels, "Jacques Dupuis — Theologie unterwegs," *Stimmen der Zeit* 126/4: 217-218.

2002

M. Barnes, *Theology and the Dialogue of Religions* (Cambridge: Cambridge University Press): 6-7.

J. Cornwell, *Breaking Faith. The Pope, the People and the Fate of Catholicism* (London: Penguin Books): 214-220.

Alberto Cozzi, "Le religioni nel magistero postconciliare," *Teologia* 28/3: 268-309.

———, "Il Logos e Gesù/ Alla ricerca di un nuovo spazio di pensabilità dell' incarnazione," *La scuola cattolica* 130/1: 77-116, at 85-96.

H. Donneaud, "Chalcédoine contre l'unicité absolue du Médiateur Jésus-Christ?" *Revue thomiste* 102/1: 43-62.

"Jacques Dupuis: A Select Bibliography of Reviews and Reactions, *Toward a Christian Theology of Religious Pluralism*," *Louvain Studies* 27/4: 406-410.

J. Fuellenbach, *Church, Community of the Kingdom* (Maryknoll, N.Y.: Orbis Books).

Cl. Geffré, "Perspectives," in *Un livre à lire: J. Dupuis, Vers un théologie chréetienne du pluralisme religieux,* présenté par Bénédicte Doumenge et François Nielly, nn. 57-82, 62-88.

———, "L'avenir du dialogue interreligieux après *Dominus Iesus*," *Sedos Bulletin* 34/5: 131-137.

———, "Interreligious Dialogue. A Challenge and an Opportunity," *Japan Missionary Journal* (Winter): 219-224.

G. Hall, Jacques Dupuis' Christian Theology of Religious Pluralism," *Pacifica* 15, February, 37-50.

P. F. Knitter, *Introducing Theologies of Religions* (Maryknoll, N.Y.: Orbis Books).

Robert A. Krieg, "Who Do You Say I Am? Christology: What it is and Why it Matters," *Commonweal*, March 22, 12-16.

Alberto Melloni, "Recenti notificazioni su opere di Reinhard Messner, Jacques Dupuis, et Marciano Vidal," *Concilium* 38/3: 147-171.

———, "Recent notifications on the Works of Reinhard Messner, Jacques Dupuis and Marciano Vidal," *Concilium* 38/5: 115-136.

John Perry, "The Catholic Debate over Religious Pluralism," *Perspective* (Winnepeg) 5/ 1:4-13.

S. Pié-Ninot, *La teologia fondamentale* (Brescia: Queriniana): 273-277.

S. Smith, "The Holy Spirit and Mission in Some Contemporary Theologies of Mission", *Sedos Bulletin* 34/4: 98-110; at 103.

A. Race, *Interfaith Encounter* (London: SCM Press).

Pim Valkenberg, "Jacques Dupuis as a Theologian with a Reversed Mission: Some Remarks on his Controversial Theology of Religious Pluralism," in F. Wijsen and P. Nissen (eds.), *"Mission is a Must": Intercultural Theology and the Mission of the Church* (Amsterdam: Editions Rodopi b.v.):147-158.

2003

Claude Geffre, "Verso una nuova teologia delle religioni," in Rosino Gibellini (ed.), *Prospettive teologiche per il XXI secolo* (Brescia: Queriniana): 353-372.

Gerald O'Collins, "Christ and the Religions," *Gregorianum* 84/2: 347-362.

———, "Jacques Dupuis's Contributions to Interreligious Dialogue," *Theological Studies* 64 (2003): 388-397.

V. *Responses of Jacques Dupuis*

J. Dupuis, "La teologia del pluralismo religioso revisitata," *Rassegna di teologia* 40 (1999/ 5): 667-693.

———, " 'The Truth Will Make You Free'. The Theology of Theological Pluralism Revisited," *Louvain Studies* 24 (1999/3): 211-263.

———, *Il Cristianesimo e le religioni: Dallo scontro all'incontro* (Brescia: Queriniana, 2001); E.T., *Christianity and the Religions: From Confrontation to Dialogue* (Maryknoll, N.Y.: Orbis Books, 2002; London Darton, Longman & Todd, 2002; reprint 2003).

———, *Do Not Stifle the Spirit. In Conversation with Gerry O'Connell* (unpublished).

———, "The Theology of Religious Pluralism Revisited" (unpublished).

———, "Some Reflections on Two Roman Documents" (unpublished).

———, "Le Verde de Dieu come tel et comme incarné" (unpulbished).

———, "The Word and the Christ" (unpublished).

Index of Names

Abbado, C. 21
Abelard, P. 3,
Abelé, J. 231
Abhishiktananda, Swami 75, 76, 84, 146-
    57, 219, 246, 250, 255, 257, 258, 261,
    264
Abraham, K. C. 257
Abu-Sahlieh, S. A. A. 193
Achtegui, P. S. De 241
Aebischer-Crettol, M. 278
Aherne, C. M. 246
Ahmad, K 192
Aixala, J. 238
Akhilananda, Swami 75
Alangaram, A. 71
Alemany, J.-J. 272, 275, 278
Allen, J. 275, 277, 278
Allievi, S. 275
Allison, D. C. 167
Alphonso, H. 117, 131, 132, 226
Amaladoss, M. 142, 145, 152, 245, 278
Amaldas, B. 248
Amalorpavadass, D. S. 74, 100, 238, 239
Amato, Archbishop Angelo 22, 243, 273, 274,
    277
Anderson, G. H. 12, 248, 249, 250, 253
André, D. G. 272
Andreotti, G. 21
Andrews, C. F. 156
Anselm (of Canterbury), St. 20
Aquinas, St. Thomas 23, 83, 261, 266, 279
Aratus 174
Ard, F. 272
Aristotle 56
Arevalo, C. G. 83, 132
Arinze, Cardinal Francis 9, 13, 269
Armogate, J. 247
Armstrong, A. H. 231
Arokiasamy, S. 84, 256
Asclepius 110
Ashton, J. 167

Athanasius, St. 26, 240
Augustin, G. 208
Augustine (of Hippo), St. 170, 265
Aumont, M. 235
Ayoub, M. 193
Azevedo, M. de C. 253

Balasuriya, T. 243, 275, 278
Balthasar, H. U. von 199, 208, 237, 259,
    264
Barnes, M. 33, 269, 280
Barré, H. 232
Barrett, C. K. 160, 168
Barth, K. 49, 265
Barthe, C. 272
Barzel, B. 250
Basset, B. 240, 242
Batchelor, S. 42, 44,
Baumer, O. 152
Beasley-Murray, G. 168
Bedoya, J. G. 278
Beeck, F. J. van 250
Beethoven, L. von 123
Bellitto, C. 269
Benoit, P. 231, 237, 239
Bernard, C. 119, 131, 132
Bernard, J. 250
Berryman, P. 214, 220
Bertone, Archbishop Tarcisio 22
Bevans, S. B. 260
Bezançon, J.-N. 247
Bianchi, E. 269, 271
Bianchi, H. 261
Biechler, J. E. 275
Biffi, I. 272, 277
Billet, B. 237
Boespflug, F. 59
Boff, C. 254
Boff, L. 88, 100, 246, 253, 254, 255, 259
Boismard, M. E. 231, 232
Bonhoeffer, D. 234, 236